MINNESOTA TREASURES

MINNESOTA TREASURES

DENIS P. GARDNER

✳

Foreword
by Richard Moe

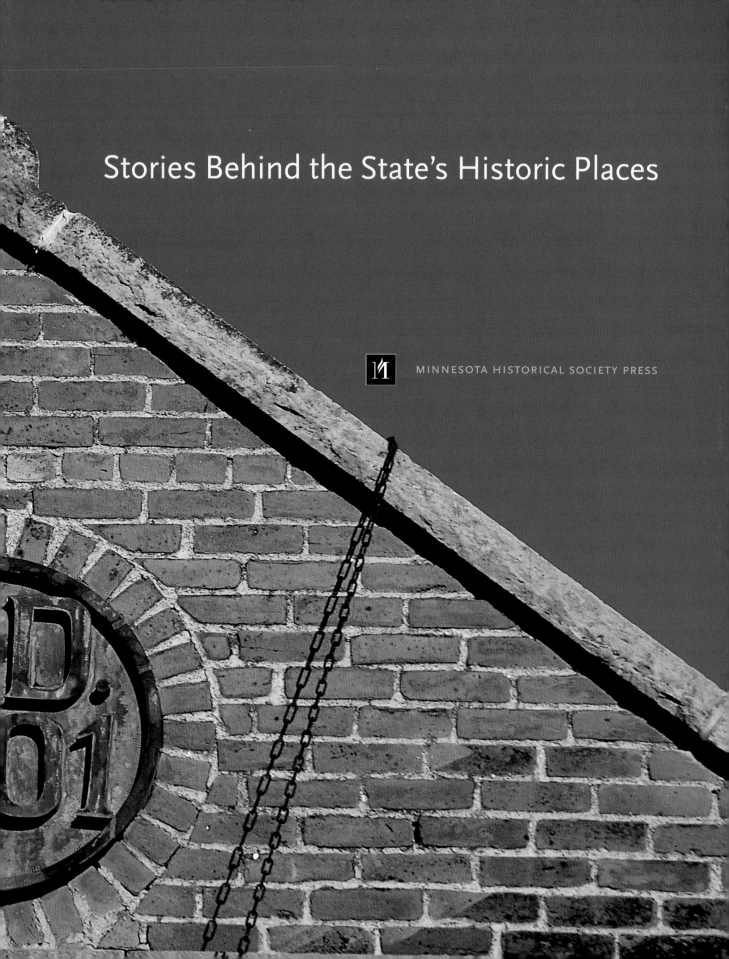

Stories Behind the State's Historic Places

MINNESOTA HISTORICAL SOCIETY PRESS

With select new photography by Doug Ohman, Pioneer Photography © 2004. Photo credits are given on page 296.

Publication of this book was supported in part by the Elmer L. and Eleanor J. Anderson Publications Endowment Fund of the Minnesota Historical Society.

www.mnhs.org/mhspress

The Minnesota Historical Society Press is a member of the Association of American University Presses.

———

Manufactured in China

10 9 8 7 6 5 4 3 2 1

♾ The paper used in this publication meets the minimum requirements of the American National Standard for Information Sciences—Permanence for Printed Library Materials, ANSI Z39.48–1984.

International Standard Book Number 0-87351-471-8 (cloth)

Library of Congress Cataloging-in-Publication Data
Gardner, Denis P., 1965–
Minnesota treasures : stories behind the state's historic places / Denis P. Gardner ; foreword by Richard Moe.
    p. cm.
Includes bibliographical references and index.
ISBN 0-87351-471-8 (cloth: alk. paper)
    1. Historic sites—Minnesota.
    2. Minnesota—History, Local.
    3. Minnesota—Antiquities.
    I. Title.

F607.G37 2004
977.6—dc22

2003020765

Minnesota Treasures was designed by Cathy Spengler and printed by Pettit Network, Afton, Minnesota

For my mother and father, both of whom have faced challenges

far more difficult than writing a book

ACKNOWLEDGMENTS

THIS BOOK WAS YEARS IN THE MAKING—that is, the idea for a work featuring the histories of many of Minnesota's National Register of Historic Places properties had floated about the historic preservation community for some time. Since Minnesota is brimming with historians of considerable ability, I am a little surprised that I became the one to write this book. True, I had spent years documenting properties, living out of a Motel 6 in Rochester, Minnesota, or a Red Roof Inn in Saginaw, Michigan, or a Super 8 in Boise, Idaho; Green Bay, Wisconsin; Lincoln, Nebraska; Bismarck, North Dakota; and so many other locales from which that familiar red, yellow, and black beacon beckons the weary traveler. Still, I feel a bit lucky. Whether it was aptitude or fortune or a combination of the two, I will always be grateful to Greg Britton, Ann Regan, and others at the Minnesota Historical Society Press for giving me the opportunity to articulate Minnesota's remarkable history through its built environment.

My exceptional editor at the Press, Pamela McClanahan, did not simply lasso roving commas or spur me to clarification. No, she also coaxed my occasionally meandering prose back on path while maintaining my voice, an editorial skill welcomed by any author. Alan Woolworth, a research fellow emeritus for the MHS, reviewed several manuscript sections and spotlighted some factual gaffes, for which I am appreciative. Scott Anfinson, the archaeologist at Minnesota's State Historic Preservation Office (SHPO) at the MHS, also reviewed parts of this work, offering sound advice and ensuring I got archaeological facts and terminology correct. In fact, all of the staff at SHPO aided my research, even if they never realized it. I spent so much time in their office asking questions, rifling through files, and making photocopies that I almost felt like a member of that unique department, a body fulfilling certain federal and state responsibilities vital to architectural history and preservation in Minnesota. The person I owe most at the SHPO, though, is Susan Roth, Minnesota's longtime National Register Historian. Besides her extensive knowledge of Minnesota history, Susan has a formidable grasp of the National Register process and an almost intrinsic sense of what makes a property "special." The advice I sought from her throughout the last two years makes this book better than it otherwise would be.

I am indebted to Abbey Christman, a superb architectural historian and former colleague who encouraged my efforts, perused early drafts, and pointed out a gaping hole in my conceptualization. I quickly patched the hole. I appreciate the assistance of several historical societies, from the

Cook County Historical Society in Grand Marais to the Fillmore County Historical Center in Fountain. These repositories provided me both written and oral local historical information. I am grateful to those who granted access to the properties highlighted in this book, welcoming photographer Doug Ohman and myself into their personal worlds. And, of course, I thank Doug for his wonderful images. Many of the National Register of Historic Places nominations I referenced were excellent, and I am obliged to their authors, most notably the historians at Gemini Research in Morris, a staff that has produced numerous high-quality nominations. Charlene K. Roise, an exceptional architectural historian I worked with for many years, weaned me from wordiness, making my prose more concise and clear, for which I am thankful. I also wish to thank Jeffrey A. Hess, maybe the most unusual personality I have ever met, and a gentleman who taught me what is truly important when documenting cultural resources: what makes a good historian. Lastly, I am grateful for a loving and supportive family, one that instilled my blue-collar values and, in a way, labored with me as I completed this book.

MAP OF MINNESOTA TREASURES

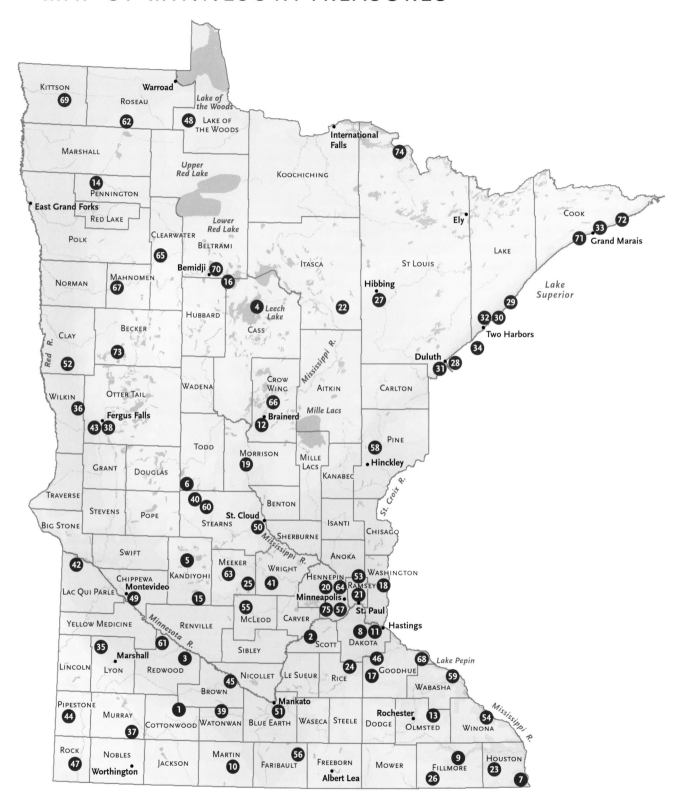

1. Jeffers Petroglyphs Site
2. Little Rapids (Inyan Ceyaka Otonwe)
3. Birch Coulee School
4. Battle Point (Sugar Point)
5. Guri and Lars Endreson House
6. St. Cloud & Red River Valley Stage Road: Kandota Section
7. Jefferson Grain Warehouse
8. Good Templars Hall
9. Lanesboro Stone Dam
10. Orville P. & Sarah Chubb House
11. Hastings Foundry
12. Northern Pacific Railway Shops
13. Viola Cooperative Creamery
14. Minneapolis, St. Paul & Sault St. Marie Depot (Soo Line Depot)
15. John Bosch Farmstead
16. Steamboat Bridge
17. Nansen Agricultural District
18. Soo Line High Bridge
19. Pine Tree Lumber Company Office Building
20. Peavey-Haglin Experimental Concrete Grain Elevator
21. Seventh Street Improvement Arches
22. Hill Annex Mine
23. Schech's Mill
24. Goodsell Observatory
25. Universal Laboratories Building
26. Bernard H. Pietenpol Workshop & Garage
27. Hibbing Disposal Plant
28. Aerial Lift Bridge
29. *Madeira* Shipwreck
30. Two Harbors Light Station
31. U.S. Army Corps of Engineers Duluth Vessel Yard
32. Tugboat *Edna G.*
33. Jim Scott Fish House
34. *Onoko* Shipwreck
35. The Big Store (O. G. Anderson & Company Store)
36. J. A. Johnson Blacksmith Shop
37. First National Bank
38. Barnard Mortuary
39. Nelson & Albin Cooperative Mercantile Association Store
40. Original Main Street
41. Howard Lake City Hall
42. Louisburg School
43. Fergus Falls State Hospital Complex
44. Pipestone Water Tower
45. New Ulm Post Office
46. Firemen's Hall
47. Rock County Courthouse & Jail
48. Norris Camp
49. Montevideo Carnegie Library
50. Minnesota State Reformatory for Men
51. Rensselaer D. Hubbard House
52. Hannah C. & Peter E. Thompson House
53. Casiville Bullard House
54. Paul Watkins House
55. Merton S. Goodnow House
56. Muret N. Leland House
57. Lena O. Smith House
58. Hinckley Fire Relief House
59. Lorenz & Lugerde Ginthner House
60. Church of St. Boniface (Church of St. Mary)
61. Odeon Theater
62. Lodge Boleslav Jablonsky No. 219
63. Grand Army of the Republic Hall
64. North East Neighborhood House
65. Gran Evangelical Lutheran Church
66. Deerwood Auditorium
67. Mahnomen County Fairgrounds
68. Frontenac
69. Lake Bronson State Park
70. Paul Bunyan & Babe the Blue Ox
71. Cascade River Wayside
72. Naniboujou Club
73. Graystone Hotel
74. Jun Fujita Cabin
75. White Castle Building No. 8

CONTENTS

Foreword by Richard Moe | xv

Introduction | xxi

NATIVE AMERICANS | 3

Jeffers Petroglyphs Site | 5

Little Rapids (Inyan Ceyaka Otonwe) | 9

Birch Coulee School | 13

Battle Point (Sugar Point) | 16

BEFORE THE RAILROAD | 21

Guri and Lars Endreson House | 23

St. Cloud & Red River Valley Stage Road:

    Kandota Section | 26

Jefferson Grain Warehouse | 28

Good Templars Hall | 31

Lanesboro Stone Dam | 34

Orville P. & Sarah Chubb House | 37

Hastings Foundry | 40

RAILROADS & AGRICULTURE | 43

Northern Pacific Railway Shops | 47

Viola Cooperative Creamery | 50

Minneapolis, St. Paul & Sault St. Marie Depot
     (Soo Line Depot) | 54

John Bosch Farmstead | 57

Steamboat Bridge | 61

Nansen Agricultural District | 64

Soo Line High Bridge | 67

MARITIME MINNESOTA | 105

Aerial Lift Bridge | 107

Madeira Shipwreck | 111

Two Harbors Light Station | 113

U.S. Army Corps of Engineers Duluth Vessel Yard | 116

Tugboat *Edna G.* | 120

Jim Scott Fish House | 123

Onoko Shipwreck | 126

INDUSTRY & TECHNOLOGY | 71

Pine Tree Lumber Company Office Building | 74

Peavey-Haglin Experimental Concrete Grain Elevator | 77

Seventh Street Improvement Arches | 81

Hill Annex Mine | 84

Schech's Mill | 87

Goodsell Observatory | 91

Universal Laboratories Building | 95

Bernard H. Pietenpol Workshop & Garage | 98

Hibbing Disposal Plant | 101

COMMERCIAL HISTORY | 129

The Big Store

    (O. G. Anderson & Company Store) | 131

J. A. Johnson Blacksmith Shop | 136

First National Bank | 139

Barnard Mortuary | 141

Nelson & Albin Cooperative

    Mercantile Association Store | 144

Original Main Street | 147

YESTERDAY'S HOUSE | 187

Rensselaer D. Hubbard House | 190

Hannah C. & Peter E. Thompson House | 193

Casiville Bullard House | 196

Paul Watkins House | 199

Merton S. Goodnow House | 202

Muret N. Leland House | 206

Lena O. Smith House | 209

Hinckley Fire Relief House | 212

Lorenz & Lugerde Ginthner House | 216

PUBLIC HISTORY | 151

Howard Lake City Hall | 154

Louisburg School | 157

Fergus Falls State Hospital Complex | 160

Pipestone Water Tower | 165

New Ulm Post Office | 168

Firemen's Hall | 171

Rock County Courthouse & Jail | 174

Norris Camp | 176

Montevideo Carnegie Library | 180

Minnesota State Reformatory for Men | 183

TOURISM & ROADSIDE ARCHITECTURE | 249

Frontenac | 252

Lake Bronson State Park | 255

Paul Bunyan & Babe the Blue Ox | 259

Cascade River Wayside | 262

Naniboujou Club | 266

Graystone Hotel | 269

Jun Fujita Cabin | 273

White Castle Building No. 8 | 276

Notes | 280

Index | 290

Photo Credits | 296

GATHERING PLACES | 219

Church of St. Boniface (Church of St. Mary) | 221

Odeon Theater | 225

Lodge Boleslav Jablonsky No. 219 | 228

Grand Army of the Republic Hall | 231

North East Neighborhood House | 235

Gran Evangelical Lutheran Church | 240

Deerwood Auditorium | 242

Mahnomen County Fairgrounds | 245

FOREWORD

A COUPLE OF YEARS AGO, in an essay that appeared in a publication titled *Saving America's Treasures,* Ray Suarez wrote that the buildings, documents, and works of art described in the book carried "the DNA of democracy." That marvelously evocative phrase applies equally well, I believe, to the seventy-five historic sites featured in the pages of *Minnesota Treasures.* These places help us understand who we are as Americans—and, more specifically, as Minnesotans. In other words, they constitute a unique family portrait of us.

And what a colorful, complex, endlessly fascinating portrait it is, with vignettes ranging from simple farmhouses to a White Castle hamburger stand, from the sunken iron-hulled freighter *Onoko* to a segment of a frontier stagecoach road, from a grand North Shore lodge to hardscrabble mines and mills. There are some very impressive architectural creations here—the Fergus Falls State Hospital, for example, is aptly described by author Denis P. Gardner as "jaw-dropping"—as well as others to which the word "architecture" hardly applies and where functional practicality clearly takes precedence over aesthetic appeal. Some of these places are puzzling: Who can look at the ancient Jeffers Petroglyphs and not be profoundly awed and mystified? Others are endowed with the simple (and all too rare) power to make us feel good: Bemidji's colossal statues of Paul Bunyan and Babe the Blue Ox are practically foolproof grin-inducers. Each is a telling detail in the vast picture of us as Minnesotans.

While our state boasts a number of historic sites whose fame extends far beyond its borders—the renowned Mayo Clinic in Rochester is a good example, as are Louis Sullivan's gemlike National Farmers' Bank in Owatonna and the thoroughfare in Sauk Centre that was the real-life inspiration for Sinclair Lewis's groundbreaking novel *Main Street*—most of the places in this book are less well known. They serve to remind us that while icons such as Independence Hall and the Golden Gate Bridge are in relatively short supply, almost every community has some landmark that makes it unique. It is these "hidden treasures"—the modest St. Paul home of brickmason Casiville Bullard, an African American craftsman working early in the twentieth century, the awesome Soo Line High Bridge near Stillwater, even the Pipestone Water Tower and the impressively monikered Peavey-Haglin Experimental Concrete Grain Elevator in St. Louis Park—that give Minnesota's family portrait much of its color and texture.

The sites featured in *Minnesota Treasures* have been chosen from the hundreds of Minnesota properties included in the National Register of Historic Places, the nation's official list of buildings, structures, districts, sites, and objects worthy of preservation. That last phrase is very important.

In their remarkable variety, the places in this book may at first glance appear to be a random collection of unrelated artifacts—but in fact they share one very important trait in common: They are all worth saving.

Having spent much of my life in Minnesota, I am proud to say that I have at least a passing acquaintance with many of the places chosen for inclusion in this book. I must admit, however, that as a boy in Duluth and a young man in the Twin Cities, I was largely unaware of the historic structures that formed the backdrop to my life. My awakening didn't come until several years later, when I was preparing to write a book about the Civil War. In the course of my research I visited several of the nation's most important battlefields, and again and again I was dismayed by the deterioration and inappropriate new development that threatened to overwhelm those hallowed fields. That's when I began to realize that the heritage embodied in America's older buildings, neighborhoods, and landscapes is perilously fragile—and, in many cases, actually disappearing right before our eyes.

Turning the pages of this book, being reminded of the interesting and evocative historic places that grace Minnesota's cities, towns, and rural areas, it's hard not to remember the many—far too many—equally important landmarks that have been needlessly destroyed over the years. Minneapolis alone has lost scores of structures—including, to name just a few, the Metropolitan and New York Life Buildings, the splendiferous Minnesota Theater (described by architecture critic Larry Millett as "Versailles in a brick box"), the sleek Art Deco Forum Cafeteria, Thomas Griffith's stone-towered suspension bridge of 1876, the elegant little Gateway Park Pavilion, and several highly distinctive houses by local architect LeRoy Buffington—structures whose disappearance has left gaping holes in both the physical fabric of the city and the collective memory of its residents.

What has happened in Minneapolis has also happened in other communities all over the state, and Minnesota's experience has been duplicated in every other state from coast to coast. It's a cultural disaster that should leave us appalled and outraged because it has left us poorer. Whether it results from shortsighted public policy, natural disaster, the misguided pursuit of "progress," or the simple, inexorable effects of weather and time, the loss of our heritage robs our communities of stylistic variety and visual richness, and robs us of the opportunity to know ourselves better.

In the middle of the nineteenth century, the famed English artist and critic John Ruskin wrote, "Architecture is to be regarded by us with the most serious thought. We may live without her, and worship without her, but we cannot remember without her."

The tangled, tragic, amusing, and enthralling story of where we came from, how we got here, and at what cost, is bound up in the wood and stone, brick and steel of historic places like those described in this book. Losing one of these places is like losing a piece of our memory of ourselves. The crash of the wrecking ball is the sound of a doorway to our shared past slamming shut forever.

We can learn about the past from books, of course, but *reading* history can't compare with the experience of *walking through* history, living with it, learning from hands-on contact with it. Every Minnesota schoolchild learns about the importance of the Mesabi Iron Range in our state's economic history, but a visit to the Hill Annex Mine (now a state park) near Calumet makes it all real. Similarly, we can try to imagine what life was like for settlers on the nineteenth-century frontier, but if we walk through the dark, cramped Endreson log cabin in Kandiyohi County, the site of an immigrant family's harrowing experience during the Dakota Conflict of 1862, our imaginings are informed by what we see and hear.

But historic places such as those described in this book aren't important solely because they are tangible and uniquely enlightening links with the past. They're also our legacy to the future. Here's John Ruskin again, writing in *The Seven Lamps of Architecture* in 1849:

> *When we build, let us think that we build for ever. Let it not be for present delight, nor for present use alone; let it be such work as our descendants will thank us for, and let us think, as we lay stone on stone, that a time is to come when . . . men will say . . . , "See! This our fathers did for us."*

Just as we learn about our fathers and mothers—who they were, what they believed, how they lived—from the buildings they left for us, our children will learn about us in the same way. They'll learn about us from what we build, of course, but it's logical to assume that they'll also learn about us from what we have the common sense to hang on to. When you strip away all the rhetoric, that's a big part of what historic preservation is all about: being wise enough to hang on to the things that matter.

When we save historic places, we strengthen a partnership that makes for orderly growth and change in our communities: the perpetual partnership among the past, the present, and the future. This partnership acknowledges that we can't live in the past, so it encourages each generation to meet its needs by taking advantage of the very best of contemporary thought and technology. But it also encourages us to realize that we can't afford to reject the history, the culture, the traditions, and the values on which our lives and our futures are built.

When this partnership falls apart, when the connections between successive generations of Americans are broken, blank spaces open up in our understanding of the long process that made us who we are. But when it's allowed to work as it's supposed to, this partnership produces a healthy society with the sense of continuity that art historian Siegfried Giedion has called "part of the very backbone of human dignity."

Ever since Ann Pamela Cunningham rallied the women of the nation to save Mount Vernon in the 1850s, a vigorous preservation movement has been working to strengthen this partnership by protecting and celebrating the places that tell America's story. Helping people save the historic places they care about is the main job for which the National Trust was created in 1949. While I'm enormously proud of what the Trust has accomplished, I'm also well aware that much of our success has been made possible by the dedication and hard work of our preservation partners at the state and local levels.

Minnesota is fortunate to have an extensive network of energetic, effective organizations whose work is guided by a vision of the future in which communities incorporate historic buildings and neighborhoods as a vital part of daily life. Advocacy groups such as the Preservation Alliance of Minnesota and 1000 Friends of Minnesota do yeoman work at the statewide level, ably assisting and encouraging the grassroots efforts of the dozens of local historical societies and preservation organizations that are in place in practically every city and town.

Minnesota is *particularly* fortunate in having the Minnesota Historical Society, which, in addition to helping recognize, conserve, and interpret the state's historic treasures, is something of a treasure itself. The Society quite literally does it all, providing exemplary stewardship of its extensive collections, producing award-winning publications and conferences, and administering school programs and a statewide collection of historic sites that attract hundreds of thousands of visitors every year. *Minnesota Treasures* is merely the latest in a long string of achievements that lead me to believe—and I am convinced that this is a wholly objective evaluation—that the Minnesota Historical Society is one of the best organizations of its kind in the United States.

The preservation efforts of these statewide and local organizations are bearing some very healthy fruit. In St. Paul, the transformation of Lowertown from a shabby backwater into a thriving urban neighborhood has won national acclaim. In Duluth, innovative renovation has made Union Depot a veritable "poster child" for the reuse of historic railroad stations. In Lanesboro, the rebirth of the downtown business district won a Great American Main Street Award. And in Minneapolis, the creation of the Mill City Museum in the ruins of the historic Washburn A Mill brings the industrial history of St. Anthony Falls to new and vivid life.

In fact, from one end of the state to the other, it's really hard to find a city or town where houses and storefronts haven't been "fixed up" with pride, where underused or obsolete buildings haven't been put to imaginative new uses, where landmarks haven't been identified and protected in some way, where historic sites aren't heavily marketed to attract tourists. In short, preservation's impact is visible everywhere, and it has made a real difference in the way our communities look and in the way Minnesotans value the heritage that is among our state's greatest treasures.

In my dictionary, "treasure" is defined as "something of great worth or value." That seems a totally accurate description of Minnesota's historic places, including those that are so expertly and engagingly described in this book—from millionaire's mansion and small-town theater to Indian school and municipal sewage-treatment plant. It is worth noting that these treasures have not survived by accident. Each is listed in the National Register because someone—state employee, professional consultant, or public-spirited citizen—noticed its significance and took the time to fill out the requisite nomination forms. In addition, many have been patiently, painstakingly restored by owners who made a significant investment of time and funding—and love.

Someone has written, "In the end we will conserve only what we love, we will love only what we understand, and we will understand only what we are taught." If this book achieves the purpose for which it was written and published, citizens all over the state of Minnesota—homemakers and business executives, elected officials and schoolchildren, card-carrying preservationists and people who would never dream of adopting that label—will gain a better understanding of, and appreciation for, the historic places that ornament our communities and inform our lives.

Inspired by that understanding, they will work to ensure that these places don't disappear. And with the success of that effort, they will enrich the lives of generations to come.

Richard Moe
President, National Trust for Historic Preservation

INTRODUCTION

FOR TWO YEARS ZHAO JINGXIN, an eighty-two-year-old former English instructor in Beijing, China, labored to convince the city not to demolish his traditional courtyard house, believing the residence a cultural resource worth preserving. According to several historians and preservationists the house dated to the mid-seventeenth century, thus meeting the local government's benchmark for declaring a structure a historical asset. Nevertheless, in October 2000 a Beijing court ruled that the house was not 350 years old and therefore deserved no protection. Within days of the decision workers were hacking at the home's gray-tile roof with pickaxes. Today, a ten-story bank occupies the site.[1]

Fortunately, Americans do not face such a formidable standard for determining the historic value of a property. Unfortunately, most rarely think about the historic value of a property at all. It is difficult to blame the country for not paying attention to its structural heritage. An increasingly suburbanized society reared on strip malls and fast-food restaurants—each looking much like the other—seems to have been numbed into a kind of architectural indifference. Yet in contrast to building efforts of previous generations, the general architectural conformity of modern society demonstrates that we are settling for less. In truth, though, indifference alone does not explain the rather ho-hum view we take toward our built environment. There also is unawareness, an ignorance of our heritage, whether architectural, technological, political, or social, and how that history is reflected in the edifices we create. This is why the National Register of Historic Places is so important.

As Richard Moe explained in his foreword, the National Register of Historic Places is an official list of properties recognized as historically significant and deserving preservation. The list includes properties significant in American history, culture, architecture, engineering, and archaeology. This honorary roll of tangible history finds its roots in groups like the Mount Vernon Ladies' Association of the Union, a mid-nineteenth-century organization of forward-thinking women convinced that preserving our first president's home was a "good" thing. This preservation notion was influenced by the inaction of the federal government, which seemed almost ambivalent toward prominent places of the nation's past. The government recognized the importance of geographical features as early as 1872, when it established Yellowstone National Park, and although Congress designated Arizona's Casa Grande ruin a National Monument in 1889, it was not until 1906 that comprehensive preservation legislation covering structures was passed; the Antiquities Act gave the president authority to designate properties on federal lands as historic. In 1916, the National Park Service was formed within the United States Department of the Interior and was charged with administering the nation's parks and federally designated historic properties. In 1949, Congress chartered the National Trust for Historic Preservation, a quasi-public organization that served as a bridge between private preservation efforts and those of the government.

Although preservation policy in the United States had progressed since the Mount Vernon Ladies' Association, its failings were profoundly apparent by the mid-1960s. Waving the banner of urban renewal, cities across the country spent much of the 1950s and 1960s demolishing whole city blocks. In Minneapolis, for instance, the city fought blight by pounding the entire Gateway District into nothingness, destroying nearly two hundred mostly nineteenth-century commercial buildings. An expanding interstate highway system created further loss as neighborhoods were wiped away so Americans could rush forward without experiencing what they were rushing past. Located at the northern edge of downtown St. Paul, Central Park Methodist Episcopal Church boasted, in the rich prose of architectural historian Larry Millett, a "playful silhouette, pale walls of Dresbach limestone, and bulging corner turrets garnished with a jolly assortment of conical roofs." The striking Richardsonian Romanesque-style church was one of many buildings leveled to make way for Interstate Highway 94. The history lost through these "improvement" efforts forced many to reconsider gutting our structural past in the name of progress. In 1965, the National Trust for Historic Preservation and a special committee of the U.S. Conference of Mayors published *With Heritage So Rich,* a report highlighting the structural heritage the country had lost. The document also proposed ways governments could carry out building projects without haphazardly destroying structures meaningful to a community's history. More importantly, the report prompted the National Historic Preservation Act, possibly the nation's most significant piece of preservation legislation.

The National Historic Preservation Act of 1966 created a new perspective as the federal government officially acknowledged what was already understood—the vast majority of our history is not found in prominent places like Mount Vernon. As important as George Washington's residence is to our history—as vital as Independence Hall and Gettysburg are to our national identity—it is the places where we live, work, play, and pray that chiefly define who we are; and in the National Historic Preservation Act we finally had a cultural policy that recognized the importance of state and local history. The Act led to the creation of State Historic Preservation Offices (SHPOs) to oversee preservation activities. The Advisory Council on Historic Preservation, a federal agency charged with advising lawmakers on preservation policy, was also born from the legislation. Additionally, the Act encouraged development of locally regulated historic districts and provided a means for securing federal funds for local preservation programs. Finally, the law established the National Register of Historic Places, an inventory of significant structures and sites that represent where the country has been.

In part, the National Register is intriguing because of its diversity. While it is common to find grand architectural places on the federal listing, such as capitol buildings or fantastically ornate churches, the National Register is also a repository of the unadorned.

Moreover, the list is not reserved for only those places where great things happened. Any property retaining historic integrity and reflecting broad patterns of our history can be part of the National Register. For example, what is more indicative of a community founded on commercial fishing than a fish house? Is there anything that defines the history of an agricultural region better than a district of farmsteads? Of course not all properties can be eligible for the National Register—if everything is special, then nothing is special. And this is why SHPOs are so important. By following National Park Service criteria for evaluating the historic significance of properties, SHPOs determine what is and is not eligible for the National Register.

The National Register is especially valuable because most of its properties are not museum pieces. Signs that read "Do Not Touch" are largely absent. A principal tenet of the program is to encourage continued use of historic structures while maintaining their original character and feel. This does not mean that owners of National Register properties cannot make changes to the structure, but if a modification significantly alters a property's historic character it likely will be removed from the list.

Ideally, a National Register property will continue to function in a manner for which it was originally intended. But this is not always possible. Many lighthouses, for instance, are now obsolete because modern ships are equipped with navigational aids that allow crews to find their own way safely to harbor. Still, National Register structures can find new life in a new role. In Two Harbors the local historical society converted the community's picturesque lighthouse into a bed and breakfast, a splendid reuse for a distinctive building. The federal government encourages reuse through tax credits, which are available to owners of income-producing National Register properties.

Minnesota has over fifteen hundred National Register listings, as well as twenty-two National Historic Landmarks, which are properties central to the history of the nation. The large number of listings reflects the importance many Minnesotans give their past. And although the state has occasionally stumbled on preservation matters, Minnesota recognized the meaningfulness of its built environment very early. In 1896, after twice being relocated and mostly forgotten, the John Stevens House, a weathered residence constructed in 1850 by the principal founder of Minneapolis, was rediscovered. The dwelling was preserved and restored once it was hauled to a seat of veneration in Minnehaha Park, an event made more memorable by the roughly seven thousand schoolchildren invited to tug on the towropes. Minnesota's archaeological story also received early attention when avocational archaeologists initiated study of the state's American Indian earthworks in the late 1800s. Analysis of American Indian rock art soon followed.

The ensuing pages feature only a fraction of the National Register places in Minnesota. The sampling is diverse, however, accurately reflecting the many property types found on the listing. Some of the structures in this work are almost shamelessly grand while others are delightfully simple. And even though a few properties may initially seem uninspiring they were actually quite innovative. Some places are archaeological sites, often hidden reminders of an important event or concealed material memories of a community that has vanished.

Since many of the legacies of our past highlighted here are historically significant for their architecture or engineering, architectural and technical terms are often clarified. Further, each property in this book is set within one of several thematic contexts: Native Americans, Before the Railroad, Railroads and Agriculture, Industry and Technology, Maritime Minnesota, Commercial History, Public History, Yesterday's House, Gathering Places, and Tourism and Roadside Architecture. The brief contexts provide historical frameworks so readers better understand how these unique places are woven into the fabric of our heritage. Finally, these diverse properties are sprinkled throughout the state. That is important because each echoes a piece of our history from a different stage, and like a puzzle, the pieces link together to tell a larger story—the story of Minnesota.

MINNESOTA TREASURES

NATIVE AMERICANS

WELL BEFORE THE FIRST EUROPEANS plodded its rolling prairies, negotiated its dense forests, waded its meandering rivers and streams, and canoed its sometimes temperamental lakes, generations upon generations of ancient Native Americans traversed Minnesota. Indeed, Minnesota's original settlement began about twelve thousand years ago, roughly eleven thousand years before Vikings landed at Newfoundland, "discovering" North America. Since we are so far removed from these earliest Minnesotans, we are forced in large part to speculate as to their cultural characteristics. Our suppositions are drawn, reinforced, and sometimes significantly altered, by the vague reminders they left behind. Artifacts like petroglyphs and pictographs, pottery sherds and projectile points, and ornaments and implements of stone, bone, shell, or copper, aid our understanding of these ancient peoples. But no matter how hard we try, we may never be able to weave a satisfactory story of their existence prior to the arrival of Europeans in Minnesota in the late seventeenth century.[2]

The story of the recent ancestors of Minnesota's contemporary Native Americans is clearer, although the Euro-American tempest that began settling Minnesota around the mid-nineteenth century wiped away many traces of indigenous populations. Our knowledge of Minnesota Indians from the last few hundred years is

3

bolstered by written documentation, but the record is sometimes skewed because victors often write the histories. Even so, conscientiously weeding subjectivity produces a reasonable picture of those occupying Minnesota as white settlers pushed into the region.

In 1898 amateur archaeologist J. V. Brower composed "Prehistoric Man at the Headwaters of the Mississippi River." The author observed that Minnesota's ancient Native Americans may not have been unlike Indians of the nineteenth century: "Probably the prehistoric race of men who occupied the upper waters of the Mississippi river basin were not extraordinarily different from the nations and tribes now receding before the enlightened encroachments of the English-speaking people." Brower may be correct in his assessment of prehistoric Indians, but his words reflect the paternalistic and condescending attitude many whites held toward nineteenth-century Native Americans, a mind-set that dearly cost aboriginal populations, including Minnesota's Dakota and Ojibwe.

At the beginning of the nineteenth century, the Dakota and Ojibwe dominated Minnesota. The Dakota were concentrated in the south while the Ojibwe mostly occupied the north. Although the tribes had been warring with each other since at least the mid-1700s, a power more formidable than either conspicuously arrived in 1819. That year the federal government began erecting Fort St. Anthony (later Fort Snelling) at the junction of the Mississippi and Minnesota Rivers. The fort was frontier muscle, first protecting traders, merchants, and others tied to the lucrative fur industry, and later watching over white settlers. The bastion was also a base for government representatives mediating differences between the tribes.

Dousing the Dakota and Ojibwe with "enlightenment" began in earnest with a treaty in 1837, when the relentless westward push of white settlement and industry essentially forced both tribes to cede their ancestral lands east of the Mississippi River below the mouth of the Crow Wing River. In 1851 further settlement pressures, as well as disappearing game and a defunct fur trade, compelled the Dakota to cede the remainder of their Minnesota lands in the Treaty of Traverse des Sioux and the Treaty of Mendota. By the end of the decade, the Dakota were confined to the Upper Sioux Reservation near Granite Falls and the Lower Sioux Reservation near Redwood Falls, along the Minnesota River in western Minnesota.

The Ojibwe fared better than the Dakota, retaining large portions of their traditional lands. The tribe benefited from its northern Minnesota location—at least for a time. Unlike the nutrient-rich soil to the south, most of the ground in the north was nutrient-poor, convincing early Minnesota immigrants to turn left at St. Paul rather than right. White settlement still pushed the Ojibwe, however, as did the timber industry. The tribe again ceded territory in 1847. Several more cessations were made in the last half of the nineteenth century to accommodate expanded timbering and iron ore development. Moreover, white settlers increasingly moved north as good agricultural lands in southern Minnesota became scarce. Eventually, most Ojibwe were placed on several reservations in central and northern Minnesota, including ones at Mille Lacs, Leech Lake, White Earth, and Red Lake.

Since, historically, Minnesota Indians frequently migrated, establishing camps in one location during summer and at another site in fall, the population rarely erected lasting buildings. But this unique cultural trait creates a National Register dilemma, since the federal listing is almost devoid of built representations of Indian communities prior to white settlement. Instead, National Register properties linked to Native Americans are often archaeological. While Indian archaeology sites are welcome additions to the listing, such as the White Oak Point Site in Itasca County and the Gull Lake Mounds Site in Cass County, our dearth of precontact buildings is nevertheless unfortunate. Several built reminders of Native American acculturation do remain, however. Although forced indoctrination of Indians in Old World values is one of this country's less sterling moments, the buildings falling within that context still represent a significant component of Native American history. The Pipestone Indian School Superintendent's Residence in Pipestone, for example, reflects Native American instruction in Euro-American ideals. St. Cornelia's Episcopal Church at the Lower Sioux Indian Community in Redwood County was dedicated to converting the Dakota to Christianity. As with these National Register properties, the four highlighted on the succeeding pages chronicle but a tiny piece of Minnesota's Indian history. Modern Minnesotans should remember, though, that while extant historical structures tied to the state's aboriginal people are lacking, their intriguing heritage is considerably longer than all other inhabitants of Minnesota.

❋ Jeffers Petroglyphs Site

VICINITY OF JEFFERS | COTTONWOOD COUNTY

In 1962 archaeologist Dean R. Snow explained a goal of his vocation: "The long range purpose of Archaeology is not simply to discover and define chronological tables of prehistoric changes and events, but also to endeavor to say as much as possible about the total culture of any specific group of prehistoric people." Sometimes, saying as much as possible is not saying much, as with the Jeffers Petroglyphs Site in Cottonwood County in southwestern Minnesota, about six miles northeast of the small community of Jeffers.[3]

Petroglyphs are generally defined as rock art, as are pictographs. Whereas a pictograph is an image painted or drawn onto a rock surface, a petroglyph is an image pecked into a rock surface using a pointed object,

The Jeffers site is marked with numerous images, including the thunderbird, a powerful spiritual symbol for many Indians.

like a pointed rock or a fire-hardened, wood stake. The roughly two thousand images at Jeffers were pecked into a section of Red Rock Ridge, a twenty-three-mile-long Sioux quartzite outcropping that bisects the grassy prairie of north-central Cottonwood County and extends from Watonwan County to the east to Brown County to the northwest. One of the oldest and finest examples of petroglyphs in the Upper Midwest, the rock at Jeffers is decorated with symbols of bison, turtles, thunderbirds, dragonflies, projectile points, shamans, and more. A frequently repeated symbol is an atlatl, a wood, spear-throwing device that looks like a two-foot-long crochet needle and was used by prehistoric hunters to increase the force of the hurled projectile. Although many have analyzed the atlatls and other carvings, they remain a mysterious pictorial tongue fully understood only by ancient Native Americans.

The first known published record of the carvings at Jeffers is found in *The Geology of Minnesota, Volume 1 of the Final Report,* an 1884 work that notes:

> *A ledge of rock, very remarkably striated . . . and bearing rude Indian inscriptions, is found on the ridge about a mile north-northeast from the Little Cottonwood falls and quarry [in Cottonwood County]. . . . Numerous figures are pecked on this rock, representing animals, arrows, etc., similar to those inscribed by the Indians on the quartzite beside the boulders called the Three Maidens, near the Pipestone quarry.*

A year after publication of *The Geology of Minnesota,* the *New Ulm Review* of August 12, wrote of a survey party that had recently recorded nine figures at the site, some of which included "a man, his head crowned by what should perhaps present feathers," as well as "a figure much resembling a bird" and "a curious figure of geometrical character, closely resembling a kite." Four years later, as part of a massive archaeological study in the Upper Midwest, Theodore H. Lewis inspected Red Rock Ridge, tracing twenty-four petroglyphs at the present-day Jeffers site and six more at another location on the outcropping. Reviewing the efforts of Lewis, archaeologist Newton H. Winchell, who was one of the authors of *The Geology of Minnesota* as well as the author of *The Aborigines of Minnesota* (1911)—a work that featured several of Minnesota's petroglyph sites—concluded the carvings were likely the work of the Dakota. Winchell, however, failed to postulate a theory as to their meaning.

In 1935 preservationist Armin Arndt wished to save the petroglyphs by removing them from their original site. Thankfully he failed. In the early 1960s archaeologist Dean R. Snow completed the first anthropological study at Jeffers, analyzing the site for cultural meaning and concluding that "a religious motive seems to be the most probable explanation" for the petroglyphs. Also in the 1960s, several preservation-minded residents of Cottonwood County published lay works on the symbols, introducing a largely uninformed pubic to the rare carvings. One of these individuals was Florence Roefer, who became the first Jeffers Petroglyphs Site interpreter when the state of Minnesota purchased the property from the Warren Jeffers Family in 1966 and turned it over to the Minnesota Historical Society (MHS). Ten years later, archaeologist Gordon A. Lothson authored the findings of the most thorough investigation of Jeffers, a study sponsored by the MHS in 1971.

Lothson's report did not provide absolute answers as to the origins, meanings, and ages of the petroglyphs, but it was certainly better than the superficial understanding scholars had lived with for years. Lothson's team of researchers painstakingly mapped and recorded almost two thousand petroglyphs. Lothson then considered several factors when analyzing their work, including "media [the Sioux quartzite outcrop]; the techniques of manufacture revealed by the carvings; the physical size of the petroglyphs; their carving style, and the spatial relationships of individual carvings and clusters of carvings." The petroglyphs were also classified by subject, which proved the most challenging task, since many of the carvings were almost impossible to identify. Lothson's conclusions suggested a cultural resource spanning thousands of years, with several prehistoric and historic native peoples contributing representations of their heritage.

Lothson dated the carvings by subject matter, comparing symbols to historically accepted cultural characteristics. For example, the atlatl symbols at Jeffers match favorably with those discovered at Indian Knoll in Kentucky, which have been dated to 3000 BCE. The Indian Knoll carvings imply that the atlatls on Red Rock Ridge, possibly the earliest petroglyphs at the site, fell within the Late Archaic period, sometime between 3000 BCE and

500 BCE. The argument was reinforced by the projectile point carvings, which reflect a projectile point design known to have been used by hunters of the Late Archaic. Prehistoric civilizations were not the only ones who left their mark on Red Rock Ridge, however. Many carvings, such as the thunderbirds, dragonflies, turtles, and shamans, are symbolic of historic Native American tribes like the Oto, Dakota, and Iowa. Lothson believed this later group of petroglyphs fell between 900 CE and 1750 CE.

While the MHS study went further than any other toward dating the petroglyphs at Jeffers, Lothson also theorized as to the purpose of the carvings, going well beyond the ponderings of Snow. The archaeologist hypothesized three explanations: "(1) the practice of hunting magic, (2) the performance of sacred ceremonies, and (3) the recording of important events in the lives of warriors, shamans, and chiefs." Hunting magic entailed creating symbols of animal kills, like the bison carvings at Jeffers with protruding atlatl darts or spears. Some analysts speculate hunters formed such images before the hunt because they believed it would give them a certain magic when stalking their prey, improving chances of a kill. And as with other sites depicting animal kills, Jeffers is located adjacent to a migratory game trail, which edges the Little Cottonwood River. The symbols of bison, thunderbirds, and other traditionally spiritual figures suggest that Red Rock Ridge was also used for sacred ceremonies. The thunderbird, for instance, is one of the most prominent spirit beings depicted in Native American rock art. The Algonkians believed it capable of morphing into a man or conjuring magnificent storms. The bison, too, was a revered spiritual symbol, and many Indians believed it possessed magical power. While many petroglyphs at Jeffers are of bison, others are of figures adorned with bison horns, as if the individuals who carved the petroglyphs were trying to possess the bison's magic. Finally,

Thousands of years ago ancient Native Americans began pecking images into a section of Sioux quartzite bisecting grassy prairie in what would become Cottonwood County, Minnesota.

the Jeffers site may serve as a historical record, especially of chiefs, warriors, or religious leaders. As Lothson writes, many human-like figures on Red Rock Ridge exhibit horned headdresses, "a well-established cultural feature on the Plains [that] was as highly prized as the feather headdress as a symbol of social status." Some of these figures may represent individuals of high standing, or possibly reflect events in their lives. The various weapons depicted at Jeffers, as well as images of stickmen with arrows protruding from their bodies, may be a reminder of the warrior tradition of those who created the carvings.

Even though the MHS study of Jeffers is far better than any previous examinations, it remains speculation, albeit well-reasoned speculation. While further study of Jeffers, or even a similar site, may reveal more specific information, it is unlikely scholars will ever completely unravel the mystery of the petroglyphs. But for some Native Americans the mystery may not need unraveling since they view Jeffers as sacred ground, not as a story with a vague plot. In his work *The Jeffers Petroglyphs: Native American Rock Art on the Midwestern Prairie* (2001), Kevin L. Callahan quotes Jerry Flute, a Dakota elder: "To the contemporary Native Americans who reside in and around the state [Jeffers Petroglyphs] is a very spiritual place. It is a place where Grandmother Earth speaks of the past, present and future." Maybe this is the only answer we need from Jeffers—maybe this special site, which was added to the National Register in 1970, should be accepted as a venue where Grandmother Earth speaks.

✳ Little Rapids (Inyan Ceyaka Otonwe)

VICINITY OF JORDAN | SCOTT COUNTY

In 1935, Paul Klammer recounted for the *Minnesota Archaeologist* his party's archaeological exploration along the Minnesota River in Scott County, about four miles north of Jordan:

> On the fourth day of May, shortly after the big May snowstorm, Judge A. G. W. Anderson, my father and I set out on an archaeological expedition. . . . We looked for new fields with little success, returning to a location which we had explored in 1934. . . . After walking about we came back to the car. There, in an old sunken excavation, Dad saw a fish spear protruding out of the bank, at which point we immediately started to dig. The first article uncovered was a spear. . . . The tip of the spear [was] broken and we were not successful in finding it. We had not dug more than a half minute before Dad tossed out an iron tomahawk. He was so excited he was speechless."

A bone-handled iron awl, an iron axe, a sandstone arrow smoother, and other items were discovered as well. Klammer was almost giddy: "Not

The Minnesota River near Little Rapids, the site of a nineteenth-century Wahpeton Dakota village.

having expected to find such things and never expecting to again, all we seemed able to say was, 'WHAT A FIND.'"[4]

Over the next two days the group uncovered numerous other artifacts, with Klammer including a list of finds in his narrative. The party had unearthed constituents of Little Rapids (Inyan Ceyaka Otonwe), the site of a nineteenth-century Wahpeton ("people of leaves") Dakota village that existed adjacent to the east bank of the Minnesota River, near some small rapids. The Klammer group was not the first to come across the place, however. Theodore H. Lewis, the surveyor who traced images at the Jeffers Petroglyphs Site in 1889, mapped Little Rapids in 1887, including twenty-nine mounds immediately south of the village. It appears, however, that the location remained relatively unknown until Klammer's piece in the *Minnesota Archaeologist*. In the 1980s the University of Minnesota studied the site and recovered numerous artifacts, many related to the once flourishing fur trade in the area. The university excavations were led by Professor Janet D. Spector, a professional archaeologist who was ultimately inspired to write *What This Awl Means: Feminist Archaeology at a Wahpeton Dakota Village* (1993), an intriguing account of Little Rapids that is also a tribute to the accomplishments of Dakota women, a frequently neglected population in archaeological and historical scholarship. Spector's book, as well as the various excavations and modest historical records, give us a glimpse into the lives of the Wahpeton at Little Rapids during the 1800s.

The Wahpeton, along with the Mdewakanton, Sisseton, and Wahpekute tribes, make up the Eastern Dakota, while the Teton, Yankton, and Yanktonai comprise the Western Dakota. During the late 1600s, the Wahpeton were generally situated northeast of Lake Mille Lacs, but by the early 1700s the tribe had migrated south, into the lower Minnesota River area. The Wahpeton appear to have occupied Little Rapids beginning in the early 1800s, but since the tribe journeyed into the region the previous century, the Indians may have been at the site earlier. The Wahpeton were not the first aboriginal people to leave traces of themselves at Little Rapids, however. The mounds, which are artificial earthen banks that are likely burial or ceremonial sites, were probably created by ancestors of the Dakota centuries before Euro-Americans arrived in the region. Prehistoric pottery sherds and stone tools discovered at the village site also imply a precontact civilization.

Little Rapids consisted of about 325 Wahpeton living in several pitched-roof lodges made of wood and bark. The largest shelters were about 20 to 30 feet long and roughly 15 to 20 feet wide. Each shelter housed four families, one family in each corner. Since the village was only occupied during summer, the lodges were well ventilated. Scaffolds were erected above doorways and were probably used as sleeping platforms on especially warm nights. Immediately north of the village was a trading post that was established in 1802. Little is known of trading practices at the site, although French Canadian Jean Baptiste Faribault, one of Minnesota's prominent early fur traders, frequently wintered at the location.

Much of the activity in the village consisted of gathering stores for colder months. For example, the Wahpeton, like most Dakota, constructed large bark barrels for stockpiling corn. The corn was often boiled and then scraped from the cob. After the corn dried, it was placed in the barrels, which were then buried in the ground for preservation. With the arrival of autumn, the villagers would move to wild-ricing sites, and then to deer-hunting camps. The Wahpeton would return to the vicinity of Little Rapids during winter, erecting tepees in the nearby woods where they had ready access to firewood.

A significant person tied to Little Rapids is Mazomani ("Iron Walker" or "Walking Iron"). Mazomani was a Wahpeton village leader who was later killed in the Dakota Conflict, an 1862 Dakota rebellion that began at the Upper and Lower Sioux Agencies near the Minnesota River in southwestern Minnesota. Dakota oral tradition recounts that Mazomani was mortally wounded when he entered the camp of government soldiers to negotiate the release of captives. He was apparently carried to a nearby village where he died the next morning.

In 1851, Mazomani was one of the Dakota chiefs who signed the Treaty of Traverse des Sioux, ceding much Dakota land to the federal government. The treaty forced the Wahpeton from Little Rapids and onto the reservation at the Upper Sioux Agency. By this time the Wahpeton and other Dakota bands were suffering. In part, the Indians subsisted on goods obtained

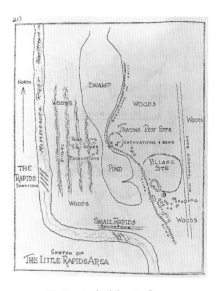

Having studied the site for years, Kenneth K. and Paul W. Klammer sketched Little Rapids in 1949.

through the fur trade. By the 1830s, overtrapping had dramatically reduced the number of fur-bearing animals. Moreover, fur markets were collapsing. When the Treaty of Traverse des Sioux was signed, opening the way for white settlement on former Indian lands, the Dakota likely viewed the Upper and Lower Sioux Agencies as their best hope for survival.

More than 130 years after the Treaty of Traverse des Sioux forever altered the lives of the Wahpeton of Little Rapids, Spector's team discovered a fascinating Dakota remembrance in a village disposal site, a finely carved and adorned bone awl handle. Spector sensed the significance of the patterns on the tool:

> When I examined the handle more closely, I felt increasingly intrigued by the person who made it. I assumed it was a woman, since women were responsible for working hides among the Dakota. She had drilled five holes down the length of the handle and etched patterns of dots and lines over all its surfaces. . . . Along one edge of the handle, she had impressed a row of fourteen equally spaced dots, marking each with a dab of red pigment. One dot was scratched over with an "X" as if she had miscounted or for some other reason wanted to erase it. On the opposite edge of the handle, another set of impressed red dots formed a different motif: six dots in a row followed by diamond-shaped clusters of four red dots each. Inscribed lines and dots covered the handle, surely signifying something to the person who crafted it and to others in the community who viewed it.

The awl handle Spector's team discovered in 1980 denotes the accomplishments of the Dakota woman who used it.

Spector later learned that the impressed, colored dots were a kind of merit badge, a symbol of the deeds of the woman who made and used the awl. Each Wahpeton Dakota woman dotted and patterned her tool to signify the wares she created with it, such as tepees or robes, as well as the number of goods fashioned. Just as the status of Dakota men was reflected in the implements they displayed, so the community standing of Dakota women was evident in the number of colored dots impressed into their awl handles.

Spector's story of the awl handle illustrates why archaeological sites like Little Rapids are important. Often, these bits of history are the only tangible evidence we have to describe those that came before us—simple markers that say "We were here, too."

Today Little Rapids is part of the Minnesota Department of Natural Resources Minnesota Valley Trail, Carver Wayside Management Unit. Unfortunately, parts of the site have been looted. Little information is available about the trading post because the location has been virtually stripped of artifacts. Some of the mounds have been plundered as well. Overall, though, the mounds and village site retain good integrity and have the potential to reveal substantial prehistoric and historic information about Native Americans in the region. Hopefully, listing Little Rapids on the National Register in 1999 will provide the location additional protection.

✳ Birch Coulee School

In December 1887, the Reverend Samuel Dutton Hinman wrote to Henry Benjamin Whipple, Minnesota's first Episcopal bishop, articulating his views on Native American education:

> *Young [Native Americans] must be provided for by giving them a thorough industrial education. They at least will grow up not helpless but fitted to bear the struggle of life in the midst of a busy civilization. Indians will continue to be Indians—in habits of mind, ideas and the stolid lethargy of their natures— until it is drilled out of them in good, practical, Christian schools where they can be separated from their home surroundings and even their native tongue and where instead they can learn thrift and industry and truth and cleanliness of mind as well as body and acquire character and learn to bow to duty instead of their own selfish and self-indulgent imaginations. With such English schools established on or near every Reserve and the children held in them as our own are—in one generation the Indian question would be settled.*

Hinman's comments are embarrassing, and addressing the "Indian question" by substituting Euro-American tradition for Native American culture—making Indians less Indian—is a supremely arrogant policy. But even though the idea of stripping heritage from another culture now makes us queasy, many government officials and missionaries in the late 1800s truly believed that converting Native Americans into Christian farmers was the right thing to do. And the sad and brutal truth is that without extensive acceptance of alien ways America's native race may never have survived.[5]

Hinman was not quite the condescending patriarch that his December 1887 letter to Whipple implies. In fact, he genuinely cared for Native Amer-

Inside Birch Coulee School in 1901, with large portraits of then-President William McKinley and his vice president, Theodore Roosevelt, on the front wall.

icans, although he steadfastly believed that the Christian life—that is, Euro-American life—was the proper life for Indians. He spent nearly half his years ministering to Native Americans, much of the time at the Lower Sioux Agency, which was established by the federal government near the Minnesota River, about ninety miles southwest of Minneapolis. Created in 1853, two years after the Wahpekute, Mdewakanton, Sisseton, and Wahpeton Dakota bands ceded their ancestral lands to the United States in the Treaties of Traverse des Sioux and Mendota, the agency was the administrative center for the southern portion of a ten-mile-wide Dakota reservation that edged the Minnesota River. The Upper Sioux Agency, about thirty miles northwest, was founded in 1856 to serve the northern section.

After arriving with his family at the Lower Sioux Agency in October 1860, one of Hinman's first acts was the construction of the Mission of St. John the Evangelist, a building that served as church, rectory, and school. The missionary also immersed himself in the Dakota language, realizing this was the only way he could effectively communicate with his congregation. In a letter to Whipple in 1861, he explained: "I so much long to speak to this people earnestly in their own tongue that I sometimes think it is my duty to banish myself from my family for a time and accompany my flock on their winter expedition that I may sooner acquire it." The comments are curious, since a quarter-century later he seemed to want to silence the Dakota language. It is likely Hinman concluded that the Dakota needed to abandon their tongue if they were to fully assimilate into Euro-American society. In any event, Hinman had learned much of the native language by 1862, when he translated the church service into Dakota. The translation was published as a booklet, which was further refined into the "Niobrara Service Book," a work still used by many Dakota late in the twentieth century.

Hinman's congregation outgrew its mission house within two years. Construction of a larger building began in July 1862, with Whipple laying the cornerstone. The structure was never completed, however, for the next month hundreds of Dakota on the reservation revolted against white authority, attacking the Lower Sioux Agency and nearby communities. There are many reasons that led to the Dakota Conflict of 1862, but the immediate trigger was crop failures in the region and late annuity payments from the federal government to the bands—in other words, the Dakota were starving. At the Lower Sioux Agency one trader is purported to have remarked: "If the Indians are hungry, let them eat grass." Apparently, he later was found dead with his mouth filled with grass. By the time hostilities subsided in late September, hundreds of white settlers and many soldiers had perished. More than three hundred Dakota were sent to Mankato for execution, although President Abraham Lincoln commuted the sentences of all but thirty-nine convicted of the most atrocious acts. Regrettably, almost all of the Dakota, including those who helped white settlers during the unrest, were exiled to the Crow Creek Reservation along the Missouri River in the Dakota Territory (now central South Dakota). Refusing to abandon his ministry, Hinman accompanied the Indians. A few years later the Dakota were again relocated, this time on the Santee Reservation near the junction of the Missouri and Niobrara Rivers in Nebraska.

In the early 1880s the Dakota began trickling back into Minnesota, most establishing farms near the sites of the Upper and Lower Sioux Agencies. In 1886, as the area began to thrive again, Hinman returned to teach young Native Americans. Instructing more than forty pupils in his home, he appealed to Whipple to convince government officials to erect a schoolhouse in the Lower Sioux Community. In 1888, $1,000 was appropriated for the task, and the following year an additional $1,000 was approved. The T-shaped building was completed in 1891, the same year as nearby St. Cornelia's Episcopal Church, a building that was placed on the National Register in 1979. Hinman never witnessed the completion of either structure, dying from pneumonia in March 1890.

Birch Coulee School was a simple, wood-framed, clapboard-covered building topped with a gable roof that was punctuated with a louvered belfry. A chimney pierced the roof's ridge at both the north and south ends. Three entrances, each with tiny, gable-roofed porches, were located at the building's east facade. Rectangular multipane windows marked the walls. Although Hinman and Whipple had hoped that the school would be maintained by the Episcopal Church, the Bureau of Indian Affairs managed it as a day school. Hinman's son, Robert, became the school's first teacher, overseeing instruction until about 1918.

Birch Coulee School closed in 1920, and the students attended the local rural school or the Indian boarding schools in Pipestone, Minnesota and

The louvered belfry is no longer extant, but the Lower Sioux Community has brought back much of Birch Coulee School's 1891 appearance.

Flandreau, South Dakota. The school reopened in 1939, but then closed again in 1969 when the state consolidated the rural school system. The building operated as a pottery shop until the mid-1980s, featuring hand-craft items with traditional Dakota designs. At some point, the louvered belfry was removed from atop the building. In the late 1980s the Lower Sioux Community restored the school, converting it into a library and community center. The "earliest and best preserved building associated with Indian education in Minnesota," the Birch Coulee School was added to the National Register in 1990.

❋ Battle Point (Sugar Point)

VICINITY OF WALKER │ CASS COUNTY

Early in the fighting, Brevet Major Melville C. Wilkinson stalked the skirmish line, directing fire and encouraging his mostly raw recruits to hold their position within the clearing that served as their base. He was felled by a bullet through his left thigh. The major was carried behind a log cabin, the only substantial protection from the intense gunfire erupting from the surrounding trees. The crude dwelling belonged to Bug-O-Nay-Ge-Shig (Hole-in-the-Day), a member of the Pillager band of Ojibwe whose reservation nestled against Leech Lake in north-central Minnesota, just north and east of Walker in Cass County. Bug-O-Nay-Ge-Shig was the reason the soldiers from Fort Snelling in St. Paul found themselves in such a precarious predicament. Intent on arresting the Pillager, the troopers had steamed across the lake from Walker, landing at Bug-O-Nay-Ge-Shig's allotment on Sugar Point, a peninsula that pierced the northeast section of Leech Lake. Instead of discovering Bug-O-Nay-Ge-Shig the soldiers stumbled into a fight. It was a bad day for the United States Army.[6]

The conflict at Sugar Point on October 5, 1898, finds its roots in the mistreatment heaped upon Bug-O-Nay-Ge-Shig by local officials, although all of the Pillagers had been abused for some time. Members of the band were frequently arrested for trivial reasons and taken far from home for trial. Witnesses to supposedly criminal acts were detained as well. Even more unsettling, the Pillagers experienced direct threats to their survival. In the 1880s the United States Army Corps of Engineers constructed dams in the Mississippi River headwaters, including one at Leech Lake. The dams flooded Indian lands, displacing villages and destroying much of the subsistence base of the band. The Pillagers also suffered injustices from logging interests. Logging companies paid annuities to the Pillagers for harvesting dead and fallen timber from the band's reservation. The value of the timber was often underestimated, and payments made to the Pillagers

One year before the conflict at Sugar Point, Bug-O-Nay-Ge-Shig (left) poses with two companions.

were frequently late. Moreover, some loggers resorted to extraordinarily devious tactics, burning the foundation of live trees to create dead timber. A day after fighting erupted on Sugar Point the *Cass County Pioneer* published the Pillagers' timber grievance. In part, the petition to the federal government read:

> *We, the undersigned chiefs and headmen of the Pillager band of Chippewa [Ojibwe] Indians of Minnesota . . . respectfully represent that our people are carrying a heavy burden, and in order that they may not be crushed by it, we humbly petition you to send a commission, consisting of men who are honest and cannot be controlled by lumbermen, to investigate the existing troubles here. . . . We now have only the pine lands of our reservation for our future subsistence and support, but the manner in which we are being defrauded out of these has alarmed us. The lands are now, as heretofore, being underestimated by the appraisers, the pine thereon is being destroyed by fires in order to create that class of timber known as dead and down timber, so as to enable [others] to cut and sell the same for their own benefit.*

Since the Pillagers were often exploited, it seemed only a matter of time before some event sparked a clash with white authorities. That event happened on September 15, 1898, when Bug-O-Nay-Ge-Shig and Sha-Boon-Day-Shkong traveled to Onigum, an Indian village near Leech Lake. While in the village the men were seized as witnesses in a bootlegging case. As they were being led away Bug-O-Nay-Ge-Shig pleaded for help from onlookers. The two men managed to escape when several Pillagers overpowered United States Deputy Marshal Robert Morrison and Indian agent Arthur M. Tinker. Bug-O-Nay-Ge-Shig had good reason to avoid being hauled a hundred miles east to Duluth as a witness. Five months earlier he had been taken to the port city on Lake Superior as a witness in another bootlegging trial. After authorities finished with him he was forced to find his own way home. It was a long walk back to the reservation, especially for a sixty-two-year-old.

Soldiers at the dock near Sugar Point at Walker in 1898

Realizing they did not have the numbers to retake Bug-O-Nay-Ge-Shig and those who assisted his escape, authorities in Cass County appealed for help to the military. Twenty soldiers of the Third Regiment United States Infantry under the command of Lieutenant Chauncey B. Humphreys were dispatched from Fort Snelling to Onigum. Humphrey and his agents soon discovered that Bug-O-Nay-Ge-Shig and the others had no intention of surrendering. The lieutenant also grasped that his tiny command was insufficient to take the Pillagers by force. Another unit of the Third Regiment was sent from St. Paul to Leech Lake. The seventy-seven troopers were led by Brevet Major Melville C. Wilkinson, who was accompanied by General John M. Bacon, acting commander of the Department of Dakota. Early in the morning of October 5, Wilkinson's soldiers boarded the steamers *Flora* and *Chief of Duluth* and sailed from Walker across Leech Lake to Sugar Point, hoping to find Bug-O-Nay-Ge-Shig and other wanted Pillagers. Several civilians were part of the force, including a couple of marshals and deputy marshals, Indian police officers, and a few reporters.

Soon after disembarking at Sugar Point the soldiers arrested two Pillagers who were part of the group that helped Bug-O-Nay-Ge-Shig flee. Bug-O-Nay-Ge-Shig, however, was absent, and the elderly Indian would not take part in the ensuing fight. The troopers made camp on his allotment, then started searching the surrounding woods and nearby Indian villages for Pillagers with outstanding warrants. None were found. Actually, few young Pillager men were seen anywhere—but they were there. General Bacon later claimed that the battle began when one of the soldiers' rifles mistakenly discharged, convincing concealed Pillagers they were being fired upon. Pillagers argued that the conflict started because several soldiers shot at a canoe carrying Indian women as it rounded Sugar Point. Regardless of how it began, around 11:30 AM the woods edging the clearing exploded with gunfire. The troopers dropped to the ground, but were quickly roused by officers and formed into a crescent-shaped skirmish line around Bug-O-Nay-Ge-Shig's cabin, with Leech Lake at their rear. The first thirty minutes were the worst, and several men in Wilkinson's force were soon killed or wounded. The wounded, including Wilkinson, were placed toward the lake side of the cabin, which offered some protection from the gunfire.

Major Wilkinson did not remain behind the cabin for long. Immediately after his leg wound was dressed he was back in front of the dwelling encouraging his troopers. It must have been disheartening to the young recruits when the major was again shot, this time through the abdomen. The officer lingered for more than an hour before dying. As Sergeant William Butler rushed to inform General Bacon of the major's mortal wound, Butler was killed by a round through the head. Gunfire from the Pillagers eventually eased, although occasional shots erupted throughout the remainder of the day. Late in the evening an Indian police officer was killed when one soldier mistook him for a Pillager attacker. The following morning a hungry soldier was shot and killed as he tried to dig potatoes from a patch in the clearing. He was the last casualty of the battle. The Pillagers apparently dispersed by the third day and the Third Regiment unceremoniously departed Sugar Point. Besides Major Wilkinson, five other soldiers had died, and ten were wounded. The Indian police officer was the only fatality among the civilians, although four were injured. It does not appear that the Pillagers suffered fatalities, and it was later learned that only nineteen of the band had taken part in the fight.

Initial panic that Indian attacks were imminent in places like Deer River, Grand Rapids, Bemidji, and Aitkin eventually subsided when the public realized the Pillagers never intended to start a war. In fact, after the federal

Even though it appears Bug-O-Nay-Ge-Shig's grave marker is misspelled, it is possible his name was spelled phonetically here.

government promised to investigate the grievances of the Pillagers, most of the Indians with outstanding warrants surrendered to authorities. They were sentenced to jail terms varying between two and ten months, although by the middle of 1899 each was pardoned. Bug-O-Nay-Ge-Shig never forfeited himself, however—his long walk from Duluth a powerful memory. Authorities chose to ignore the matter. Bug-O-Nay-Ge-Shig died in 1916 at the age of eighty. Not much effort was made to discover which Pillagers took part in the fight at Sugar Point, authorities willing to leave things alone. Within a few years much of the Pillager land was purchased from the band and converted into a national forest.

Today, all that is left of Bug-O-Nay-Ge-Shig's cabin is its foundation. Remains of trenches troopers dug for protection the night of October 5 are also visible. The boat landing where soldiers came ashore and the trail through the woods used while searching for Pillagers is present as well. The Pillager cemetery where Bug-O-Nay-Ge-Shig is buried is located nearby. The name on the gravestone reads "Pug-O-Nay-Ge-Shig," but it is possible the name was spelled phonetically. In fact, the Smithsonian Institution's National Anthropological Archives spells the name "Po-Go-Na-Ke-Shik." Interestingly, signs of an earlier Native American civilization are also apparent at the Sugar Point Site. Sandy Lake ceramics, triangular stone projectile points, and socketed antler points are all materials left by the Wanikan culture, a people who occupied the location sometime between the twelfth and eighteenth centuries. Several Wanikan burial mounds also remain. Eventually, Sugar Point—reputed as the site of the last battle between the United States Army and Native Americans—was renamed "Battle Point." It was listed on the National Register in 1990.

BEFORE THE RAILROAD 2

IN 1912, JOHN H. RANDALL wrote a story of early railroad development in Minnesota. Randall was a former employee of the St. Paul and Pacific Railroad (StP&P), successor of the Minnesota and Pacific Railroad—and predecessor to the Great Northern Railway. Randall's narrative explored an industry staggering through years of uncertainty before finding its feet in 1862. The piece in *Collections of the Minnesota Historical Society* is detailed scholarship, but toward the end of the history he observed that the StP&P "construct[ed] its line ahead of settlement." He probably should have left the statement out, or at least qualified it, because it is not entirely accurate.[7]

Many years later Timothy Rowley, a resident of Martin County in south-central Minnesota, told another story. It opened:

> *Picture in your minds, if you will, a young couple in an eastern state who have just taken the marriage vows. They are trying to solve the problem of procuring a home. Their financial circumstances will not permit them to purchase one there. The trades and professions are overcrowded. They have heard that somewhere in the West, Uncle Sam is practically giving away quarter sections of land to actual settlers. They decide to avail themselves of this opportunity of having a home of their own.*

Rowley's colorful and descriptive address on the ordeals of pioneering was delivered to the Martin County Historical Society in 1929. Although a fictional story, it aptly expressed the hardships of immigrating to Minnesota and making a new life in the mid-nineteenth century. And Rowley should know, since the seventy-three-year-old speaker had traveled west in a canvas-covered wagon with his family, settling in Martin County in the late 1850s. If Randall was correct, then Rowley's family, as well as his imaginary couple, would have ridden the train into Minnesota. But that was impossible, because no rail line existed in Minnesota in the 1850s, and those established in the 1860s mostly served small sections of the state. Minnesota was not connected to another state by railroad until the late 1860s, and even that was a circuitous route. Substantial railroad development awaited the 1870s.

Many settlers began arriving in Minnesota about the time it became a territory in 1849. Statehood was still nine years away. Fur traders had traipsed the land since the seventeenth century, and the timber industry began carving its way through regional forests by the late 1830s. It was these new arrivals, however, who initiated a lasting industry: agriculture. The settlers came by wagon and steamship. By the early 1850s, steamers carried pilgrims up the Mississippi River from the railhead at Rock Island, Illinois, and St. Louis, Missouri. Additional railheads were soon established in Galena and Dunlieth, Illinois, and Prairie du Chien and La Crosse, Wisconsin. Whether coming by wagon or steamer, settlers usually flowed west, northwest, or southwest of the river city of St. Paul, although extensive expansion west was limited until the signing of further treaties with the local Native American populations. Other settlers established residence in southeastern Minnesota. Houston, Minnesota, for instance, was platted in 1852, roughly twenty miles west of Wisconsin, and about the same distance north of Iowa. Many of the settlers built farmsteads and raised wheat, at least until the land could no longer sustain a one-crop routine.

As farmsteads began dotting the countryside so did additional river communities. With the exception of Minneapolis, none would compare with the industrial might of St. Paul, although many still became economic heavyweights. Hastings, for example, which was founded along the banks of the Mississippi River about fifteen miles southeast of the capital city, became a conduit for regional agricultural produce shipped downriver by steamboat. It had already incorporated as a city by 1857, well before Minneapolis. Mankato in Blue Earth County, roughly seventy-five miles southeast of Minneapolis, had regular commerce with St. Paul via the Minnesota River by the early 1850s. During these early settlement years, the produce that gave towns like Hastings and Mankato their economic muscle came from surrounding farmers who were finally capable of cultivating cash crops after years of subsistence farming.

As important as the rivers proved to the early development of Minnesota, they were not the only means of transportation during the period. As early as the 1830s, the Red River Trails extended from the Red River, a waterway that eventually marked the northwestern boundary of Minnesota, all the way to St. Paul. Oxcarts carrying furs traveled east over these crude pathways, while settlers desiring to locate beyond frontier boundaries journeyed west. The staging industry was booming by the 1850s, providing at least a modicum of overland mass transit. By 1854, a stage road even connected Dubuque, Iowa, with St. Paul.

Minnesota before the railroad was surely advancing, although it remained a rather humble place to be. Nevertheless, its star shone bright enough to attract many looking for better opportunity, like the Rowleys. Indeed, the land's fertile soil and rich timber resources brought multitudes into the area. When the railroads were finally established, multitudes upon multitudes came—giving rise to Randall's assertion that settlement followed the railroad. But even though the historian overreached, he was partly correct, since settlement of some of Minnesota followed the rail lines or was at least occurring contemporaneously with railroad advancement. Before that happened, however, immigrants to Minnesota still managed to stake out an existence and build communities by initiating modest industry and commerce. And while some today may be surprised, Minnesota retains many properties dating to this early settlement period. Situated in Pickwick, about 120 miles southeast of St. Paul, Pickwick Mill is one of the oldest water-powered mills in the state, a limestone edifice erected in 1854. Nine years later, the graceful Zoar Moravian Church was raised in Lakeside Township, about three miles southeast of Waconia in Carver County. Both of these National Register structures are worthy representatives of the period just prior to the railroad's emergence, as are the historic resources that follow.

✳ Guri & Lars Endreson House

DOVRE TOWNSHIP | KANDIYOHI COUNTY

Guri and Lars Endreson emigrated from Norway to the United States in 1856, looking to the Midwest to make a new life. In 1857 the Endresons settled in sparsely populated western Minnesota, in what soon would become Kandiyohi County. The following year they erected a small cabin near West Solomon Lake, about five miles northwest of Willmar. Since industrially manufactured materials were mostly unavailable in newly settled regions of Minnesota in the mid- to late 1800s, settlers relied on their immediate environment for resources to erect a house. In wooded areas, this often meant humble dwellings formed of timber, like the Endreson House. But although the Endresons' one-and-a-half-story cabin wasn't much, it was home. Formed of square-hewn logs, the gable-roofed structure was notched at the corners in a dovetail, the quintessential cabin-construction method of Scandinavian immigrants. The Endresons formed the notch by shaping the ends of each wall timber into a tenon, or projecting member, broader at its end than at its base—like a dove's tail. Overlapping the dovetailed ends of the timbers, the family raised a rectangular house over a rock-walled cellar. The dwelling had a few windows and doors but displayed no aesthetic embellishment. The interior consisted of an undivided main floor, as well as a loft accessed by a ladder. While no longer extant, the cabin likely included a hearth or stove for cooking and heating. The house the Endresons built was so durable that almost 150 years later it continues to mark its original plot near West Solomon Lake.[8]

Like most immigrants, the Endresons just wanted a shot at prosperity, and in the mid-nineteenth century America was the land of chances. By the early 1860s, Lars and Guri Endreson and their children were succeeding, cultivating several acres of farmland and maintaining a significant number of livestock, including cows, sheep, pigs, and chickens. Their eldest daughter, Gjaertru, was married and living on a nearby farm. Life was hard, but it was good. Unfortunately, it did not last.

On August 21, 1862, the family was surprised at their home by a party of Dakota. Starving and angry, hundreds of Dakota confined to the Upper and Lower Sioux Agencies in southwestern Minnesota had rebelled three days earlier. Now commonly known as the Dakota Conflict of 1862, the rebellion depopulated much of the southwestern part of the state. Many white settlers perished, and even more fled east toward Forest City, Paynesville, and St. Cloud. At the Endreson House, Lars was killed as he mowed grass, and Endre, one of the Endresons' sons, was murdered as he picked potatoes for dinner. Another son, Ole, was wounded and daughters Brita and Guri were taken captive. The elder Guri escaped notice by sheltering in an outside cellar with Anna, her infant daughter.

The next day Guri and her son buried Lars and Endre and then traveled to the Erickson farmstead, home of Gjaertru. Unsure of the voices emanating from the Erickson cabin, Guri and Ole returned home, but revisited the Erickson place the following day, where they discovered two dead men and two wounded men. One of the injured may have been Gjaertru's husband. Apparently Gjaertru made her escape earlier with another woman and some children. Dressing the wounded, Guri loaded the men in a wagon and took them to Forest City, where she was reunited with her two daughters, Brita and Guri, who had managed to flee their captors. The next several weeks brought hundreds of deaths throughout southwestern Minnesota, but Guri's small Lutheran church congregation in Kandiyohi County seemed especially affected, losing twenty of its members.

Although the Dakota Conflict lasted only about six weeks, it took much longer before settlers from Kandiyohi County began returning to their homes in significant numbers, many likely waiting until the Dakota were banished from the state. Guri finally returned to the area in 1866, but she shunned her cabin for a period and stayed with friends. In December 1866, she wrote another daughter in Norway, explaining the family's ordeal, her bitterness toward the Dakota at times apparent:

> *I do not seem to have been able to do so much as to write to you, because during the time when the savages raged so fearfully here I was not able to think about anything except being murdered, with my whole family, by these terrible heathen. . . . I had to look on while they shot my precious husband dead, and in my sight my dear son Ole was shot through the shoulder. But he got well again from this wound and lived a little more than a year and then was taken sick and died. We also found my oldest son Endre shot dead, but I did not see the firing of this death shot. . . . To be an eyewitness to these things and to see many others wounded and killed was almost too much for a poor woman, but, God be thanked, I kept my life and my sanity, though all my movable property was torn away and stolen. But this would have been nothing if only I could have had my loved husband and children. . . .*

At some point Guri moved back into her cabin with her daughters Anna and Brita, remaining there for several years. After Anna married, Guri left the cabin and stayed with her daughter's family, passing away in June 1881. Eventually, the cabin was incorporated within a frame farmhouse, although a later owner, Paul E. Anderson, removed the framed building, reexposing the cabin. The structure was purchased by the Kandiyohi County Historical Society in 1962 and restored eight years later by the Ekeberg Foundation as a tribute to local historian and legislator Victor E. Lawson, who died in 1960.

The Guri and Lars Endreson House, a frontier log home displaying the dovetail joinery common to nineteenth-century Scandinavian immigrants

Maintained by the Kandiyohi County Historical Society, the cabin is now a historic site. One of the oldest buildings in the county, constructed several years before the arrival of the railroad forever altered life in Minnesota, this excellent example of a frontier dwelling was added to the National Register in 1986.

✳ St. Cloud & Red River Valley Stage Road: Kandota Section

VICINITY OF WEST UNION | TODD COUNTY

Charles Dickens, the nineteenth-century English novelist acknowledged for his uncommonly descriptive and expressive prose, reflected on a stage-coach trip he took while in Ohio:

> *At one time we were all flung together in a heap at the bottom of the coach, and at another we were crushing our heads against the roof. Now, one side was down deep in the mire, and we were holding on to the other. Now, the coach was lying on the tails of the two wheelers; and now it was rearing up in the air, in a frantic state. . . .*

Dickens exaggerated, of course, but not by much.[9]

Like Dickens's ordeal in Ohio, stagecoach travel for many in Minnesota in the mid- to late nineteenth century was often a trial. Former Minnesota Lieutenant Governor Ignatius Donnelly is purported to have spurned Iowa as a home in part because he believed he would have to travel almost everywhere by coach. With the abhorrent road conditions it is little wonder that passengers rarely enjoyed the ride. Roads were often poorly graded dirt trails that became poorly graded mud trails when the rain came, and few took pleasure paying a fare and then being forced to exit the coach and push when the wagon became stuck. Nevertheless, between 1849, when Minnesota became a territory, and 1880, when the railroads reached into almost every section of the state, stagecoach transportation was vital, opening Minnesota's interior to settlement.

Stagecoach travel did not become common in the New World until about 1760, although a stage line existed between Burlington and Perth Amboy, New Jersey in 1706. A line linked the cities of Boston and Newport, Rhode Island, in 1716, and another was established between Philadelphia and New York in 1750. In the 1760s several lines opened in New Jersey, and connections between Delaware and Maryland were also established. Links between Boston and New York were created as well, and several shorter connections were made between areas near major northern cities. The lines eventually pushed west, following the migration of Americans deeper inland. Staging opened in St. Louis in 1818 and in Illinois the following year, receiving a boost in the 1830s when the Jackson administration began awarding mail contracts to stagecoach companies to stimulate development of transportation corridors. By the late 1830s the program had encouraged the creation of stage lines in Wisconsin and Iowa.

Although a series of simple caravan trails already existed between the Mississippi River and the Red River Valley, Minnesota's first attempt at significant stagecoach transportation came in 1849, when Amherst Willoughby and Simon Powers operated a route between St. Paul and St. Anthony. Other staging concerns and routes soon followed. In 1852, a road was established between St. Peter in south-central Minnesota and St. Paul. Around the same time routes from Lake Pepin and Read's Landing on the Mississippi River to locations along the Minnesota River were surveyed. In 1854, Martin O. Walker, an enterprising although seemingly abrasive personality, created a road from St. Paul to the Iowa border, giving him stage routes in Minnesota, Iowa, Wisconsin, Illinois, and Missouri. Minnesota's most expansive staging period continued through 1859, capped by the completion of the Minnesota Stage Company's Red River Valley Stage Road.

In 1857 the Northwestern Express and Transportation Company gained the contract to haul goods to the Red River Valley outposts of the Hudson's Bay Company. Two years later, after merging with another stage firm to form the Minnesota Stage Company, the concern acquired the mail contract from St. Cloud in central Minnesota to Fort Abercrombie in the Red River Valley, an outpost in the Dakota Territory near the present-day Minnesota town of Breckenridge. Under the guidance of partner Russell Blakely, the Minnesota Stage Company carved a roughly 160-mile road from St. Cloud to the Red River Valley by felling trees, erecting bridges, and building stage stops. The task was mostly finished in about a month, implying that the road wasn't much. Travelers on the line lamented all the holes, tree stumps, crude bridges, swamps, and mosquitoes. On July 7, 1859, the (St. Paul) *Weekly Pioneer and Democrat* complained that the road "winds spirally like a grapevine round the twisted stem of the Sauk River—over it and under it, and on both sides of it." Specifically, the road traversed the Sauk River about four miles northwest of St. Cloud, crossing the waterway again near New Munich, before running to Melrose and Sauk Centre. In Kandota Township in Todd County, the route bisected the Sauk River for the last time, and then passed near Osakis Lake and through Alexandria, extending to a point near present-day Fergus Falls, before finally reaching Breckenridge and Fort Abercrombie near the Bois de Sioux and Red Rivers. While the road was not straight or unobstructed, it was still the best route between the Red River Valley and settlements in central and southeastern Minnesota.

Settlements began springing up along the road within a year of its construction, and by 1863 so much traffic was passing over the route that the Minnesota Stage Company had to advertise for extra teams. With the com-

Stagecoach travel in early Minnesota was a chore, and merely the thought of a long journey over the Kandota Section of the St. Cloud and Red River Valley Stage Road made the bones ache.

pletion of another road from St. Paul to Superior, Wisconsin, the Minnesota Stage Company was the state's leading carrier, operating roughly thirteen hundred miles of roads. The heyday of the stage road in Minnesota was brief, however, as railroads began laying tracks in the state beginning in the 1860s. Railroad development was at first timid, but greatly expanded during the 1870s. The stage lines were eventually supplanted by the railroads as the principal mode of land transportation because staging could not offer the same capacity as the rail lines. Traffic was already being siphoned from the Minnesota Stage Company after the St. Paul and Pacific Railroad (later the Great Northern Railway) reached Breckenridge in 1871. The Northern Pacific Railway built into Fargo the following year. For a time, stage service survived by feeding passengers, mail, and freight to the railroads, but as the rail lines continued to expand stage transportation increasingly became less profitable. By 1880 almost every part of the state was linked by the railroads and the few stage lines that still existed were only a shadow of what they had been. While staging would eventually disappear, a line from Roseau to Marshall managed to stay in business until the early years of the twentieth century.

Today, only remnants of some early stage routes can be found. In 1990, the Minnesota State Historic Preservation Office pinpointed three fragments of stage roads that continue to reflect their historic character, including the Kandota Section of the St. Cloud and Red River Valley Stage Road built by the Minnesota Stage Company in 1859. Situated in the southeast quarter of Section 30 in Kandota Township, the unimproved road runs a few hundred yards northwest, "long enough to evoke a sense of destination or direction." Moreover, the woodland setting remains much as it was when teams ushered passengers and freight between St. Cloud and the Red River Valley. The Mantorville Section of the Mantorville and Red Wing Stage Road in Dodge County, as well as the Mount Pleasant Section of the Lake City and Rochester Stage Road in Wabasha County, have also been identified as reminiscent of their original transportation and settlement purpose. All three segments were added to the National Register in 1991.

✳ Jefferson Grain Warehouse

JEFFERSON TOWNSHIP | HOUSTON COUNTY

Steamboat transportation in the Upper Mississippi River Valley was immensely prosperous in the early and middle parts of the nineteenth century. With little railroad competition in the region the steamers dominated the freight traffic. The Mississippi River between St. Paul and St. Louis was a bustle of activity as steamboats plied the waters with cargoes of grain harvested from the wheat fields of Iowa and Minnesota and earmarked for

The slough behind the Jefferson Grain Warehouse vanished after a series of dams were constructed on the Mississippi River in the 1930s, but it no longer mattered since the steamboat age had long since passed.

urban centers in the East. It was a "Golden Age" for the steamers and a potential financial boon to those who tied their fortune to the steamboat industry. So went the thinking of William Robinson, a native of Allamakee County, Iowa, when he established a steamboat grain warehouse along a Mississippi River slough—or inlet—in southeastern Minnesota in 1868.[10]

Built of limestone and wood, the 22- by 40-foot warehouse was constructed about one mile north of the Minnesota-Iowa border in Houston County. Area farmers welcomed the one-and-a-half-story, gable-roofed structure since it was the only grain storage facility along the river for miles. Oriented on an east-west axis, the rear of the building edged the water, providing easy transfer of grain from the structure's basement to vessels moored in the slough. To complement the warehouse Robinson and another man from Allamakee County, R. P. Spencer, platted a village that they named Jefferson. When the plat was filed in 1869 the village consisted of several 40- by 80-foot lots bordering either side of a single half-mile-long street. A few houses and hotels were soon constructed and Jefferson seemed a community on the rise. With no railroad to siphon freight traffic away from the steamers the future of Jefferson, with its grain warehouse edging a major commercial waterway, looked bright. But the railroad was coming, and management behind the line had little interest in the prosperity of Jefferson.

Maybe Robinson should have realized his venture was doomed from the outset. After all, the railroads were relentlessly pushing west. It was simply a matter of time before the Mississippi was bridged and rail lines were constructed paralleling the river. Robinson may have been lulled into a belief that steamboat and rail transport would work in consort. During the Civil War steamboats in the Upper Mississippi River Valley frequently hauled cargoes to the nearest railheads where the freight was shipped east. The earliest railheads were established in the region during the 1850s and originated from Chicago and Milwaukee. Rock Island, Illinois (1854), Dunlieth, Illinois (1855), Prairie du Chien, Wisconsin (1857), and La Crosse, Wisconsin (1858), were all fixed railroad shipping points on the east bank of the Mississippi River by the start of the Civil War.

Whatever Robinson's grand ambitions for the future of his grain warehouse and village, it was clear by the early 1870s that the railroad did not share them. The railroad had the resources to usurp Robinson's small-scale operation, and when the Chicago, Dubuque, and Minnesota Railroad reached the Jefferson vicinity it chose to plat another town one and a half miles to the south. The community of New Albin, Iowa, was born in 1871 on a site the railroad considered well suited to expansion. Grain storage facilities were soon constructed and the town quickly flourished. It hardly mattered that New Albin was not located on the river since the community's fortunes would rise and fall with the railroad, a means of transport technologically superior to the steamboat. And in 1871, along the Minnesota-Iowa border in the Upper Mississippi River Valley, it was obvious where the real promise lay. After only a few years of operation Robinson's steamboat warehouse was obsolete, and the village of Jefferson would never fulfill its anticipated potential. In a cruel twist of fate William Robinson would die one year after the founding of New Albin. That same year his former partner, R. P. Spencer, joined with the Chicago, Dubuque, and Minnesota Railroad in replatting the village of Jefferson. By the end of the year the railroad had laid its tracks though Jefferson, essentially following the village's main road that was laid out three years earlier.

It is uncertain if steamboats, or even the railroad, ever utilized the grain warehouse in Jefferson after 1872. If so, it was not used for long. Four years after the railroad came through the facility was abandoned. The grain warehouse and all the lots east of the railroad line were sold in 1881 for $12.00 in back taxes.

The community of Jefferson eventually faded away. Like so many villages established along the Mississippi River in the nineteenth century it proved a "paper town"—a town officially documented in local county records that failed to survive. Most of the structures that comprised the village remained until the 1940s, when they were finally demolished to make way for Minnesota State Highway 26. One remnant of the old town endured, however. More than 130 years after it was constructed, the Jefferson Grain Warehouse continues to stand as a reminder of a period when the steamboat was the primary mode of freight transport in the Upper Mississippi River Valley. It is one of three steamboat grain warehouses remaining in Minnesota, and it is clearly the state's best example of the property type. It was placed on the National Register in 1994.

✳ Good Templars Hall

NININGER | DAKOTA COUNTY

In part, the circa 1857 poster read:

> *The city of Nininger, situated on the Mississippi River, 35 miles below St. Paul,*
> *is now a prominent point for a large commercial town, being backed by exten-*
> *sive agricultural, grazing and farming country. [It] has fine streams in the inte-*
> *rior, well adapted for milling in all its branches, and manufacturing water-*
> *power to any extent.*

Boosterism in the mid-nineteenth century was nothing new. In fact,
it was expected. Many entrepreneurs made a fortune platting towns in the
West and then promoting them to an economically disenfranchised populace in the East. The sky was always bluer in the West, the grass perpetually
greener, and, most importantly, the financial opportunities invariably better.
For many boosters, truth was an option, but exaggeration was essential.
To hear Ignatius Donnelly tell it, the small community of Nininger, about
fifteen miles southeast of St. Paul and only a few miles northwest of Hastings, was the nearest thing to heaven on earth: "It is delightfully situated
on an abrupt eminence on the west bank of the Mississippi River . . . [it]
charms the eye with the scenery it commands." Unlike many boosters,
Donnelly seemed to truly believe what he was saying. He tirelessly promoted
his town, even as it was vanishing.[11]

Donnelly was born into a devoutly religious family in Philadelphia in
1831. He graduated from high school in 1849 and was accepted to the Pennsylvania bar three years later. He immersed himself in Pennsylvania politics, campaigning for the state legislature in 1855. He bowed out and supported the Whig candidate when he realized he would not win the election.
About this time he became intrigued with land speculation in the West.
Heeding Horace Greeley's advice, Donnelly and his wife, Katherine, liqui-
dated their assets and headed west. He ruled out Ohio because civilization
had already enveloped it. He disliked Kansas because the state embraced
slavery. Iowa was apparently rejected because he felt he would have to travel
almost everywhere by stagecoach, something he found terribly uncomfort-
able. But the Minnesota Territory he liked. He was delighted with his steamboat trip from Davenport, Iowa, to St. Paul, enamored by the picturesque
country edging the Mississippi River. Moreover, Minnesota was in the
midst of an economic boom. For Donnelly, the rosy financial scene in Minnesota was as inviting as its landscape.

Soon after arriving in Minnesota in late 1856, Donnelly formed a partnership with land speculator John Nininger, a Philadelphia acquaintance
who had recently laid out a townsite carrying his moniker. John Nininger
was also the brother-in-law of Alexander Ramsey, the former territorial gov-

ernor of Minnesota. Donnelly's role in the partnership was to promote the townsite, lauding its favorable location along the Mississippi River. John Nininger was responsible for lot sales. Both men believed the community of Nininger had the potential to become a major commercial center, serving as a distribution point for commodities coming upriver, and as a shipping point for agricultural goods going downriver. With Ramsey providing influence, the two men were convinced they had a winner. Others thought so as well. Persuaded by Donnelly's hard-charging advertising campaign, settlers soon began arriving in Nininger, certain the town was destined to be a Minnesota metropolis. By 1858, the community's population was nearing a thousand, including one physician and several lawyers and real estate agents. About this time, Nininger could boast seven or eight merchant establishments, a few blacksmith and wagon shops, a sash and door manufacturer, a plow factory, two sawmills, a gristmill, three hotels, and a drugstore. Moreover, the young town had six saloons, which probably explains why the Independent Order of the Good Templars chose to establish a chapter there.

The Good Templars were a national temperance society founded in the early 1850s. The organization evolved into the largest temperance fraternal group in American history. The Good Templars provided members with support and friendship, encouraging addicts to remain free from alcohol. Constituents were urged to "run and speak to that young man who is contracting vicious habits—gain his consent that you shall propose his name for membership in the lodge." Constructed in spring 1858, the Good Templars Hall in Nininger was a two-story, wood-framed building with a gable roof and wood lap siding. Its Greek Revival style was reflected in gable

Now a one-story building, but still loosely reflecting Greek Revival style, the Good Templars Hall is all that remains of a nineteenth-century dream.

returns and decorative, corner pilasters, a shallow, rectangular and vertical architectural element reminiscent of a column. Measuring about 20 by 38 feet, it rapidly became one of the principal social centers in town. Unfortunately for the Templars, the hall's popularity was not enough to keep the group in business in Nininger.

The Templars owned the hall for only one year. Financial problems plagued the chapter in Nininger and they were forced to sell the building to the town for $200. The town converted the hall into a school. Financial woes were not reserved for the Templars. The entire country was suffering through the financial panic of 1857, a crisis initiated by the failure in August of the New York branch of the Ohio Life Insurance and Trust Company. Nininger was especially vulnerable at this time. Only an infant settlement, it had been built on expectation—the promise of a bright tomorrow. That is, it had been built on a mountain of debt. The year the Templars erected their hall proved the town's high point. As investment in the community waned, the town faltered. Many citizens could not follow through with improvements that were stipulated in their deeds and John Nininger began forfeiture proceedings, an action that made him profoundly unpopular. Donnelly continued to champion Nininger, as well as Minnesota, which officially became a state in 1858. Donnelly even attempted to use the nation's economic misfortune to generate interest in the state. One of his promotional pamphlets employed a tongue-in-cheek pitch: "Cure for the panic. Emigrate to Minnesota! Where no banks exist." The marketing ploy was more amusing than successful. With a populace now hoarding its dimes, Nininger was finished.

The town's citizens exited in droves, some taking their buildings with them. The Handyside House, one of the community's hotels, was removed from Nininger and reestablished in Hastings. Many other businesses and homes were torn down or abandoned. The Good Templars Hall remained, however, operating as a rural school. By the 1870s it was suffering from wood decay and a poor foundation. A new stone foundation was constructed and the original first floor was torn away. The second floor was then lowered onto the foundation, thus converting the building into a single-story structure. The walls were lined with soft brick for insulation. The building continued as a school until 1949, when it was sold to Nininger Township and began functioning as a town hall. In the 1970s, the Nininger Chapter of the Dakota County Historical Society wanted to preserve the building since it represented a significant piece of the area's history. The hall was modified with new siding and corner pilasters, as well as new shingles. The building has undergone additional modification since that time. The decorative corner pilasters installed in the 1970s have been replaced with less embellished elements. The transom above the front door has also been removed.

Neither the National Park Service nor State Historic Preservation Offices provide plaques for National Register properties, although owners of historic places often have one manufactured, as the Nininger Chapter of the Dakota County Historical Society did for the Good Templars Hall.

In this circa 1860 image of the original two-story Good Templars Hall, modest Greek Revival style is evident in the gable returns and corner pilasters.

For many years the Good Templars Hall shared its Nininger heritage only with the Ignatius Donnelly House, which was located just northwest of the hall. Donnelly had remained committed to Nininger, calling it home even after everyone else had left. During the years following the town's collapse, he gained distinction, first as lieutenant governor of Minnesota and later as a member of Congress. He also wrote books, including *Atlantis* (1882), as well as *Ragnarok: The Age of Fire and Gravel* (1883). Through it all he lived in Nininger, passing away in 1901. Despite efforts to save his home, it was razed in 1949. The Good Templars Hall is now the last vestige of the former boomtown, although modern development in the area makes the old building look somewhat out of place. The hall was added to the National Register in 1979.

Lanesboro Stone Dam

LANESBORO | FILLMORE COUNTY

In summer 1868 officials of the newly established village of Lanesboro in southeastern Minnesota began building a dam across the South Branch of the Root River. The dam was comprised of several stone tiers, each set back several inches from the one just below, like steps of a stairway. It proved a poor plan, and even before the dam was finished the river washed it away. Undeterred, workers began again using a different design. This time they were successful, erecting a stone dam that was built along an arc that curved upstream. The dam was constructed so well that almost 140 years later it continues to mark the western edge of Lanesboro.[12]

Lanesboro, roughly a hundred miles southeast of the Twin Cities in Fillmore County, was founded in 1868 by the Lanesboro Townsite Company. Some members of the townsite company were also invested in the Southern Minnesota Railroad Company, which began constructing a rail line across southern Minnesota to the Dakota Territory in the late 1860s. The creation of Lanesboro coincided with the railroad reaching the townsite. Officials of the townsite company were convinced the new community had the potential to become an industrial center by milling wheat, the cash crop of southern Minnesota, and shipping it east via the Southern Minnesota Railroad. Several buildings were soon erected, including a stone hotel, a frame boarding house, and a company office. A number of other commercial establishments and houses were also built. Two of the most significant contributions to the community, however, were a dam on the South Branch of the Root River and a diversion canal that paralleled the waterway. The dam directed some of the river's flow into the canal, while most of the river cascaded over the dam's crest. Flow in the canal provided the motive force for turning the turbines of three flour mills that were situated adjacent to the canal.

Lanesboro's dam was an arch constructed from locally quarried stone. The design was technically demanding, and it is somewhat surprising that the infant community in sparsely settled Fillmore County was able to muster the expertise to build it. Erecting an arch dam after the failure of the earlier dam, which used a less challenging plan, was bold. Other communities may have been more conservative and constructed a gravity structure, the most elementary, and therefore most common, form of dam. A gravity dam is simply a mass of material like wood, stone, or concrete that

The arch dam resists hydrostatic loads pressing its upstream face by flexing against the hard rock walls at either end of the dam.

is placed in a waterway. The weight of the material is so great that the hydrostatic load (water pressure) cannot move it. Officials in Lanesboro were probably tempted to build an arch dam because the walls at either side of the river channel were made of hard rock, a necessary geographical feature for constructing this type of dam. Unlike a gravity structure, an arch dam does not rely on weight to withstand hydrostatic loads. Instead, it resists water pressure through "arch action." Pressure against the upstream face of the dam is carried through the arch and into the walls at either side of the structure. In other words, the hydrostatic load forces the dam to press against the rock walls, thus resisting the water pressure.

The engineer for Lanesboro's dam was a man named Porter. Porter was also the engineer for the first dam, implying that he received some technical advice from another quarter the second time around. W. H. Walrath

Nearly 140 years old, the Lanesboro Stone Dam may not look special, but it is major engineering for a nineteenth-century Minnesota community.

served as foreman, and Frank Erickson, Nels Benson, and Olaf Olson were the stonemasons. The masons cut the stones so well that the dam was pieced together without mortar. The structure was comprised of two principal components: a main spillway and a headgate section. The headgates were vertically sliding timber gates that covered openings in the stone dam segment that blocked the river from the diversion canal. Raising and lowering the headgates controlled flow into the canal. The arched main spillway was roughly 193 feet long, and rose about 25 feet above the riverbed. The headgate component was considerably smaller.

Lanesboro's $15,000 dam created a picturesque lake near the southwest corner of the community. The lake was about two miles long and roughly a mile wide, with depths up to thirty-five feet. The lake was mostly gone by the turn of the twentieth century. Soil erosion caused the water body to fill with silt, leaving only the river channel. Lanesboro's flour milling industry vanished as well. Wheat farming so depleted the soil that the ground could no longer sustain the crop and the mills were forced to close. But even though the enterprise that the dam and diversion canal were originally constructed to support was gone, the structures remained vital to the community. In 1895, Lanesboro built a hydroelectric facility, which was rebuilt in the 1920s. The plant relied on the dam and diversion canal to provide water to its turbines for generating electricity. The dam and diversion canal were added to the National Register in 1982 as part of the Lanesboro Historic District, which includes much of downtown Lanesboro. The Lanesboro Stone Dam, however, is also significant as a stand-alone feature of the district, since it is one of the earliest masonry arch dams remaining in the country.

Orville P. & Sarah Chubb House

FAIRMONT | MARTIN COUNTY

By 1990 the Martin County Board of Commissioners was seeking additional parking for the county courthouse in Fairmont, a south-central Minnesota town about ten miles north of the Minnesota-Iowa border, and roughly fifty miles west of Albert Lea. The board purchased a lot and house on Lake Avenue, immediately north of the courthouse, intending to replace the old dwelling with a parking lot. But the house had friends, local citizens who realized what they were about to lose, the oldest residence in Fairmont, and the city's only extant building constructed of brick manufactured in the region's first brickyard. Home to one of Fairmont's founders, the Orville P. and Sarah Chubb House sidestepped the wrecking ball when the Martin County Preservation Association acquired and restored the property in the early 1990s.[13]

Orville and Sarah Chubb

Born in Nankin, Michigan, in 1830, Orville P. Chubb studied medicine at Cincinnati Medical College. After graduating he married Sarah E. Gorton and opened a professional practice in Tuscola County, Michigan. Not long after the Civil War erupted he enlisted as a private in the Fifth Michigan Regiment of the Union Army. But doctors do not remain privates for long, and Chubb was soon functioning as an army surgeon. In spring 1865 he traveled to Martin County in southern Minnesota as representative of several Fifth Michigan Regiment officers who wished to purchase the undeveloped townsite of Fairmont. Completing the transaction, he returned to his regiment and finished his military service. Chubb was back in Fairmont with his family in 1866, likely joining the loud chorus calling for a rail line into the area to make the county's wheat production profitable. A railroad remained years away, however.

One year after settling in Fairmont, Chubb and his partners replatted the community. The doctor was also responsible for the form of the local cemetery and the county fairgrounds. To generate interest in Fairmont, Chubb and fellow officer Colonel Lounsberry partnered in a brickyard near the southwestern edge of Buffalo Lake, roughly two miles north of town. The brickyard was soon abandoned, however, because some brickmakers believed the soil at the site contained too much lime to manufacture quality brick. It was too late for Chubb and Lounsberry, though, since Chubb had constructed his house of the supposedly substandard material and Lounsberry had built his basement with the brick. The brick was also employed for the basement of the local school. Early residents of Fairmont likely eyed the structures with trepidation, wondering if they might collapse at some point.

The Greek Revival–style Chubb House was completed in 1867 by John R. Dalton, an Irish-born mason who became one of Martin County's natural oddities, living to the ripe age of a hundred, despite smoking and chewing tobacco every day since his early youth. When Dalton was ninety years old he reflected on the Chubb House:

Detail of stones used to construct the cellar, many of which were pulled from a nearby lake

> We had to go into the lake to get enough stones for the cellar. My wagon ran out of grease, and I went to Reuben Ward to buy some. He didn't have it, and there wasn't enough in Fairmont for my wagon. He then sold me some brown soap and I used that. . . . I drew three dollars a day for the team and wagon and four dollars a day for myself. . . . I'm sure that this was the first brick house in the territory, including Jackson, Faribault, and Martin Counties.

Greek Revival architecture was largely popular from about 1830 to 1860, so the Chubb House was somewhat out of style by the time it was built, although in tiny Fairmont, separated from the outside world, it was probably the height of residential fashion. The architecture often features low-pitched gable or hip roofs, gable returns, and small, rectangular windows near a wide frieze at the cornice. Bolder examples of the style are often embellished with porches accented with Doric columns supporting an entablature, a horizontal band formed of classical architectural elements, or a pediment, a low-pitched gable with classical detailing. Narrow sidelights and transoms around the main entrance are common as well. The modest-

sized, one-and-a-half-story Chubb House was more reserved in style, how-ever. The gable-roofed, rectangular building exhibited gable returns at its east facade, a wide, simple frieze near the cornice, and small, rectangular frieze windows at the north and south sides. Vertically aligned rectangular win-dows marked the center of the east facade, just north of the main entrance.

The Chubb family remained in their brick home for eight years. Much of that time Orville was the only physician in Fairmont. He became a partner in a local drugstore and invested in a steam-powered sawmill as well. Appar-ently concluding that he was not a newsman, he soon resold a local news-paper he purchased in 1872. Believing family more important than his busi-ness dealings in Fairmont, the doctor moved with his wife and children to Omaha, Nebraska, in 1875, allowing his daughter, Lottie, to attend college while still being near her parents. Three years later the Southern Minnesota Railroad (later the Chicago, Milwaukee, and St. Paul Railway) reached Fair-mont, triggering a county population boom. By 1880 the Chubb family had returned to Fairmont to care for Lottie, who was gravely ill. She soon passed away, her mother following two years later. Orville remarried and moved to California in 1883. After his death in 1894, his body was returned to Fair-mont and laid near Sarah and Lottie in Lakeside Cemetery.

When the Chubbs left for Omaha, their brick house was sold to George S. Livermore, who operated the dwelling as one of Fairmont's first hotels.

Fairmont's oldest extant residence was completed in 1867, but now the Orville P. and Sarah Chubb House is a historical museum.

About 1895, Livermore made a sympathetic one-story, gabled-roof addition to the south side of the building. He erected a summer kitchen at the rear of the house as well. The next owner, David Wade, replaced the summer kitchen with a wood-framed addition in 1920. Roughly ten years later, Wade constructed a tiny Classical Revival–style porch at the front entrance. The dwelling passed through other owners before being rescued from destruction by the Martin County Preservation Association. More than 130 years old now, Fairmont's oldest residence accentuates the ignorance of those who claimed that the soil near the town was too poor for brickmaking. Presently a historical museum, the Orville P. and Sarah Chubb House was listed on the National Register in 1995.

The foundry's window sash appears tired today, but the rough stone walls are ready for the new century.

✳ Hastings Foundry

HASTINGS | DAKOTA COUNTY

The prairies, throughout the county, fairly laughed with fertility and paid their tribute to the husbandman, who in turn paid tribute to the town. Commerce climbed the river and wedded Minnesota to the gulf states and the east. Prosperity drew her scepter over all this youthful country, in which Labor was the sole potentate and the plow the one great instrument of conquest.

Early county histories are wonderful. While sometimes romantic and verbose, they provide a wealth of historical context, as with the passage above composed by historian Edward D. Neill for *History of Dakota County and the City of Hastings*, which clearly, although somewhat quixotically, articulates why the town of Hastings succeeded. A Mississippi River town in Dakota County, about fifteen miles southeast of St. Paul, Hastings became the thriving agricultural distribution center that Nininger, a few miles to the northwest, always wanted to be. By the mid-1850s, as Nininger was trying to find its feet, Hastings was already well on its way to becoming a city, propelled by its lock on agricultural produce, chiefly wheat, shipped from the Dakota County region down the Mississippi River. Incorporated as a city in 1857, Hastings was sustained by steamboat commerce for a number of years, but by the early 1870s the end for the steamers was near. The St. Paul and Chicago Railroad constructed a line from the Twin Cities to the Hastings area in 1869, but did not cross the river into the city until two years later. The line eventually became part of the Milwaukee Road, reaching all the way to Chicago.[14]

Almost two decades before the railroad moved into Hastings, A. R. Morrell constructed an iron foundry along the banks of the Mississippi River in the eastern part of the city. The purpose of the foundry was to manufacture castings, which are objects formed from pouring molten iron into molds. This was a vital effort in the mid-1800s, since the ironsmith created much of the shaped material used to build communities, such as the framework for buildings or bridges. In fact, the small foundry Morrell established is purported to have made some of the metal members for the Hastings Spiral Bridge, one of the most unusual crossings ever erected in Minnesota. Built in 1895, and demolished in 1951, the through truss bridge featured a precariously spiraling entrance/exit ramp reminiscent of an amusement park ride.

Little is known of Morrell before he came to Hastings. In September 1859, as his foundry was under construction, the *Hastings Independent* admitted its ignorance of the ironsmith from Vermont, but nonetheless expected much from him:

> *We are not personally acquainted with Mr. Morrell, the proprietor, but are assured that he is a gentleman of character and ability, well posted in regard to everything that pertains to the Foundry and Machine business, and by his management we expect every variety of castings and machine work to be executed in superior style. Hastings, in a couple of months, will have the best Foundry and Machine works in the State.*

Morrell's foundry was in no way architecturally impressive, but of course few industrial buildings in infant mid-nineteenth-century communities were designed to make an aesthetic statement. The roof of the single-story stone structure had an extremely shallow pitch and its walls were marked with a number of entrances and many rectangular windows. A

The Hastings Foundry is an 1850s reminder of the community's riverboating legacy.

brick, furnace chimney rose from the 90- by 70-foot building, although in the early 1900s the chimney was removed and the foundry's size reduced to 50 by 70 feet.

Morrell managed the business through early 1862. During his tenure he is credited with manufacturing the first steam engine made in Minnesota, a motor employed in a grain warehouse. In 1861, he was tapped to create the iron components and steam engine for the *Stella Whipple,* the first steam freighter constructed in Hastings. The *Stella Whipple* regularly plied the Mississippi River between Hastings and La Crosse, Wisconsin. In May 1862, soon after Morrell sold the business to John L. Thorne, the foundry's interior was consumed by fire, causing about $40,000 in damage. The building was repaired, but Thorne could not turn a profit and he sold the enterprise to a stock company in 1866. One year later the foundry began operation under the name "Star Iron Works." Unfortunately, Star Iron Works was no more successful than Thorne and the business eventually failed.

Under management of local ironsmith Andrew Warsop, the foundry reopened in 1875. Five years later Harris K. Stroud began working at the business, purchasing the property from Warsop in 1904. Stroud was born in Middletown, Connecticut, in 1848, and was trained as a machinist in New York City. He arrived in Hastings with his family the same year he started working at the foundry. Stroud is likely the owner who reduced the building's size, using the facility chiefly to construct marine engines and launches. His son, Charles, was working at the foundry at least by the early 1900s. A man with many skills, Charles was employed as an electrician and a photographer before joining his father. While at his father's shop he designed and built several automobiles. One of his most unique creations was a pneumatic automobile wheel. Each spoke of the wheel was actually an air-filled cylinder that contained a piston, which supposedly absorbed shock to the automobile as it traveled over the road. In 1906, Charles received a license to operate a motorized vehicle within the corporate limits of Hastings, purportedly the first such license issued in Minnesota.

The Hastings Foundry eventually passed through a succession of owners, finding its way to Lauren E. Heselton in 1976. Today it serves as an equipment repair shop for Heselton Excavating Company. While the roof has been covered with newer material, the building still looks like a mid-nineteenth-century industrial structure. One of the oldest industrial buildings remaining in Minnesota, and a reminder of the time when Hastings was a riverboat town, the Hastings Foundry was placed on the National Register in 1979.

RAILROADS & AGRICULTURE

3

IT IS DIFFICULT TO OVERESTIMATE the importance of the railroads to the development of Minnesota. Even though settlers were planting roots in the region well in advance of the rail lines, the labyrinth of tracks that had spread throughout much of Minnesota by the 1880s had stimulated mass immigration, which led to extensive social, political, commercial, and industrial development. In truth, the railroad was often the seed for institutions reflected in common edifices like city and town halls, churches and common lodges, hardware stores and drugstores, factories and flour mills—the list goes on and on. Without the economic link to the world provided by the railroad, many of these institutions in communities throughout the state would never have existed—in fact, many of the communities themselves would never have existed. Surely, some of the earliest settlers lamented being chased by the railroad. Still, an overwhelming number welcomed the enterprise as a progenitor to economic prosperity. The considerable value of the rail lines to infant Minnesota is evidenced in almost any early local history, where the railroad is either praised for passing through the community or cursed for avoiding it.[15]

No industry in Minnesota owes more to railroads than agriculture. Like steamboats, railroads linked the state's farming regions with eastern commercial markets. Railroads, however, were far more efficient than steamers, haul-ing much more freight much faster. Moreover, rail lines did not suffer the same geographic limitations as steamships. Railroads could lay track almost anywhere but steamers were confined to rivers—specifically, water-ways that could support freight-carrying vessels. The advantages of the railroad, coupled with the fertile soil and affordable acreage in Minnesota, enticed significant numbers of settlers into the state to farm the land. While timbering and the iron ore industry substantially contributed to the growth of Minnesota, it was agriculture that chiefly supported an ever-expanding population. And it was agriculture that was the impetus for a rail system in Minnesota—that, and what seemed like a far-fetched dream to connect the eastern half of the country with the Pacific Ocean.

For a state significantly shaped by railroads, Minnesota's early attempts at railroad building were hardly inspiring, although in June 1854 some may have believed Minnesota had divine guidance. It was at that time that a St. Paul minister uttered a curious sermon: "The voice of him that crieth in the wilderness, Prepare ye the way of the Lord. Make straight in the desert a highway for our God. . . . Every great invention is an aid to religion. The telescope, the printing press, the telegraph, the ocean steamers, a Pacific Railway, are ordained by God." Well . . . maybe. One year earlier, President Franklin Pierce asked Issac Stevens, newly appointed governor of the Ter-ritory of Washington, to survey a railroad route from St. Paul to the Pacific Ocean. The Northern Pacific Survey ended in Olympia, Washington Terri-tory, in late November 1853.

As difficult as the survey proved, it was still the easy part. No railroad had yet connected any parts of Minnesota, and looking beyond the horizon to the Pacific seemed almost absurd. Four years later, however, Minnesota took baby steps toward building a railroad when the federal government authorized the territory to convey congressional lands for that purpose. Four railroads were quickly chartered. The Transit Railroad was to con-struct a line across southern Minnesota from Winona, while the Root River Valley and Southern Minnesota Railroad was granted rights to a western route edging the Root River, from the Mississippi River near La Crosse, Wisconsin, to Rochester. This company was also authorized to lay a line from St. Paul to the Minnesota River Valley to the south. The Minneapolis and Cedar Valley Railroad planned to link Minneapolis to the Iowa border. The boldest plans, though, were for the Minnesota and Pacific Railroad (M&P), which was to originate in Stillwater, move through St. Paul and St. Anthony on the Mississippi River, and then march west to the Pacific Ocean. It never happened, because the M&P did not meet the building timetables set out in its charter. Actually, it never came close to completing even a small section of line. Neither did the three other original railroads—nor did the nearly two dozen railway companies chartered within months of those first four. The Territory of Minnesota foreclosed on each enterprise, gaining possession of its properties. For all of the enthusiasm surrounding these early railroads, there simply was not enough money to build them, a dilemma caused in part by the failure of the New York branch of the Ohio Life Insurance and Trust Company, a pecuniary uppercut that triggered the financial panic of 1857—the same panic that sunk the boomtown of Nininger.

In 1858 Minnesota again tried to build a railway, awarding forty-six railroad charters. As before, no railroad met the time limits and construction ceased. At least the public could rejoice that Minnesota was now a state. Attempts at railroad building puttered along for a few more years until the St. Paul and Pacific Railroad (StP&P), successor to the M&P, finally completed a line from St. Paul to St. Anthony in June 1862. It may not have been the long-awaited route to the Pacific Ocean, but at least it was a step in the general direction. Railway construction slowed over the next few years, as railroad companies treaded the poor economic tide generated by the Civil War. In 1867, however, Minneapolis was joined to Chicago, the eastern gateway for Minnesota's agricultural produce, via northeastern Iowa and the rail lines of the Minnesota Central Railway, McGregor Western Railway, and the Milwaukee and Prairie du Chien Railway.

By 1870, rail lines were branching from the Twin Cities to the west, southwest, northwest, and almost due north to Duluth. A westward line from Winona bisected the southeastern section of the state. These routes mostly followed pre-railroad settlement patterns, linking established communities with Chicago and the East primarily through Minneapolis and St. Paul. But the railroads also created new towns, deliberately seeding parts of the state with infant communities that would grow into agricultural distribution points and provide produce to the carriers. Litchfield, for example, was an agricultural town platted roughly sixty-five miles west of Minneapolis by the StP&P in 1869. Willmar, another twenty-seven miles further west, was platted the same year by the same railroad. Those without financial interests in railroads also founded communities along rail lines. Ten miles east of Rochester in southeastern Minnesota, the tiny community of Viola was established adjacent to a line of the Chicago and North Western Railway in 1878.

The 1870s proved a phenomenal period of railroad development, led by the Northern Pacific Railway (NP), which began construction of a route from Carlton, just south of Duluth, toward the Pacific Ocean, supplanting the StP&P as the first Minnesota railroad that would link the left and right coasts. The NP accomplished the feat in 1883, fourteen years after the Union Pacific Railway and the Central Pacific Railway tied together near Promontory, Utah, creating the first transcontinental railroad. The NP route merged with the line of the Oregon Railway and Navigation Company, which had a route running from Wallula, Washington, to Portland, Oregon. The St. Paul, Minneapolis and Manitoba Railway (StPM&M), incorporated in 1879 to assume the routes of the financially strapped StP&P, reached Seattle on the Pacific Ocean ten years later. The StPM&M later became the principal constituent of the Great Northern Railway (GN), the railroad most closely associated with James J. Hill.

A man who never intended to reside in Minnesota after arriving in St. Paul in 1856, Hill found financial opportunities in the region too great to ignore. Hill was an agent for the StP&P by 1866, but he began his rail-roading conquest of Minnesota and the American Northwest thirteen years later as the general manger of the newly formed StPM&M. By the time Hill died in 1916, he truly deserved the title "Empire Builder," his monument the GN, a vast collection of founded, acquired, and leased rail lines span-ning thousands upon thousands of miles. Indeed, tracing Hill's immense rail system is like tracing a vat of spaghetti.

By 1880, as Hill was beginning his quest for the history books, Min-nesota had nearly 3,100 miles of track, about triple the total from a decade earlier. The lines were chiefly concentrated in the lower two-thirds of the state, and especially in the southern one-third, a region of prodigious agri-cultural production. The impact of the railroad on the state was evidenced in its increased population. When the StP&P inaugurated rail travel in Minnesota the population was about 172,000. Eighteen years and many railroads later, the state claimed almost 800,000 citizens. Railroad expan-sion during the 1880s mostly filled the gaps between the rail lines in the lower two-thirds of the state, although there was modest movement into the sparsely settled north, reaching principally to the few agriculturally fer-tile areas, such as the Red River Valley in northwestern Minnesota. This decade introduced the Iron Range railroads to northeastern Minnesota, as the state began exploiting its iron resources. Logging railroads were built in parts of northern Minnesota as well, mainly inland from Lake Superior.

At the close of the nineteenth century Minnesota was laced with rail lines, and the first decade of the twentieth century would bring additional routes to northern portions of the state. The total amount of acreage in farms about this time was remarkable. In 1860 when Minnesota was still pining for a railroad, only about two million acres were in farms, but by 1898 that total had risen to roughly twenty-five million acres, proof the rail-road was more than pulling its weight. And even though the railroad some-times acted like an eight-hundred-pound gorilla, prompting farmers to join organizations that tempered railway influence, the rail lines can claim con-siderable credit for building the state into an agricultural haven.

The symbiotic relationship between railroads and agriculture is one of the principal contexts explaining Minnesota's growth. Thankfully, the state retains a number of National Register listings that help tell this story, including the Duluth Union Depot, a striking Chateauesque-style building, as well as the quaint Sioux City and St. Paul Railroad Section House in Dundee in Nobles County, the community's first residence and home to the rail line's depot agent and section foreman. The Wulf C. Krabbenhoft Farmstead in Elmwood Township, Clay County, was a very successful turn-of-the-twentieth-century Red River Valley farm. In Wacouta Township in Goodhue County, Henry Damon erected an unusual circular barn to aid his dairy farming. Each of these properties is an unambiguous reminder of our railroading and agricultural heritage, as are the properties highlighted on the ensuing pages. It must be remembered, however, that less obvious property types are also tied to this context. Railroads, after all, brought the world to community doorsteps, promoting agricultural production and spurring economic growth, which turned settlements into villages and villages into cities.

✳ Northern Pacific Railway Shops

BRAINERD | CROW WING COUNTY

With many resorts and hundreds of nearby lakes, Brainerd, about 115 miles southwest of Duluth, is popularly known as a playground for tourists. Throughout much of its history, however, the city was a railroad hub. But the railroad abandoned Brainerd in the early 1980s, leaving behind an industrial monument to its once formidable presence. Adjacent to Thirteenth Street, only a half mile east of the city's downtown, is the brick and steel legacy of the Northern Pacific Railway (NP), a collection of massive, cream-colored buildings that symbolize the period when the railroad set Brainerd's agenda.[16]

The NP was born in May 1864, when Congress passed a land grant bill providing the railroad a right-of-way to construct a line from Lake Superior to Puget Sound on the Pacific Coast. The enterprise foundered for several years until it secured financial backing from the banking house of Jay Cooke and Company. Construction of the line finally began in early 1870 near Carlton, just southwest of Duluth. Within two years the railroad had reached Fargo in upper Dakota Territory. One year later the New York branch of Jay Cooke and Company failed, followed by a succession of bank closings, plunging the country into financial panic. Many blamed the NP, considering it a fiscal albatross perched atop Jay Cooke. Nevertheless, the country survived the economic despair, as did the NP.

Three years before the NP became the whipping boy for financial investors the railroad had reached the Mississippi River in central Minnesota, choosing to erect a Howe deck-truss bridge (a truss type patented by William Howe in 1840 that is formed of wood, diagonal compression members, and metal, vertical tension members) over the waterway near the present-day site of Brainerd. Initially, the location was simply called "The Crossing," but when the NP opted to make the site its headquarters the obvious was no longer sufficient. Some suggested "Ogemaqua," a somewhat elegant moniker Native Americans applied to Emma Beaulieu, apparently a local woman thought quite stunning. The name means "Queen" or "Chief Woman." But since the NP set the agenda, it also set the name of the new community. The town was christened "Brainerd," the maiden name of Ann Eliza Smith, the wife of John Gregory Smith, then-president of the NP.

The NP began a massive construction program in 1871, erecting several wooden railroad maintenance buildings just north of the present-day main complex. In 1882 the railroad raised many of the current brick and steel buildings that comprise the main facility. These rectangular structures included the Boiler, Machine, and Blacksmith Shops, as well as the Office and Storehouse Building, an edifice embellished at its west facade with a pyramidal-roofed clock tower. The NP also built a second roundhouse in 1882, a singularly unique building type that resembles a giant donut. A roundhouse is a maintenance building consisting of numerous stalls, or bays, for locomotives. Engines move into the building via a turntable—a revolving, tracked deck located at the center of the donut. After a locomotive pulls onto the deck, the turntable is rotated until the engine aligns with the designated bay. The engine is then directed into the stall. Roundhouses were often built in sections, so structures resembling partially eaten donuts were not unusual. As a railroad expanded and the number of locomotives increased, more sections were added to the building until it formed a circle.

The enlargement of the NP complex in the early 1880s indicated the rail line was doing well, as was Brainerd, since an expanding NP meant more employment for the city's citizens. In 1886, however, the railroad facility suffered a devastating fire, and many of the original wood buildings were destroyed. The *Brainerd Dispatch* reported the event:

> The blaze started in the engine room of the planing mill, having been kindled by a spark falling into the shaving tower, and was first discovered by the night watchman, but a heavy gale was blowing at the time, and before he could get the shop hose unreeled the flames had gained such headway as to make it impossible to stop their ravages. . . .

The blaze destroyed the planing mill, office, machine shop, and upholstery department, as well as the original roundhouse. Much of the rolling stock was also ruined or damaged. The *Dispatch* seemed somewhat perversely taken by the inferno: "The flames lighted up the country for miles around and in the darkness of the night, with the flames roaring skyward, and the clouds of sparks and cinders being carried by the wind out over the city, made a grand sight."

Measuring almost five hundred feet long, the Office and Storehouse Building, the most prominent structure remaining at the Northern Pacific Railway Shops, was erected in stages: 1882–83, 1907, and 1918.

The NP immediately announced it would rebuild many of the burned-out buildings, replacing them with structures of brick and steel. The *Dispatch* sounded a revivalist note, thrilled that no jobs would be lost: "Let the people of Brainerd rejoice that the question of her future prosperity is forever settled." A little hyperbolic, maybe, but the shops were the operating and engineering headquarters for the entire line, and by the late 1880s they were employing more than a thousand Brainerd residents.

The good times at Brainerd continued into the twentieth century. In fact, several buildings received additions. The Boiler, Machine, and Blacksmith Shops were all expanded in the early 1900s, as was the Office and Storehouse Building. But a gradual decline in work began in the 1930s, when the NP Shops in Livingston, Montana, a maintenance facility strategically positioned about halfway between the railroad's shops in Minnesota and those in South Tacoma, Washington, assumed more control. After the Second World War, the Brainerd complex shifted from construction and maintenance of rolling stock to reclamation. In 1970, the NP merged with the Great Northern Railway; the Spokane, Portland and Seattle Railway; and the Chicago, Burlington and Quincy Railway to form the Burlington Northern Railroad (BN). The shops at Brainerd continued to service the BN, but their role consistently diminished. The BN finally closed the complex in 1981, selling it two years later. By this time much of the facility had been razed, most notably the roundhouse. Several other major structures remained, however, including the Boiler, Machine, and Blacksmith Shops, as well as the Office and Storehouse Building. Additional buildings built after 1882, like the Lavatory Building (1907), Foundry Boiler House (1910), Pattern Shop and Storehouse Building (1911), Acetylene Generator Plant (1924), and Power Plant (1924), are still in place.

Although the railroad moved on, so did Brainerd. The city was forced to wean itself from the NP and BN as the railroad shops stooped into decline. Today, with a more diverse economy and thriving tourist industry, the community seems to be doing well. Still, the NP is the key constituent in the city's history, and it left for posterity an unmistakable marker to prove it. Presently, some of the shops are employed for light industrial manufacturing. The current owner of the complex plans to rehabilitate many of the buildings and offer them for other manufacturing enterprises. The most important industrial facility ever in Brainerd, and a fine collection of late nineteenth- and early twentieth-century railroad buildings, the Northern Pacific Railway Shops were added to the National Register in 1989.

✳ Viola Cooperative Creamery

VIOLA | OLMSTED COUNTY

There is strength in numbers, which explains why so many rural communities feature cooperatives. A cooperative, or co-op, is an enterprise owned and operated by a group that uses the services the cooperative provides. Co-op members receive benefits that are not available to those functioning independently. For instance, farmers gain by coming together to establish cooperative stores near their homes, eliminating the chore of traveling to faraway towns for supplies, a task that was especially burdensome before paved roads and motorized transportation. Grocery stores, hardware stores, and feed and fertilizer distributors are examples of common co-ops. Attempts to date the cooperative practice are nearly impossible, since individuals have banded together for the commercial benefit of all for as long as there have been businesses.[17]

Creameries are also popular cooperatives, formed by groups of dairy farmers who realized the cost-effectiveness of delivering milk to well-equipped, centralized facilities that produced butter and cheese. In Minnesota, many cooperative creameries extended the collaborative notion by creating a cooperative of cooperatives, the Minnesota Cooperative Creameries Association. Founded in 1921, the association changed its moniker to Land O'Lakes Creameries, Inc. in 1926, a name that matched its popular product label. The organization standardized the product produced by its members and helped stabilize railroad shipping rates for creamery goods.

It does not appear that the creamery in the tiny community of Viola was ever part of Land O'Lakes, apparently convinced it could maintain high production standards and negotiate acceptable shipping charges without oversight by an association. Viola Cooperative Creamery was established in 1900, twenty-two years after Viola was founded. Located in Olmsted County in southeastern Minnesota, only ten miles east of Rochester, Viola was born adjacent to a line of the Chicago and North Western Railway. Platting a community near a rail line was usually a foregone conclusion, since the railroads were lifeblood in the late 1800s, a town's economic link to the rest of the country.

The basis for a creamery in Viola came from its rail connection to out-side markets and the diversification of local farming. For much of the late nineteenth century farming in Minnesota was based heavily on a single crop—wheat—a practice that depleted soil nutrients and saturated markets, driving down prices. While crop raising remained an important part of farming practice, dairying gained favor throughout much of the state as a way for farmers to insulate themselves against tired cropland and depressed wheat markets.

Like most creameries in Minnesota, the Viola Cooperative Creamery manufactured butter. Cheese was rarely made in Minnesota creameries since Wisconsin and New York had captured the cheese markets by the late 1870s. Whole milk brought to the creamery by Viola-area dairy farmers passed through a centrifugal separator. The separator whirled the milk, creating layers of cream, which were then skimmed off and used to make butter. Farmers were compensated for the amount of cream pulled from their product, while taking home the resultant skim milk. Butter produced at the creamery was often shipped to New York markets.

In its first eight months of operation the Viola Cooperative Creamery produced almost 42,000 pounds of butter. August Radke, a butter maker from Elgin, about five miles north of Viola, joined the cooperative during its second year of operation, promptly winning an award for his butter in a national competition. But although the creamery seemed to start with a sprint, within a matter of years it stumbled, closing its door in 1910 because of poor management and declining support from local farmers. The cooperative began again in 1916, but eight years later it was dealt a setback when the wood-framed creamery building caught fire. The *Elgin Monitor* reported the event:

> *The Viola co-operative creamery was totally destroyed by fire early Saturday morning with a loss of about $10,000, including building and equipment. What caused the fire is unknown. E. B. Hampel, the butter maker, discovered smoke coming from the attic over the boiler room at about six o'clock and on rushing to investigate found that the fire had gained such headway that he could not enter.*

Minnesota—indeed, the country—is sprinkled with communities that have been visited by fire at some point in their history. Cannon Falls, roughly thirty miles southeast of the Twin Cities, endured a terrible fire in 1884, only to be scorched worse three years later. Fire is a great motivator, however, often prompting citizens to create better and safer communities. Numerous late-nineteenth- and early-twentieth-century brick and stone buildings in towns in Minnesota and elsewhere found the impetus for their beginnings in the burned-out shells of their wooden forerunners. So did the new creamery in Viola, which was completed as a fireproof building six months after the old structure was destroyed.

The Viola Cooperative Creamery was designed by Harold Crawford, a Rochester architect who created the plan for a number of creamery buildings, including the Eyota Farmers Cooperative Creamery, a National Register property in nearby Eyota. The facility in Viola was a one-and-a-half-story, rectangular building with a projecting bay at the south facade that was fronted with a triple-arched arcade labeled "Viola Cooperative Creamery." Formed of reinforced concrete faced with red and brown brick, the creamery rested upon a concrete foundation and featured a clipped gable roof pierced by a corbelled chimney and two ventilators. Brick quoining, a kind of toothed pattern of projecting and receding rectangular blocks, often masonry, decorated the corners. Rectangular windows marked the walls and entrances were covered by wood doors. The *Elgin Monitor* boasted: "Nothing has been omitted to make this creamery a model in sanitation and efficiency. It is a credit to its builders and will be an enduring monument to posterity."

With its new building and new equipment, and seemingly renewed

The current owners of the creamery display a circa 1940s image of the building with its arcade.

enthusiasm, the creamery produced nearly 143,000 pounds of butter in 1924, about 35,000 pounds more than in 1923, the year before the fire. At this time the creamery was one of eleven operating in Olmsted County, a formidable dairy region that produced 3.5 million pounds of butter in 1924, although by this time many farmers were separating whole milk on the farm and delivering only the cream to the creameries. By 1936, the creamery in Viola manufactured almost 173,000 pounds of butter. Maybe more importantly, the cooperative paid off the mortgage on its building that year, inviting J. H. Hay, Minnesota's Deputy Commissioner of Agriculture, to the annual meeting for the ceremonial mortgage burning. While things appeared good for the creamery in the mid- to late 1930s, bad times were just around the decade. The 1940s ushered in trouble for all creameries as butter prices fell, convincing many farmers to sell their whole milk rather than use it for butter production. Moreover, World War II drained labor from the industry. Some larger creameries converted from butter production to whole milk production, which required new equipment. Smaller operations like Viola, however, were unable to stay in business. In March 1948, the Viola Cooperative Creamery closed.

The creamery was purchased in 1957 by Maurice Williams, a gentleman who planned to use it as a service station or as rental units. Williams removed the deteriorating arcade but never completed his plans for the building. He sold the structure to Robert D. Applen in 1961, who employed the building as a beekeeping enterprise until 1979. Applen removed much of the butter equipment and enclosed some of the window openings with brick. The building was vacant until 1998. The present owners have converted the creamery into a restaurant. While the creamery's integrity has suffered some from the alterations, most notably the loss of the arcade, it still reflects its original purpose. Even more, it represents a period when many small cooperative creameries dotted the rural landscape, bolstering the economic fortunes of those they served. The Viola Cooperative Creamery was placed on the National Register in 1999.

✳ Minneapolis, St. Paul & Sault Ste. Marie Depot (Soo Line Depot)

THIEF RIVER FALLS | PENNINGTON COUNTY

In early March 1913, the Minneapolis, St. Paul and Sault Ste. Marie Railway (Soo Line) deposited Pauline Carpentuer and John Vineir in Thief River Falls, a northwestern Minnesota community roughly fifty-five miles north of Mahnomen, the betrothed couple's hometown. The two were traveling to Crookston, about thirty miles southwest of Thief River Falls, and were departing the following day on the Great Northern Railway (GN). A rural community that featured two major rail lines was unique, since many small towns were fortunate to claim only one. But Thief River Falls benefited from location, and the desire of Soo Line management to connect the wheat fields of northwestern Minnesota and North Dakota with flour millers in Minneapolis. While the GN resented competition in a region it had ruled alone for years, the arrival of the Soo Line in Thief River Falls in 1904 proved a financial boon to the town. The community evolved into a significant distribution center for the region's agricultural produce. It also became a connecting point for travelers transferring from one rail line to the other, which is what Carpentuer and Vineir had hoped to do. The pair was unsuccessful, for the local sheriff rushed to the Great Northern Depot and placed both in custody before they could board the train for Crookston. It seems young Miss Carpentuer was just too young, and her parents refused to sanction the marriage. While it is uncertain if Carpentuer and Vineir eventually found a successful life together, the early twentieth-century union between the Soo Line and Thief River Falls lasted for almost sixty years.[18]

In 1883 the St. Paul, Minneapolis and Manitoba Railway (StPM&M), which later became part of the GN, constructed a line to St. Hilaire, about seven miles south of Thief River Falls. The inconvenience of hauling freight from St. Hilaire convinced Thief River Falls to entice the railroad north with a $750 incentive. In 1890 the GN began leasing the routes of the StPM&M, and it was the GN that accepted the village's offer, completing an extension into Thief River Falls in October 1892. While Thief River Falls was now a link in the railroad chain, it was only a minor one. That changed twelve years later when the Soo Line laid its way into the community en route to Winnipeg in southern Manitoba.

The Soo Line was incorporated in 1888 when the Canadian Pacific Railway helped finance a merger of the Minneapolis, Sault Ste. Marie and Atlantic Railway; the Minneapolis and Pacific Railway; and the Minneapolis and St. Croix Railway. The new railroad was welcomed by those tied to the wheat trade in Minnesota and North Dakota, since it functioned independently of the railroads operating out of Chicago and Milwaukee, lines that traditionally set wheat and flour shipping prices. With the formation of the Soo Line, millers in Minneapolis, some of whom had financial interests in the railroad, were assured of getting a steady supply of wheat at more favorable shipping rates. Transportation costs also improved for flour shipped from Minneapolis to the East via Soo Line routes.

As the Soo Line constructed its road toward Winnipeg, it passed through traditional GN territory, upsetting James J. Hill, owner of the GN. Despite Soo Line assertions that it had no desire to take business from the GN, industry observers thought differently: "The line is decidedly an invader of [GN] territory, no matter how strong are official denials to antagonize Jim Hill. It cuts across [GN] lines and will certainly draw Twin City traffic from the northern Minnesota lines of that system." The Soo Line undoubtedly realized that it would cut into the bottom line of the GN, but it was determined to establish a powerful presence in northwestern Minnesota and North Dakota.

The Soo Line left Thief River Falls many years ago, but the community remembered its railroading heritage by rehabilitating its 1914 depot.

Thief River Falls had graduated from a village to a city by the time the Soo Line arrived in 1904. One year later the railroad demonstrated its commitment to the city by making it the line's western division point, constructing a roundhouse, mechanic shop, derrick house, passenger depot, several warehouses, and more. Thief River Falls flourished as people flocked to the community to work for the railroad. Commercial investment followed, and more than twenty businesses edged the Soo Line tracks by 1906. The Soo Line was also booming, driven in large measure by the agricultural largesse passing through the city. In a short period the Soo Line had far outpaced the tonnage being shipped into and out of the city by the GN. In 1913, the Soo Line punctuated its coupling with Thief River Falls by removing its old depot and constructing a large and handsome new one. The wonderful building would serve as a monument to the rail line's superiority over the GN in the region.

Minneapolis architects William Kenyon and Maurice Maine were commissioned to design the building. The Soo Line had previously employed Kenyon for its passenger depot in Minot, North Dakota (1911), a structure that was added to the National Register in 1977. While most Soo Line depots followed a relatively simple standard plan, the railroad demanded that the depot in Thief River Falls be a kind of trophy. Material for the depot began arriving in July 1913, and the building was completed in April 1914. The two-story, bungalow/Craftsman–style depot cost $60,000 and measured 140 by 50 feet. Formed of brick in a Flemish pattern, the structure featured a cross-gambrel roof with shallow parapets and limestone copings accented with diamond-shaped limestone finials. The base of a five-sided, two-story bay centered at the east facade held an entrance and the bay's upper section was flanked by shed dormers. A limestone panel reading "Thief River Falls" was situated just above the entrance. The depot's west rear was dominated by two gambrel end walls holding rectangular windows, a window design common to all sides of the building. The asymmetrical south side had two entrances, one covered by a gable-roofed porte cochere, a vehicular passageway, usually near a building's entrance, with battered columns surmounted by limestone bands. Another "Thief River Falls" limestone panel was located near the second floor. The north side was somewhat similar to the south, although a single-story, 25- by 80-foot wing extended parallel to the railroad tracks from the east end of the north wall.

Although the depot represented the success of the Soo Line and Thief River Falls, the good times failed to last. Both the railroad and city were dependent on Minnesota and North Dakota farmers, but the Depression of the 1930s, a severe drought in 1936, and an increasing reliance on trucks to ship freight broke the back of the railroad. The Soo Line filed for reorganization in 1937, reemerging a humbled company that discontinued passenger service and concentrated on freight shipping. The railway eventually

Large, ornate brackets and earthy colors decorate Kenyon and Maine's marvelous building.

consolidated its division points, and closed the train dispatcher's office in Thief River Falls in 1961. Two years later only three division points remained: Enderlin, North Dakota; Shoreham, Minnesota; and Stevens Point, Wisconsin. Thankfully, Thief River Falls embraced its railroad history, renovating the depot instead of demolishing it. The picturesque building now serves as city offices. It was included as part of the National Register in 1995.

✳ John Bosch Farmstead

VICINITY OF LAKE LILLIAN | KANDIYOHI COUNTY

When John Bosch was three years old a family acquaintance asked him his name. "I am a Populist," he replied. It was an unusual response, but one that delighted his family. Political discourse and allegiance to the Populist movement were part of being a Bosch, a large rural family residing near Prinsburg in southwestern Kandiyohi County at the turn of the twentieth century. The Populist movement was faltering by the time John was born in 1898, but many rural citizens were still convinced that the political and social ideology of the "People's Party" best reflected their agrarian values. By the time John was an adult, however, the original movement had all but vanished. Even so, John Bosch would always remember his roots, and thousands of like-minded farmers eventually rallied behind him to preserve the farming heritage of numerous families on the edge of ruin.[19]

The Populist platform was formalized in Omaha, Nebraska, in 1892. The doctrine called for elimination of private banking, public rule over railroads and communications, public control of money, and the return of corporate land to the people. At first glance, these demands seem extreme, but for the small farmer in the late 1800s this was a strategy for survival. For many years farmers had suffered as America became increasingly industrialized, exemplified by the exorbitant rates the railroads charged to ship agricultural goods from west to east. It was not unusual for a farmer to pay the equivalent of a bushel of wheat to the railroad to have a second bushel shipped east. Moreover, as agricultural prices dropped in the late nineteenth century, farmers were still expected to pay mortgages given when market prices assured a reasonable standard of living. Since capitalism is a system of fluctuating markets, this seems just. But in the late 1800s, the market value of agricultural goods was obscenely low, merely a fraction of farmers' expense and labor. As a result, no matter how hard farmers worked they could not get out from under their debt. The government blamed miserable market prices on overproduction, but saying that there was an abundance of food seemed absurd because so many people were enduring the privations of a national depression that began in 1873 and continued into the 1880s. As one Arkansas farmer explained: "To say that overproduction is the cause of 'hard times' is to say that the people are too industrious; that they could make a better living if they did not work so hard; that they have raised so much they are starving to death." For farmers, outrageous shipping costs, and an appalling medium of exchange were what needed fixing. This was what the Populist Party hoped to accomplish. Unfortunately for farmers, it failed.

Although the Populist Party had subsided by the early part of the twentieth century, the movement spawned similar organizations. One was the Farmers Union, a cooperative designed to secure fair shipping and exchange rates for agricultural products. Since the loss of farms in the late 1800s and early 1900s was staggering, farmers needed little incentive to join the Farmers Union. In 1870, 50 percent of the population were farmers, but by 1930 that number had fallen to about 22 percent. Even with the Farmers Union, and other similar organizations like the Grange and Farm Bureau, farmers continued to struggle. Well before the nation sank into depression in 1929, the farmers were already there. Urged by the federal government to produce at maximum levels during the First World War and immediately after, farmers were pinched when market prices and land values plunged. As if salting the wound, federal economic policy was increasingly turning from agricultural to industrial production. About the only solace farmers garnered from the economic doldrums of the late 1920s and early 1930s was knowing the rest of the country was now sharing the misery.

The concrete silo was erected in 1936, but the barn dates to around 1900, although two sections at the east end were added later.

The Victorian-style dwelling was built by former state senator Gustav A. Glader before becoming home to a family of Populists.

By this time John Bosch was schooled in the financial pitfalls of farming. He was living with his parents and siblings on a farm the family purchased in 1914. The farmstead was located in Section 9 of Lake Elizabeth Township, between the towns of Atwater and Lake Lillian, about fifteen miles southeast of Willmar. Gustav A. Glader, a Swedish farmer who became a state senator, established the farmstead in 1868. Around 1885, he expanded it from 280 to 600 acres. About this time he built a two-and-a-half-story house, which was remodeled in 1912. The large, Victorian-style dwelling was dressed in clapboard siding and had an intersecting gable roof and stone foundation. The south facade and half the east side were edged by an L-shaped porch with a hip roof braced by columns of the Tuscan order, the simplest of the five classical orders, which also includes the Ionic, the Doric, the Corinthian, and Composite. The Bosch Farmstead also included a gable-roofed barn built around 1900. The barn rested upon a stone foundation and had clapboard siding. A gable-roofed, clapboard-covered granary was built about the same time as the barn. The property also included various sheds, as well as a chicken coop, all of which were constructed around 1910. About 1920, the Bosches added a metal covered hog house and windmill.

Encouraged by his father, John Bosch joined the Lake Elizabeth unit of the Farmers Union. In 1930, he became president of the county chapter. The following year Robert E. Lee, a farmer who had recently arrived in Kandiyohi County from Stevens County, sought the chapter's help. Lee had given a chattel mortgage on his herd not realizing he needed the mortgage holder's permission to move the cattle outside Stevens County. Since he did not seek consent, the bank foreclosed. The bank did not alter its position after Bosch lobbied on behalf of Lee. But Bosch had another plan. When the bank representative and county sheriff arrived at Lee's farm to auction the herd they were greeted by a large group of farmers who earlier agreed to purchase the cattle for pennies and return the property to Lee, a tactic called a "penny auction." The auction never took place, however, because the farmers had also hung nooses from the trees. Seeing the ropes, the banker and sheriff drove directly to Willmar, the county seat of Kandiyohi County. The mortgage was sold to a bank in Willmar, placing the agreement in the same county as the chattel property—a victory for the local Farmers Union.

This small success was only the beginning for Bosch and his supporters. In May 1932 Bosch and an Iowa farmer named Milo Reno initiated a splinter group of the Farmers Union. The organization was called the Farmers Holiday Association. The Holiday Association's aim was to force the federal government to guarantee that farmers would recoup their expenses for growing and marketing their product. The group demanded embargoes against agricultural goods sold at less than the cost of production, as well as a ban on agricultural imports. The organization also wanted a moratorium on farm and chattel foreclosures. If the demands were not met members of the association would declare a farm strike, or a "farm holiday," halting agricultural production. Mass demonstrations and penny auctions also would be implemented.

The Holiday Association rapidly evolved into a national movement, although it was strongest in Minnesota, especially in the southwestern and west-central part of the state. In Swift County, for example, roughly 1,700 of the county's 1,900 farmers were members. The movement's first major strike in Minnesota began on September 21, 1932. Many rural communities celebrated the event with parades. Willmar actually had fireworks. Members picketed the marketing centers of Montevideo and Worthington, as well as other western Minnesota cities. In October, the Holiday Association blockaded Minneapolis and St. Paul, eventually closing ten major thoroughfares. Additionally, a creamery in Montevideo was seized, and a meat processing plant in Marshall was shut down. The group's biggest successes were against farm foreclosures. During the early 1930s hundreds of foreclosure sales were halted across Minnesota. Banks in other states also succumbed to pressure. In early 1933 lenders in several regions of the county halted foreclosures.

The Holiday Association developed a reputation as the most aggressive Depression-era agricultural protest movement. While Minnesota did not experience the level of violence other states did, fisticuffs were common. One picketer was shot to death at a mass demonstration in Canby in early October 1932. A riot involving eight hundred people erupted the following week in Howard Lake and several people were injured. The aggressiveness

of the movement paid dividends, though. Governors in eight states eventually declared a moratorium on foreclosures. The Holiday Association even influenced the substance of President Franklin Roosevelt's New Deal agricultural policies. At one point, Roosevelt even sought John Bosch's advice.

The influence of the Holiday Association subsided after 1933. Membership declined as farmers felt less threatened by foreclosure. They were also generally enthusiastic about Roosevelt's stimulus initiatives. Even though the movement was brief, it made a significant impact on the nation, and thousands of farm families across the country were indebted to its members. Ironically, John Bosch eventually walked away from farming and became an urbanite. Bosch moved to Minneapolis and worked as an agent for an insurance company. He died in Minneapolis in 1978. But the Bosch Farmstead, once a refuge for discussion and planning concerning how to save a vanishing way of life, remains. It was included in the National Register in 1987.

✳ Steamboat Bridge

VICINITY OF CASS LAKE │ CASS COUNTY

In 1974 historian David Plowden finished an exceptional book on bridges, a work that featured many of the most impressive crossings ever erected in North America. Included in his book was the magnificent Stone Arch Bridge spanning the Mississippi River in Minneapolis. Completed in 1883, the bridge is a defining symbol of James J. Hill and his Great Northern Railway (GN), although it was actually commissioned by the Minneapolis Union Railway, one of the railroad tycoon's interests that later became part

The 1914 Steamboat Bridge rotated like a turntable atop its center pier, opening the river channel to steamboats and logs.

of the GN. Plowden described the 2,100-foot-long, National Register crossing as "a tour de force in every sense of the word." Not surprisingly, the historian never uttered a word about Steamboat Bridge, another GN crossing that spanned Steamboat River in Cass County, roughly twelve miles north of the county seat, Walker. Steamboat Bridge could never hope to compete for space in Plowden's book, since it is in no way a sexy bridge. Instead, it is a rather small, unattractive crossing that few notice as they zoom past on the adjacent State Highway 371. Still, unattractive does not mean uninteresting.[20]

In 1898, the Park Rapids and Leech Lake Railway constructed the first bridge over Steamboat River, the eastern outlet of Steamboat Lake that coursed its way one-half-mile southeast to Steamboat Bay on Leech Lake. The low bridge was part of a forty-nine-mile line connecting Park Rapids in Hubbard County with Cass Lake in Cass County. An independent railroad, the Park Rapids and Leech Lake Railway nevertheless operated chiefly as an extension of the GN. Hill's railway finally purchased the smaller road in 1907. It is uncertain what type of bridge the Park Rapids and Leech Lake Railway erected over Steamboat River in 1898, but a plate-girder crossing seems likely. GN records indicate as much, but the documentation also notes that the span was 150 feet long, which is clearly a mistake because the waterway is not nearly wide enough for a bridge of that length. A plate-girder bridge, however, is a reasonable assumption, since railroads welcomed the design for crossings of less than a hundred feet. In truth, railroads absolutely loved plate girders for their simplicity and durability. In his 1916 treatise *Bridge Engineering*, J. A. L. Waddell lauded the humble bridge type: "Although plate girders are of necessity as unscientific structures as a bridge specialist ever has to design, they are without doubt the most satisfactory type of construction possible for short spans. . . . One rarely hears of the failure of a plate-girder span."

A plate-girder bridge is usually composed of two load-bearing beams that have been "built up." The beams are formed of wide, thin, metal plates with flanges riveted to the edges at the top and bottom. Metal angles riveted vertically across the width of the plates, between the top and bottom flanges, stiffen the beams. The built-up beams support floor beams, which in turn carry the deck.

Besides their simplicity and strength, plate-girder spans were also extremely convenient. A railroad could literally build a plate-girder bridge in its maintenance shops, place it on a flatcar, and haul it to the bridge site and set it atop the abutments and piers. Since this utterly practical bridge design suited the utterly practical railroad, it is hardly surprising that the GN employed a fifty-eight-foot-long plate-girder span when the railroad replaced the first bridge over Steamboat River in 1914. While it is unlikely that it was any more unusual than its predecessor, the new Steamboat Bridge was certainly more remarkable than most plate-girder crossings.

The appellations "Steamboat Bridge," "Steamboat River," "Steamboat Lake," and "Steamboat Bay" hint at why the GN crossing needed to be different from most. Cass County was part of a major north-central Minnesota logging region in the late nineteenth and early twentieth centuries, although modest timber cutting in the area began as early as the mid-1800s, an occurrence colorfully described in a local history: "The ring of the ax striking into the hearts of the giant pine trees shattered the silence of the wilderness, which had for years known nothing but the swish of moccasined [sic] Indian feet, the soft thud of the trapper's horse, and the occasional tramp, tramp of a lone hunter." Beginning in the late nineteenth century, after the "tramp, tramp" of the pioneer hunter had faded, much of the region's cut timber was transported from cutting areas via steamboat. These vessels frequently towed log booms across area lakes to nearby rivers. Logs dumped into Steamboat Lake, for instance, were directed into Steamboat River. The logs floated downriver to Leech Lake, where they were again gathered into booms and hauled by steamboat to the next river. Eventually, the logs made it to the Mississippi River and the sawmills farther downstream. But how did large quantities of logs get beyond the low bridge obstructing Steamboat River? Moreover, how did steamboats navigate between Steamboat and Leech Lakes? Simple; the bridge was swung out of the way.

There are different types of movable bridges (often called drawbridges), including bascules and vertical lifts. A bascule consists of roadway leaves supported on a trunnion, or hinge. The bridge operates by rotating the leaves upward from the hinged ends to a nearly vertical position. The main span of a vertical lift, however, rises between towers that support and flank it. At the turn of the twentieth century, the most common type of movable bridge was a swing span, the same kind of bridge the GN erected over Steamboat River. Steamboat Bridge was positioned over a large-diameter, steel ring, which in turn rested atop many small-diameter, steel wheels. The wheels moved over a circular rim that was fixed to the top of the wood-pile, center pier. By retracting the steel, wedge shoes at either end of the bridge, the "unlocked" structure was manually pivoted, opening the waterway.

It is unclear precisely how long Steamboat Bridge regularly operated. Substantial logging in Cass Lake ended in the 1920s, and the heyday of the industry in Minnesota was already becoming a distant memory when the last major sawmills closed in the 1930s. The Burlington Northern Railroad (BN) eventually gained control of the structure when the GN became part of that line in 1970. In 1972, the BN abandoned the road, and three years later it conveyed the bridge to the state of Minnesota. The rails over the crossing have long since been removed and the bridge is probably a good fishing spot these days. The bridge should not be viewed as just another place to cast a line, though, since it reflects an innovative solution to what was a very real concern in early twentieth-century Cass County. Moreover, the bridge is a rare surviving symbol of the cooperation between timber interests and the railroads during northern Minnesota's logging period. As such, Steamboat Bridge was honored with a National Register listing in 1980.

✳ Nansen Agricultural District

VICINITY OF NANSEN | GOODHUE COUNTY

Holden Township in southwestern Goodhue County was the childhood home of two influential social thinkers of the late nineteenth and early twentieth centuries. Thorstein Veblen, author of *The Theory of the Leisure Class* (1899), was an economist who decried the accumulation and demonstration of wealth and the man who coined the phrase "conspicuous consumption." A towering intellect, Veblen was once described as "the last man who knew everything." Andrew Volstead was a politician, a Minnesota congressman forever tied to the 18th Amendment to the Constitution. Volstead sponsored the National Prohibition Act, commonly known as the Volstead Act, which defined intoxicating beverages as those containing more than 0.5 percent alcohol. Both men came from Norwegian immigrant families that settled in Holden Township in the 1850s, joining countrymen who began arriving in the Goodhue County area as early as the 1840s, well before Minnesota became a state. Norwegians in the region established farmsteads and raised wheat, the early cash crop of southern Minnesota, but later diversified when the land could no longer sustain one-crop farming. As with many rural areas, advancing years brought residential, commercial,

A section of the tranquil
Sogn Valley at the beginning
of the twenty-first century

and industrial development, until much of Goodhue County lost agricultural cohesiveness. The county's historical footprint remains prominent in a roughly seven-square-mile area, however. A collection of thirty farmsteads located in the southern portion of the Sogn Valley, which includes parts of Holden and Warsaw Townships, exhibits little intrusion, a substantial feat for an agricultural locality dating to the mid-nineteenth century.[21]

In Harold Severson's work *We Give You Kenyon: A Bicentennial History of a Minnesota Community*, historian Peter Brandvold Sr. paints a portrait of the Sogn Valley: "Nestled in a picturesque area south of Cannon Falls and along the Little Cannon River is the Sogn Valley, surrounded by wooded hillsides and fertile farmland. . . . The similarity of the landscape of the Sogn Valley to that of Norway may have had some bearing on why so many Norwegians settled among these steepsided hills, wooded hollows and bold outcroppings." While the Sogn Valley was chiefly dominated by Norwegians, German immigrants established homes in the area as well.

Due to the sloping landscape, farmstead size in the Sogn Valley was comparatively modest, usually no more than two hundred acres. As with other locations in Goodhue County, early dwellings were simple, consisting of log cabins or dugouts, the latter formed by burrowing into the side of a hill and erecting log or limestone walls at the sides and front. These dwellings were an indication of the farming, which was principally subsistence, at least for the first several years. During the 1860s, when farmers became established and transportation routes to distribution centers were

NANSEN AGRICULTURAL DISTRICT | 65

created, production included cash crops. One regional distribution center was at Red Wing on the Mississippi River, but farmers in the Sogn Valley typically delivered their wheat crop to Hastings, also on the great midwestern waterway, where it was loaded on steamboats and sent to rail points south. In 1870, as the railroads were usurping the steamers as the principal mode of freight transportation in Minnesota, the Minnesota Central Railway reached Owatonna, giving farmers in southwestern Goodhue County a nearby rail connection. Eight years later the Rochester and Northern Minnesota, a branch of the Winona and St. Peter Railroad, built a line into Zumbrota in southeastern Goodhue County, establishing a rail link that was closer yet, only about a dozen miles east of the Sogn Valley.

As farmsteads in the valley became economically stable, farmers erected houses and outbuildings that reflected their growing prosperity. Sometimes farmhouses were built atop the original dugouts, which then served as basements. The current Anders Erickson Haugen Farmhouse that was constructed sometime in the 1870s was built over a dugout raised in the 1860s. The cross-gabled house is not elaborate, but does exhibit some Italianate-style flourishes. The generally vernacular architecture of farmhouses in the valley is frequently displayed in the two-story cube with hip roof that was popular between 1900 and 1920. The Bestal Farmhouse,

A view along a corncrib toward the gable-roofed barn with gambrel-roofed addition at the Simon Gjellum/Neseth Farmstead

for example, is a two-story cube erected around 1913. The house hints at Colonial Revival style with its Palladian window and classical porch. Outbuildings in the valley also are structure types common to specific periods of history. While many farmsteads contain gable-roofed granaries, reminders of when wheat dominated agriculture in southern Minnesota, numerous properties also have dairy and stock barns, symbols of farming diversification that began in the late nineteenth and early twentieth centuries after continual wheat raising drained nutrients from the soil.

Even though development eventually crept into the northern part of the Sogn Valley, the southern section enveloping Nansen, a hamlet founded in 1898 that was named for Arctic explorer Fridtjof Nansen, has remained virtually free of modern intrusion. Of course, the farmsteads in the Nansen Agricultural District do not exist within a glass box and are dotted with farm structures of more recent construction. Most buildings, however, date to an earlier period. More significantly, agriculture continues to dominate land use. Indeed, some current farmers are working land first worked by their great-grandparents. Owing a great deal of uniformity to geography, the hills serving as natural buffers to sprawl stemming from the Twin Cities, the Nansen Agricultural District aptly reflects the familial trade so prominent in southern Minnesota before industrial revolution radically altered Minnesota's agrarian way of life. One of the state's best examples of a cohesive agricultural area, the district was placed on the National Register in 2000.

✳ Soo Line High Bridge

VICINITY OF STILLWATER | WASHINGTON COUNTY

The big bridge over the St. Croix river at Somerset suffered a mishap quite serious this week and which cost the contractor perhaps $20,000 or more. On the Minnesota side portions of the false work gave way, which was supporting the heavy steel spans above. Several sections of the span began to give way and it looked as though many feet of the mammoth bridge would topple into the river. . . . Three inch steel bolts that had been riveted into the section were snapped off in a twinkling and the big girders and beams slid eight or ten inches and the numerous workmen rushed off the bridge, scrambling to a place of safety. . . . In the excitement several workmen were bumped and bruised and one man was hit in the forehead with the arms of a steel drill. It knocked him unconscious and he was taken to the hospital at Stillwater with his skull almost split open. . . . The bridge is so high that it looks frail and delicate to one on the ground, although it is regarded as one of the strongest steel bridges ever built. So far not a single workman has been killed in prosecuting this difficult and gigantic engineering feat. When finished the structure will be one of the sights of the Northwest.

While the Great Northern Railway had its own arched "statement" crossing in the Minneapolis Stone Arch Bridge, the Minneapolis, St. Paul and Sault Ste. Marie Railway had its spectacular Soo Line High Bridge over the St. Croix River, linking Minnesota with Wisconsin about five miles north of Stillwater. The bridge was completed in June 1911, three months after the *Chippewa Falls Herald* reported the near collapse of one of the spans. Even though the account noted the safety record at the bridge site, the *Herald* omitted the fatality four months earlier near Arcola, Minnesota, about a mile west of the crossing. John Bohlman of Chicago, who was helping lay a new Soo Line extension to the St. Croix River, which made the high bridge necessary, was crushed when a jack elevating a flatcar he was working on failed.[22]

Nearly a hundred years old, the graceful Soo Line High Bridge is hidden within the St. Croix River Valley north of Stillwater.

The extension Bohlman helped construct was part of a huge improvement effort connecting St. Paul with New Richmond, Wisconsin, and came about after the Soo Line acquired controlling interest of the Wisconsin Central Railway (WC) in 1909. The WC already had a route from St. Paul to Chippewa Falls, Wisconsin, roughly sixty-five miles east of New Richmond. The road included an enormous bridge over the St. Croix River that was built in 1884. Measuring almost 2,400 feet long, it was comprised of a pinned, double-intersection, through-truss flanked by nine pinned, double-intersection, deck trusses that were approached by twenty plate girders. It was interesting bridge, but looked somewhat utilitarian for this picturesque section of the St. Croix River Valley. Even so, the Soo Line likely would have used the crossing instead of erecting a new bridge if the railroad had believed it worthwhile. In truth, though, the line the WC laid to

St. Paul was tortuous, especially east of the St. Croix River. Historian Patrick Dorin explained: "The section of railroad from Chippewa Falls to the west of the St. Croix River is extremely rough with many hills and ravines occurring in regular succession. St. Croix River was bridged as inexpensively as possible with sharp grade descents to both approaches and was a real operating problem. . . ." By building a new bridge and rerouting the road, the Soo Line shortened the mileage between St. Paul and Chippewa Falls and eliminated the precarious operating conditions.

Initially, the Soo Line considered erecting a concrete bridge but was deterred by the high cost of creating the huge piers required to support the tremendous weight of the spans. Moreover, work was scheduled through the winter of 1910–11 and the railroad believed that cold weather would delay concrete construction. Instead, the railway opted for a steel arch—specifically, a five-span, steel, riveted, three-hinged, spandrel-braced arch with deck-plate-girder approaches. The delightful setting for the new bridge deserved the graceful curves of an arch, although economics, not aesthetics, were the Soo Line's principal concern. Arches are rarely economical, but site conditions frequently determine what form a bridge will take. Along the St. Croix River, five miles above Stillwater, an arch seemed ideal.

The bridge was designed by Claude A. P. Turner (commonly known as C. A. P. Turner), a professional from Minneapolis described by historian David Plowden as "one of America's most brilliant engineers." Interestingly, by the time Turner engineered his huge steel arch, he was nationally recognized for his innovative efforts with reinforced concrete, especially his work with flat-slab framing, an economical means of erecting multistory buildings that incorporated supporting columns with flared capitals, commonly called mushroom capitals.

Turner's bridge for the Soo Line was also innovative. In fact, it is now considered a classic three-hinged arch. Most steel-arch bridges in America are fixed, which means there are no hinged joints incorporated within the arch, making bridges of this type rigid. Occasionally, though, conditions demand a more yielding, hinged arch—the more hinges, the more yielding. Most hinged arches are of the one- or two-hinged variety, making Turner's structure unique. Turner's bridge included a hinged joint near the springing line at opposing ends of each arch, but also incorporated a hinged joint at arch crowns. J. A. L. Waddell, one of the foremost bridge engineers of the early twentieth century, noted that this type of arch bridge has "no temperature stresses or indeterminate stresses of any importance." What truly made Turner's arch fascinating, however, was the sliding lap joint that "locked" each crown hinge when a live load (a train) passed over the bridge, essentially making the three-hinged crossing as rigid as a two-hinged structure.

Construction of the bridge began on June 1, 1910, just north of the 1884 crossing. While the Kelly-Atkinson Construction Company of Chicago

Taken about 1909, this image not only depicts some brave lads within a deck-truss section of the Wisconsin Central crossing, but also the "pinned" joints where vertical, horizontal, and diagonal bridge members intersected.

This 1914 photograph shows the Soo Line High Bridge north of the old Wisconsin Central crossing, which featured a through-truss main span flanked by several deck trusses.

erected the bridge, the American Bridge Company, a subsidiary of the United States Steel Corporation, actually fabricated the structure. Formed in the early 1900s through the merger of twenty-six bridge enterprises, the American Bridge Company is responsible for numerous crossings throughout this country, including the Portage Lake Bridge, a huge, double-deck, vertical-lift structure joining Houghton with Hancock across Portage Lake in Michigan's Upper Peninsula.

Finished in June 1911, the $500,000 Soo Line High Bridge was almost 2,700 feet long and rose 185 feet above the St. Croix River. It was christened on June 10, when a trainload of Soo Line officials and other dignitaries passed over the arches. Curiously, the engineer for the novel bridge was not among them, sending a representative in his place. Turner's bridge engineering prowess was again demonstrated in the late 1920s, when he modified the Duluth Aerial Ferry Bridge spanning the Duluth Ship Canal into the present vertical-lift structure (see page 107).

Today, the nimble Soo Line High Bridge remains a familiar sight to those plying the St. Croix River north of Stillwater. From a distance, it looks almost too fragile to have remained standing for nearly a century. Regrettably, most never get a chance to see the elegant crossing because of the densely-wooded river banks and the bridge's rather obscure location. Considered by Plowden "the most outstanding example" of a steel, multiarch railway bridge, and "one of the world's most beautiful steel structures," the Soo Line High Bridge became part of the National Register in 1977.

INDUSTRY & TECHNOLOGY

IN 1823 SOLDIERS FROM FORT SNELLING
completed a gristmill at St. Anthony Falls on the
Mississippi River near present-day Minneapolis.
The flour the mill produced was not very good,
mainly because the wheat was poor, the processing
equipment inadequate, and the workers were
soldiers, not farmers or millers. Still, this tiny
enterprise that milled flour for bitter-tasting bread represented the early stages
of industry in Minnesota.[23]

Despite this effort, or maybe because of it, many in the East were unim-
pressed with the long-term industrial and economic potential of Minnesota, a fact
James J. Hill reflected on many years later in a speech at the annual meeting of the
Minnesota Historical Society in January 1897. The railroad baron explained that in
the mid-nineteenth century some in the East had to be convinced that "Minnesota
was not an utterly barren waste, that it was not a country limited to the raising of a
few cranberries and some muskrat skins." Some doubters were swayed after examin-
ing high-quality ears of corn Minnesota entrepreneurs delivered to the East. More
were persuaded after being informed that much of the choice flour labeled "Musk-
ingum Mills, Troy, Ohio—The Genuine," was really from Minnesota. These efforts
spurred agricultural development in the Upper Mississippi River Valley region,

and agriculture ultimately became Minnesota's primary early industry. Timber and iron ore, however, also aided the transformation of this cranberry and muskrat land into a significant industrial power.

Logging began in the late 1830s, and was possibly Minnesota's first major industry, although some may argue the fur trade was first, since traders were active in the region by the mid- to late seventeenth century. Fur trading, however, does not fit as neatly within the concept of industrialization as does logging. Industrialization conjures images of expansion, not just in the size of factories or machines, but also in the size of systems and organizations. (Agriculture, for instance, became an industry after the volume of produce for exchange was large enough to warrant a substantial system devoted to its processing and delivery to large markets.) Further, industrialization typically brings considerable population growth, as well as extensive civic and commercial development. The fur trade fits some characterizations of industry. As example, by the latter half of the eighteenth century Minnesota was marked by numerous British and American fur-trading posts, demonstrating the enterprise's importance. A circuitous means for delivering goods to markets was also in place. Fur trading, though, never promoted generous population and community growth in Minnesota, yet agricultural development and logging attracted sizeable settlement and triggered substantial improvement even before the railroad arrived. If fur trading was an industry, then it was a qualified one.

Unlike agricultural interests, those tied to logging did not hesitate to move into Minnesota. Minnesota's large tracts of white pine were obvious simply by peering across the St. Croix River from Wisconsin. Moreover, in contrast to those desiring fertile planting fields year after year, timber companies rarely viewed forests as renewable resources (replanting was not common until the 1930s). Instead, tracts were routinely devoured and abandoned as timber companies moved west in search of the next coniferous mouthful. By the time the last of Minnesota's major sawmills closed in the 1930s, the state was left with acres upon acres of surreal landscapes resembling war zones.

Minnesota logging peaked around the turn of the twentieth century. By then Minnesota was the third largest lumber-producing state. Even so, agriculture, enhanced by an extensive rail system, was the state's chief economic driver at the start of the new century. Minneapolis, for example, had become a leading flour-milling city, thanks in large measure to St. Anthony Falls. As early as 1880, one-third of the output of Minneapolis mills was destined for foreign markets. By 1885 the world craved Minneapolis flour, a want partly resulting from the use of the middlings purifier, a processing machine employed by the mills near St. Anthony Falls that greatly improved flour quality. By this time, roller mills had replaced millstones in many Minnesota flour mills, an innovation making grain grinding much more efficient.

The middlings purifier and roller mills were only a couple examples of the technological advances influencing development in early Minnesota. In 1899 grain merchant Frank Hutchison Peavey erected a circular, concrete elevator near the western edge of Minneapolis in present-day St. Louis Park. Peavey's elevator was the first of its type in the country, and likely the first cylindrical, concrete grain elevator in the world. The structure type is now common for grain storage. Roadway infrastructure evidenced technological leaps as well. The Seventh Street Improvement Arches immediately east of downtown St. Paul, for instance, is one of the most unusual bridges ever erected in Minnesota. Completed in 1884, the skewed crossing employed a helicoidal plan, a technically demanding design most late-nineteenth-century engineers were loathe to attempt. Bernard H. Pietenpol, a mechanical wizard from Fillmore County, added his unassuming personality to the creative and technological lore of the state when he began erecting airplanes in his garage in the 1920s.

In the early 1880s, as Minneapolis mills were becoming what historian Robert M. Frame III termed the "Millers to the World," Minnesota welcomed the raw iron wealth of the northeastern section of the state. In the years 1883–84, the Vermilion Iron Range was opened by the Minnesota Iron Company. By the early 1890s, the production of the Vermilion was augmented by the Mesabi Iron Range to the south. The Cuyuna Iron Range southwest of the Mesabi opened during the first decade of the twentieth century. In the 1930s, as logging was fading, these three ranges were contributing about $100 million annually to the coffers of Minnesota.

Minnesota developed other important industries as well, including quarrying and commercial fishing. At the close of the nineteenth century, Minnesota was one of the nation's top stone-producing states, supported by quarries in counties like Rock, Sandstone, Sherburne, and Stearns. Lake Superior was a reservoir of game fish that begged a fishing industry. By the mid-1930s, commercial fishermen were pulling nearly eight million pounds of trout, ciscoes, whitefish, and particularly herring from the freshwater sea. Meatpacking, a constituent of the agricultural industry, was also substantial, especially in South St. Paul, which was home to the St. Paul Union Stock Yards. At the beginning of the Great Depression, almost 30 percent of Minnesota's farm income was derived from selling livestock to stockyards.

Today, reminders of Minnesota's industrial and technological history are evident in many places, such as Sandstone in Pine County, the site of the Kettle River Sandstone Company Quarry, a National Register property that was the most extensive sandstone quarrying operation in the state in the late nineteenth and early twentieth centuries. Phelps Mill, a National Register structure straddling the Otter Tail River in Maine Township in Otter Tail County, was erected in 1889. The mill is a fine example of the pioneering agricultural industry in that region. The Kern Bridge in Mankato Township in Blue Earth County represents mid- to late-nineteenth-century bridge technology. Erected in 1873, the crossing was added to the National Register as the only bowstring arch through-truss bridge in the entire state. Near Mazeppa in Wabasha County, the Lake Zumbro Hydroelectric Generating Plant is a 60-foot-high, 900-foot-long gravity dam and powerhouse. The National Register edifice was built in 1919 to supply electricity to Rochester in Olmstead County. As with each of these properties, the historic structures noted in this chapter symbolize economic growth and innovation during Minnesota's formative years.

✳ Pine Tree Lumber Company Office Building

LITTLE FALLS | MORRISON COUNTY

Commercial logging in this country began soon after the founding of Jamestown, Virginia, in 1607. The following year a shipload of timber products gleaned from the forests of the New World was delivered to England. Timber morsels during early colonization merely whetted an appetite that later became voracious. As historian Mary Swanholm observed: "For the next 300 years Americans fell upon their forests with the fury of a chosen people opening the way to a heavenly city, testing their faith against towering pines, clearing the land for cultivation and settlement, converting their fallen adversaries into huts and firewood, towns and cities, and eventually newsprint and particle board." While devastating huge tracts of forests now seems obscene, the timber industry inaugurated prosperity in this country, providing the resources to erect the nascent infrastructure of a nation that would become an industrial behemoth. Moreover, cleared timberland induced settlement, attracting waves of immigrants seeking opportunity largely unknown elsewhere.[24]

Until the early 1800s logging was concentrated mostly in the East, chiefly in Maine. As the population shifted west, however, so did timber enterprises. By the late 1830s timber companies were sweeping through Michigan and Wisconsin and eyeing the pine forests adjacent to the St. Croix River. Minnesota was still two decades away from becoming a state when timbering was initiated on the west side of the waterway in 1839, two years after the Dakota and Ojibwe ceded much of their land near the river to the federal government. The first commercial sawmill, Marine Lumber Company, was prospering by 1850, but its production was soon surpassed by mills in nearby Stillwater. Much of the timber not used in the region was rafted down the St. Croix River to the Mississippi River, and then on to Iowa, Illinois, or Missouri.

By 1848 the first commercial sawmill was established on the Mississippi River near St. Anthony Falls, a geographic benefaction that gave rise to the immensely successful Minneapolis flour-milling industry. Incorporated as a city in 1867, Minneapolis was thriving by the 1880s, as was its sister city, St. Paul. Minneapolis sawmills supplied the metropolitan area with about 300 million board feet of lumber annually between 1880 and 1890. By this time, however, timber tracts in the southeastern part of the state were nearly exhausted and lumbermen were looking north and northwest for new forests. In 1890 officials of the newly formed Pine Tree Lumber Company purchased more than 200,000 acres of pineland in northern Minnesota from the Northern Pacific Railway (NP) for nearly $500,000. The company founded a sawmill to process the pine on the east bank of the Mississippi River at Little Falls, a Morrison County town thirty-three miles north of St. Cloud.

The Pine Tree Lumber Company was incorporated by a group of prominent lumbermen, including Peter Musser and Frederick Weyerhaeuser. Musser was from Muscatine, Iowa, remembered by the *Muscatine News-Tribune* as a man "passionately fond of music and flowers." A forceful personality, "tempered by a conservative business ability," Musser was commonly known as "Uncle Peter." Weyerhaeuser, a German immigrant described by Swanholm as "the most powerful of the timberland generals . . . more of a diplomat than a dictator," began his journey into lumbering immortality when he started working at a small sawmill in Rock Island, Illinois, when he was twenty-one.

Pine Tree Lumber Company was only one component of the Musser and Weyerhaeuser empires, and as such the two magnates let the kids manage it. Richard "Drew" Musser was twenty-five and Charles A. Weyerhaeuser twenty-six when the childhood friends moved to Little Falls, living in a local hotel for a time until room was available near the company plant.

This interior photo, taken sometime in the 1890s, captures the work of running the Pine Tree Lumber Company.

In 1891 the roughly 40- by 40-foot, two-story, Pine Tree Lumber Company
Office Building was constructed adjacent to the east bank of the river, and
Drew and Charles moved into the attic. The brick building rested upon a
granite foundation and had a hip roof with a flat, center section, a feature
likely appreciated by the attic's occupants since it provided headroom
unavailable with a gable roof. Dormers pierced the north and south sides
of the roof, allowing light into the attic and large, rectangular windows
surmounted by flat arches marked first- and second-floor walls. The main
entrance was situated at the east facade, garnished with a decorative porch.

Drew and Charles lived in the building's attic for several years, managing the business from the offices below. Initially, the duo supervised the
lumber production of an old sawmill that was erected on the east bank of
the river many years before Pine Tree purchased the site. While the old
mill was in operation, the company constructed a much larger plant on the
west bank of the river. Eventually, the new mill grew to over a hundred acres,
employing roughly four hundred men during the milling season and producing millions of board feet of lumber annually that was shipped to markets via the NP. Spin-off industries, such as sash and door manufacturing,
brought further growth to Little Falls. Between 1890 and 1900, the population of the community increased from about 2,300 to almost 6,000.

In 1898, finally convinced the business was stable, Drew and Charles
built homes in Little Falls. Designed by well-known Minnesota architect
Clarence H. Johnston, the two houses were constructed within feet of each
other along the Mississippi River, about a half-mile south of the town's

commercial core. Charles married Frances Maud Moon of Duluth the same year his home was completed, while Drew wed Sarah Walker of Glens Falls, New York, five years later.

Charles and Frances left Little Falls for St. Paul in 1920, the year the mill closed after the timber ran out. Drew and Sarah remained in Little Falls until their passing. Production at the mill had peaked in 1902, reaching about 75 million board feet, but after 1907 annual totals continually dropped. By the time the mill stopped, the glory days of Minnesota logging were reaching an inglorious end. Lumbermen were moving to woodlands in the South and West, leaving behind stump forests of little commercial value. By the 1930s, however, as the federal and state government surveyed the aftermath of unregulated logging, new policies were initiated that controlled future cutting and demanded replanting. Much of Minnesota is again lush with trees, although the white pine cherished by early lumber companies is all but gone.

Gone, too, is almost every constituent of the Pine Tree Lumber Company in Little Falls. Still standing, though, is the Pine Tree Lumber Company Office Building, from which Charles A. Weyerhaeuser and Drew Musser managed one of Minnesota's mammoth timber operations. Even though the building has been altered somewhat, most notably the front porch, which has been enclosed, the structure still denotes its period of construction. One of the few remaining tangible reminders of Minnesota's early logging heritage, the industry that primed the state's economic engine, this unfussy building was added to the National Register in 1985, the same year the Charles A. Weyerhaeuser and Richard D. Musser Houses were so honored.

✳ Peavey-Haglin Experimental Concrete Grain Elevator

ST. LOUIS PARK | HENNEPIN COUNTY

Frank Hutchison Peavey had a difficult childhood. He was born in Eastport, Maine, in 1850. When he was only nine years old his father died, leaving young Frank to work odd jobs to help the family survive. By the time he was a teen he felt the inexorable pull of the West. Like so many disenchanted Easterners in the mid-nineteenth century, he was convinced that his destiny lay in the vast, fertile plains of Middle America. Kissing his mother goodbye, fifteen-year-old Peavey boarded a train for Chicago and the better life he was certain awaited him. Within three years he was a managing partner for a farm implement company in Sioux City, Iowa. One year later his uninsured business burned to the ground and he found himself almost $2,000 in debt.[25]

Although Peavey lost his company, he did not lose his will to succeed. He secured another partner and plunged back into the farm implement business. The destruction of his earlier enterprise had taught him a valuable lesson. He vowed to never again own a business without adequate fire protection. A superb salesman with a tireless work ethic, Peavey was soon free of his debt. In 1873, Ned Bucknam, a friend of the young entrepreneur, noted Peavey's unremitting determination and remarkable salesmanship:

> We started out in November on this trip to sell implements and wagons. It seemed to me a hopeless business, but he knew that there must be some demand for his goods. He would get to a frontier trading post composed of a dozen shanties or sod houses and almost as many stores. 'This doesn't look like a good prospect for doing business,' I would say. 'No, but wait until I get done with it,' Frank would reply confidently. And then he would go to work. He sold goods in every town. They might tell him they didn't want anything, but he always changed their minds. He was the most wonderful salesman and solicitor I ever knew.

On that single trip with Bucknam, Peavey secured over $50,000 in orders. His business was going so well that he brought his mother and two siblings to live in Sioux City. He also established the new firm of Peavey Brothers, forming a partnership with his brother James Fulton Peavey. About this time Peavey began operating as a grain merchant, the vocation that would ultimately make his name throughout the Midwest. Promising flour millers in Minneapolis a steady supply of grain, he began buying as much harvest as he could from regional farmers. Initially, Peavey stored the grain near rail lines in flathouses, which were low, wooden warehouses near the tracks. Flathouses consigned grain in sacks, but railroads found handling sacked grain very inefficient. As incentive to eliminate the practice, the railroads offered free land near their tracks to companies that would build grain elevators on the sites. It's likely Peavey was a recipient of some of these locations, for he soon abandoned flathouses for elevators. Elevators were specially designed square- or rectangular-shaped wooden structures capable of storing and distributing grain in bulk. Much higher than flathouses, elevators received their moniker because they elevated grain. Grain delivered to an elevator was drawn upward by a bucket conveyor. Near the top of the facility the buckets emptied their contents into chutes that directed the grain into storage bins. A bucket conveyor was also used to deliver grain to distributors that directed flow into railroad cars.

By the late 1800s country elevators began dotting the rural landscape. These buildings were frequently smaller versions of terminal elevators, which were often mammoth structures in terminal markets, such as rail centers. Whereas country elevators received grain in small wagonloads and transferred it to railroad cars, terminal elevators received grain from the railroad cars and conveyed it to ships, barges, or other railroad cars.

Now a National Historic Landmark, Frank Hutchison Peavey's turn-of-the-twentieth-century cylindrical, concrete grain elevator is an original.

At first, Peavey was chiefly occupied with building country elevators, often employing crews to erect the structures in rural towns even before the railroads had reached the communities. By 1886 he had become so successful that he constructed his first terminal elevator in southeast Minneapolis. Unfortunately, the St. Anthony Elevator was devoured by fire the following year. It was insured, however, and Peavey quickly replaced it with the Interior Elevator on the outskirts of Minneapolis in present-day St. Louis Park. But high fire insurance premiums were always a sore point with him, since insurance companies often charged close to two percent the value of the grain in the elevator for coverage. Although this may not seem like much, at large terminals the annual premium could be hundreds of thousands of dollars. Moreover, insurers often required that elevators be constructed some distance from one another so as to limit damage should one elevator catch fire. This was a prudent policy, except that it increased costs for elevator owners. What seemed to irk grain merchants most, though, was that oftentimes insurers would not grant insurance at all, concluding that some elevators were not worth the risk. For insurance providers, large, wooden terminals were tinderboxes easily ignited by an errant spark from a passing train. To prevent fire catastrophes, some elevator owners sheathed their wooden elevators in sheet metal. Other owners were more creative, searching for elevator designs that eliminated wood as a construction material. Around the turn of the twentieth century elevators of steel, tile, and brick were being built.

Peavey had his own idea of how a fireproof grain storage structure should be built, and in the late 1890s he conceived a plan to develop a relatively thin, cylindrical, poured-concrete terminal elevator. After consulting with Charles F. Haglin, a prominent Minneapolis contractor, the duo decided to erect a cylindrical, concrete elevator near the western edge of Minneapolis, near Peavey's Interior Elevator. Since the practicality of the design was uncertain, it was intended solely as an experiment. Some dubbed the plan "Peavey's Folly" because conventional wisdom held that shifting forces from grain pouring out of a slender concrete grain storage structure would cause it to collapse. Nevertheless, Peavey and Haglin began construction in summer 1899.

Concrete was poured in one continuous operation, a building method known as monolithic construction. Curved "slip forms" were used to shape the structure. After concrete for the lower section had been poured and hardened, the forms were slipped upward, braced, and the next section poured. Steel hoops embedded within the concrete provided reinforcement. Work continued into the fall until the elevator was sixty-eight feet high.

Having an inside diameter of twenty feet, the elevator's walls were only twelve inches thick at the base and merely eight inches near the top. Peavey then filled the elevator with grain and awaited spring, at which time he would draw off its contents and hope the storage facility did not crumble.

In the meantime Peavey sent associates to Europe to discover how others were storing their grain. The representatives visited Hamburg, Brunswick, Copenhagen, Budapest, Vienna, Paris, and Amsterdam, as well as cities in Romania and Russia. The men discovered some interesting grain handling and storage practices, but nowhere did they find an elevator like Peavey's. In Minneapolis in late spring 1900, hundreds of spectators gathered around Peavey's Folly as he prepared to drain the elevator. Those who came to watch the tower fall to pieces were disappointed. When the elevator was opened and the grain rushed out nothing happened. For some it must have seemed anticlimactic, but for Peavey it was vindication. His monolithic folly continued to mark the skyline like an enormous finger that he could jab in the eye of any critic. More importantly, the successful experiment represented the birth of a new age in grain storage. While terminal elevators of wood, steel, tile, and brick would still be built for some years, eventually each gave way to Peavey's innovative design. Insurance companies took notice of the new technology, slashing rates on grain stored in concrete elevators.

The elevator hatched by Peavey and built by Haglin was raised to 125 feet soon after the experiment. Constructed only as a test, it was never used to store commercial grain. For the past century the first cylindrical, concrete grain elevator in the country—and probably the world—has stood as a monument to the foresight of its planner and builder. It is situated near the intersection of State Highway 100 and State Highway 7. The Nordic Ware Company has owned it for decades, and it has become a familiar landmark to passing motorists who smile at the Viking head painted on its side. The Peavey-Haglin Experimental Concrete Grain Elevator was placed on the National Register in 1978. Three years later its major contribution to the agricultural history of this country was recognized when it was christened a National Historic Landmark.

✳ Seventh Street Improvement Arches

ST. PAUL | RAMSEY COUNTY

In summer 1916 the Great Northern Railway (GN) and the Northern Pacific Railway (NP) were battling with the city of St. Paul over who was responsible for repairing or replacing a failing section of the East Seventh Street Bridge. The NP had built the truss bridge section in the 1880s, a time when much of Seventh Street east of downtown St. Paul was improved. The GN and NP believed the original agreement with the city held St. Paul liable for maintaining the roadway bridge over their tracks. The city disagreed, apparently arguing that the roadway was in place before the railway lines, thus the railroads were responsible for building and maintaining the crossing. The historical facts of the dispute are a bit muddy, but each side appeared to make valid points. In the end, however, District Judge J. C. Michael ruled in favor of the city. The state supreme court upheld the ruling.[26]

Just up the road from the faltering NP bridge was another crossing that passed over the tracks of the St. Paul and Duluth Railroad (StP&D). It was constructed a few years before the NP structure, and unlike the NP bridge, it was built to last. Moreover, it was one of the most unusual bridges ever erected in Minnesota, a skewed, double-arched, stone roadway bridge that utilized a helicoidal plan. Constructed by Michael O'Brien of St. Paul and McArthur Brothers of Chicago, the bridge's designer was a "bluff, undiplomatic, outspoken" engineer named William Albert Truesdell, a man who spent a good deal of free time studying mathematics and the U.S. Constitution.

Truesdell was born in New York City in 1845. A short time later his family moved to Wisconsin, settling on a farm at Wautoma. As a young man Truesdell studied engineering at the University of Wisconsin, graduating in 1867. He taught school briefly before engaging in railroad and land survey work. In 1880 he began working as an engineer for the St. Paul, Minneapolis and Manitoba Railway (later the Great Northern Railway), although he did consulting as well. One of his consulting efforts was for the city of St. Paul, which hired him in 1883 to supervise the improvement of Seventh Street, including the design of the arch bridge over the StP&D line.

Truesdell was handed a formidable task, since Seventh Street crossed the StP&D tracks at a 63-degree angle. The skewed angle required a skewed bridge. Truesdell observed: "Nothing of this kind had ever been built in this western country. Very few of our masons in St. Paul had ever seen [such a bridge], and no one knew anything about the stone-cutting necessary." The engineer considered building an oblique arch bridge using a series of ribs, a design method often employed for skewed crossings. He concluded that the plan would never work. Using ribs was fine for simple roadway bridges, but his structure had to also hold city water and sewer lines, which required a substantial amount of fill over the arches; the ribs would not withstand the weight. Truesdell next considered the French method of oblique arch construction, also known as the logarithmic method. The voussoirs (shaped stones) used to form the arch are made of many different sizes and pieced together like a puzzle. Truesdell understood that a bridge constructed in this way would be incredibly strong, but it would be extraordinarily difficult and expensive to build. He moved to his next option, a helicoidal arch.

English architect Peter Nicholson pioneered helicoidal arch construction in the early 1800s. The plan was adopted for a number of skewed bridges in England and Scotland, but rarely employed in America. And for good reason—few engineers in this country knew how to build a helicoidal arch. In the late 1880s one American writer noted: "The general opinion has arisen that helicoidal arches are of the most intricate construction . . . often their consideration has been abandoned with disgust." Truesdell, however, understood the demanding mathematics required for designing such arches. He also knew that the construction technique offered practical advantages over other arch building methods. The design is stronger than a ribbed arch, and unlike the French method, which required voussoirs of varying size, each stone in a helicoidal arch is cut to the same dimensions, except for the ring stones (the outermost voussoirs of the arch). Helicoidal construction utilizes voussoirs that are warped. Picture a rectangular stone that appears slightly twisted—although it is not really twisted at all, it simply has been carved to look that way. When several warped stones with identical measurements are placed end-to-end they form a spiraling course.

The Seventh Street
Improvement Arches,
a rare bridge type formed
of many spiraling, stone
courses, was completed
in 1884.

This is how Truesdell created the arches for his bridge over the StP&D line,
by using numerous parallel spiraling courses.

Constructing the bridge began in September 1883. The abutments and
single pier were made from locally quarried limestone, while the voussoirs,
ring stones, and spandrel walls were formed from a buff-colored limestone
drawn from Mankato, Minnesota. The masonry work for the bridge was
finished in November 1884. A trestle was then built atop the bridge so dump
cars could pass over the structure and empty fill over the arches. The structure was completed around mid-December. The west arch measured twenty-
seven feet in width, while the east arch was thirty-seven feet wide. A six-foot-
wide pier with rounded cutwaters separated the two arches. At the time
the bridge was built the arches accommodated five lines of railroad tracks.
Today the tracks are gone and an asphalt pedestrian and bicycle
path runs beneath the west arch.

Truesdell's arch bridge was named the Seventh Street Improvement Arches because it was part of the Seventh Street improvement he supervised. Many of his peers considered the structure "the most important piece of masonry in the city." Interestingly, this unusual bridge is the only crossing that can be directly tied to Truesdell. He passed away in 1909, lauded by fellow engineers for his exceptional accuracy and thoroughness. His substantial arch bridge remains, however, virtually hidden from the bustling traffic on Seventh Street east of downtown St. Paul. The Seventh Street Improvement Arches is one of only a handful of helicoidal arch bridges known to exist in America. The bridge was placed on the National Register in 1989.

✳ Hill Annex Mine

VICINITY OF CALUMET | ITASCA COUNTY

Many may never fully appreciate the significance of the Upper Midwest to the industrial development of the United States, but it was here that the raw material that built much of modern America was buried. Six great iron ranges were situated within three states. The Marquette and Menominee Iron Ranges were in Upper Michigan, while the Gogebic Iron Range stretched from Upper Michigan to northern Wisconsin. The Vermilion, Mesabi, and Cuyuna Iron Ranges were all in northeastern Minnesota. While prodigious quantities of iron were pulled from all of the ranges, it was the Mesabi that ultimately proved king. Ironically, iron speculators tramped over the exceptional range for years, believing the Mesabi not worth the financial investment or sweat.[27]

The iron ranges in Michigan and Wisconsin were surveyed and exploited before those in Minnesota. Douglass Houghton, Michigan's first geologist, found the Marquette Range in 1844, as he and a work crew completed land surveys and mineral investigations along the Upper Escanaba River in northern Upper Michigan. Houghton was actually looking for copper and the iron find was a surprise. Geologists discovered the Menominee Range, situated near the Upper Peninsula's border with Wisconsin, in the late 1840s. The first hint of a third range in the region was revealed about the same time the Menominee was found, although the Gogebic Range near the Montreal River was studied for several years before it was recognized as a cohesive unit stretching from Upper Michigan to northern Wisconsin.

In the late 1800s, while iron was being extracted from deposits in Michigan, surveyors were searching for the raw material on the opposite side of Lake Superior. For more than a century iron was known to exist in the lands that would eventually form northeastern Minnesota. In fact, Native Americans in the area described mines of iron as early as the 1730s. A scientific record of iron deposits in the region was not recorded until the mid-1800s, however. Even then the record was sparse, since geologists

A conveyor descends into the Hill Annex Mine, an open pit mine formed from decades of stripping away earth to retrieve iron ore.

were chiefly interested in copper. More detailed investigations were conducted later in the century when private parties decided to exploit the state's iron resources. The first successful mining operation was initiated in 1882 with the formation of the Minnesota Iron Company, an enterprise begun by Charlemagne Tower, a financier from Philadelphia. Although Tower concentrated his efforts on the Vermilion, it was understood that another iron field known as the Mesabi existed to the south. The Mesabi was largely shunned, however, because early study of the range convinced many that its iron was poor quality. It was—at least where speculators were digging.

Some believed the Merritt family of Duluth was not being rational when the brothers set out to find high-quality iron deposits on the Mesabi in the late 1880s. Like many speculators, the Merritts understood that serious study of the range had been concentrated at its east end where iron content in the rock formations was less than 45 percent. Unlike most, the brothers refused to believe that the low iron level in this small area was representative of the entire range. In 1890, after searching farther to the west, they found a large, high-quality iron deposit about twenty-five miles southwest of the community of Tower. The deposit was not buried very deep, a characteristic common to much of the Mesabi. Leonidas Merritt later recalled the ease with which ore could be removed from the range, an observation recorded in David A. Walker's *Iron Frontier: The Discovery and Early Development of Minnesota's Three Ranges*: "If we had gotten mad and kicked the ground right where we stood we would have thrown out 64-percent iron." Of course removing the ore was not quite as simple as Leonidas made out, but unlike the deep underground mining that was required on the Vermilion, Mesabi iron could be extracted by stripping away layers of earth with a steam shovel. Word of the Merritt's discovery quickly spread, converting doubters and bringing more iron-searchers into the area. Many speculators would leave disenchanted, but others would make a fortune.

One of the Mesabi's successful mining operations was the Hill Annex Mine, immediately north of Calumet. The Arthur Iron Mining Company, a subsidiary of James J. Hill's Great Northern Railway Company, initially developed the mine. A large body of iron had been confirmed at the site by 1908, the same year that mining commenced on the Cuyuna Range, roughly sixty miles to the southwest. Construction at the Hill Annex site began in 1912. Interestingly, the property actually belonged to the state. The Territorial Act of 1848 stipulated Sections 16 and 36 of each township in the Northwest Territory be set aside for educational purposes. Since the Hill Annex fell within Section 16 of Greenway Township, James J. Hill, through his Great Northern Iron Ore Properties, was forced to lease the site from the state. The agreement required that royalties be paid into Minnesota's School Trust Fund for all ore removed from the mine.

Stripping at the site began in 1914, and over the next two years the limits of the ore body were determined. In 1917, the property lease was assigned to Inter State Iron Company, an affiliate of Jones and Laughlin Steel Corporation. Jones and Laughlin hired A. Guthrie and Company of St. Paul to continue stripping operations. In the first year of Guthrie management the mine produced over 250,000 tons of ore. Nearly 5 million tons of the raw material had been shipped by 1924. Much of the product was merch, ore that contained very high quantities of iron. Unlike low-grade ores, which required processing to separate the iron from the silica, merch could be shipped direct to steel mills.

Like all iron mines, the Hill Annex suffered during the Great Depression as demand for steel plummeted. The industry rebounded with the onset of the Second World War. In fact, the Hill Annex had its best year in 1941 when it shipped over 3.6 million tons of ore. But even though the total was a milestone, it was also a precursor that the end was coming, since over 75 percent of the total was drawn from low-grade ore. By the early 1950s, the merch at Hill Annex was gone and management was forced to construct more processing equipment to refine and concentrate the low-quality ore. Between 1952 and 1958, the mine produced only 3.5 million tons of concentrates. While the mine continued to operate for another twenty years, its volume steadily declined. Unable to squeeze further profit from the Hill Annex, management finally closed it in 1978.

Over its long history the mine contributed almost 64 million tons of ore to the total volume coming out of the Mesabi, a range that produced 85 percent of the nation's iron ore in the first half of the twentieth century. Moreover, the mine proved a financial windfall for the state, adding roughly $27 million in royalties to the School Trust Fund. Today, the Department of Natural Resources operates the Hill Annex as a state park. Many of the mine's buildings and structures remain, which help visitors to the site understand how the mine functioned during its heyday. A fine example of early twentieth-century mining practice on the most prolific iron range the world has ever known, Hill Annex Mine was listed on the National Register in 1986.

Many pieces of equipment at a strip mine are super-sized, as evidenced by this 1940 photograph of a power shovel at Hill Annex Mine.

✳ Schech's Mill

VICINITY OF SHELDON | HOUSTON COUNTY

Schech's Mill is situated within Beaver Creek Valley State Park in southeastern Minnesota, only a mile southeast of the small, Houston County community of Sheldon and about six miles northwest of the county seat, Caledonia. Houston County draws its name from a town within its borders christened for Sam Houston, a curious namesake since the Texas legend who hailed from Tennessee does not appear to have ever visited Minnesota. General Houston, however, was a favorite of William George McSpadden, a Scots-Irish immigrant who served under the commander for a time. When McSpadden sought a name for the townsite he platted in southeastern Minnesota in 1852, the audacious general came to mind.[28]

It is unlikely that most think of Sam Houston when they consider Houston County. Instead, many probably imagine the striking panorama of rocky bluffs, serpentine rivers, and lush valleys. While early settlers to the region were impressed by the scenery as well, most were summoned because the landscape foretold financial opportunity. Although timbering quickly became a major industry in the area, it was gristmilling, the act of grinding grain into flour or meal, that ultimately defined the county. Indeed, as early as 1858 promoters gushed:

> We venture to assert, without fear of contradiction, that no part of Southern Minnesota offers a greater number of available sites for mill seats than this, and we believe, too, that the day is not far distant when in no other portion of the State the same in extent of territory, will be more intimately blended the interests of manufacture and agriculture.

One individual who embraced the milling opportunity in Houston County was John Blinn, an entrepreneur who constructed a wood-framed saw and gristmill on the west side of Beaver Creek, just a mile southeast of Sheldon, a community some in the county viewed as a diamond in the rough:

> We consider the town of Sheldon as one destined to be of no second or third rate importance in the history of our progress. . . . Her superiority as a good point for the interchange of all kinds of commodities must and will place her in a prominent position among the towns of Southern Minnesota.

Optimistic sentiments, but it was not to be, for when the Southern Minnesota Railroad laid its line toward Lanesboro and points west in the late 1860s it bypassed Sheldon. As a result, the community never evolved into a significant commercial center. One late-nineteenth-century historian expressed Sheldon's unlucky fate in the poetic prose so common for the period:

> Certain causes . . . put a check to [Sheldon's] progress, the construction of the Southern Minnesota Railroad, six miles or so away, with the warning bell of the locomotive, proved to be the curfew that tolled the hour to extinguish its light, as it has many another promising village, to cause others, however, to appear in unexpected places, and thus to fulfill the law of compensation.

Although the "law of compensation" was fulfilled elsewhere, that was little comfort to those in and around Sheldon.

Even though the Sheldon area would never blossom into a significant financial hub, it was still home to John Blinn, who demonstrated his commitment to the region in 1875 when he replaced his wooden mill with one made of locally quarried stone. The two-and-a-half-story, rectangular structure had a gable roof pierced at the ridge by a ventilating cupola. Multipane windows dotted the walls. The interior was a maze of milling equipment, the most important being four run of millstone driven by two Leffel turbines. Turbines had been improved earlier in the century and were considerably more efficient than the picturesque vertical waterwheels that have been romanticized by artists and writers. Vertical waterwheels are propelled by impulse, the action of water moving in the direction of the wheel's motion. Turbines, however, operate by harnessing the power of the water's action and reaction. In other words, water entering the turbine propels it by impulse, but the reaction of the water as it exits moves the turbine as well. Turbines were so much better than vertical waterwheels that the latter could scarcely be found in Minnesota by the 1890s.

The turbines at Blinn's Mill were mounted near the base of the building within a penstock, which is a large casing that holds water. A pond created by a wood dam across Beaver Creek fed a head race canal that funneled water to the mill and into the penstock through an arched opening at the bottom of the mill's south wall. Water passing through the turbines inside the penstock exited the building through two arched openings at the base of the north wall. A vertical driveshaft rising from the turbines turned the wheels and belts that powered the milling equipment, including the millstones used to grind grain.

It appears that John Blinn died before he witnessed the completion of his new mill. The enterprise continued to be known as Blinn's Mill until sometime later in the nineteenth century, when it became the Caledonia Grist Mill. The concern was named Schech's Mill when Michael Schech, a Bavarian who was the head miller at the St. Paul Roller Milling Company, purchased the property in 1887. About this time Minnesota was on its way to becoming a milling goliath, in large measure because of the mills in Minneapolis adjacent to St. Anthony Falls on the Mississippi River. By the turn of the twentieth century, the mills in the state were producing almost $85 million in ground flour and meal, roughly twice that of New York, Minnesota's nearest competitor.

Eventually, many mills outside of Minneapolis closed, unable to compete with urban giants like C. A. Pillsbury and Company, Washburn-Crosby Company, Washburn Mill Company, and Pillsbury-Washburn Flour Mills Company. The larger enterprises were better able to finance improvements to their mills as milling technology advanced. Moreover, they had a larger supply base, so if wheat production was down in one agricultural region they could draw from another. Being dominated by Minneapolis may not have bothered Michael Schech as much as it did some other millers outside the Twin Cities. Without easy access to a rail line, his mill was never going to be a major milling player and he was probably content to service the farmers in his part of the state. That did not mean he refused to improve his mill, however. When roller mills replaced millstones as the primary means of grinding grain in the 1880s and 1890s, Schech included them

Since Schech's Mill operates infrequently nowadays, water in the head race canal is usually placid.

in his mill, although he continued to employ his millstones as well. He also added middlings purifiers.

Schech's Mill passed to Michael's son in 1913. In 1922, Edward Schech improved the mill further when he replaced the wood dam across Beaver Creek with one of concrete. Two years later he added a third turbine to the mill. Edward operated the mill until his death in 1941. While merchant milling at the site ended with his passing, his wife continued custom grinding until 1946. Feed-mixing was started by Ivan Krugmire, her son-in-law, soon thereafter. Krugmire still owns the mill today, although it functions chiefly as a private museum. Krugmire grinds grain occasionally, and sometimes operates the machinery for tour guests. The roller mills have been removed from the building, but the original millstones, turbines, and other equipment remain. A superb example of a rural nineteenth-century Minnesota gristmill, Schech's Mill was placed on the National Register in 1978.

✳ Goodsell Observatory

CARLETON COLLEGE | NORTHFIELD | RICE COUNTY

It is hard to imagine now, but as late as the 1880s cities within the same region of the country measured the hours of the day by a local standard—not a regional or national one. For example, Pittsburgh is about 160 miles south of Buffalo, but it is only slightly further west, and yet Pittsburgh clocks were set earlier than Buffalo's. Variation in time from one city to the next was rarely a problem for homebodies, since time in their community advanced at a constant rate. When a Pittsburgh steelworker took his lunch break at noon on Tuesday, he understood that twenty-four hours later he would take his lunch break at noon on Wednesday. But it was not as simple for a traveler. When a traveler left the East Coast heading west, he encountered numerous cities and regions running on their "own" time—Boston Time, Albany Time, Buffalo Time, Pittsburgh Time, and so on. The traveler was continually resetting his watch—and likely getting a migraine. Furthermore, railroads published their time schedules based on the time in their headquarters city, which made connecting to a different rail line an unwelcome adventure. The time differences between towns, and thus the railroads, came about because cities are located along different lines of longitude. As the earth rotates the sun reaches some cities before it reaches others, so it is impossible for time to be the same everywhere. Interpreting time in a literal way is honest, but it is also chaotic.[29]

By the early 1880s railroads agreed the confusion over time needed to end. In 1883 rail lines began adopting a uniform time system, although the changeover was not completed until 1887. Standard Railway Time divided the country into four regions: Eastern, Central, Mountain, and Pacific.

Time within each region advanced at a constant rate, while moving from one region to the next altered time by exactly one hour. Although efficiency forced railroads to suspend literal interpretations of time from one geographic area to the next, the rail lines still needed precise time. Indeed, everyone requires precise time, since it serves as the point of reference from which all time schedules are made. Railroads and cities relied on "time stations" to provide precise time—and one of these stations was located at a tiny liberal arts college in Northfield, a Rice County town forty miles south of Minneapolis.

When Carleton College was established in 1866 its benefactors probably never envisioned that a university specializing in the humanities would develop one of the leading time stations in the country. After all, operating a time station is a scientific endeavor, a task that involves studying the position of celestial bodies with respect to the earth. In 1871, the college hired William Wallace Payne as Professor of Mathematics and Natural Philosophy. Payne had limited training as an astronomer, although his mathematics background gave him an adequate foundation for studying the cosmos. In 1877, he convinced university officials to build and equip a small observatory, arguing that Carleton would be the only university in the state with such a facility. Moreover, if the observatory operated as a time station it would bring significant publicity to the modest school. The observatory was completed in 1878 and was equipped with several astronomical instruments, including a Clark 8-1/4-inch refracting telescope, as well as a 3-inch Fauth

Completed in 1888, the Goodsell Observatory's principal viewing platform is situated near the south facade and a smaller observation room is located at the northwest corner.

transit circle, a device that precisely measured the positions and movements of planets and stars. Soon after it was finished the observatory began providing precise time to railroads operating in the Northwest.

Carleton's observatory determined precise time by monitoring both solar time and sidereal time. Solar time is based on the rotation of the earth with respect to the sun, while sidereal time is based on the earth's rotation with respect to the stars. The Fauth transit circle measured sidereal time by tracking a distant star to determine when it was on the meridian of the observatory. The reading was then compared to the time depicted on the observatory's sidereal clock. If a discrepancy existed the clock was corrected. Time on the sidereal clock was then compared to time on the observatory's solar clock. Understanding that a sidereal day is nearly four minutes shorter than a solar day, astronomers determined whether the solar clock was displaying proper time. If not, the time was adjusted. The observatory then relayed the correct solar time by telegraph to various railroads.

By 1887, the same year the railroads completed the transition to Standard Railway Time, Carleton was constructing a more expansive observatory near the west edge of the campus. Designed by St. Paul architect J. Walter Stevens, the Romanesque Revival–style building was finished the following year. The one- and two-story structure was chiefly comprised of St. Louis red brick, although red sandstone provided the foundation. Sandstone also crowned window and door openings. The building was formed of two sections joined by a single-story space. An observatory with a hemispherical roof dominated each section. The primary observatory was centered at the south facade and a smaller observatory marked the structure's northwest corner. The Clark telescope from the previous building was installed inside the northwest observatory, although the south observatory would not receive its 16.2-inch Brashear refracting telescope until 1890. The Clock Room was situated on the first floor, immediately beneath the south observatory. A circular pier surrounded by wood and glass cabinets occupied the center of the room and provided support for the observatory's large telescope. A sidereal clock was mounted on one side of the pier and a solar clock was set at the other side. A meridian circle, an instrument similar to the Fauth transit circle, was housed in a room just east of the Clock Room. James J. Hill of the Great Northern Railway donated $5,000 toward the instrument's purchase. The room immediately west of the Clock Room served as a library.

Initially, the facility was simply known as "New Observatory," although its name soon changed to "Goodsell Observatory" in honor of Deacon Charles Moorehouse Goodsell, the school's founder. The elegant building reflected Carleton's growing significance as a time station and college. In fact, in the early twentieth century Carleton and the U.S. Naval Observatory were the only time stations left in existence, and every major railroad from

The observatory's solar clock marks one side of a circular pier supporting the Brashear telescope and a sidereal clock is positioned at the other side.

The observatory's
16.2-inch Brashear
refracting telescope was
acquired in 1890.

Chicago to Seattle relied on Goodsell Observatory to set time. Furthermore, Carleton had developed a prominent undergraduate astronomy program, stoked in part by *Popular Astronomy,* a scientific journal established by William Wallace Payne in 1893. But Goodsell's days as one of the premier observatories in the country were numbered. By 1930, most railroads depended on the U.S. Naval Observatory for time signals, and in 1931 Goodsell stopped broadcasting time to its few railroad clients. Moreover, by this time huge telescopes were being installed in observatories in the mountains of the West.

These new telescopes had tremendous "seeing" power, and the high elevations limited atmospheric interference. The small, prairie observatory in Northfield simply could not compete and Goodsell's prestige faded, as did the prominence of Carleton's astronomy program. By 1970, it appeared the observatory might be torn down to make room for a student union building. Fortunately, subsequent events favored the observatory. In 1975, the building that brought so much early recognition to Carleton was listed on the National Register. Today, it remains a pristine example of a late nineteenth-century astronomical laboratory.

✳ Universal Laboratories Building

DASSEL | MEEKER COUNTY

Lester R. Peel was a former schoolteacher turned businessman who became interested in the digestive tracts of hogs and poultry. It was an unusual concern, but not to the people of Dassel, a farming town in Meeker County, about sixty miles west of Minneapolis. Peel managed Rice Laboratories, a Dassel business established in 1935 to manufacture yeast for livestock feed. The yeast carried vitamins and enzymes, which helped control diseases of the digestive tract. Specifically, enzymes from yeast fermenting inside the bellies of hogs and poultry helped break down food cell walls so stomach acids could more readily reach food elements, thus improving nutrient absorption. In other words, the yeast made hogs meatier and chickens more productive—"Yeast increases egg production because it keeps the flock healthy and a healthy bird is a good layer," explained the *Dassel Dispatch*. Two years after Rice Laboratories was formed, Peel embarked on an endeavor that would make people healthier.[30]

In 1937, Rice Laboratories constructed a new, utilitarian-looking building on the west side of First Street North at the northern edge of town. The generally rectangular, wood-framed structure rested upon a concrete foundation and was divided into two main parts. The two-story south section had a north-south gable roof and the somewhat higher north section featured an east-west gable roof. A gable-roofed freight elevator wing was located on the east side at the junction of the north and south building sections. The entire building was covered with pressed-metal siding that resembled bricks. Walls of the south section held several rectangular windows, but only a few marked the north part. A personnel entrance was located in the structure's south facade and a larger, sliding door overlooked a loading dock at the west side.

While the building was intended specifically for yeast production, the same year it was constructed Peel initiated an ergot enterprise in the northwest corner of the structure's first floor. Earlier, Peel learned that local farmers were discarding rye infected with the fungus sclerotia, a toxic purplish growth commonly known as ergot. Ergot poisoning can be deadly, and farmers did not want the tainted rye infecting flour or feed. But Peel understood that ergot also contained alkaloids with medicinal value. In fact, as

The Universal Laboratories Building appeared worn when placed on the National Register in 1996, but thanks to the efforts of preservation-minded citizens the old processing plant now looks fantastic.

early as the sixteenth century midwives employed ergot to induce labor, although by the twentieth century its use in obstetrics was limited to derivatives for treating postpartum bleeding. By this time, however, other therapeutic uses for ergot had been discovered, including treatment for vasoconstriction, hypertension, vascular headaches, and migraines. Studies also showed that ergot helped treat combat stress or "bomb shock," a condition many would experience during World War II.

In the early 1900s Russia was the world's principal exporter of ergot, but supplies were disrupted with the onset of the Russian Revolution in 1917. Spain supplanted Russia as chief exporter of the material, but quantities again dropped when Spain fell into civil war in 1936. By the late 1930s, with war raging across Europe, the only European country still exporting ergot to the United States was Portugal, although a small amount was also coming from Canada. More than two decades of political unrest on the opposite side of the Atlantic demonstrated the tenuous nature of European ergot exports to the United States, making Peel's entrance into the ergot market fortuitous.

Peel named his ergot business Universal Laboratories. Initially, he purchased ergotic rye from local farmers, then Universal Laboratories staff fed the material through small mills that broke it up and delivered it to conveyors. Employees lined the conveyor and picked the grain from the belt, leaving the ergot to fall into a storage receptacle for bagging. Others in Dassel picked and bagged ergot at their homes, paid by Universal Laboratories for the amount of pure ergot delivered to the company. Peel soon began a publicity campaign to educate farmers in other regions on the importance of ergot. He was joined in the effort by Eli Lilly and Company, a major pharmaceutical enterprise that was Peel's principal customer. The Lilly Management Report of January 1952 noted the company's pains a decade earlier to teach farmers about ergot: "The northwestern states were blanketed with publicity. Stores displayed pamphlets; grain publications and rural newspapers printed stories; a dozen radio stations told the facts; Lilly medical service representatives and county agents talked to farmers personally." The campaign was successful and Universal Laboratories began receiving considerable quantities of ergotic rye, which was stored in an elevator the company leased in downtown Dassel.

Much of the interior of Peel's building was altered to facilitate the ergot operation. New machines made the earlier labor-intensive picking unnecessary, as much of the ergot was removed from the rye when it passed through mills that directed flow to gravity separators, where the lighter ergot kernels were mechanically segregated from the heavier rye. The increased output from Universal Laboratories kept ergot stores in the United States viable after imports plummeted during the Second World War. In 1940, 60,000 pounds of domestic ergot were collected, and 100,000 pounds were gathered the following year. The vast majority of domestic ergot passed through Universal Laboratories in Dassel.

Universal Laboratories continued its success after the war, even though foreign ergot supplies became more stable. This was due chiefly to its intimate relationship with Eli Lilly, which continued to receive the bulk of its ergot from Universal Laboratories. In 1952, Peel added a larger elevator leg inside his building, which necessitated the construction of a small, gable-roofed monitor at the west side of the building's north end. By this time the original yeast manufacturing operation was thoroughly overshadowed by the ergot business. At some point yeast production ceased, but it is uncertain if this happened before or after Peel died of a stroke in 1959. Losing its leader was a sad event for Universal Laboratories, but things got sadder in the late 1960s when Eli Lilly dropped the company as its ergot supplier in favor of European distributors. Peel's company hung on a little longer by providing ergot to Britain-based Burroughs Wellcome Company, but the Dassel enterprise eventually ceased operation in 1975. As late as 1995, the building remained empty. One year later, however, the country recognized the business as a pioneer in the production of domestic ergot when the Universal Laboratories Building was placed on the National Register. The building looks fantastic today, thanks to the efforts of local citizens and others who rehabilitated the structure. Now home to the Dassel Area Historical Society, it is one of the most unusual historical society buildings in Minnesota.

Close-up view of the spiraling chutes of a gravity separator used at Universal Laboratories to divide ergot from rye

❋ Bernard H. Pietenpol Workshop & Garage

CHERRY GROVE | FILLMORE COUNTY

According to one local legend, it began as Bernard H. Pietenpol was zooming down the road on his motorbike. He was between Wykoff and Cherry Grove in southeast Minnesota. The gravel road snaked over a steep rise known as Turner Hill. As Pietenpol negotiated the rise he lost control of his motorbike and hit the gravel. He was lying on the road gathering his wits when a thought occurred to him—there must be a better way to travel than this! Aviation was in its infancy the day Pietenpol greeted the ground, but he figured it had to be safer than riding his motorbike.[31]

Minnesota claims history's most famous aviator, Charles Lindbergh. It also claims Bernard H. Pietenpol. Pietenpol never garnered the fame of Lindbergh, but he too was an aviation pioneer. Pietenpol was born in Spring Valley in 1901, a small community near the western border of Fillmore County in southeast Minnesota. While still a lad he moved with his family to North Dakota. When he was a teen, the family moved back to Fillmore County, to the hamlet of Cherry Grove, about thirty-five miles south of Rochester. Pietenpol would remain there for the rest of his life.

The early 1900s were the pioneering age of aviation. After Wilbur and Orville Wright made the first powered flight at Kitty Hawk, North Carolina, in 1903, many adventuresome spirits wished to duplicate the effort. Minnesota had its share of daredevils, two of whom were young men from Minneapolis. In autumn 1908, A. C. Bennett and Ralph Wilcox built an aircraft modeled on the Wrights' biplane. The men assembled the airplane at the Wilcox Motor Company on Marshall Avenue, a business owned by Wilcox's family. The grand experiment was ready in January 1909. The men hauled the aircraft to Lake Minnetonka, lashed it to a tree, and started its 25-horsepower, four-cylinder motor. With the engine at full power the rope was cut. The airplane lurched down the icy runway and . . . hopped. Several years later Ralph Wilcox's brother, Harry, recalled the event: "The machine barely got into the air . . . I've seen skiers go higher." Hardly disenchanted, Wilcox and Bennett tried again the next year with a more powerful motor. Their aircraft may have hopped a little higher this time, but it was scarcely flight. The two gave up.

Wilcox and Bennett may have failed, but they gave it a good try. With a technology that few knew anything about, all an aspiring aviator could do was try. About a decade after Wilcox and Bennett made their attempt, Bernard H. Pietenpol decided he also wanted to touch the clouds. Pietenpol had an advantage over Wilcox and Bennett, though. Aviation made significant strides over the 1910s, due in large measure to the First World War. By the early 1920s, as Pietenpol was preparing to take wing, the physics of flight were better understood and aircraft were more soundly constructed.

Pietenpol's portrait, as well some of the aviator's memorabilia, can be found at the Fillmore County Historical Center in Fountain.

Of course, Pietenpol had only about four hours of flight instruction. He shrugged off this detail and figured he would learn as he went.

In 1921 Pietenpol erected a small, wood-framed workshop and garage near the heart of Cherry Grove. It had a low-pitched, gable roof and a false front. A vehicle entrance and a pedestrian entrance marked its west facade. Several windows of various dimensions punctuated the walls. Although he built his first airplane in a local church barn, the workshop became his principal place of business. Here he would design and construct numerous aircraft over the next several decades.

Pietenpol's first airplane was ready for flight in 1923. Since airplane engines were expensive, he adapted a Ford Model T motor to the biplane, a design characteristic that became a signature. He was almost a natural pilot. He could take off and fly the biplane pretty well, but he could never land the machine without damaging it. His brother-in-law later explained the problem: "Bernard would go up 50 feet and come back down 75." When Pietenpol destroyed the plane altogether, he opted for more flying lessons.

The instruction paid off and Pietenpol was a better pilot by 1926, when he built his second biplane. In 1929 he constructed another aircraft, although this one was a monoplane. He replaced the original engine with a Ford Model A motor and christened the two-seater the "Air Camper." In 1930 Pietenpol read an editorial in *Modern Mechanics and Inventions* asserting that automobile engines would never work in airplanes. He contacted the magazine's editor, E. L. Weston Farmer, and informed him the editorial was wrong. Farmer demanded proof, so Pietenpol and a friend, Donald Finke, flew two Air Campers from Cherry Grove to Robbinsdale Airport near Minneapolis. Farmer was thrilled, publishing the event in his magazine and making Pietenpol famous. The aviator was inundated with requests for plans for his plane. But Pietenpol had sketched out the design

Every building, even the inconspicuous, has a story, like the Bernard H. Pietenpol Workshop and Garage, a humble, framed structure erected in 1921 by one of Minnesota's aviation pioneers.

on his shop floor, never anticipating he would need plans. With help from his neighbor, Orrin Hoopman, Pietenpol began producing formal plans for his Air Camper. A set cost $7.50.

In part, the Air Camper was a hit because it was easy to build and materials were readily available. His directions were often simple: "Go to the lumber yard and buy materials for the Air Camper and then watch the papers for a yard-goods sale and purchase several bed sheets." The plane became so popular that Pietenpol offered it in a kit. Later, he began pre-assembling kits so customers could put the aircraft together quicker. He also designed a single-seat monoplane that used the less powerful Model T

A Sky Scout presently on display at the Fillmore County Historical Center

engine. Dubbed the "Sky Scout," it became immensely popular as well. Eventually Pietenpol made a deal to publish plans of the Air Camper in *Flying and Glider Manual*. Plans for the Sky Scout were published in *Modern Mechanics and Inventions*.

Between the early 1920s and 1975, Pietenpol designed and constructed over twenty airplanes in his workshop in Cherry Grove, gaining him world-wide recognition. He became popularly known as "the father of the home-built aircraft movement in the United States." In April 1969, Bob Whittier, a writer for *Sport Aviation*, paid tribute to Pietenpol's pioneering spirit, his words later re-recorded for Noel E. Allard and Gerald N. Sandvick's *Minnesota Aviation History, 1857–1945*:

> As to the Man, after seeing where he lived and what he had accomplished, working largely alone and isolated from the rush and bustle of commercial aviation, I could not help but reflect on what an impressive object lesson he is to those who explain away the emptiness of their lives by the excuse, 'I never had a chance.'

Bernard H. Pietenpol died in 1984. His memory endures through the International Pietenpol Association, and the many Pietenpol airplanes that can be found at aircraft shows across the country. Every year Brodhead, Wisconsin, hosts a "Pietenpol Fly-In," attracting pilots devoted to Pietenpol airplanes. Pietenpol's legacy is also reflected in his workshop and garage in Cherry Grove, which still stands today, so many decades after he crashed his motorbike and was inspired to take flight. The Bernard H. Pietenpol Workshop and Garage was added to the National Register in 1981.

✳ Hibbing Disposal Plant

HIBBING | ST. LOUIS COUNTY

In 1930 only 99 communities in Minnesota had sewage disposal plants. This represented merely 12 percent of the state's urban population. Over the next decade a tremendous effort was undertaken to decrease the amount of raw sewage pouring into natural water systems by constructing sewage treatment plants throughout the state. Much of the work was completed through federal relief programs like the Public Works Administration (PWA), one of Franklin Roosevelt's initiatives to alleviate the effects of the Great Depression by putting Americans to work. By 1939 sewage disposal plants existed in 187 communities that comprised 78 percent of Minnesota's urban population, a phenomenal increase in only ten years. One of these towns was Hibbing, Minnesota, which embraced the unusual concept of housing the trickling filters for its new sewage disposal plant beneath elliptical dome roofs, one of the earliest and largest examples of concrete thin-shell construction in the United States.[32]

Domes date to the ancient world, as demonstrated by the Roman Pantheon, which was constructed in the first century. During the reign of Emperor Justinian in the sixth century, Santa Sophia was raised in Constantinople (now Istanbul). Lacking reinforcement, domes such as these demanded relatively thick dimensions. The dome of St. Peter's Cathedral, for instance, is nine feet thick near its base. Heavy dome construction was common for centuries, although few were built because of the immense amount of material required. Not until reinforced concrete was adopted as a standard building material in the early twentieth century did domed roofs of exceedingly thin dimensions become possible. Metal members laced within the concrete strengthened the dome while substantially limiting the amount of material necessary to build the structure.

Initially, thin concrete roof construction, more commonly known as "concrete thin shells," was concentrated in Europe. The Italians, Spanish, and Germans all pursued architectural expression through thin shells, but how each went about it varied. The Italians and Spanish were chiefly drawn

The domes shielding the trickling filters of the Hibbing Disposal Plant were erected using the Zeiss-Dywidag System, an innovative early-twentieth-century technique for constructing incredibly thin concrete roofs.

to the aesthetic qualities of the form. In Italy, engineer Pier Luigi Nervi constructed many ribbed, thin-shell, domed roofs between 1935 and 1959. The Little Sports Palace in Rome, often considered Nervi's thin-shell masterwork, incorporated a two-way ribbed system supporting a slender, domed roof. The dual ribbed system hugged the roof's interior and created a spectacular lattice pattern. Engineers in Spain approached thin shells differently, although their designs were just as visually inspiring as those in Italy. Eduardo Torroja and Felix Candela, Spanish thin-shell experts during the early and mid twentieth century, primarily viewed concrete shells as ribless. Torroja, for instance, constructed slim concrete roofs employing hyperboloidal shapes, a characteristic that makes these roof-types very stiff. In 1935, Torroja successfully demonstrated the design for the roof of the Zarzuela Hippodrome near Madrid. Candela used eight extremely thin hyperbolic paraboloidal vaults for his elegant roof over the Xochimilco Restaurant in Mexico City in 1957.

While the Italians and Spanish stressed the pleasing aesthetics of thin shells, the Germans emphasized numeric calculations that would bolster their thin-shell plans. Certainly the Italians and Spanish considered load stress when building thin shells, but the Germans sought mathematical perfection when figuring load stress. Artistic statement was not as imperative to German engineers as were numeric formulations that validated their thin-shell aspirations. In fact, in 1928, German engineer Franz Dischinger penned a mathematical treatise confirming that extant thin shells tidily fell within his computations. The tireless number-crunching of Dischinger and other German engineers was rewarded in 1929 with the construction of the impressive Leipzig Market Hall. The roof of the hall consisted of two 76-meter concrete domes. Each dome was 11 meters larger than the dome roof that was built for the Market Hall in Breslau, Germany, in 1913, and yet each was two-thirds lighter than the Breslau dome.

The Germans proved the chief protagonists in the growth and promotion of thin-shell construction in the first half of the twentieth century, and it was primarily German concepts adopted by engineers in the United States in the early 1930s. Viennese engineer Anton Tedesko came to America as the representative for the German engineering firm Dyckerhoff-Widmann (Dywidag). Dywidag was an affiliate of the Carl Zeiss Company, an enterprise that developed intricate projectors used to cast moving images of celestial bodies over the hemispherical ceiling of planetariums. Dywidag and Zeiss developed engineering techniques for erecting thin shells known as the Zeiss-Dywidag System. The Zeiss-Dywidag System involved an elaborate construction process whereby a self-supporting steel skeleton of a dome was erected and covered with wire mesh. Forms were then placed against the interior skeleton and concrete distributed over the steel framework. The steel skeleton thus became the dome's reinforcement. The tricky part of construction was figuring out just how much load stress a particular dome shape could bear. It was this thorny problem that the Germans proved so adept at solving, and no system worked better than Zeiss-Dywidag.

One of America's earliest recipients of Zeiss-Dywidag thin-shell domes was Hibbing, a St. Louis County town seventy-five miles northwest of Duluth. Work began on a $439,946 sewage treatment plant for the community in 1938. The PWA financed 45 percent of the project, while the remaining expense was funded through a bond issue. The plant was one of the largest federal relief undertakings in northern Minnesota. Plans for the plant had actually been announced in August 1933, but delays pushed construction back several years. J. C. Taylor of Hibbing was the project architect and Charles Foster of Duluth served as consulting engineer. The plant had all the components of most sewage treatment facilities, including a flocculator, pumping plant, clarifiers, sludge drying bed, stage digesters, and a chlorinating basin, as well as an office and garage. The remarkable feature of the plant, however, were the two dome roofs that shielded the plant's trickling filters. The thin-shell, elliptical domes were designed and built by Roberts and Schaefer Company of Chicago, the American patent holder of the Zeiss-Dywidag System and the employer of Zeiss-Dywidag's representative in this country, Anton Tedesko. Each dome was 150 feet in diameter, with a shallow rise of only 32 feet. Four layers of round bars, two meridional and two ring, served as the reinforcement for the domes. In part, the elliptical shape of the roofs was possible because the base of each dome was designed with no horizontal thrust. The thickness of the shells at their base was just six inches, and at the crown it was only five inches. Amazingly, roughly half of each dome had a thickness less than four inches. This was major engineering, and the Hibbing Disposal Plant received considerable press in prominent engineering journals from the period. The disposal plant's trickling filter roofs can also be found in more recent architectural and engineering publications, and they are noted as fine examples of early concrete thin-shell construction. As a major federal relief undertaking in northern Minnesota and, more importantly, as a recipient of pioneering concrete building technology, the Hibbing Disposal Plant was placed on the National Register in 1991.

MARITIME MINNESOTA 5

GRIFFIN WAS A SMALL SHIP. By modern standards she was puny, weighing somewhere between forty-five and sixty tons. But size is relative to many things. For the weary mariners who were forced to tow *Griffin* through the rapids above Niagara Falls to the waters of Lake Erie, the vessel seemed enormous. The sailors realized the effort was worthwhile, however, because *Griffin* was special. In August 1679, under the guidance of Robert Cavalier de La Salle, the ship became the first merchant sailing vessel to voyage upon North America's Great Lakes, the largest freshwater system on earth. Her adventure lasted less than two months. After crossing Lakes Erie and Huron and reaching Green Bay on Lake Michigan, La Salle sent the ship back to the Niagara River. Loaded with furs and outfitted with only a skeleton crew, the vessel never reached its destination. What tragedy befell *Griffin* was never discovered.[33]

Although *Griffin* perished, La Salle demonstrated that the Great Lakes could be employed as a commerce transportation system, eventually enticing other merchant ships to venture onto the inland seas. These early vessels were used in the same manner that La Salle employed *Griffin*—as a means for moving large quantities of pelts from the region of the Great Lakes to points in eastern North America, the ships often returning with supplies for the fur-trading posts. By the 1770s Scottish immigrant John Askin was regularly supplying Grand Portage via Michili-mackinac and Sault Ste. Marie using a fleet of small sailing ships, although during the Revolutionary War the British substantially limited merchant vessels on the Great Lakes. Commercial shipping again increased in the late 1780s, but nevertheless remained modest and few navigational improvements were made on the waterway. In 1825, the Erie Canal was constructed between the city of Buffalo on Lake Erie and the Hudson River in eastern New York, thus creating a continuous water route from the Atlantic all the way to Lake Michigan. While the canal promoted shipping, it was not until copper was discovered in Michigan near the shores of Lake Superior in the 1840s that large-scale commercial transportation began. Shipping access to Lake Superior was incredibly difficult, however, because vessels had to be hauled around the rapids of the St. Mary's River, the water passage connecting Lake Huron with Lake Superior. Frontier entrepreneurs like John Askin managed the difficult task, but the chore became unnecessary in 1855 when the St. Mary's Falls Ship Canal was constructed at Sault Ste. Marie, conveniently linking Lake Superior with the other Great Lakes.

About the time the canal was being carved at Sault Ste. Marie, an agreement was reached in Wisconsin between the United States government and the Ojibwe. The 1854 Treaty of La Pointe effectively opened lands on the west side of Lake Superior to white settlement. The communities that soon developed along Minnesota's North Shore tied a good deal of their livelihood to the lake. Commercial fishing rapidly evolved and fish houses sprang up along much of the coast. Moreover, harbors developed as shipping points for the state's natural resources such as lumber and grain. As these goods moved east, manufactured goods from eastern industrialized areas flowed west. Duluth ultimately evolved into a major port city because of its choice location at the base of Lake Superior, a site endowed with a very large natural harbor. While the city was perfectly positioned to be Minnesota's principal shipping and receiving port, other harbors also gained a measure of notoriety. Grand Marais, for example, was linked with commercial fishing as early as the 1830s. The town was a fishing industry hub by the late 1800s. Two Harbors was founded in the early 1880s with the birth of the Duluth and Iron Range Rail Road, the land transportation arm of the Minnesota Iron Company, an enterprise initially formed to extract ore from the Vermilion Iron Range. Iron shipped from the ore docks at Two Harbors helped build twentieth-century America. Actually, ore from the state's iron ranges, especially the mighty Mesabi Iron Range, is partly responsible for the continuation of Minnesota's maritime story.

Today, Minnesota's rich marine history is reflected in the many properties developed to augment our Great Lakes commerce, some well over a century old. A number of these cultural resources have been designated historic as exceptional examples of the property type, although some structures no longer exist as a cohesive whole. Each has an interesting story. For instance, the noble U.S.S. *Essex,* an Enterprise Class wooden screw sloop that reflected a technological shift from sailing ships to steamers, came to an ignoble end when her owners purposely grounded her near Duluth and set her ablaze. Remnants of this once proud ship are now buried by beach sand. Then there is the Minnesota Point Lighthouse, the first high-powered navigational light beacon erected on Lake Superior. Constructed in 1858, decades before picturesque Split Rock Lighthouse came into existence, its tower still stands near the tip of Duluth's Minnesota Point. The lighthouse marks the "zero point"—the point of reference from which Lake Superior was first mapped. The North Superior Lifeboat Station Lightkeeper's House in Grand Marais and the U.S. Fisheries Station–Duluth are also maritime resources placed on the National Register because of their significant contribution to our history. There are many more.

The following narratives relate the stories of some of the historic resources constructed and maintained to serve Minnesota's Great Lakes trade. While a diverse group of properties, all were developed for a practical purpose, and each denotes a history not often associated with a heartland state known better for its fields of grain.

✳ Aerial Lift Bridge

DULUTH | ST. LOUIS COUNTY

On June 27, 1679, Daniel Greysolon, Sieur du Lhut, and his companions beached their canoe on a finger of land near the head of Lake Superior. Greysolon was on a mission for his king. A French soldier-explorer, he was seeking a truce between the warring Dakota and Ojibwe in the region, a conflict that disrupted French fur trading. Greysolon had canoed down the lake from New France (Canada), eventually finding himself on this narrow peninsula that jutted southeasterly across the head of the great lake. Surveying his surroundings, he must have been impressed by the huge natural port created just to his south by the raw breakwater he was standing upon. Greysolon's peacekeeping sortie would achieve success within a matter of months, but it would be another two centuries before the potential of the harbor was realized.[34]

Since the spot where Greysolon and his party came ashore was the narrowest point for portaging along the sandy strip, it was named "Little Portage." In time, the sandy strip would be known as "Minnesota Point." For nearly two hundred years the only Europeans to cross the point and enter the territory that eventually became northeastern Minnesota were fur traders and missionaries. White settlement in the area finally began when the Treaty of La Pointe was signed in the mid-1850s. By this time, across the bay in Wisconsin, the community of Superior was already established. Superior had a natural port created by another narrow strip of land that reached northwesterly toward Minnesota Point. Not surprisingly, it was called "Wisconsin Point." Superior also claimed a harbor channel, which was formed by the breach between Minnesota and Wisconsin Points. The channel gave the city an advantage over the infant community of Duluth on the Minnesota side of the bay. Ships could readily access Superior's large port through its channel, while Duluth had no comparable facility to entice freighters its direction. But the citizens of Duluth refused to remain the poor neighbors across the lake. Community officials convinced the Lake Superior and Mississippi Railroad to terminate in Duluth instead of Superior. They also built a breakwater and dock just north of Little Portage to attract shipping. Unfortunately, the brutal Lake Superior winter proved too much for the breakwater and it was soon destroyed. By early 1870 officials were convinced that a channel through Minnesota Point was imperative.

Construction of Duluth's harbor channel began in summer 1870 on the spot where Greysolon and his companions grounded their canoe almost two centuries earlier. While the people of Duluth were excited about the project, those in Superior were not. The St. Louis River fed the bay from the southwest and officials in Superior feared the flow of the river into the bay and out the natural channel into the body of Lake Superior would be interrupted. An interruption could cause Superior's channel to fill and shoal. Although a legitimate concern, competition for shipping traffic with a large harbor in Duluth must have also weighed on some in Superior. Superior petitioned the U. S. War Department to halt construction of Duluth's harbor channel. The mayor of Duluth, J. B. Culver, received telegraph notice of the War Department's response on Friday evening, June 9, 1871. The news was not good, for an official of the War Department had been dispatched to Duluth to stop work on the channel. Consulting the train schedule, the mayor realized the government representative could not reach Duluth until Monday. The dredge *Ishpeming* had already excavated two-thirds of the channel. If the *Ishpeming* worked around the clock, receiving help from townsfolk with their picks and shovels, it was possible to complete work before the War Department thwarted construction. The ensuing labor marathon was successful and by Sunday evening the thirty-foot-wide channel was finished. There was little the federal official could do when he arrived the following morning except admonish the Duluthians. It is doubtful the War Department remained angry for long, however, for the federal government had been eyeing Duluth as a potential Great Lakes port for some time.

Duluth now had a harbor channel, but carving the passageway had separated Minnesota Point from the heart of the community. If Minnesota Point's lake frontage was to be sufficiently employed, a means for crossing the channel without obstructing shipping into the harbor was essential. For several years officials wrestled with various bridge schemes but could not find an acceptable design. Meanwhile, a ferryboat transported people and materials from one side of the channel to the other. In 1898 the federal government widened the channel to 350 feet. One year later, finally, the city adopted a plan for bridging the waterway. City engineer Thomas F. McGilvray's design consisted of two vertical truss towers, one on either side of the channel, surmounted by a horizontal truss. A large gondola hung from the horizontal truss by movable vertical truss supports. Electric motors propelled the gondola along fixed rails mounted inside the lower chord of the horizontal truss. Although an interesting design, it was not original, for it was an adaptation of the Anodin Bridge in Rouen, France.

Construction of the bridge began in 1901, but was halted the following year for lack of funds. Work again started in 1904, with the Modern Steel Structural Company of Waukesha, Wisconsin, providing the bridge's steel framework and gondola. Completed the next year, the "Duluth Aerial Ferry Bridge" was the first of its kind in the country. Costing a little over $100,000, it measured about 400 feet long, and with a vertical clearance of 135 feet it was able to accommodate the passage of any vessel on the Great Lakes.

The gondola held up to 125,000 pounds, the equivalent of a loaded streetcar, two wagons and their teams, and 350 passengers. It made about twelve trips an hour across the canal, except in the early morning when fewer crossings were required. Duluth was growing, however, and as its population increased so did its daily traffic. By the late 1920s the gondola system would no longer do. C. A. P. Turner, a nationally recognized engineer who once worked for the city of Duluth, developed a plan for modifying the ferry bridge into a vertical lift structure. His design entailed replacing the gondola with a single truss span that joined Minnesota Point with the rest

The freighter *Roger Blough* passes beneath the elevated lift span of the Aerial Lift Bridge in 1990.

At night, the lighted
Aerial Lift Bridge is always
impressive.

of the city, allowing a relatively steady flow of pedestrians and vehicles across the channel. When lake vessels required passage into or out of the harbor, the truss span could be shifted upwards between the towers, clearing the channel. Duluth flirted with this concept in the early 1890s, but the idea never moved beyond the design phase. In 1929 Duluth pushed forward with the $400,000 plan, lengthening the vertical truss towers and installing the truss span. By December of that year the Duluth Aerial Ferry Bridge had been modified into the present "Aerial Lift Bridge."

Although an engineering marvel for its day, the Aerial Lift Bridge's operation was remarkably simple. Gravity was key. The movable span was attached by cables to counterweights positioned within the vertical truss towers. The cables passed over sheaves near the top of each tower. An electric motor initiated movement, causing the lift span to begin to rise and the counterweights to descend. The tonnage of the descending counterweights was the primary force that pulled the lift span upwards. For more than seven decades the bridge has operated in this manner with only occasional maintenance. During that time Duluth has grown into one of the busiest ports in the country, evidenced by the fact that the Aerial Lift Bridge must be raised and lowered about 5,500 times a year. The reliability of the structure is testament to its innovative technology. The bridge is intimately tied to the history of Duluth, and it represents the "western gateway" to the Great Lakes–St. Lawrence Seaway. Each year more than 500,000 people visit the city's harbor and watch freighters from all over the world pass beneath this grand symbol of Duluth. The practical yet imaginative Aerial Lift Bridge was placed on the National Register in 1973.

Madeira Shipwreck

She was neither beautiful nor fast. Instead, she was long and flat, with no mechanical propulsion of her own. But *Madeira* represented a vital implement of commerce on Lake Superior in the early twentieth century. She was a schooner-barge, a vessel designed to accommodate the shipment of bulk cargoes throughout the Great Lakes region and along the coasts. Although not the first of her type built, she is the last to remain. Ironically, the price of her longevity was a violent burial beneath the waves of Lake Superior in the worst storm to ever strike the lake.[35]

The Chicago Shipbuilding Company of Chicago, Illinois, constructed *Madeira* in 1900. With a hull formed of riveted, steel plates, the ship weighed around 5,000 tons. She was over 400 feet long and about 50 feet wide, with a hold depth of roughly 24 feet. *Madeira*'s deckhouse was positioned at the centerline of the ship, and the pilothouse sat above a stern house that was surrounded by a solid rail. The barge also carried three masts. At the beginning of the twentieth century she was a new breed of schooner-barge, a type of ship little documented in maritime history. These vessels evolved from wooden sailing ships that were cut down into barges and towed behind wooden steamships, a practice common in coastal areas of the United States by the late 1800s. Transports like *Madeira* appear to have first developed as a distinctive type along the New England coast in the 1880s. Commercial carriers operating on the Great Lakes later adopted the design for transporting midwestern grain, as well as for moving iron ore from Minnesota mines to processing centers in the East. The steel barges carried much larger loads than their wooden forerunners, but they still operated in the same manner. Attached by towlines to steamers, barges were dragged to their destination. Steam-engine technology improved considerably in the last half of the nineteenth century, and by the time *Madeira* was constructed one steamer could haul two or three comparably sized barges. The steamer sometimes needed aid, however, so the barges were fixed with a minimal rig of five to seven sails.

Madeira entered the fleet of the Minnesota Steamship Company of Cleveland, Ohio, the same year she was built. After only one year of service she was sold to another Ohio shipping concern, the Pittsburgh Steamship Company. Although little is known of the career of *Madeira,* she gained worldwide notice when she collided with the International Bridge at Sault Ste. Marie in early June 1902. Her name surfaced again about three years later when she became a casualty of the infamous "Maatafa Storm."

Early in the morning on November 28, 1905, *Madeira* was under tow of the steamer *William Edenborn*. The vessels were caught in a fierce tempest that had been raging since the previous afternoon. Winds gusted seventy to eighty miles per hour, almost blinding the crews of both ships with blowing snow while kicking up huge swells. Fearing for his own vessel, and believing *Madeira* stood a better chance of survival if she was free of the tow, the captain of *William Edenborn* cut the towline to the schooner-barge. Accounts from the period suggest that *Madeira* tried to set anchor and ride out the storm. Interestingly, when the wreck site was initially examined the ship's anchors were still intact at the bow. Roughly two hours after her release from the steamer, the waves hurled *Madeira* against a rock cliff known as Gold Rock, just northeast of the community of Split Rock. As the vessel began to break up one of her crewmen, Fred Benson, leapt from her deck with a safety line, landing at the base of Gold Rock. As waves pounded over him, Benson climbed the sixty-foot rock face to safety. He then tied a rock to the safety line and dropped it to crewmen on the dying *Madeira*. He was able to pull three men from the bow section to the top of the cliff, and then five more from the stern deck. The first mate perished, pulled down with the ship as he tried to jump from the mizzenmast. The survivors were rescued two days later by the tugboat *Edna G*. The crew of the tug also pulled the body of the first mate from the icy waters.

Madeira, shown here in 1900 soon after she was completed, was over four hundred feet long and rigged for sails.

The storm destroyed or damaged about thirty vessels on Lake Superior. Coincidentally, one was *William Edenborn,* which was thrown aground near Split Rock about the same time *Madeira* went under. Widely considered the most ferocious storm to ever strike the Great Lakes, it would take its name from one of its wrecks, *Maatafa*. The storm smashed the steel steamer just outside Duluth Harbor, within full view of the city's citizens.

Although *Madeira* plunged to the bottom of Lake Superior in pieces she remains the last surviving example of a schooner-barge of her type. Moreover, the principal diagnostic components of her hull, the bow and stern sections, remain relatively unaltered. She was placed on the National Register in 1992.

✳ Two Harbors Light Station

TWO HARBORS | LAKE COUNTY

In the mid-1850s Thomas Sexton erected a log cabin near Agate Bay on Lake Superior. The Treaty of La Pointe had only recently been signed and Sexton was one of many on the east side of Lake Superior to scamper to the opposite side of the lake and establish a "preemptive claim"—a means of validating prior rights to land by demonstrating occupancy. Born in Ireland in 1825, Sexton immigrated to Canada with his family when he was very young. In 1854 he moved to Ontonagon, Michigan, working in the copper mines there for one winter. He then relocated to Superior, Wisconsin, where he was employed for a short time as a bridge builder. More importantly, he was in the best position to access lands on the Minnesota side of the lake when white settlement in the area was authorized. And so in summer 1855, Sexton found himself constructing a 14- by 16-foot dwelling overlooking Lake Superior and Agate Bay, thereby substantiating his rights to the land. He officially purchased the parcel in 1863 for $145. As Sexton looked out over the bay in those early days he probably never realized what that body of water would mean to the commercial development of Minnesota—what it would mean to the economic growth of a young nation on the cusp of an industrial revolution.[36]

While Sexton is credited as the first settler in the area that eventually spawned Two Harbors, it was Charlemagne Tower, a lawyer and financier from Philadelphia, who had the political and financial muscle to bring the community to life. More than twenty-five years after Sexton built his cabin, Tower was convinced that a fortune lay in Minnesota's Vermilion Iron Range northwest of Agate Bay. In the early 1880s he incorporated the Minnesota Iron Company to mine the Vermilion. He also built Minnesota's first Iron Range railroad, the Duluth and Iron Range (D&IR), to haul the raw iron to Agate Bay for shipment across the Great Lakes to manufacturing centers in the East. The ore loading docks erected on the bay were also the state's first. Of course, to do all this Tower purchased a considerable amount of land, including 150 acres from Thomas Sexton. Deriving substantial profit from the sale of most of his land, Sexton now enjoyed watching the bustle of activity that dominated the once sedate region. The community of Two Harbors was born in these early days of Tower's enterprise, as the mining operation and its railroad drew skilled and unskilled laborers into the area in search of a new adventure, a better life, or both.

Two Harbors was platted in 1885. Its name reflects its location, with Burlington Bay bordering it to the east and Agate Bay edging it to the south. The following year Two Harbors became the county seat for Lake County and was incorporated as a village two years later. The village was the obvious choice as the center of government in the county since it was growing so quickly, fueled by D&IR investment in housing and mercantile establishments. Moreover, in 1886 the D&IR had constructed a line to Duluth, giving citizens of Two Harbors and the surrounding area easy access to the blossoming metropolis to the south. By the late 1880s, however, Charlemagne Tower was no longer guiding the Minnesota Iron Company and the D&IR. In 1887 a Chicago mining syndicate led by Henry H. Porter, the head of the Illinois Steel Company, forced Tower to give up his interests in the Vermilion. Although management at the mining company and railroad changed, trains loaded with iron ore continued to roll toward Agate Bay. The year Tower lost his mining interests in northern Minnesota almost 400,000 tons of ore passed over the Two Harbors loading docks. The following year more than 450,000 tons were shipped from the bay. In coming years several million tons of iron ore and other goods would be shipped from Agate Bay annually. By the 1910s the tonnage coming out of Two Harbors rivaled that passing through the Suez Canal.

About the time Charlemagne Tower was being supplanted as head of the Minnesota Iron Company and its railroad, the U.S. Army Corps

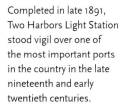

Completed in late 1891, Two Harbors Light Station stood vigil over one of the most important ports in the country in the late nineteenth and early twentieth centuries.

of Engineers developed a plan for protecting the port at Two Harbors. The plan included building an east and west breakwater, as well as constructing a lighthouse on an elevated parcel located at the edge of Lake Superior between Burlington and Agate Bays. At this time, all lighthouses in the country fell under the jurisdiction of the Lighthouse Service. The Lighthouse Service became a formal administrative unit of the government in August 1789, when Congress established federal authority over the nation's lighthouses. The secretary of the treasury oversaw the Lighthouse Service until 1903, at which time responsibility for the agency passed to the newly created Department of Commerce and Labor. To improve governmental efficiency, President Franklin Roosevelt ordered the Lighthouse Service assimilated into the U.S. Coast Guard in 1939.

Work on the east breakwater at Two Harbors was completed in 1888. Duluth contractor T. R. McDonald began construction of the west breakwater in spring 1891. In midsummer of that year a crew of ten men built a track from Agate Bay to the lighthouse site. Construction of the lighthouse commenced in August under the supervision of the Lighthouse Service. Building material arriving at the bay was moved to the construction site along the track. By the end of October the lighthouse keeper's family had joined him in Two Harbors and was awaiting the completion of the navigational aid, which was finished the following month, although the lantern was not lit until April 1892. The brick, two-story, gable-roofed keeper's residence had an L-shaped plan. The brick light tower was tucked into the corner created by the intersecting walls of the residence, giving the combined structures a generally square footprint. The tower measured almost 13 feet square and roughly 50 feet high. The octagonal cast-iron lantern atop the tower held a Fourth-Order Fresnel lens that rotated around a fixed flame lit with kerosene. Invented by French physicist Augustin Fresnel, these lenses were works of art, each composed of a pattern of prisms that boosted the brightness and strength of a lighthouse beam.

The light beacon came at an opportune time, since by the early 1890s ship traffic at Two Harbors was exploding. The same year the lighthouse went online roughly 1,300 vessels visited the harbor. The large volume of ships into and out of Two Harbors increased the likelihood of accidents, so the navigational aid was a welcome safety measure. For the next several decades the lighthouse remained mostly unchanged, guiding commercial vessels, homebound fishermen, and others safely into port. In the early 1970s the Coast Guard removed the lighthouse's Fresnel lens and replaced it with an aerobeacon. The original lens is now on display at the Great Lakes Maritime Museum in Ohio. The light station was automated in the early 1980s and a lighthouse keeper was no longer required. As navigational aids aboard ships became more sophisticated the light itself became obsolete. It has remained the only continually functioning lighthouse in

From Agate Bay's east breakwater, the lighthouse tower and lantern peek above the treetops, while a ship's pilothouse provides an excellent vantage from which to view Lake Superior.

Minnesota due largely to the efforts of the local historical society, which has operated the light station as a historic site since 1987. In 1998 ownership of the structure passed to the Lake County Historical Society. The organization now also employs the lighthouse as a bed and breakfast, with the profits going toward the restoration of the old beacon. Presently, the historical society is working to procure the lighthouse's Fresnel lens, an integral component of the original structure. As the sentinel of Minnesota's most important iron ore port in the late nineteenth century, the Two Harbors Light Station was listed on the National Register in 1984.

✳ U.S. Army Corps of Engineers Duluth Vessel Yard

DULUTH | ST. LOUIS COUNTY

Duluth Harbor at the base of Lake Superior is a jewel, a naturally sheltered bay created by the geographic blessing, Minnesota Point. Lake Superior was tied to the other Great Lakes in 1855, when the St. Mary's Falls Ship Canal was constructed at Sault Ste. Marie, thus creating a continuous waterway from the Duluth-Superior region all the way to the Atlantic Coast. Much of the grain, lumber, and coal from the Middle West could now be shipped East via the Great Lakes. In the late nineteenth century, the federal government recognized a good thing when it saw it. If the port at Duluth were improved the harbor could serve as the western launching point for a great deal of these commodities. So in 1871 the U.S. Army Corps of Engineers appeared in Duluth to shape a first-class harbor.[37]

The Corps began work on the harbor soon after Duluth cut a channel through Minnesota Point to open the port to shipping. Within two years the federal government assumed authority over the channel. It would be another fourteen years, though, before ownership of the structure officially passed from the city to the federal government. During that period much of the Corps's work involved building and repairing breakwaters, as well as constructing docks. Most of the government's efforts, however, were directed toward dredging the harbor and the channel. In its natural state the harbor was only about eight to nine feet deep, yet if the harbor was to develop as a meaningful shipping hub capable of accommodating large freighters it had to be much deeper. Over time, as commercial carriers grew ever larger and the volume of goods passing through the harbor mushroomed, dredging became even more important.

Corps activities in Duluth Harbor increased by the 1890s, spurred by the development of the Vermilion and Mesabi Iron Ranges. In 1895 the Vermilion produced over 2 million tons of iron ore, while almost 1.6 million tons of the raw material were pulled from the Mesabi. Five years later

the Vermilion accounted for roughly 4 million tons and the Mesabi produced only slightly less—iron ore was rapidly becoming a major contribu-
tor to Minnesota's economy. But at the beginning of the 1890s Duluth did
not have an iron ore dock in its harbor. At that time much of Minnesota's
iron ore was shipped from the docks in Superior, Wisconsin, or from those
on Agate Bay in Two Harbors, Minnesota. When the Duluth, Missabe, and
Northern Railway finally completed its dock in Duluth's harbor in summer
1893, the city was finally able to compete in the iron ore shipping trade with
Superior and Two Harbors. The dock had 384 ore pockets and jutted into
the harbor roughly 2,300 feet, making it the largest ore dock yet erected on
the Great Lakes. Two additional ore docks were in place by 1902.

The commercial importance of iron ore to the nation was evidenced
by the federal government's commitment to Duluth and Superior in 1896.
That year Congress authorized $3 million for harbor improvements in both
ports. The government also created the Duluth-Superior Harbor Authority,
an entity born to oversee maintenance and construction in the harbors.
This legislative action essentially treated the harbors in Duluth and Superior as a single large port. In 1897, to aid the government's efforts, a vessel
yard for the Corps was established at the foot of Duluth's Seventh Avenue
West, along the northwest edge of the harbor. The yard included a warehouse, oil house, and a dock, as well as boathouses.

A dredging bucket frames
the symbol of Duluth.

Between the years 1897 and 1902 the Corps dredged almost 22 million cubic yards of material from the bottom of Duluth-Superior Harbor, efforts that opened about 17 miles of channel and created a roughly 360-acre harbor basin more than 20 feet deep. The labor proved worthwhile, and by 1906 the quantity of goods passing through the harbor amounted to almost 30 million tons, which made Duluth-Superior the third busiest port in the nation, behind only New York and Philadelphia. The fact that the shipping season at Duluth-Superior was limited to the nine months between April and December further exemplified the port's significance.

Only seven years after the Corps built its vessel yard near Seventh Avenue West it relocated the facility, constructing a new slip to the east, across the harbor on the sandy peninsula of Minnesota Point. The location for the vessel yard appears to have been chosen because it was more centrally positioned than the previous site. Comprising 44,000 square feet, the new harbor frontage cost the agency $6,700. A dock and the wrecked tugboat *James Bardons* occupied sections of the property. It is likely that the abandoned tug served as fill (earth, stone, or another material used to raise an existing grade) for the vessel yard. The Corps relocated a boathouse, launch house, warehouse, and paint/oil house from the old vessel yard site to the new one. All of the buildings were wood-framed structures topped with gable roofs.

After the vessel yard was moved to Minnesota Point in 1904, the Corps continued its dredging, maintenance, and pier construction activities. In the mid-1920s it also supervised the reconstruction of the Duluth Ship Canal. About this time the vessel yard consisted of a dozen buildings, but less than two decades later almost all of the structures were removed when the vessel yard was reconstructed. The new brick buildings that were erected mostly between 1940 and 1941 were utilitarian in design, exhibiting few architectural embellishments. One of the few structures to survive this rebuilding phase was a brick warehouse with stepped gables that was built in 1926.

Today, the Corps continues its chore of keeping Duluth-Superior Harbor navigable to commercial shipping. In some ways the job is harder because modern-day freighters are several hundred feet longer than those the Corps worked to accommodate in the late nineteenth century. Presently, the vessel yard mostly resembles its 1940s construction, generally displaying a cohesive architectural style. It consists of a slip (formed by a north and south pier and a sliphead) and six buildings. Four of the six buildings date to the early 1940s reconstruction. The 1926 warehouse also remains. A welding shop made of prefabricated steel sheets that was erected in 1977

The U.S. Army Corps of Engineers Duluth Vessel Yard has been situated on Minnesota Point for a century, with Duluth Harbor on one side and the great expanse of Lake Superior on the other.

occupies part of the yard as well. The vessel yard was listed on the National Register in 1995 as the site of activities crucial to the development of Duluth and its harbor—activities that helped make the port a vital shipping link to eastern manufacturing centers. And although the vessel yard is composed mostly of aesthetically reserved buildings, its general architectural uniformity makes it a notable example of a federal construction project.

✳ Tugboat *Edna G.*

TWO HARBORS | LAKE COUNTY

The tugboat *Edna G.* was launched in Cleveland, Ohio, in 1896. She promptly sank. It was not that the tug was top-heavy or had holes in her bow or some other unrecognized ailment. She was as well crafted as a tug could be. Fault lay with those who launched her. The angle of her sideways drop into the water was just too steep, and when she hit the surface she continued down. She was soon raised by her builders, the Cleveland Shipbuilding Company, and sent properly on her way. Although her beginning was unlucky, the shipbuilding concern had constructed a fine Great Lakes vessel. So fine, in fact, that more than a century later her pudgy profile continues to grace the shores of Agate Bay in Two Harbors, Minnesota.[38]

Tugboats have served as a vital shipping tool on the Great Lakes for many years. It is the role of the tug to help guide freighters through the harbor and safely dock. This was a difficult task in the mid-nineteenth century when wooden schooners ranged in size from 150 to 160 feet and carried over 400 tons of cargo. The chore became especially arduous by the end of the century when 400- to 500-foot steel freighters became common. Many of these ships often towed one or two barges as well, vessels about the same size as the ships that hauled them. Since they had no mechanical power of their own the barges were particularly dependent on aid from the tugs. As the new century dawned the size of commercial vessels continued to increase. By the 1910s freighters measuring almost 600 feet in length were appearing—the tug's job was getting tougher.

The first tugs on the Great Lakes were Canadian. By the early 1840s the vessel type had reached the American side of Lake Ontario. As commercial shipping on the Great Lakes increased so did the number of tugs. In the 1850s about four hundred tugs were constructed to serve shipping on the inland seas and an additional seven hundred were built in the 1860s. These tugs were fabricated with wooden hulls, but around the beginning of the twentieth century tugs with steel hulls became commonplace.

Edna G. was built for the Duluth and Iron Range Rail Road (D&IR). She was chiefly designed to guide ore carriers to the railroad's ore loading docks, although the boat was employed for other purposes as well. The tug was named for Edna Greatsinger, the daughter of Jacob Greatsinger, who was president of the D&IR from 1886 to 1896. Developed in the early 1880s, the D&IR was constructed for the single purpose of moving iron ore from the Vermilion Iron Range to Agate Bay on Lake Superior. Agate Bay was chosen as a shipping port because its stable bottom of clay provided a good foundation on which to erect ore docks. A settlement sprang up just north of the bay and was christened "Two Harbors." Two Harbors would be home to *Edna G.* for most of her years.

Moored on Agate Bay adjacent to the DM&IR ore docks, *Edna G.* is in remarkable condition for a centenarian.

Costing roughly $50,000, the steel-hulled tug was more than 100 feet long, with a width of 23 feet. Her heart was a coal-fired, steam-driven engine. When she came into service in 1896 she replaced the D&IR tug *Ella G. Stone,* a wooden tug brought to Agate Bay in 1884 when the D&IR ore docks were constructed. The tug was underpowered, however, and by the mid-1890s the railroad opted for *Edna G.* and her 750-horsepower engine.

The crew of *Edna G.* consisted of a captain, chief engineer, deckhand, and fireman. It was the role of the fireman to keep the tug's boilers hot at all times during the shipping season since the boat had to be ready to move quickly. The fireman usually shoveled about twenty-five tons of coal a week into the ship's boilers. The vessel's motive power was achieved when heat generated by the boilers turned water into steam. The pressure from the steam drove the pistons within the engine, turning the propeller shaft that spun the propeller. When an incoming freighter blew its whistle, *Edna G.* would "steam" into the lake and guide the big ship into the harbor under tow. During the early years the tug communicated with her tows by whistle signals. In later years radios were used.

The tug's interior is surprisingly roomy, as shown in this 1987 view of the aft cabin.

The tug's funnel obscures the rear view somewhat, but the many windows of the pilothouse allow an almost 360-degree field of vision.

While *Edna G.* spent most of her days maneuvering freighters into and out of Agate Bay, she was sometimes called upon for other duties as well. She was modified for use as a fire tug, with a "fire gun" on her upper deck that could pump 2,600 gallons of water a minute. If fire broke out on another ship or in one of the commercial fish houses or shanties along the shore, the tug could assist in quelling the blaze. More importantly for the D&IR, if fire erupted on one of the wood ore docks the tug was there before the blaze became uncontrollable. By the mid-1920s the railroad had replaced its wood ore docks with steel structures and fire on the docks was no longer a principal concern. *Edna G.* also assisted in rescue missions. In late November 1905, for instance, she rescued the crew of the ill-fated *Madeira*, a schooner-barge that went down off of Gold Rock in a fierce storm.

The only time *Edna G.* was absent from the Two Harbors area was during World War I when she was requisitioned by the federal government, although from the D&IR perspective the tug had been "commandeered." Between the years 1917 and 1919, *Edna G.* operated out of Norfolk, Virginia, towing a variety of vessels along the Atlantic Coast. It was probably at this time that the tug's wooden superstructure was modified with one of steel. Back in Two Harbors after the war, the tug continued her traditional chore of moving ore carriers into and out of Agate Bay. Around the middle of the twentieth century many tugs were refitted with more powerful diesel engines. *Edna G.* never underwent this modification, although she did receive new boilers in 1948, which increased her capacity to 1,000 horsepower. Technology eventually caught up with the tug, though. New freighters were constructed with bow thrusters, a maneuvering system that allowed carriers to position themselves alongside ore docks. In 1981 the railroad concluded the services of *Edna G.* were no longer required, and three years later the city of Two Harbors purchased the ship for one dollar. More than

$200,000 has been spent on the tug's restoration since that time. Today, *Edna G.* is displayed on Agate Bay, adjacent to the ore docks of the Duluth, Missabe and Iron Range Railway (DM&IR), successor to the D&IR. *Edna G.* is the last steam-powered tug to serve the Great Lakes, and she was included in the National Register in 1975.

✳ Jim Scott Fish House

GRAND MARAIS | COOK COUNTY

In 1849 Alexander Ramsey, the first territorial governor of Minnesota, remarked: "The abundant fisheries of the western extremity of Lake [Superior] will, under proper development, prove additional rich sources of revenue to the Territory." The governor was right, although it would take some time before his prophecy was fulfilled.[39]

During the nineteenth century the waters along Minnesota's North Shore were inhabited by vast schools of whitefish and lake trout, fish varieties prized in commercial markets. In the mid-1850s a modest fishing industry was in place, but transportation to population centers was limited. When steamboat transportation from the North Shore to Duluth was improved in the 1880s, the region finally gained commercial importance as a source for fish. As the significance of the Lake Superior fishing industry continued to grow, more individuals were drawn to the vocation. Aspiring fishermen either purchased their own boats and equipment or were fronted the capital by fish wholesalers in Duluth. By the early 1900s a substantial number of people along the North Shore made their living fishing the lake. In her *Minnesota History* piece "Commercial Fishing on Lake Superior in

Although now showing fatigue, the Jim Scott Fish House remains a superb example of an early-twentieth-century North Shore commercial fish house.

Presently boating and fishing equipment is stored in the fish house.

the 1890s," June Holmquist quotes a North Shore writer who noted in 1917: "There is almost one fisherman for every half mile of shore all the way from Duluth to Grand Portage." One of these fishermen was James (Jim) Garfield Scott.

Jim Scott was born in Grand Marais in 1881. His father, Andrew Jackson Scott, came to the community in the 1870s. Initially, Andrew made his living primarily as a trapper, but around the turn of the twentieth century he shifted focus to commercial fishing. His son soon joined him. Jim would eventually become one of the most successful commercial fishermen on the North Shore. In 1907 Jim purchased waterfront property along the west edge of Grand Marais Harbor and constructed a gable-roofed fish house and an adjacent dock. While only a humble rectangular building measuring 25 by 30 feet, it generally matched the dimensions of most like structures. It may have been during its initial construction that the fish house was sided with wood shingles, a decorative feature giving the building a bit more architectural flair than most fish houses, which were often sided only with wood boards. During the fishing season Jim Scott used the fish house for dressing and packing fish, and in winter the building was employed for storage and maintenance of fishing equipment.

Not long after the fish house was erected Jim entered into a partnership with another commercial fisherman, Eugene Clark. Clark was a bachelor who resided within the fish house, sleeping in the building's small loft. Besides commercial fishing, the partners also became well known locally as fishing-boat builders. The partnership between the two men came to an end when Clark passed away in 1915. Possibly as a tribute to the late fisherman, his bunk in the fish house remained at least until the 1980s. Scott eventually acquired another partner, his son Roger. Together they constructed the *Nee Gee*, a fishing vessel the team would operate for years. The good-sized boat had a 110-horsepower engine and a 24-inch propeller. A large cabin with wooden doors that opened toward the bow dominated the deck. The pilot's station was slightly elevated and provided a clear field of view. The boat's design allowed the fishermen to manage the equipment for setting the fishing nets without leaving the interior of the cabin.

The Scotts began fishing early in the season, as soon as the ice in the harbor was gone. The days were long, with the fishing vessel usually clearing the harbor about five o'clock in the morning. The destination was often a spot to the south, not far from Outer Island, an area favored by lake trout. The thirty-five-mile trip took about four hours. The crew spent another six hours working on-site, setting over four miles of net and, later, reeling it aboard with the day's haul. On the return trip crewmen cleaned the catch, but the fish could not be packed on ice until the Scotts reached the fish house. During the fall, the Scotts would sail to a site near Duluth in search of herring.

Jim Scott fished Lake Superior for half a century, but in 1947, while working on the dock near his fish house, he collapsed and died. With his passing, Grand Marais lost more than just a premier commercial fisherman. Although he had dedicated most of his life to fishing Lake Superior, he also found time to be an industry and community leader. He helped found the North Shore Cooperative Fishermen's Association and the North Shore Fish and Freight Trucking Company. Moreover, the same year he built his fish house he established the local Congregational church, where

Local carpenter Dennis Bradley is currently helping restore Jim and Roger Scott's trusty *Nee Gee*.

he occasionally served as deacon. At the time of his passing he was also the president of the local bank, a position he held since 1920.

After Scott's death the fish house remained within the family. During the 1980s the structure was still being used in the manner for which it was designed. By this time, however, commercial fishing on the lake had dramatically declined. Much of the trout and whitefish that once occupied the lake had been overfished or pushed out by herring. Smelt eventually succeeded the herring. Native fish populations were further reduced when the sea lamprey appeared.

Today, the Jim Scott Fish House is owned by two of the fisherman's grandchildren. No longer used for packing fish, the structure is employed for storage of boating and fishing equipment. The fishermen now using the fish house have an adjacent building for filleting and packing fish. Looking much like it always has, with its familiar wood-shingled exterior walls, the Jim Scott Fish House was added to the National Register in 1986 as an excellent example of the small, wood-framed commercial fish houses that once marked the North Shore of Minnesota.

✳ *Onoko* Shipwreck

VICINITY OF KNIFE ISLAND | LAKE SUPERIOR

Lake Superior was calm when *Onoko* sailed out of Duluth Harbor on the morning of September 14, 1915. The freighter was headed for Toledo, Ohio, with 100,000 bushels of wheat. The ship had only recently survived a harrowing Great Lakes storm on its trek from Collingwood, Ontario, to the Minnesota port city. At one point the fierce winds turned the ship completely around. So the crew must have felt pleased with the tranquil weather conditions of this early autumn day as the 287-foot freighter glided from the security of the harbor into Lake Superior. Less than two hours later a crewman rushed on deck in search of the captain. "She's sinking, she's sinking!" he exclaimed.[40]

Onoko was the first of her kind on the Great Lakes, an iron-hulled bulk freighter, the prototype for hundreds of commercial carriers that would follow. Development of Great Lakes bulk freighters began in the late 1860s to meet the shipping needs of a growing iron ore industry. The ships had double decks, with a pilothouse situated on an elevated forecastle. Machinery spaces were placed at the stern. Large hatches were positioned evenly along the deck and aligned with the loading spouts of the prominent ore docks of the day. The first freighters of this type were *R. J. Hackett* and *William T. Graves,* both constructed in 1869. During the next decade over fifty additional bulk freighters were built, and another thirty-nine were fabricated between 1880 and 1881. While the design rapidly gained acceptance, all of these ships were made from wood. By this time England already embraced iron as a shipbuilding material. The English realized that a ship of iron could be made larger than one of wood and still be lighter and capable of carrying larger cargoes. Certainly the initial investment in an iron carrier was greater than that of a wooden ship, but this added cost was trumped by the lighter vessel's increased efficiency. Most American shipbuilders, however, were not yet convinced that a ship formed from metal was superior to a ship made of wood. And although a small number of iron-hulled vessels did exist in America at this time, none were bulk freighters. A few forward-thinking entrepreneurs in Cleveland, Ohio, were eager to change that. In 1880 the newly formed Globe Shipbuilding Com-

pany of Cleveland was commissioned to build a bulk freighter made with
an iron hull. In spring 1882 *Onoko* made her debut.

Just under 300 feet in length, *Onoko* was about 45 feet wide, with a
hold depth of 25 feet. She was the largest vessel on the Great Lakes. Her
hull was comprised of riveted, iron plates and she was powered by a steam
engine, although the ship was also rigged for sails. Built to carry up to
3,000 tons of iron ore, she far outpaced the 300- to 400-ton maximum
capacity of many of the commercial carriers of the period. Still, many were
not convinced that she could do what her designers said she could, some
even christening her the "White Elephant." Nine days after *Onoko* steamed
from Cleveland, she discharged a mammoth 2,400 tons of ore, persuading
at least some of her naysayers that the ship was as good as advertised.

Onoko remained the largest vessel on the Great Lakes for nearly a decade
as traditionally conservative ship owners remained hesitant to expend the
extra sum on a ship of metal. But *Onoko*'s presence—her impressive load-
carrying capacity—did not go unnoticed, and eventually commercial ship-
pers warmed to the idea of carriers made from iron or steel. While only
7 percent of bulk freighters constructed for the Great Lakes during the 1880s
were made of metal, during the 1890s almost 75 percent were formed from
the material.

For more than three decades *Onoko* navigated the Great Lakes, earning
her cost many times over. By 1915, however, she was no longer the largest
vessel on the Lakes. In fact, ships about twice her size were becoming com-

The first freighter of her type on the Great Lakes, *Onoko* went down stern first on September 14, 1915.

monplace. Even so, she was admired as an efficient and dependable commercial carrier. Moreover, she was remembered as the first of her kind, a test case that introduced a new shipping technology into one of the world's major commercial transportation arteries. Her crew must have felt a certain satisfaction with her reputation and reliability. When *Onoko* steamed from Duluth Harbor on September 14, they believed the ship would perform as she always had. On this trip *Onoko* showed her age.

Onoko was about thirteen nautical miles northeast of Duluth when water started rushing into the engine room. The chief engineer immediately started the bilge pumps, but by the time he reached an exit ladder the water was already up to his waist. Heeding the call that the ship was sinking, the captain quickly surveyed the situation and realized that his boat was lost. Ordering the ship abandoned, the sixteen crewmen and a single passenger gathered their belongings, including their mascot, a bulldog named Rex, and pushed off in the lifeboats. From a safe distance, the saddened crew watched as *Onoko* dipped stern first into Lake Superior. An explosion rocked the old freighter and she threw her bow into the air and arced over onto her deck. The Standard Oil Company tanker *Renown* was only a short distance away when *Onoko* started going down. *Renown* pulled alongside *Onoko*'s lifeboats and gathered the dying freighter's crew.

Some theorized that agents of the German-Austrian alliance sabotaged the freighter. After all, conspiracists speculated, the destination for the grain aboard *Onoko* was England, an enemy to both Germany and Austria-Hungary. The finding of an investigation conducted immediately after the sinking was less dramatic, concluding that a worn iron plate had dropped from the aging freighter's hull, allowing water to flood the ship's hold and send *Onoko* 220 feet to the bottom of Lake Superior. The freighter's final resting place was discovered in 1988. She lies upside down with a break in her hull near the stern. Although concealed beneath the waves of Lake Superior for almost ninety years, *Onoko* remains the premier example of a vessel of her type. She was added to the National Register in 1992.

COMMERCIAL HISTORY

INFANT COMMUNITIES in mid- to late-nineteenth-century Minnesota resembled infant communities in newly settled areas most anywhere. Whether straddling a river or rail line, newborn towns were usually a collection of small, mostly unadorned, wood-framed buildings. As communities labored to become economically viable, the aesthetic appeal of constituent parts was simply not a primary concern. Occasionally, though, a building exhibited modest flourishes, like a false front—a facade extending above the roof offering the impression of a larger structure. Still, substantial embellishment typically awaited financial stability.[41]

Many Minnesota towns had gained a measure of economic security by the late nineteenth century. Construction at this time was more elaborate and permanent, characteristics often exhibited in public buildings like city halls, courthouses, libraries, and schools. The City Hall of Lake City, for example, was an eclectic mix of Romanesque and Queen Anne–style elements. Constructed in 1899, the building's facade was dominated by a central tower crowned with a pyramidal roof. Formed of red brick and resting on a limestone foundation, the delightful National Register structure projected solidity, signaling Lake City residents it intended to stay. Financial stability was also apparent on Main Street, the seasoned metaphor for central commercial districts across America. Merchants and others who established enterprises in simple, wooden buildings usually graduated to architecturally detailed edifices of stone or brick once they realized business success or, as with members of the Viola Cooperative Creamery, after fire convinced them of the worthiness of masonry.

Central commercial districts, whether large or small, represent the hearts of communities. Usually built around one or two primary routes, and oftentimes flanked by municipal buildings, churches, and residences, they are the most obvious manifestation of capitalism in many towns. In late-nineteenth- and early-twentieth-century Minnesota, they were frequently the first section of a community to receive improvements such as road grading or street lighting. While chiefly a venue of exchange, the district was often the center of social activity as well, a place that invited visitors to linger. As historian Carole Rifkind explains: "Even if it was no more than a dozen facing structures across a wide space, Main Street was a magnet for human activity. Residential, religious, civic, educational, recreational, commercial and ceremonial use took place side by side." Much of this activity was in commercial buildings that also served as town gathering halls. In Blooming Prairie, a Steele County community in southeastern Minnesota, the basement of the First National Bank was intentionally designed as a community center, a meeting place for local farm families who flooded the town on Saturday afternoons to purchase supplies and other goods.

Merchants, bank owners, and others promoted the primacy of commercial areas by the fanciful buildings they constructed. General stores, hardware stores, drugstores, banks, hotels, and more were erected as aesthetic augmentation to a streetscape rapidly transforming from humble to handsome. But besides visually enhancing the commercial experience, entrepreneurs wanted their monuments to capitalism to be a kind of merit badge to their industriousness, a symbol of their success and commitment to the community. In Minnesota near the turn of the twentieth century, this often meant buildings garnished with Italianate or Queen Anne–style elements. Beaux Arts Classicism soon became popular as well, especially for banks. Ornamentation often included pilasters and window hoods. An attractive cornice, which is a molded projection crowning a wall and sometimes resting upon ornate brackets (frequently lending visual support rather than structural support), was common as well. Often the cornice was edged below by a decorative band, or frieze.

In the first half of the twentieth century, merchants sometimes altered the look of their original storefront, an effort to convince customers that the store their parents frequented was still relevant. Many shop owners decorated storefronts with structural glass panels when Streamline Moderne style became prominent in the 1930s and 1940s. While many of these storefronts are impressive, they sometimes sharply contrast with the buildings' Picturesque- or Victorian-style upper levels.

The dominance of Minnesota's central business districts vanished after the Second World War as automobiles and superhighways transported people to locales other than Main Street. Many of Minnesota's early commercial buildings are now enduring a lingering death. Some towns, however, are trying hard to resuscitate their hearts. Cities like Blooming Prairie and Cannon Falls now have early business cores on the National Register, a revitalization effort acknowledging the districts' historical contribution to community development. Many individual commercial properties are also on the federal listing, such as the Esselman Brothers General Store in the hamlet of Mayhew Lake in Benton County in central Minnesota and the Hotel Atwater in Atwater, a Kandiyohi County town in the west-central part of the state. The Hotel Atwater is described by architectural historian Susan Granger as "one of west-central Minnesota's finest extant railroad-era downtown hotels." The Nelson and Albin Cooperative Mercantile Association Store in Godahl, a Watonwan County village in south-central Minnesota, is a rare example of the cooperative general stores that were once so common in the state's rural agricultural areas. The Big Store in Minneota in Lyon County, not far from the South Dakota border, is a superb example of a turn-of-the-twentieth-century, small-town retail outlet. Accounts of the Big Store and the Nelson and Albin Cooperative Mercantile Association Store follow, as do the stories of other National Register commercial entities that contributed to the growth and heritage of their respective communities.

✳   The Big Store
(O. G. Anderson & Company Store)

MINNEOTA | LYON COUNTY

*The elderly women move out over the worn wooden floor at the close of every
 business day, threading their way between the old cast-iron radiators and
 the clothing counters, spreading sheets over the counters to protect the goods
 from dust. It matters little that there no longer is any dust from which to protect
 the goods; the dirt streets, once kicked up by passing teams of horses and sput-
 tering Model T's, have long since been paved. It matters only that the daily
 ritual of covering the items has been followed for more than seven decades and,
 like so much else about this store, has become a tradition and—perhaps—
 an anachronism.*

In summer 1972, only a few weeks after a journalist for the *Minneapolis Tribune* penned the words above, The Big Store closed its doors.[42]

The Big Store was the brainchild of Olafur Gudjon Anderson and Sigurdur Arne Anderson. The two were not related, although both arrived

Officially O. G. Anderson and Company, the enterprise was commonly known as "the Big Store," which is evident from the sign still adorning the building.

in Minnesota from Iceland in 1879. Both were members of the large Icelandic community that was established in the late nineteenth century in Lyon, Lincoln, and Yellow Medicine Counties in the southwestern part of the state. Olafur, commonly known as O. G., worked for a railroad and farmed for a period before entering the mercantile business as a clerk for the Verzlunarfelag Islendinga (V.I.), or Icelandic Mercantile Company, a consumers' cooperative of Icelandic families. Sigurdur also worked for the V.I. for a time. In spring 1896 O. G. opened a small dry goods company in Minneota, a Lyon County community about twelve miles northwest of Marshall, the county seat. Sigurdur became a partner in the O. G. Anderson Company the same year the store opened.

O. G. Anderson Company quickly flourished and expanded its product line. In September 1897 O. G. advertised that the company "had the largest stock of goods ever shown in Minneota: dry goods, underwear, jackets, clothing, shoes, duck coats, groceries, and crockery." The company grew so quickly that by 1899 the partners were planning a new, larger building to house all their goods. By summer 1901, work on the store was underway at the corner of Jefferson Street and Second Street. It was completed within a few months.

The Queen Anne Commercial–style building was designed by Mankato architect H. G. Gerlach and constructed by Mahlke and Franksen, also of Mankato. Costing somewhere between $12,000 and $15,000, the two-story structure was 50 feet long and 100 feet wide. Large display windows separated by a main entrance marked the building's first floor at the northwest facade. A large window set within a semicircular-arched opening was centered at the facade's second floor. An engraved tablet reading "Opera Hall" was situated just above the window. The facade's remaining second-floor windows were mounted within segmental-arched openings, a window-opening design common to most of the building. Pilasters framed facade windows and also accented the store's southwest wall. The southwest wall was marked by another entrance that was recessed within a semicircular-arched opening near the rear of the building. The handsome store's roofline was further embellished with a low-relief frieze and corbelling, which is overlapping units or courses of masonry projecting from a vertical wall, with each unit or course projecting slightly farther than the one just below, like an inverted stairway. A small pediment holding an engraved date tablet was situated above the frieze at the facade.

The building's interior had wood floors and pressed metal ceilings.

The Big Store, an elegant Queen Anne Commercial–style building designed by Mankato architect H. G. Gerlach, was Minneota's main retail attraction for seven decades.

The first floor was the display and sales area, and the second floor was designed as an opera house with a stage at the northwest end. An opera house was common to select commercial buildings in many rural towns in the early twentieth century and was an indication that a community was maturing. Access to the opera house was from the arched opening at the southwest side of the building.

Impressed by the size of the structure, locals immediately began calling it "Stora Budin"—the Big Store. Even though the store's name remained O. G. Anderson and Company, it was the sobriquet that stuck. O. G. Anderson did not enjoy his "Big Store" for long, dying of tuberculosis two years after it was built. He was only forty-four years old. For the next forty years Sigurdur would manage the business, although he received help from O. G.'s son, Carl, as well as his own son, Theodore William, commonly known as Billy. In time, the enterprise developed into a major retail outlet in the tri-county area.

The store seemed to have something for everyone: housewares and hardware, toys, groceries, and clothes for all family members—it was like an early-twentieth-century Wal-Mart. Moreover, the opera house became the main venue for community entertainment, hosting theatrical performances, socials, dances, and lectures. It was even used for roller skating and basketball games. But the Big Store was more than the sum of its parts. It also represented a personal story of family and community, of Icelandic immigration and acculturation to America. As Minneota native Margaret Pennings explains: "The ethnicity of the store was probably best seen in its

The Big Store in 1922—staffed by people who were more than managers and salesclerks, but rather members of an extended family that included the entire community of Minneota.

strong ethnic family bonding. This concept of family did not turn inward but instead . . . extended the sense of family to the entire community. . . . [It was] part of the personality of the Big Store." Sigurdur often demonstrated this familial notion by sending residents home wrapped in loaner coats or blankets during foul weather because he genuinely cared about their health. This "human" touch, rarely encountered in our often impersonal twenty-first century, helped make The Big Store a success. But The Big Store also thrived because its immigrant founders embraced the American tenet that everyone has the right to try—a concept alien to most of the world when Icelanders left the rocky shores of their native land in the nineteenth century for the rolling prairie of southwestern Minnesota. Like other immigrants, opportunity was all that Icelanders wanted—it was all O. G. and Sigurdur wanted, and the two entrepreneurs succeeded admirably.

By the early 1970s the Big Store no longer was the major commercial draw it once had been. The opera house had stopped functioning as the town's cultural and recreational core many years earlier. Like so many commercial businesses in small towns across the nation, The Big Store withered under an onslaught of retail chain stores. An improved highway system and a stubborn fondness for the automobile compelled many to abandon traditional small-town commercial districts in favor of large roadside retail outlets or major urban centers. The Big Store also suffered because the community's demographics were changing. The store "could not retain the close ties of family and ethnicity because an aging process was taking place. The Icelandic settlement was dying out." Finally, although the store might have been able to endure a while longer, there seemed to be no one that could assume control and run the enterprise the way the Anderson families had managed it.

Billy Anderson, Sigurdur's son, was still heading the Big Store when it went out of business in 1972. At the age of seventy-five, he had little idea what he was going to do: "A fellow that's been here as long as I have, who comes down here at 7:30 every morning and hangs around all day, then quits and has nothing to do—he's going to miss it, don't you think?" Billy passed away three years later. His ninety-five-year-old aunt, Anna Anderson, who worked at the store for more than six decades, died a day later. The legacy of the Andersons is still standing, however. Although no longer operating as a retail outlet, the Big Store continues to grace downtown Minneota. Today it is owned by the Society for the Preservation of Minneota's Heritage. The organization has restored much of the opera house and plans to once again use it as an entertainment venue. The main floor currently functions as storage, but many in Minneota hope it will one day house a community library. This "outstanding component of rural commerce" was added to the National Register in 1982.

J. A. Johnson Blacksmith Shop

ROTHSAY | WILKIN COUNTY

For since the birth of time, throughout all ages and nations,
Has the craft of the blacksmith been held in repute by the people.

HENRY WADSWORTH LONGFELLOW, "EVANGELINE"

The line from Longfellow's 1847 poem was displayed in Johannes Arndt
(J. A.) Johnson's Blacksmith Shop in Rothsay for decades. Johnson died
in 1978, after spending more than sixty years being held in repute by his
neighbors. He was a unique fellow who adapted his ancient craft to a rapidly changing world. Long after there were no more horses to shod, the
forge in Johnson's smithy continued to glow.[43]

Rothsay, a small community situated in northeastern Wilkin County,
about forty-five miles southeast of Moorhead, was incorporated in 1879
adjacent to the St. Paul, Minneapolis and Manitoba Railway (later the Great
Northern Railway). The town was named by an official of the railroad for
his Scottish hometown. The area around Rothsay was chiefly settled by Norwegian families in the 1860s, although Danish and Swedish immigrants
also made homes in the region. J. A. Johnson's roots in northeastern Wilkin
County were planted eight years before Rothsay was incorporated, when
his Norwegian grandparents settled in the area after spending two years in
Fillmore County in southeastern Minnesota. By 1880 the land surrounding
Rothsay was scattered with farmsteads and the community had developed
a modest agricultural trade. At this time the town consisted of a couple of
stores, four saloons, a railroad section house, a hotel, several homes, and
a blacksmith shop.

Blacksmithing was vital to emerging rural communities, since the
trade provided services necessary for economic survival, as John Hudson
observed in *Plains Country Towns:*

> *Blacksmiths were, second to general stores, the most common business in the*
> *inland towns. . . . Many [blacksmiths] forged farm tools of various sorts and,*
> *if they also possessed woodworking skills, manufactured farm implements.*
> *The blacksmith offered a general store of another sort: often a jack-of-all-trades,*
> *his skills could be applied to a variety of problems.*

Rothsay had its second blacksmith shop by the early 1880s. Others
followed, including a shop constructed by John Helgeson and Emil Krogh
in 1903. In 1912 J. A. Johnson became an apprentice to Helgeson, learning
the craft by shoeing horses and repairing wagon wheels, drills, and diggers.
Three years later he purchased the business from Helgeson.

Johnson's shop was located on Main Avenue West at the edge of the
business district. It was a simple structure indicative of most blacksmith

shops in Minnesota. Covered in clapboard siding and resting on a concrete foundation, it was a modest-sized, one-and-a-half-story, rectangular building with a gable roof and a false front accented with a bracketed cornice. A large door opening was centered at the south facade and another entrance marked the rear of the building. Rectangular windows flanked the entrances, a feature familiar to other parts of the structure. Much of the blacksmithing equipment inside the building was located near the windows, although light into the shop was also provided from the south entrance, which Johnson usually kept open during working hours. While a dirt floor surrounded the forge, most shop flooring was either concrete or wood planks.

Johnson forged many of his tools, including tongs, chisels, and hammers. He even built a threader and coupler, equipment employed as blacksmithing moved into the modern age. During the early years he spent much time sharpening and pounding plowshares and shoeing horses. The rafters in his shop were lined with numerous horseshoes varying in size. Smooth shoes were used during the warmer months and studded shoes were tacked to the hooves of horses in winter. Johnson usually fired his forge in the morning and ran it all day. Plowshares and other implements were heated in the forge, making them malleable so they could be hammered into proper shape on the adjacent anvil and then dipped in a nearby quenching tub. As the years passed and agricultural practices advanced, the equipment brought to Johnson's shop for repair changed—wagon wheels became rare and tractor wheels common, for example. While Johnson continued to fire his forge, it was not employed as often since much of the newer farming equipment was repaired by welding, a skill the blacksmith learned that continued to make him indispensable to the community. In 1936, local postal worker W. A. Redmann asked Johnson if he could build a vehicle to handle the mail carrier's snow-covered mail route. The result was a "snowmobile," an odd machine that many of today's off-roaders would envy. A mix of Ford Model A and Model T car parts, the vehicle's rear moved on tracks while the front was balanced on balloon airplane tires. For especially snowy roads, the front of the vehicle also featured runners. After driving the machine for nearly two decades, Redmann gushed to Cale Dickey, editor of the *Fergus Falls Daily Journal:* "There was not anything that rig couldn't run through."

In Johnson's later years he was unwilling to pine for the old ways. Without regret he changed as his craft changed. "I hated wagon work," he stated in 1973, "but not enough to quit," he finished with a grin. Johnson continued working at his shop until his death in 1978. His son Walter, who worked at the shop for many years, continued the business until his retirement in 1986. The Johnson family donated the shop to the Wilkin County Historical Society after Walter died the following year. The historical society has been a good steward of the property, restoring much of the building to its early twentieth-century form. Rothsay is presently considering purchasing the shop for use as an educational tool. Described by architectural historians Susan Granger and Kay Grossman as a "rare, intact example of the type of blacksmith shops which were common in small midwestern agricultural communities in the early to mid-twentieth century," the J. A. Johnson Blacksmith shop was included in the National Register in 1996.

Today the J. A. Johnson Blacksmith Shop is managed by the Wilkin County Historical Society.

First National Bank

On May 2, 1919 the *Fulda Free Press* boasted: "When the First National Bank of Fulda opened its doors for business on Thursday, April 24, 1919, this community became possessed of an addition to its business enterprise unequalled in a similar location anywhere in Minnesota." The newspaper's hyperbole can be forgiven since it was simply reflecting Fulda's excitement and pride in its new Beaux Arts–style financial building, an ornate structure that implied strength and security, demonstrating that the small agricultural community was growing up.[44]

Fulda, about ten miles southeast of Slayton in Murray County, was established along the northern edge of Seven Mile Lake in 1881. Four years later the Dickinson brothers formed the Bank of Fulda, a private financial institution that operated from a local commercial building, a common characteristic of midwestern banks in nascent communities in the late 1800s. Besides lending money and securing residents' savings, the bank of Fulda sold steamship tickets. Immigrant families that made a successful living in this country could purchase passage to America for family members residing in the homeland. Six years after the Bank of Fulda was founded the Martyn brothers also established a private bank. In 1897 the Martyns constructed a new brick building on St. Paul Street, Fulda's principal thoroughfare. Most of the building functioned as a general store, but a section was set aside for the brothers' bank. In 1901 the Martyn Brothers Bank was sold and the new owners obtained a state charter and operated the institution as the Farmers State Bank. By this time the Dickinsons' bank had been a state-regulated facility for almost a decade, but in 1902 the brothers acquired a national charter and renamed their State Bank of Fulda the First National Bank. In 1908, after they sold the business, a state charter was obtained by the new owners and the institution renamed the Citizens State Bank.

In 1910 local stockholders purchased the Farmers State Bank. After the state charter was dropped and a national charter obtained, Fulda had its second First National Bank. Eight years later management constructed a building solely for bank use. A symbol of Fulda's maturation, the structure was one of the most decorative buildings in the community and exhibited architectural elements common to late-nineteenth- and early-twentieth-century bank buildings. Historically, there has been no standard plan for banking houses, although their architecture often reflected the significance of the institution to the community. While some designs were simple and elegant, others were elaborate, even ostentatious. But whether graceful or extravagant, the architecture was intended to draw attention. Often Greek or Roman schemes were adopted, and sometimes Beaux Arts styles were employed, as with the Indiana National Bank in Indianapolis. For archi-

Today, First National Bank's architecture continues to reflect the strength and security that boosted the confidence of depositors in the early twentieth century.

tects and bankers, these ornate styles evoked confidence, a sense of security. Such emotional bolstering was important in an age without a Federal Deposit Insurance Corporation. Even if a bank was fiscally unstable it was commercially imprudent to convey that image.

The architectural style of the First National Bank in Fulda was reminiscent of Beaux Arts Classicism, a design popular from about 1890 to 1920. Although not nearly as grandiose as the Indiana National Bank, Fulda's national bank was definitely an eye-catcher, especially for a small town. The building was constructed by the Lytle Company of Sioux City, Iowa, a firm known for its distinctive commercial structures throughout southern Minnesota and Iowa. Situated adjacent to St. Paul Street, between Front Street and Second Street, the two-story bank was formed of gunmetal-colored brick and cream-colored terra cotta, a hard, fired clay often used for architectural ornamentation. The east facade of the two-story, rectangular structure featured single and paired pilasters accented with fluting, a series of rounded, parallel grooves, as well as decorative capitals. The pilasters framed large windows and a centrally located entrance that was highlighted by an ornate, flat hood, or miniaturized entablature, resting upon scrolled brackets, also known as consoles. Single and paired brick pilasters marked the north side of the building. A terra cotta bandcourse spanned the length of the east facade and north side just above and below window openings. The bank's cornice was accented with dentils, a series of small, rectangular blocks, and a brick parapet rose above the roof. The building's interior was dominated by marble and mahogany.

First National Bank became integral to the community. The financial institution was used for traditional banking purposes, but its large basement evolved into a meeting hall. Residents gathered in the basement for celebrations and banquets, and on election nights returns were received at the bank. But the financial institution was unable to remain solvent. On October 7, 1926, three years before the stock market crashed and the country plunged into economic depression, the bank closed its doors. First National's bankruptcy was a precursor of what was to come, but the financial house was hardly the first bank to tumble into receivership before depression "officially" arrived. Indeed, many banks were already failing by the early 1920s, victims of poor lending policies, declining farm prices, and low wages in mining and manufacturing. Excellent management at Citizens State Bank, however, allowed it to march through the Great Depression and emerge financially sound. In fact, only a month after the stock market destroyed the economic fortunes of millions, Citizens State Bank was seeking a larger building. The obvious choice was the wonderful structure erected by the stockholders of the defunct First National Bank.

Citizens State Bank operated from the former First National Bank Building for almost sixty years; however, management in the mid-1980s was not as fiscally vigilant as that which guided the institution through the tumultuous 1920s and 1930s. The bank closed in 1985, but was purchased by Bancorporation three years later. Bancorporation, whose chief shareholder is Frank Farrar, a former governor of South Dakota, now operates the facility as . . . First National Bank. Noted by Minnesota's National Register Historian Susan Roth as a well-preserved building that "commands an unusual prominence among the commercial buildings of Murray County's small towns," the First National Bank was added to the National Register in 1982.

✳ Barnard Mortuary

FERGUS FALLS | OTTER TAIL COUNTY

Everyone dies, which possibly makes mortuary science the vocation with the most job security. It is a profession that demands controlled squeamishness and a sensitive touch, qualities that Edward T. Barnard exhibited for nearly half a century as a mortician in Fergus Falls, an Otter Tail County community in northwestern Minnesota, roughly fifty miles southeast of Fargo-Moorhead. Barnard was well known and well liked, acquainted with numerous Otter Tail County families who looked to him and his earnest compassion when they lost someone dear. At his passing, local reverend Colvin G. Butler eulogized: "If one had the wisdom of a Solomon, the language of a Shakespeare, and the eloquence of a Demosthenes, he could not do full justice to the integrity, the achievements and the character of our beloved friend." Powerful sentiments—and if Barnard was only half the man the reverend lauded, he was more admirable than most.[45]

In this 1940 photograph, Edward T. Barnard stands at far right.

Barnard did not start out as a mortician. Born in Minneapolis in 1865, he was the son of a furniture craftsman. His father taught Edward the trade, skills the young man would employ later in life. Barnard initially chose to make his way in the newspaper business, arriving in Fergus Falls in April 1880 to work for A. J. Underwood, founder of the *Fergus Falls Journal*. Eight years later he married Lillian Nichols, a Fergus Falls resident who studied music in St. Paul before returning to her hometown. Barnard remained with the *Journal* for two decades, spending much time traveling throughout Otter Tail County soliciting subscriptions to the newspaper, a task that made him well acquainted with families in the region. Around 1900 he left the newspaper, opening a small furniture manufacturing and undertaking business at the corner of Lincoln Avenue and Court Street. A man who viewed the past as a treasure, he helped found the Otter Tail County Historical Society in 1927, serving as its secretary for twenty years, and later as its president. Besides amassing much of the historical society's collection, Barnard occasionally authored historical pieces. In the article "E. T. Barnard Recalls First Journal Press" he narrated an early history of the Journal and its old press. In part, Barnard wrote:

> *Mr. A. J. Underwood . . . was an old time country printer who served his time as an apprentice as well as a soldier in the Civil War. He looked over the field in this section, Fergus Falls, Ottertail City and Detroit Lakes, and finally decided to start the* Journal *in Fergus Falls. . . . As he was limited on capital he was compelled to buy an outfit that was secondhand. This included the press, which was as good as new, because a Washington Hand Press never wore out if decently taken care of.*

Penning histories and laboring for the historical society remained avocations, however, and most of Barnard's time was dedicated to his furniture and undertaking enterprise. By 1930, the undertaking business must have been good, for Barnard closed the furniture operation and concentrated full-time on mortuary science. That same year he and his son, Arthur, constructed a new, large mortuary on North Union Avenue, about a block and a half north of the Otter Tail River. The *Journal* noted that changing living conditions dictated a change in tradition, which influenced the Barnards to erect a larger building: "The modern trend of people living in small homes and apartments necessitates the care of the dead and the holding of the funeral outside the home."

The Barnards adopted the Mission style for their new building, a curious design since it was chiefly popular in California and the southwestern states and had passed from favor a decade earlier. Perhaps the Barnards believed that the design's simple, graceful forms best reflected their unique business—or maybe they just wanted to be different. The style is often defined by stuccoed walls, tile roofs, and Mission-shaped parapets and dormers. Also sometimes present are bell towers, one-story porches, balconies or balconets, arches, and quatrefoil windows, a window design formed of four intersecting foils, or rounded leaves, and loosely resembling a four-leafed clover.

Walter R. Dennis, a Fergus Falls architect, designed the Barnards' rectangular mortuary and local contractor J. P. Johnson erected it. Completed in November 1930, the two-story, stucco structure had a pent roof sheathed in tiles, as well as an asymmetrical east facade, a feature common to many

Completed in 1930 but no longer a mortuary, Edward T. Barnard's Mission-style building remains one of the most distinctive structures in downtown Fergus Falls.

Mission-style buildings. The first floor was dominated by a projecting bay composed of two entrances surmounted with arches flanking a large window opening and picture window. Another large window opening and picture window was adjacent the south end of the projecting bay. The facade's second-floor windows were crowned with arches and edged to the south by a larger opening covered by French doors and accented with a balconet with wrought-iron balustrade. The facade was further embellished with a Mission-shaped parapet above the balconet opening, which carried around to the east end of the building's south side. The remainder of the exterior was mostly unadorned, although a narrow porte cochere resembling a gateway to a southwestern ranch extended from the facade over the driveway at the south side of building. The mortuary's interior held an office, chapel, reception room, preparation room, and "slumber room," presumably a euphemism for body storage area. Casket display rooms were located in the basement.

Clearly pleased with the mortuary, the Barnards held a three-day open house in late November, inviting the public to view the handsome facility where someday they would be prepped for the hereafter. A section of the full-page open house advertisement read:

> It is with a certain degree of pride that we announce this formal opening of a new institution in Fergus Falls. It is not going to be formal so far as dress is concerned for we want you to come just as you are, inspect every part of the building and become better acquainted with what a modern mortuary really is.

The Barnards managed the mortuary together until 1945, the year Arthur died. Edward sold the business the following year to Benson and Wheeler, another mortuary firm, which resold the operation in the early 1950s to mortician Daniel Gearhart. It became the Nilson Funeral Home when it passed to Bruce Nilson in 1962. Edward Barnard was not around for all the transfers, having passed away in 1953. Today, Barnard's uniquely designed building with its uniquely commercial purpose continues to mark North Union Avenue in Fergus Falls, although it is now a residence. It was added to the National Register in 1986.

✳ Nelson & Albin Cooperative Mercantile Association Store

GODAHL | WATONWAN COUNTY

"We can all win together or we lose together, it's that simple." So wrote Melvin Nundahl, a citizen of Godahl, a tiny crossroads community straddling the border between Watonwan and Brown Counties in southern Minnesota, about eight miles north of St. James. The words reflect the collaborative spirit of the citizens of Nelson Township in Watonwan County and

Albin Township in Brown County, who have depended upon the Nelson and Albin Cooperative Mercantile Association Store in Godahl since its construction in 1894. Like the Viola Cooperative Creamery in Viola, the store in Godahl was possible because citizens banded together to create and manage an enterprise that would have been difficult to launch and operate by a single individual.[46]

Around 1891 the Norwegian and Swedish citizens of Nelson and Albin Townships first demonstrated their commitment to bettering the whole when area farmers established a cooperative creamery in Godahl. While Godahl is technically part of Nelson Township, the community actually extends over the boundary line into Albin Township as well, which seems fitting since the unincorporated village has been an important part of the commercial history of both townships. The name Godahl is drawn from the Norwegian words "Gode" and "Dahl." Together, the words mean "good valley." It is a pleasant name, but it is not the most accurate description of the region because south-central Minnesota is chiefly characterized by flat and sometimes rolling topography.

The successful operation of the creamery in Godahl convinced some area residents that a cooperative mercantile store should also be part of the village. A meeting was organized about spring 1894 to gauge public interest in the enterprise. Many at the gathering supported the idea, but many more were less enthusiastic. The notion was dropped and the meeting adjourned. But one of the plan's advocates, an individual whose name is seemingly lost to history, had not yet arrived at the gathering because he was soliciting supporters along the way. The success of his labors con-

Continuing to mark the southwest corner of Godahl's lone intersection, the Nelson and Albin Cooperative Mercantile Association Store has changed little since its facade was modified.

vinced residents to reconvene the meeting at a later date and again discuss the possibility of a cooperative general store. On April 20, 1894, citizens of Nelson and Albin Townships agreed to undertake the venture and formed the Nelson and Albin Cooperative Mercantile Association. Shares in the business cost $20, with $10 paid immediately and another $10 due within three months.

Several local men received contracts for completing various parts of the building. The roughly $1,000 structure was finished by August 1894. Resting on a stone foundation, the two-story, wood-framed building had a rectangular plan and a gable roof. The store was sheathed in clapboard siding and its east facade held an entrance flanked by rectangular windows. Smaller windows marked the facade's second floor as well as the building's sides.

The store was stocked with groceries, clothing, dry goods, farm implements, and hardware purchased in St. James and La Salle. Shoes sold for $1.25 a pair, while socks were 8 cents. Overalls cost 50 cents. Coffee was 25 cents a pound and syrup 30 cents a gallon. The store also acquired produce from local farmers, paying a penny a pound for potatoes and 11 cents a pound for butter, while eggs were purchased at 7 cents a dozen. Besides buying and selling goods, the store became a community link to the outside world by housing the local post office. The first telephone in the area was installed in the store in 1905. In later years the store even served as a branch of the Watonwan County Library. Along with the cooperative creamery, which was located just across the street, the store became a meeting and social event venue.

The store expanded the year after it was constructed, when a modest wood-framed warehouse was erected behind the building and stocked with

This photograph was likely taken sometime between 1896 and 1916, after the L-shaped addition was made to the north side and east rear and before the building received its current false-front facade.

nails and fencing. In 1896 the store was enlarged with a single-story addition that wrapped around its north side and west rear. These improvements demonstrated that the business was succeeding, and while the co-op would never evolve into a significant moneymaking venture, it always managed to stay afloat, even during the difficult period of the Great Depression. The same was not true of the cooperative creamery, which failed in 1956, unable to survive the transition from dairy farming to mostly cattle and crop farming that followed the Second World War. The Nelson and Albin Cooperative Mercantile Association purchased the creamery building, using it to warehouse feed, seed, and fertilizer.

The Nelson and Albin Cooperative Mercantile Association Store received exterior modifications in 1916, but it is uncertain precisely what the alterations included. It seems likely that the current false-front facade with large display windows was part of the modification. The small, wood-framed addition at the west end of the south wall was probably included in the effort. The building seems to have changed little since these alterations, however. Moreover, it still functions as a cooperative mercantile business, a remarkable achievement in an age of chain stores. Its somewhat remote location is likely partly responsible for its survival, but its longevity can also be attributed to its strong ties to the citizens of Nelson and Albin Townships, hardworking people with a stake in the success of the business. In fact, shares in the store are often passed from one generation to the next. Residents hope the community bond represented by the co-op is enough to keep the store operating for several more generations. Regardless of what the future holds, citizens of Nelson and Albin Townships will always be tied together by their common commercial heritage—"We can all win together or we lose together, it's that simple." The Nelson and Albin Cooperative Mercantile Association Store, the oldest continuously operating cooperative general store in Minnesota, was placed on the National Register in 1987.

✸ Original Main Street

SAUK CENTRE | STEARNS COUNTY

Main Street in Sauk Centre perhaps is in a class by itself as a National Register listing in Minnesota. It is also one of the most unusual National Register honorees in the country. Historic districts are typically placed on the National Register because of architectural cohesiveness, the constituents comprising the whole belong together. Not entirely so with Sauk Centre's Main Street, since the historical profiles of many of the commercial buildings edging the roadway have been altered, as have parts of the residential areas bordering the street to the north and south of the business core. But Sauk Centre's Main Street is the "original" Main Street, although

"Main Street," no longer a synonym for unenlightenment, represents a concept— a simpler, more sincere and upright way of life.

that does not mean it was the first thoroughfare tagged with the label. It was, however, the Main Street of great literature, the Main Street that startled, but then soothed, the American psyche. It was the Main Street that became a symbol, a metaphor for Anywhere, U.S.A.: "The town is, in our tale, called 'Gopher Prairie, Minnesota.' But its Main Street is the continuation of Main Streets everywhere. The story would be the same in Ohio or Montana, in Kansas or Kentucky or Illinois, and not very differently would it be told up York State or in the Carolina hills," wrote Sinclair Lewis.[47]

Even though Gopher Prairie was the stage for Main Street, a 1920 classic penned by Sinclair Lewis, citizens of Sauk Centre, the author's hometown, quickly surmised that their town was the writer's inspiration. But the Stearns County agricultural community about forty miles northwest of St. Cloud was hardly flattered, since Lewis's book was not a tribute to the virtues of small-town America. Instead, it was a scathing assault on the notion of the quaint, amicable village, depicting citizens who were often hypocritical, churlish, and just plain boring. For Lewis, village life consisted of "an unimaginatively standardized background, a sluggishness of speech and manners, a rigid ruling of the spirit by the desire to appear respectable. It is contentment . . . The contentment of the quiet dead, who are scornful of the living for their restless walking."

While literary critics applauded Lewis's insights, Sauk Centre was understandably miffed. At least the community could take solace knowing that Lewis was skewering small towns everywhere and was not just picking on Sauk Centre. Nevertheless, Sauk Centre was not anxious to acknowledge Lewis as a native son. In fact, the *Sauk Centre Herald* waited six months after publication of the runaway hit before admitting that Lewis was a hometown boy. Even so, time eventually mended Sauk Centre's wounds and today the city proudly proclaims itself the author's birthplace. More interestingly, time has altered the public perception of Main Street, not just in Sauk Centre, but everywhere. The negative connotation Lewis pasted to the moniker has peeled away and Main Street now means quite the opposite of what the Nobel Prize–winning author intended.

It is difficult to determine precisely when the transformation took place, but by the 1930s and 1940s filmmakers and writers were again espousing the goodness of small-town America. Main Street, the label for benightedness, was evolving into a synonym for genuine simplicity. It was a term that increasingly conjured an image of a more upstanding, although fading, way of life. Perhaps the conversion was complete after *Life* magazine journalist Henry Anatole Grunwald visited Sauk Centre in 1947, more than a quarter-century after the release of Lewis's book. Grunwald could not resist taking a few pokes at the town, noting Main Street's commercial environment consisting "chiefly of flat, boxlike two-story buildings, [with] wood still deceptively disguised by stucco," as well as the "cozy shallowness" of life along the thoroughfare. Grunwald also noted, however, that Sauk Centre and Main Street were not quite the unsophisticated entities that Lewis described so many years earlier.

Sauk Centre's Main Street about five years after the release of the best-selling novel that rattled small-town America

Sauk Centre earned a kind of special dignity after weathering Lewis's satirical pen. As Grunwald explained, the novel

> . . . lifted Sauk Centre, Minn. from among the other 1,422 American towns of approximately its own size, and carried its bigotries and bedroom secrets, its sturdy faiths and ridiculous foibles to the great world beyond. . . . Sauk Centre has finally, if dimly, realized that the world is watching and that it has a right to watch.

In the end, though, the "bigotries and bedroom secrets," the "ridiculous foibles," were largely forgotten, replaced with a view of a comforting Main Street, with a slower pace and intimacy commonly acknowledged before Lewis unfurled his literary whip.

The concept of Main Street is still prominent, probably because life appears so hurried today. What seems surprising is that variations on the notion are appearing in the Twin Cities area, with mixed-use developments such as "Park Commons" in St. Louis Park, "Gateway Village" in St. Paul, and "Heart of the City" in Burnsville. Some of these communities have never had a component even resembling a Main Street, yet they now want one, which should flatter outlying towns and convince city officials to follow the lead of places like Pipestone and Northfield, communities that preserved their late-nineteenth- and early-twentieth-century commercial cores and now attract visitors to an increasingly novel, welcoming streetscape.

As for Sauk Centre, it will remain forever tied to one of the greatest American authors. Sinclair Lewis, a man once damned as the "devil's own ghostwriter," is now viewed by the community—and the world—as a literary giant. His austere, wood-framed childhood home in Sauk Centre was made a National Historic Landmark in 1968. For many decades, now, the city has promoted itself as home to "The Original Main Street," a district of mostly simple commercial and residential buildings that gave rise to, in the words of architectural historians Jeffrey A. Hess and Heather E. Maginniss, a "profoundly influential concept . . . a way of analyzing, visualizing, and symbolizing the American small town." Original Main Street was placed on the National Register in 1994.

After *Main Street* hit the bookshelves, it took some time before Sauk Centre warmed to its native son, Sinclair Lewis.

PUBLIC HISTORY 7

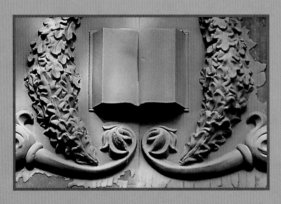

THE COURTHOUSE IN LAC QUI PARLE, a west-central Minnesota community near the eastern border of Lac qui Parle County, was only a temporary resident. In 1886 the simple, wood-framed, gable-roofed building was heisted—literally—off its foundation. The seat of government when the county was formed in 1871, Lac qui Parle officially lost the honor in 1889. In truth, though, county seat status all but vanished five years earlier after the Minneapolis and St. Louis Railway spurned the village and instead constructed a line through neighboring Madison to the west and Dawson to the southwest. Since many county residents believed it bad form to have a county seat without a rail line, Madison and Dawson became rivals for Lac qui Parle's crown. Two years after the railroad shattered the county status quo, 150 Madison residents guided forty teams to Lac qui Parle, lifted the courthouse from its site, and transported the structure fifteen miles west to Madison. The townsfolk in Dawson were peeved, of course, and many in Lac qui Parle were likely irked as well, but after three years of litigation the court awarded Madison the county seat.[48]

Madison and Dawson were not the only nineteenth-century Minnesota towns dueling to become government administration centers. In fact, in the late

1850s, there was a concerted effort to transfer the biggest prize, the Minnesota capital, from St. Paul on the Mississippi River to St. Peter on the Minnesota River in Nicollet County. Although the endeavor ultimately failed, it was a very early demonstration of how highly valued seats of government were to burgeoning Minnesota communities, the accompanying prestige almost always attracting settlement and increasing economic opportunity.

St. Paul's significance as the center of government in Minnesota was unashamedly evidenced in the late nineteenth century with the construction of the current State Capitol Building, one of the earliest properties added to the National Register in Minnesota. While counties could never hope to erect courthouses matching the architectural sophistication of Cass Gilbert's Renaissance-style structure in the capital city, they nevertheless built attractive venues for government administration, although it usually required some county prosperity first. The original Lac qui Parle County Courthouse, for example, was in keeping with the structural austerity so common to newly settled areas in nineteenth-century Minnesota. By 1899, however, one year after work began on the State Capitol Building, Madison had an aesthetically powerful Romanesque Revival–style courthouse composed of red brick trimmed with sandstone. Now a National Register building, it was a symbol of Madison's maturity, as well as an explicit acknowledgment of county leadership. Still, it was much more than a trophy awarded to Madison; it was an architectural beacon radiating civic responsibility and adherence to democratic ideals, a building that spoke to all in Lac qui Parle County.

Courthouses clearly are not the only attractive public structures in communities. City and town halls, police and fire stations, public schools and libraries, museums and park buildings, and even water towers can aid the visual appeal of towns, as can private construction like churches, lodges, commercial buildings, and houses. But whereas non-government architecture reflects the desires of a few, public design generally holds to the wishes of the masses. In late-nineteenth- and early-twentieth-century Minnesota, as in most of the country, that often meant public buildings architecturally demonstrating lofty morals and principles, a concept echoed by R. W. Sexton in his piece "Municipal Buildings Set Standards in Architectural Art," the first chapter for the 1931 volume *American Public Buildings of Today*:

> *Our public buildings encourage pride in the community, in the city, in the state and in the nation. They serve as a symbol of the civilization, culture and ideals of our country. It is fitting that they be beautiful, that they be designed in good proportion, in good taste, and that their beauty be accented by noble inscriptions, by beautiful mural paintings and by appropriate pieces of sculpture.*

Although *American Public Buildings of Today* was published at a time when the designs of public buildings were becoming less lavishly ornamented, Sexton nevertheless argued that many should remain monumental—that is, they should be designed and constructed as "monuments." While the monument notion faded somewhat during the architecturally reserved decades immediately following the Second World War, the concept was ingrained in pioneering Americans, an idealistic population attempting to cultivate prosperity and cultural enlightenment in a young nation. This idealism helps explain why many public buildings in early Minnesota and elsewhere, from hefty courthouses to petite libraries, drew so heavily from the styles of antiquity, designs described by Sexton as "the highest standard of architectural perfection." Even though some may deny the author's assertion, there is little debate that classical columns, pediments, domes, arches, and the like decorating public buildings of brick and stone symbolize the idea of monument.

Minnesota retains a number of extant monumental public buildings, many on the National Register, but not all reflecting Greek or Roman influences. The Mahnomen City Hall in Mahnomen, Mahnomen County, for instance, in no way resembles a Greek or Roman temple. Even so, the rustic building has a subtle dignity. Moreover, it is a tribute to its region of construction and will always stand as a reminder of depression-era relief efforts. In contrast, the diminutive Madison Carnegie Library, erected only a short time after the Lac qui Parle County Courthouse was built in Madison, clearly exhibits classical elements. Actually, its columned and pedimented main entrance coupled with the small dome projecting from its flat roof produces a building reminiscent of a miniaturized Roman Pantheon.

The following narratives tell the stories of a variety of National Register public structures, some more architecturally impressive than others. A government property like Norris Camp in Lake of the Woods County was never designed to visually compete with courthouses or city halls, and especially not with the truly fantastic institutional complexes the state built in the nineteenth and early twentieth centuries. Instead, Norris Camp reflects pragmatic government architecture, the aesthetics of the buildings far less important than the camp's purpose of construction. Of course all public structures, even those designed to impart a noble message, were created solely to make people's lives better. In other words, no matter how glorious or restrained, public construction exists for the supremely practical purpose of governance.

Howard Lake City Hall

HOWARD LAKE | WRIGHT COUNTY

The village of Howard Lake was reaching maturity by the end of the nineteenth century. Situated about forty-five miles northwest of the Twin Cities, the community nestled alongside a lovely body of water that gave the town its name. Improvements in the area that would eventually form Howard Lake began in the 1850s, although a village would not be incorporated until 1879. It was thriving by the 1890s, consisting of several merchant establishments, two hotels, two livery stables, two grain elevators, a bank, a lumberyard, mill, and more. Howard Lake even had three law firms. It was likely a healthy place to live since medical treatment could be obtained

Constructed in 1905, the Howard Lake City Hall is sometimes noted as a Romanesque-style building, most evident by its many arched openings, but its dominate architectural feature is its octagonal corner tower, which articulates Queen Anne style.

from four physicians. Seven churches were available for treating the soul. Maybe the most obvious sign that Howard Lake was headed in the right direction was its large and attractive village hall. Constructed in 1891, the two-story, brick-veneer building featured a mansard roof punctuated with a steeple. The prominent structure signified Howard Lake's pride, as well as its faith in the future. But while things appeared rosy for the village at the beginning of the new century, 1904 would prove a very bad year.[49]

Early in the morning on January 17, 1904, fire erupted in Thomas Jordan's saloon. Although the tavern was a total loss, thankfully no one was in the building at the time. This would not be Howard Lake's only major blaze during the year. In late September, another fire consumed the Howard Lake Roller Mills, one of the chief commercial enterprises in the village. Again, the entire building and its contents were lost. The fire that stung the community most, however, was that which consumed the town's principal landmark, its handsome village hall. Coming only a month after Thomas Jordan's place was destroyed, the fire wiped out the building and all town records. Records for the local Masonic lodge that were stored in the hall were lost as well, as were files from a physician's office and law firm. What was sadly ironic was that the fire department also filled a portion of the public structure, a practice common to rural communities. Luckily, most of the equipment from the fire department was saved, but firefighters had to rouse the town by pulling the fire bell rope while standing outside the building. Fortunately, no one was hurt in the fire. While citizens were again grateful that no one was injured when the Howard Lake Roller Mills flamed several months later, the run of bad luck must have felt like piling on. By the end of that devastating year, the populace of Howard Lake could at least take comfort in the knowledge that a new and better village hall was almost complete.

Discussion of building a new village hall began immediately after the old one was destroyed, and the village council was under pressure to come up with a construction and funding plan that was acceptable to the public. The *Howard Lake Herald* applied a good deal of the pressure. In late February, it printed a column voicing its opinion on the matter. The article noted what type of building should be constructed and how it should be financed. Although the *Herald* explained it had "no desire to dictate to the village council nor to anyone in authority, but simply to give the facts as they are for the benefit of [the] reader," it quickly became apparent that public officials were attentive to what the newspaper had to say. The plan embraced by the village council essentially mirrored the recommendations of the *Herald*.

With the fire still fresh in the public's mind, officials decided to erect a hall made of brick, a building that would be more durable than the previous brick-veneer structure. The cost of construction was limited to no more that $9,000, a figure determined by combining $4,000 in insurance from the old building with a $5,000 bond issue. The construction contract was awarded to F. A. Hancock in late July for $7,925, although it was later increased by $300 when the village council decided to add a few more embellishments to the new building. Hancock began work right away and within two months the building's walls had reached the second-story level. The building was formally opened in early January 1905, even though some minor work still remained. Interestingly, by the time the structure was dedicated it was known as "City Hall," implying that either the community's status had been upgraded from a village to a city just prior to the building's completion, or officials figured that incorporation as a city was inevitable.

Dedication ceremonies for the new building included a few speeches from dignitaries, a couple of piano and vocal solos, and a reading. A formal ball with orchestra capped the celebration. Of course, the talk of the festivities centered on the new city hall. It was an elegant building and probably more attractive than the structure it replaced. Like the old building, the new city hall was the most architecturally distinctive edifice in Howard Lake. While exhibiting Romanesque architectural elements, the building's outstanding feature was its octagonal-shaped corner tower, which reflected the Queen Anne style. The tower supported an open balcony that was crowned by a pointed roof. The rectangular, core section of the building was covered by a steep-pitched hip roof. Two brick chimneys punctuated the north side of the roof, one near either end of the building. The ground level of the south and west facades held several semicircular-arched openings accented with molded brick hoods. Many of the structure's other openings were surmounted by flat arches formed from stretcher bricks. A decorative brick stringcourse, a horizontal masonry course, often molded and projecting from a building's face, separated the first floor from the second floor.

Like many small-town public buildings, Howard Lake's city hall was a multifunctional facility. A post office filled the southwest corner of the first floor and was accessed through the entrance at the base of the tower. A postal workroom occupied the remaining first-floor space at the west end of the building. A barbershop was situated immediately east of the post office. The barbershop abutted the main hallway, which was gained through an entrance in the south facade. The hallway led to city offices, a community reading room, and the courtroom at the north side of the building. Additional office space was located adjacent the north wall of the hallway. The fire department occupied the east end of the city hall. Entrance to the fire department was made through one of the arched openings at the east end of the building's south facade. Double doors shielded the large opening. The department's pumper (fire engine) and hose cart were likely stored just beyond the double doors. The building's second floor was dominated by an auditorium, which was accessed through an arched entry immediately east of the fire department entrance.

The Howard Lake City Hall evolved over the years but maintained its multipurpose use. The auditorium was being used as a basketball venue by the 1920s. (Games must have been scheduled when courtroom proceedings were finished for the day.) A municipal liquor store was established in the building in the 1930s. The city hall also began housing the public library at some point. Eventually the post office moved out of the building. The city, however, continued to use the structure, but now municipal offices were located in the space vacated by the post office. The fire department also moved to a new location. The department's large arched entrance was filled with brick. At the close of the twentieth century this end of the building was being used for an off-sale liquor store. By 2001 the city realized that its aging city hall was in need of maintenance and initiated a reuse and rehabilitation study. Placed on the National Register in 1979, the century-old city hall was still the most prominent building in town, and the city wanted it to remain for a while longer. Today, the picturesque building continues to edge the lake that inspired the community's name.

✳ Louisburg School

LOUISBURG | LAC QUI PARLE COUNTY

Sin pays. At least many early residents of Louisburg believed so. At the beginning of the twentieth century the town had one saloon, an enterprise that generated considerable controversy. Some in the community did not want the tavern, arguing that the sale and consumption of alcohol was morally reprehensible. Others disagreed, believing pious busybodies should mind their own business. There was also a practical reason why the "wets" wanted the "drys" to ease up. The annual license fee on the saloon funded a great deal of improvements to the town. During 1906, one year after the bar was established, the liquor license fee was $600. The following year it was $700, and by 1910 it was $800. For a tiny town with a tiny treasury, those sums were significant incentive to keep the saloon. But even though the wets were getting their way, Ole Anderson, one of the leading voices for the drys, continued to believe the prohibitionist cause would eventually succeed: "A ship may be driven backward or out of its course by storms. A good course may suffer setbacks or seem to be completely sidetracked by unprincipled men, but I still believe the time will come when intemperance will meet its David." The wets in Louisburg met their "David"

A circa 1911 photograph of Louisburg, with its new schoolhouse in the background near the edge of town

in 1912, when Ole Anderson and others filed a lawsuit to halt the sale of spirits in the town. At the heart of the legal strategy was Louisburg's brick schoolhouse, an attractive Victorian building that had only recently been constructed.[50]

Ole Thompson and William R. Thomas founded Louisburg in 1887, almost twenty years prior to the battle between the wets and drys. Located near the South Dakota border in northern Lac qui Parle County, the community came about after the St. Paul, Minneapolis and Manitoba Railway (later the Great Northern Railway) constructed a siding into the area. The siding provided local farmers a means for shipping their grain to metropolitan centers. But even though Louisburg was tied to a major rail line, it would never evolve into a notable shipping or receiving point. Its modest economic future was set early on when the railroad decided that Louisburg had limited financial potential. As a result, the railroad made few improvements to the town. In fact, for several years Louisburg did not even have a railroad depot, even though it had a depot agent. The agent, a man named Clifford, was eventually transferred to Albin, South Dakota, where he committed suicide. In 1893, not long after Clifford decided this world was not for him, Louisburg finally received its depot.

While Louisburg did not get a depot until late, it at least had a schoolhouse by 1891, an indication of the importance newly founded towns placed on education. It is uncertain how the school looked, but it was probably a simple one-room building. Between the early 1700s and mid-1900s, rural school buildings were frequently one-room structures. As a community grew, the schoolhouse was often enlarged by adding a second one-room building. If the population decreased, the second building could easily be removed. As some rural towns matured, however, citizens chose to build more architecturally grand schoolhouses. This is what Louisburg decided to do in 1911. Officials chose Kilroy T. Snyder to design the building. The construction contract was given to Fred Knepfer, and E. Schake was awarded the excavation work. Unfortunately, little is known about any of the men. The site for the school building was located just north of the town's core, immediately outside the community's incorporated limits. Excavation at the site was finished around mid-July and the schoolhouse's concrete foundation was almost done by the end of that month. The entire building was nearly complete by the start of the fall session in early September. All that remained was the installation of the school bell, which was taken from the old schoolhouse. It was hanging in the new building's belfry by mid-September.

The two-story, brick school building was impressive. It had a hip roof that was accented with a rectangular, wood-framed bell tower at its southeast corner. The tower was capped with a pyramidal roof and its belfry had semicircular-arched openings with wood balustrades. Narrow window

Appearing somewhat worn by the turn of the twentieth century, the Victorian schoolhouse was vital to the prohibitionists' agenda in Louisburg in 1912.

openings surmounted by segmental arches surrounded the building at both the first and second floors. Smaller window openings marked basement walls. The recessed main entrance was crowned with a semicircular arch. The entrance was shielded by double doors, each holding a single light. The doors were edged by narrow sidelights and topped by a fanlight. A concrete panel reading "Public School" was situated immediately above the entrance arch. The Victorian design of the school building was appropriate, since the style reflected the importance of the institution to the community—its nobility of purpose.

It is unclear if the drys in Louisburg influenced the placement of the schoolhouse just outside the town's corporate limits, but one year after the school building was constructed they took advantage of its location to push their no-alcohol agenda. State law declared that no liquor establishment could be located within 1,500 feet of a schoolhouse that was situated in unincorporated territory. Although Louisburg's tavern was within the corporate limits of the town, it was still only 1,100 feet from the schoolhouse, and thus its owners were in violation of state statute. The local sheriff issued injunction papers to the saloon's proprietors only a short time before the bar's liquor license was due for renewal. Legal maneuverings followed on both sides. The argument eventually found its way to the Minnesota State Supreme Court, which lightly brushed it aside, stating that because the saloon's liquor license had long since expired there was no issue for the Court to address. Surely disappointed, it is likely the wets wished to rebuild in Louisburg farther from the school, but at least for the next several years the drys had greater influence in town and no liquor license was granted.

Although employed as a political tool early on, Louisburg School went on to function admirably as an institution of higher learning, educating the community's youth for several decades. As originally planned, the first floor was for younger students and the second floor was intended as a high school. Curiously, it appears that high school courses were never taught in the school. It is possible that resources for a high school were lacking, or maybe there just were not enough students to warrant a high school. Historically, it was not unusual for some children in rural areas to attend early grades but not later ones. Some of the children were from farming families and parents often expected teen children to help with labor on the farm. Moreover, Louisburg never evolved into a town with a large population. As late as the mid-1980s the community only had about fifty citizens. It may simply have been more economical for the area's few high school students to attend classes elsewhere. Eventually, the school stopped serving younger students as well. In the 1960s, rural schools in Lac qui Parle County were consolidated and many children were bussed to other schools, including those children in Louisburg. As a result, many small country schools were left vacant. By 1985, Louisburg School was privately owned and was being used for storage, but the building was remarkably intact. One year later it was listed on the National Register as one of the best examples of Victorian school architecture in west-central Minnesota. Presently still used for storage, the school looks more worn than it did in 1985, but its substantial brick construction implies that it will remain for some time.

✳ Fergus Falls State Hospital Complex

FERGUS FALLS | OTTER TAIL COUNTY

Minnesota has many architecturally exceptional National Register buildings. The National Farmers' Bank in Owatonna, for example, is a striking Prairie-style structure that was listed on the National Register in 1971. It received National Historic Landmark status in 1976. Duluth Central High School at the intersection of Lake Avenue and Second Street in Duluth is also inspiring. The grand Richardsonian Romanesque–style building was added to the National Register in 1972. New Ulm may have the most visually arresting building in Minnesota. Its early-twentieth-century post office resembles a magnificent gingerbread house, superbly reflecting the community's German heritage. It was placed on the National Register in 1970. While each of these structures elicits adjectival gushing, none is as jaw-dropping as the Fergus Falls State Hospital in Fergus Falls, about fifty miles southeast of Fargo-Moorhead.[51]

Construction of the Fergus Falls State Hospital began atop a hill at the northern edge of the city in 1888, nearly three years after the state legislature determined that a new mental health facility was required to alleviate

A sprawling facility, the Fergus Falls State Hospital Complex is one of the most architecturally impressive properties in Minnesota.

pressure on Minnesota's other two state psychiatric hospitals. The state's first mental health complex was built at St. Peter in 1866 and was followed by a hospital at Rochester in 1877. Coincidentally, the Center Building at the St. Peter facility was listed on the National Register in 1986. It took nearly twenty years for the Fergus Falls State Hospital to be completed, although patients were admitted as early as 1890 when the first section was finished. Construction of the facility proceeded from west to east throughout the 1890s and was mostly done by the beginning of the twentieth century. Final components of the Administration Building would not be finished until 1907, however.

Prominent Minneapolis architect Warren B. Dunnell designed the million-dollar crescent-shaped hospital. Dunnell designed several public buildings during his career, including the Minnesota Training School for Boys in Red Wing and the Owatonna State School Administration Building in Owatonna. For the hospital in Fergus Falls, Dunnell generally adhered to the design concepts of Thomas S. Kirkbride, an internationally recognized mental health practitioner convinced that thoughtful planning of psychiatric hospitals could aid the treatment of patients. In his 1854 book *On the Construction, Organization and General Arrangements of Hospitals for the Insane,* Kirkbride advocated narrow buildings, which allowed every room to have an outside window. He also believed that patients should have single rooms and that the patient wings flank a prominent administration section. Fireproof construction was also essential. Additionally, the hospital site should be large enough for gardening and farming, and grounds should be available for patient exercising and privacy.

Dunnell's design for the Fergus Falls State Hospital blended Chateauesque, Beaux Arts Classical, and Romanesque Revival elements,

Ornate octagonal towers flank the central tower and are crowned with steeply pitched roofs punctuated with elaborate finials.

creating a stunning, almost majestic, tribute to Kirkbride's ideal. The imposing Administration Building marked the center of the hospital and was flanked by east and west wings that served mainly as patient wards. The wings were recessed from the Administration Building and together measured nearly a third of a mile long. The entire structure was chiefly formed of cream-colored brick manufactured at nearby Pelican Rapids. The symmetrical three-story wings had full raised basements and finished attics. The wings were composed of a number of parts. The east wing was made up of the East Center Wing, Northeast Wing, and East Detached section, while the West Center Wing, Southwest Wing, and West Detached section formed the west wing. The pitched-roofed wings were accented with semicircular and square pavilions. Semicircular pavilions were capped with cone-shaped roofs, while flat roofs covered square pavilions. Each wing also featured barred verandas, as well as single and paired windows set within either rectangular or arched openings. Hip-roofed dormers pierced the roof of each wing. The roofs of the East Detached and West Detached sections were further embellished with brick and sandstone cupolas covered by pyramidal roofs.

Even though the ornate patient wards were impressive, the wings were trumped by the Administration Building, a fantastic structure that exuded strength. The three-story, hip-roofed building had a dentil cornice and featured single and paired windows set within either rectangular or arched openings. The building's dominant features were three towers that marked the southeast facade. The square, eight-story central tower was capped with a steeply pitched pyramidal roof that flared near the eaves. The point of the roof was punctuated with a finial. The tower was accented with a corbel cornice and was pierced by rectangular and arched window openings. A large, semicircular opening was located at the base of the tower and held a recessed entrance. Four-story octagonal corner towers flanked the central tower. Each tower had a pendant cornice and was crowned with a mock balustrade and a steeply pitched octagonal roof that terminated in a finial. Like the central tower, the corner towers had both rectangular and arched window openings.

The hospital began receiving patients on July 29, 1890, when an Otter Tail judge sentenced two men to the facility. The next day another eighty-one patients were admitted, all but one from the hospital in St. Peter. These early patients were all men with occupations that included farmer, laborer,

The stunning Fergus Falls State Hospital in 1915, eight years after its principal showpiece, the Administration Building, was completed.

blacksmith, carpenter, shoemaker, baker, sailor, and "tramp." Most were foreign-born and suffered from a variety of ailments such as overwork, fright, loneliness, epilepsy, and typhoid fever. Others were admitted because they were heartbroken over the loss of a wife or girlfriend. Still others were processed into the hospital for what seem like odd or vague reasons, such as "financial troubles" or "hereditary" problems. As more of the complex was completed women were admitted into the hospital as well. Eventually, Fergus Falls State Hospital grew to have the largest population of any of the state mental health hospitals. By the late 1920s, it had an average daily commitment approaching 1,700.

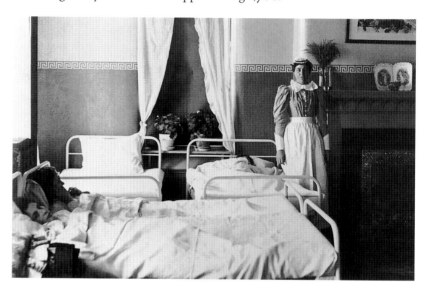

Women were first admitted to the hospital in 1893, seven years before this photograph was taken.

From the beginning the hospital had a somewhat progressive view of mental health care, a characteristic instilled by its first superintendent, Alonzo P. Williamson, a graduate of Hahnemann Medical College in Philadelphia. Williamson believed that voluntary admission to psychiatric facilities was better than forced incarceration because disorders were often advanced by the time the court assigned a troubled individual to a hospital. Williamson argued: "If the law was changed so as to admit these people before their cases became so severe, they would have a better chance of recovery." By 1910 the law allowed for voluntary admissions. Williamson also advocated limited restraint of patients: "Absolute non-restraint is not always practicable . . . [but] when restraint is deemed necessary, only the minimum amount to meet the necessities of each case should be applied."

By the late 1970s, society viewed many mental health hospitals as antiquated rather than progressive. The concept of "deinstitutionalization" became the standard, and mentally impaired individuals were often placed in group homes instead of large hospitals. As with other state psychiatric facilities, the population at Fergus Falls plummeted. Today, Fergus Falls State Hospital is known as the Fergus Falls Regional Treatment Center. Presently, it has a population of about one hundred, most with addiction disorders. The hospital is suffering neglect and there is concern among many that the complex may eventually be demolished. Some are hoping that the stately hospital, which was placed on that National Register in 1986, will find a new purpose, possibly as a college campus, or maybe as offices, apartments, or a grand resort. But the sheer size of the complex (179 acres encompassing numerous buildings) makes its reuse problematic, and preservation of the hospital has ardent opponents. One local resident remarked: "Let's face it; it needs to be blown up. . . . I doubt if my wife would want to go to a luxury hotel that used to be a 2,000-bed mental hospital." Perhaps others are less squeamish and more open to finding a way to make the fantastic facility economically viable.

✳ Pipestone Water Tower

PIPESTONE | PIPESTONE COUNTY

In 1892, the *Engineering Record* sponsored a water tower design competition. Since the minds behind the publication believed that water tower planners "should not erect structures . . . to be an offense to the eyes of this and future generations," they demanded that entrants illustrate towers that were practical yet handsome. The winning entry, announced the following year, was a stone octagonal structure crowned with a belvedere. Whether or not a water tower employing the design was ever constructed is uncertain, but the Highland Park Water Tower in the northwestern corner of St. Paul's Highland Park closely approximates the plan. Architect Clarence W. ("Cap") Wigington's wonderful brick and stone octagonal sentry was placed on the National Register in 1986.[52]

Unlike the structure in Highland Park, most water towers are rarely handsome, since many communities seem to view them as utilitarian forms not worthy of architectural effort. But for an edifice that often rises hundreds of feet into the air, literally blotting out the sun at times, aesthetic embellishment would seem a requirement. In the early 1920s, the citizens of Pipestone bucked the trend of no-frills water towers when they erected an eye-catching elevated tank near the intersection of Second Street Northeast and Sixth Avenue Northeast. Of course the folks in Pipestone were always a creative lot. In 1894, for instance, while suffering through a horrendous drought, townspeople tried to induce Mother Nature to shed some tears by pummeling the clouds with cannonballs, an event recorded in a local history:

On June 15 the heavens were bombarded, but without the desired results, although there was a heavy dew that night. On the evening of June 20 a cloud appeared in the sky and the experiment was tried again, and for more than an hour the continual boom of Pipestone's artillery was heard. The whole sky became overcast, but no rain fell. . . .

The rain eventually came, though, and Pipestone blossomed into an attractive agricultural community.

Situated in southwestern Minnesota less than ten miles east of the South Dakota border and about forty miles southwest of Marshall, Pipestone was named for the pipestone formations in the area. Technically known as catlinite, the soft, red stone was quarried for centuries by Native Americans, who often used it to make ceremonial pipes. Pipestone was platted in the mid-1870s and within only a few decades its prosperity was showing. The impressive Calumet Hotel, a stone Italianate structure,

Since Pipestone's 1921 water tower demands visual homage from residents, the community ensured it was worth looking at.

was erected in 1888. The Richardsonian Romanesque city hall followed in 1896, only to be topped four years later by a striking Beaux Arts courthouse. Each building has since been honored with a National Register listing. To quench the thirst of a growing population, the town erected a waterworks plant in the years 1887–88. The facility was antiquated by the early 1920s, convincing officials to launch a huge water works construction program to keep pace with the ever-expanding community.

In 1920, the *Pipestone County Star* gushed over Pipestone's growth during 1919: "All Previous Years Outdistanced in Matter of Local Improvements—Mammoth New School Building—Nearly Fifty New Residences Erected—Many Homes Remodeled—All Parts of City Thrive." The newspaper also noted expectations for 1920: "Buildings and Other Work Already Planned, Amount to an Enormous Total—Immense Oil Distributing Plant to be Constructed—More Factories to be Built—New Water Works Plant." The planned water works plant consisted of a well, a brick and tile pumping station, a 500,000-gallon concrete reservoir, a 150,000-gallon concrete storage tank, and numerous water and sewer lines. Even though the city was eager to complete the facility, legal wrangling held up construction for several months. By June 1920, the legal dispute resolved, the city council voiced its anxiousness to continue the project: "It has been fully demonstrated and agreed upon that absolute necessity demands that the new proposed water plant be proceeded with as little delay as possible." The Campbell Construction Company of Minneapolis was awarded the contract for the reservoir in August and J. W. Hunt and Sons of Pipestone was given the contract for the pumping plant building the next month. Campbell was also chosen to erect the water tower, although the contract was not let until the following April. Together, the expense of the structures totaled almost $40,000.

Pipestone's water tower was designed as an elevated tank rather than as the more common standpipe. Reflecting older technology than elevated tanks, standpipes are tall, columnar holding receptacles often encased within masonry towers. Rising from a ground-level foundation, they usually contain water throughout their length. In contrast, elevated tanks are large holding vessels raised well above a ground-level foundation, frequently resting upon a framework of metal members. Although standpipes were built well into the twentieth century, as demonstrated by the 1932 Washburn Park Water Tower in South Minneapolis, an intriguing National Register structure reminiscent of a pilastered bullet, the technology eventually gave way to elevated tanks. Elevated tanks were often cheaper and more stable than standpipes. They matched or surpassed the capacity of the old water tower design because they were formed with a larger-diameter tank. Moreover, standpipes demanded a large body of water to support the effective head, a problem ameliorated with elevated tanks.

Only a few years after he finished the design of the Brainerd Water Tower, St. Paul engineer L. P. Wolff completed the plan of the Pipestone tower. Not surprisingly, the structures were almost identical, although the Pipestone tower was somewhat more svelte. Like the Brainerd tower, Wolff understood that the Pipestone Water Tower would be a landmark—a landmark that greeted visitors even before they entered the corporate limits, so he shunned the utilitarian water tower form of a metal tank supported upon a metal framework. Instead, the 140-foot-high Pipestone tower was engineered as a poured concrete structure resembling the handle of a torch. The 28-foot-diameter shaft, decorated with pilasters and punctuated with several arched window openings, was crowned by a 40-foot-diameter holding tank. The shaft and tank were visually divided by a walkway with balustrade that encircled the tower.

In 1975, engineer Edmund C. Percey lamented ho-hum water tower designs, noting that the conspicuous structures should "be able to be lived with and not . . . just tolerated." Of course officials in Pipestone understood that more than fifty years earlier, as if realizing their water tower would one day become a defining symbol of the community. Percey's argument generally echoed the view of the *Engineering Record* from 1892—that water towers not be "an offense to the eyes." The attractive Pipestone Water Tower still stands, even though it was removed from service in 1976 after developing severe leaks. Refurbished in 1990, it is currently a component of a roadside rest area. It was listed on the National Register in 1980, six years after its sister tower in Brainerd.

✳ New Ulm Post Office

NEW ULM | BROWN COUNTY

What a difference a week can make. On April 18, 1908, the *Brown County Journal* in New Ulm, roughly ninety miles southwest of the Twin Cities, declared that construction of the community's new federal post office would likely be delayed for some time. New Ulm wanted a larger appropriation for the building and it did not appear that Congress would address the issue during the current session. But it helps to have friends in high places, and New Ulm had a friend in James T. McCleary, a former congressman from western Minnesota who happened to be the Second Assistant Postmaster General. On April 25, the *Brown County Journal* gleefully reported that events had suddenly changed: "James T. McCleary . . . came to the rescue and appeared before the [Committee of Public Buildings and Grounds] and at his request the committee increased the appropriation for New Ulm by $20,000. . . . This will give New Ulm an excellent public building and will answer all purposes for many years to come." Excellent public building

Looking like an elaborately carved giant gingerbread house, the New Ulm Post Office remains one of the most aesthetically pleasing buildings in Minnesota.

was an understatement, since the New Ulm Post Office would be one of the most visually impressive buildings in Minnesota.[53]

New Ulm was founded by German immigrants in 1854, many of whom hailed from Ulm, Germany. New Ulm was a "planned" German settlement, as were Amana, Iowa; Teutopolis, Illinois; New Harmony and Ferdinand, Indiana; New Braunfels and Fredericksburg, Texas; and Germantown, Ephrata, and Bethlehem, Pennsylvania. After immigrating to America, the families that established New Ulm made their way to Chicago. Representatives of the group then traveled to Iowa and Minnesota to find an acceptable location for a new town. Although the Iowa contingent failed to locate a place for the colony, the Minnesota party found a promising site along the west bank of the Minnesota River, only a few miles from Le Sueur. When families arrived at the place from Chicago, however, many were unhappy with the location. Another site further up the Minnesota River, just north of the junction of the Cottonwood River, was determined a better spot for the settlement. Even though no town had yet been platted, on October 7, 1854, the association had found New Ulm.

In the years 1855–56, a German immigrant group from Cincinnati merged with the settlers in New Ulm to form the German Land Association. The association rapidly built up New Ulm by clearing land for farming and building homes, stores, and even a log courthouse. In spring 1857 the community was incorporated as a town. As the town matured and finer residences and commercial establishments were erected, no pure architectural style emerged. Instead, residents, many of whom were artisans, skilled stonemasons, and brickworkers, adapted styles from their homeland with their own designs. This independent spirit would also be reflected in the design of the community's federal post office.

Prior to the early 1900s New Ulm's post office had been located in various commercial structures, but in 1901 the federal government approved a building specifically for the postal service. Delays pushed construction back several years. One of the delays was brought about by the citizens of New Ulm, who believed that the modest original plan of the post office was embarrassing, "plainly [showing] a lack of architectural beauty." The residents of New Ulm sought a better building through a larger appropriation than the $30,000 the government had set aside for the project. Just when it appeared the government would sit on the request, Congressman McCleary came through. Apparently Congress really liked McCleary, and James Knox Taylor, the government's supervising architect, must have been fond of him as well, for he promised McCleary and the people of New Ulm that the new post office would be "special."

Steward and Hagar Construction Company of Janesville, Wisconsin, began erecting the building at Center Street and Broadway Avenue in March 1909. The 72- by 55-foot, one-and-a-half-story post office was completed in spring 1910. The building was the most striking structure in New Ulm and one of the most impressive buildings in Minnesota. Designed with the heritage of New Ulm in mind, the post office reflected elements of the German Renaissance style, including decorative detailing and the use of both brick and stone. It also featured stepped gables, like the German Renaissance–style firehouse erected by the city of Elmira, New York, in 1898. But to say New Ulm's post office was strictly German Renaissance style would be unfair, since it also included baroque elements like scrolls, cartouches, and a very steeply pitched roof. The building's walls were formed of red brick interrupted by light-colored terra cotta courses, which created an arresting visual contrast. A granite water table marked the base of first-floor walls. The walls were pierced by paired windows surmounted by multipane transoms and the south facade featured a main entrance embraced by pilasters supporting a Doric pediment. Three elaborate dormers crowned the south facade, with the two outside dormers accented with pinnacle pediments. The peak of the stepped central dormer held a blunt-end finial, a design that matched that of the building's gable ends.

Clearly a "special" building, New Ulm's post office served the community for generations, but its "brutally dramatic" design was not enough to keep it functioning as the community's postal center. With an expanding population and increased mail load, the city was forced to build a larger post office in 1976. The old post office is presently owned by Brown County and the city of New Ulm and currently houses the Brown County Historical Society. The wonderful New Ulm Post Office was added to the National Register in 1970.

Tucked into a residential section of Cannon Falls, Firemen's Hall looks quaint today, but in 1888 it was a welcome improvement to a community that had suffered two major fires.

✳ Firemen's Hall

CANNON FALLS | GOODHUE COUNTY

Mrs. O'Leary's cow probably got a bad rap. For more than a century the Great Chicago Fire has been blamed on a bovine that supposedly kicked over a lantern, igniting the O'Learys' barn and initiating one of the worst fire disasters in American history. There is little doubt the blaze started in the O'Learys' outbuilding the evening of October 8, 1871, but recent evidence indicates it was likely the fault of a one-legged man named Daniel Sullivan. It seems Sullivan went into the barn to milk one of the O'Learys' cows. Apparently the match he lit to illuminate the darkened building was not completely extinguished when he tossed it aside. The inferno that followed devastated almost all of Chicago's downtown and north side, killing roughly 250 people. Around the time the Windy City was in flames, another huge fire was burning about 250 miles to the north in northeastern Wisconsin. The fire swept through the pine forests surrounding the community of Peshtigo. Unlike big cities, tiny Peshtigo had only one fire engine, a hand-operated pumper. It didn't help. Only an hour after the conflagration ignited Peshtigo's first building, every structure in town was gone. Other communities and farms near the town suffered a similar fate. As awful as the death toll was in Chicago, it hardly compared with the loss of life near Peshtigo, where nearly 1,200 perished.[54]

Handicapped by a lack of firefighting equipment, Peshtigo never had a chance. But Peshtigo was no different from many small communities in the late nineteenth century, since few possessed adequate resources to fight a major fire. About thirty miles southeast of the Twin Cities, the village of Cannon Falls discovered how poorly equipped it was to combat fire in May 1884. After flames erupted in one of the town's commercial establishments, townspeople fought the blaze with a "bucket brigade," pails filled with water from a nearby pond and passed hand-to-hand to the site of the fire. By the time the flames were doused several buildings were ash. The damage would have been far worse if it had not started raining. Unfortunately, Cannon Falls failed to learn from the experience. Three years later, fire again visited the village. As before, the town was ill prepared to battle it and this time the loss of property was much greater. Cannon Falls was fortunate that no one died.

Interestingly, Cannon Falls had a volunteer fire department as early as 1874, although it was not much of a force and firefighting equipment was lacking. After the ruin wrought by the 1887 blaze, the local newspaper bluntly admonished the town for its inability to protect itself from fire:

> *It is useless to speak in any detail of the fight with the flames. When there was no organized force little could be expected. The only regret and the only thing to be severely condemned was the want of this very organization and [a need for] fire apparatus. Had such fire apparatus as a town of this size and enterprise should have had . . . there is no doubt that the fire could have been confined.*

Cannon Falls concluded that two fire disasters in three years were enough. Village officials introduced sweeping measures to improve fire safety in the community, including a construction ordinance requiring new buildings be made more fire resistant. Fire equipment was purchased and a new volunteer fire department formed. A few years later the village completed a water distribution system consisting of a 3,000-gallon cistern erected on a nearby hill with water mains leading to hydrants in town. The most obvious sign Cannon Falls was taking fire seriously was the erection of a new building on Mill Street intended solely as a firehouse.

A. Doner, presumably a local architect, designed the two-story fire station. The building was a simplified Italianate style, an architectural form common for both residences and commercial buildings in the late 1800s. It was popular for firehouses as well. In fact, the fire station for Supply Hose 2 in Chicago was almost identical to the firehouse built in Cannon

Falls. A more elaborate example was erected for the Independent Fire Company of Baltimore, Maryland. The Baltimore firehouse's chief architectural feature was its imposing 117-foot-high Italianate-style tower. Obviously little Cannon Falls did not require a structure so grandiose. Costing $1,300, the Cannon Falls fire station was completed in late October 1888. Named "Firemen's Hall," the limestone building measured 35 by 24 feet. The south facade had two entrances and four windows, all surmounted by segmental arches. One large entrance punctuated the wall at the center of the first floor, which allowed access to the interior for the department's pumper and hose cart. This entrance was edged to the east by a narrow, double-hung window, and to the west by a pedestrian entrance accented with a glass transom. The facade's second floor held three windows matching the design of the one window at the first floor. An incised tablet bearing the date "1888" was situated within a recessed panel just below a parapet embellished with a low gablet. A stone coping protected both the parapet and gablet. Rectangular windows marked the building's east and west sides. In the early 1890s, a bell tower was constructed near the southwest corner of the building's nearly flat roof.

Firemen's Hall served its intended function for several decades. When fire emergencies arose, firefighters pulled the hose cart and pumper out of the firehouse and hitched them to teams of horses, then raced to the blaze. The most "spirited" member of the department was a white horse named Prince, who was owned by A. L. Clifford, a local agent of the Wells Fargo Express Company. Clifford kept Prince tethered outside his office, but when the fire bell rang Prince would pull free and bolt toward the firehouse. When the department replaced its hose cart and pumper with motorized vehicles, horses were no longer necessary.

In 1946 Cannon Falls purchased a local creamery building and modified it for use by the fire department. The new building was much larger then the old structure and could better accommodate modern firefighting equipment. The old fire bell had been taken down several years earlier and stored at the rear of the firehouse. Unfortunately, it was stolen in the early 1940s. Since World War II was raging at the time and iron was fetching a good price, it seems likely it was sold and melted down. Firemen's Hall eventually began serving as an auto body shop. Later, it was the Cannon Falls Library. Today, it seems appropriate that it is home to the local historical society and museum. Firemen's Hall was listed on the National Register in 1980 as a worthy example of a late-nineteenth-century firehouse. It is one of the few freestanding fire stations in Minnesota so honored.

Rock County Courthouse & Jail

LUVERNE | ROCK COUNTY

The 1870s courthouse in Luverne wasn't much, a feeble-looking, wood-framed structure that would probably tumble over if all the townsfolk congregated at one side and started blowing, hardly a worthy symbol of local government in a county named "Rock." Many in the region were agitating for a new courthouse by the mid-1880s. Unfortunately, many more were not eager to foot the bill. Further lobbying, especially by the *Rock County Herald,* convinced most county residents that a new courthouse was worth the expense. By summer 1888, Rock County was proud owner of a prairie castle.[55]

Rock County is situated in the southwesternmost corner of Minnesota, with Luverne at its heart. Dominated by fertile prairie, the county evolved into an agricultural bastion very early. Entrepreneurs were also quick to develop another county natural resource, the Blue Mounds. Located only a few miles north of Luverne, the Blue Mounds are a long, semicircular chain of cliffs and outcroppings partly comprised of Sioux quartzite, a hard, close-grained stone—superb building material. Much of Luverne and the surrounding area was built with Sioux quartzite quarried from the Blue Mounds, including Rock County's 1888 courthouse in Luverne.

Today, the Rock County Courthouse is a regional icon, but getting the imposing structure built required prodding. By 1885 most in the county agreed that the small, wooden courthouse was an embarrassment. Even so, public support for a new courthouse was slight. It was not simply the expense that engendered pause. More than half the residents of Rock County lived outside Luverne and these folk were not convinced that a new courthouse in the county seat benefited them. But courthouse advocates refused to give up and over the next two years opposition to the building softened. Much credit must be attributed to the *Rock County Herald,* which strove to sensitively persuade Rock County farmers that the courthouse was an advantage to everyone. The newspaper's approach to Luverne residents who doubted the need for the public building was harsher, continually bludgeoning citizens with lectures and shame: "Luverne has one of two alternatives—either to continue in its present condition by the pursuance of a do-nothing, penny-wise-and-pound-foolish policy, or to put new life in her veins by the expenditure of money for public improvements." The following week it noted:

> *Money judiciously employed and backed by generous, enthusiastic, wide-awake public spirit and enterprise is the life-giving principle. A town whose affairs are governed by a policy of niggardly economy must necessarily be stunted in its growth. Individual enterprise seldom goes in advance of public enterprise. Men of capital hesitate to erect fine buildings in a town that hasn't enterprise enough to make needed public improvements.*

In May 1887, the people of Rock County overwhelmingly approved bonds for the courthouse. Work on the $23,500 Richardsonian Romanesque structure began in late August. The building was occupied by early October 1888.

Designed by T. D. Allen of Minneapolis, the two-story courthouse had a raised basement and a combination hip/gable roof. The walls were comprised of heavy, rough-cut Sioux quartzite, the deep red hue of the stone contrasting with the buff-colored Kasota stone used for detailing. The walls held rectangular and arched windows and a double-arched, colonnaded main entrance was located at the base of a four-story, cylindrical tower at the southwest corner of the building. The tower was topped with an observation deck surrounded by a balustrade and crowned with a conical roof. With its heavy stone construction and corner tower the courthouse was reminiscent of a European castle. Anchored into the prairie, the building seemed immovable, as if daring some medieval army to align its catapult and take its best shot.

The residents of Rock County were so pleased with the courthouse that two years after it was completed they funded a companion structure. A two-story jail was built about a hundred feet east of the courthouse. Complementing the courthouse, the $15,726 structure was also constructed with Sioux quartzite and trimmed in Kasota stone. Its rusticated walls, semicircular main entrance, and rectangular windows further illustrated the cohesiveness of the two buildings.

In mid-April 1887, while the *Rock County Herald* labored to sway majority opinion in favor of a new courthouse, the newspaper claimed that the building would be "a credit to the county not only now but fifty years hence."

Rock County's prairie castle was completed in 1888 and its complementary jail two years later.

The weekly was too conservative. More than a century later the courthouse remains a credit to Rock County, as does the jail. The only significant threat to the courthouse came in the early 1980s. County services had expanded and the original interior design of the building proved inadequate. Moreover, the interior was showing its age, while not meeting modern accessibility requirements. Officials studied options, including razing the courthouse and building a new facility. The county realized it had a wonderful piece of local history in the courthouse, however, and at the end of the review process opted to sympathetically renovate the interior of its prairie castle. The courthouse and jail look as durable today as they did when constructed, and with proper care they are likely to be around for another century. Fine examples of Richardsonian Romanesque architecture in southwestern Minnesota, these two handsome symbols of early government in Rock County were placed on the National Register in 1977.

✳ Norris Camp

VICINITY OF ROOSEVELT | LAKE OF THE WOODS COUNTY

In the mid-1930s the federal government initiated the Beltrami Island Project, a huge Depression-era relief effort that employed hundreds of workers to restore much of the natural habitat in a 740,000-acre region spread between Roseau, Beltrami, and Lake of the Woods Counties in extreme northern Minnesota. The project received its moniker from Beltrami Island, a low elevation in southwestern Lake of the Woods County about fifteen miles south of the small community of Roosevelt. At one time Beltrami Island protruded from glacial Lake Agassiz, a body of water that once covered much of northwestern Minnesota. Because of its remote location, the Beltrami Island region was preserved for some time, but by the early 1900s timber speculators had discovered its rich forests. As the timber was stripped away, prospective farmers rushed in and staked their claim to the American Dream. It proved a mistake—and the Beltrami Island Project was the correction.[56]

Timber interests had mostly abandoned the Beltrami Island area by the late 1920s, leaving behind a vastly depleted forest of low-value timber. Many agricultural families remained, however, financially shackled to a region with bleak economic prospects. Potential farmers had blundered when they settled near the island, belatedly discovering that the land was not conducive to farming. Initially a topography perforated by bogs and swamps, much of the water was drawn off by a massive drainage program started in 1912. By 1917 more than 1,500 miles of ditches crisscrossed Lake of the Woods and Beltrami Counties. But although the ditches had dried the spongy land, crop production was abysmal because the soil contained

The austere Norris Camp was the base for a Depression-era government project to correct earlier shortsighted ventures.

few nutrients. While families survived, there was little money to pay for public services, including all those ditches that were supposed to improve the economic fortunes of farmers.

In 1928 more than 70 percent of those in Lake of the Woods County with ditch assessments were delinquent—and the percentage was climbing. One year later the state acquired all the delinquent land in the Beltrami Island area, assuming the debt and creating the Red Lake Game Refuge. In 1931 the state fashioned the Beltrami Island State Forest from six and one-half townships in Lake of the Woods County. Within three years all of the county's townships had been dissolved by the state. While these actions relieved the debt of the region, officials realized the area's citizens still required public services they could not afford. The solution seemed to be a huge relocation and restoration project, moving area residents to adjacent fertile lands while restoring the natural habitat of the newly created Red Lake Game Refuge and Beltrami Island State Forest.

The endeavor, which came to be known as the Beltrami Island Project, was announced in 1934, although serious effort would not begin for another year. Project preliminaries were supervised by the State Emergency Relief Administration (SERA), the state arm of the Federal Emergency Relief Administration (FERA), a Depression-era constituent of Franklin Roosevelt's New Deal designed to help alleviate the effects of a sour economy. Money the nation's SERAs received from the FERA was distributed to county relief organizations for use on local projects. The SERA had only started the Beltrami Island Project when much of the FERA was subsumed by the

Resettlement Administration (RA), a relief organization established in early 1935. The *Improvement Bulletin* explained the RA's resettlement plan for the Beltrami Island area and another nearby site in early November 1935:

> [T]wo removal projects are contemplated, the acquisition of sandy soil farms at Beltrami Island and Pine Island in the extreme northern part of the state, and the removal of the residents of both areas to the Rainy River Valley where good agricultural land exists. The government will purchase the area for about $670,000 and plans to transfer the families within two years to the valley strip along the Canadian border. The Beltrami Island area includes 370 farms in southwestern Lake of the Woods County. . . .

Resettlement was already well advanced when the *Improvement Bulletin* announced the project. In fact, the RA was contemplating the next step, the restoration of the Beltrami Island area. Razing farmsteads, installing dams, planting trees, and managing wildlife were some of the RA's goals. In 1936, Norris Camp was chosen as operational headquarters for the undertaking, a facility constructed by the Civilian Conservation Corps (CCC) a year earlier in the heart of Beltrami Island. The CCC was a relief entity that put people to work by engaging chiefly in forestry, flood control, and soil protection efforts. When the RA took over the CCC camp it consisted of a number of structures, including the Mess Hall, Blacksmith Shop, Recreation Building, and several storage buildings. Additional buildings were added by the RA, some of which were the Wildlife Administration Building, Meat Cooler, Paint Shop, Barn, Ice Box, Latrines, and Oil Houses. The simple, generally rectangular buildings were mostly one-story, wood-framed structures covered with shiplap siding and topped with shallow gable roofs, although some log buildings were erected as well.

Norris Camp served the Beltrami Island Project from 1936 until 1942, the entire length of the venture. Eventually, the complex came to include over fifty structures, some with a portable or sectional plan. Because of the difficulty accessing certain points in the project area, four side camps were also constructed. Ludlow Island, Oaks, Gates, and Schilling Camps were not nearly as large as Norris, but their strategic locations gave the RA logistic flexibility. Some of the work completed by crews operating from all the camps included timber dam and bridge construction, road maintenance, sign posting, firebreak maintenance, seeding and planting, lake and pond development, and wildlife reconnaissance. Ranger stations and cabins were erected as well. Even though the nature of the work remained steady throughout the project's duration, supervision of the effort did not. On September 1, 1937, the RA was absorbed by the Farm Security Administration, while the Land Utilization Division of the RA was brought into the Bureau of Agricultural Economics, a component of the United States Department of Agriculture. One year later, however, responsibility for land utilization passed to the Soil Conservation Service, the agency that monitored the

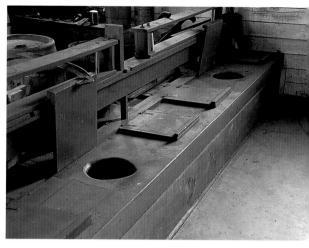

Those at the camp shared.

Beltrami Island Project until July 1940, when the Division of Game and Fish of the Minnesota Department of Conservation took over.

Considered one of the most successful resettlement undertakings in the United States, the roughly $2 million Beltrami Island Project ended in late May 1942. Most of those resettled were pleased with the developments, their net worth increasing substantially due to richer soil which produced larger and healthier yields. Furthermore, since the settlers were now more concentrated, the cost of public services decreased. At least some of the wildlife appreciated the project as well. Beavers, for instance, found an outlet for their creative energies in the many timber dams that had been erected, adding personal touches to the barriers. Jack Manweiler, one of the project game managers, welcomed the assistance: "If it makes them any happier to be puttering around with their own ideas of embellishments on our dams, we are pleased. . . . Past experience on reflooding led us to count on the beaver for any minor repair work that might occur over the years. . . ."

Over the last half-century much of Norris camp has been removed, but fourteen buildings still remain, including the Mess Hall and Kitchen, Recreation Building, Power House, Field Office and Supply Room, Blacksmith Shop, Repair Garage, Cabin No. 3, and a few bunkhouses, oil houses, and latrines. Some newer buildings have been added to the complex as well. All of the structures are used by the state to help administer the Red Lake Wildlife Management Area. Although losing a number of original buildings is often detrimental to the integrity of a historic resource, a Depression-period work relief camp that retains its principal components and continues to reflect its intended purpose is rare. As a chief element of the Beltrami Island Project, a major federal undertaking to relieve distressed settlers from submarginal lands while restoring natural habitat, Norris Camp was placed on the National Register in 1994.

Montevideo Carnegie Library

MONTEVIDEO | CHIPPEWA COUNTY

Second only to our churches and schools our public library stands as a moral factor and as an educator. Our people have always felt a pride in our library, which contains a fine selection of some of the best works of the ablest authors.

In 1907, when those words were written by the *Commercial,* the village of Montevideo in western Minnesota, about thirty-five miles east of the South Dakota border, had just dedicated its first library building. After waiting decades for the repository the community was understandably delighted. But a library is not simply a building and the citizens of Montevideo understood that very early. Well before Andrew Carnegie donated funds to construct the library building, residents of the village were enjoying great literature.[57]

The roots of the Montevideo Carnegie Library are found in the Montevideo Library Club, a society formed in 1879 by nine local citizens. Each member contributed three dollars to the club and was permitted to check out volumes from the society's collection. Rules were soon adopted that allowed any resident of Montevideo to join the organization by paying the three-dollar initiation fee. By 1881 the club's holdings consisted of 47 books. Mark Twain's *The Adventures of Tom Sawyer* (1876) was the first book in the collection, and Charles Dudley Warner's *My Winter on the Nile: Among the Mummies and Moslems* (1876) was the last. Although the society's holdings were small, interest in the group quickly grew. In 1882 the Montevideo Library Club was incorporated as the Montevideo Library Association, its purpose to create and maintain a library and lyceum (an organization sponsoring public lectures or concerts). Each member purchased interests in the company for three dollars a share and also paid annual dues of one dollar, which was used to buy books for the collection. Potential works for the library were reviewed by a selection committee. The committee wanted only what was best for the association's members, but determining what is right for someone else is a subjective task. When Thomas Henry Huxley's essay "Science and Culture" (1880) was reviewed it was rejected as heretical, as was William Robertson Smith's *The Prophets of Israel* (1882). In late-nineteenth-century America, the committee's opinion of the authors was not unusual, since Huxley was an ardent proponent of Darwinism, and Smith a revisionist Biblical historian. Regardless of the committee's personal views, the group was trying to bring some influence from the outside world to tiny Montevideo, and within a brief period the library had grown to about 250 volumes. Since the association did not have a library building to house the collection, books were stored in the Chippewa County Bank, with the financial institution's employees also acting as librarians.

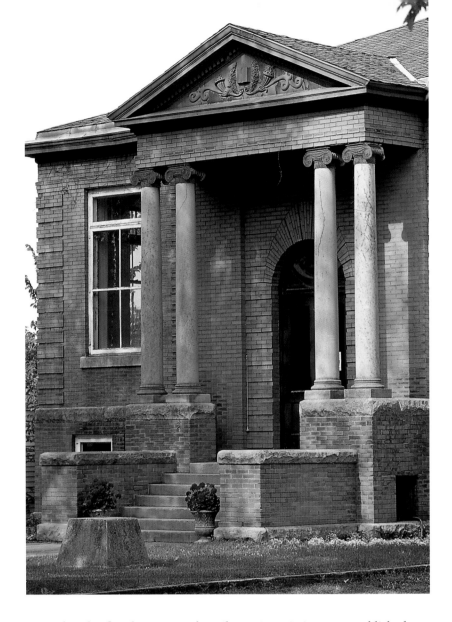

Montevideo residents rallied to save their Andrew Carnegie–endowed library, a small, noble-looking building now used as a reception hall.

A decade after the Montevideo Library Association was established, the enterprise had accumulated about 650 books, but the organization's shoestring budget convinced management that a substantial collection was only a distant dream. Realizing the future of the library was as a public appurtenance, it was offered to the village government in February 1892. The village council accepted the gift and levied taxes to raise money for the library's operation. With this additional income the size of the library's collection rapidly increased, but by the early 1900s Montevideo still did not have a library building—the town's tax base was simply insufficient to raise the funds. Fortunately, Montevideo had another option. In 1905, officials petitioned steel magnate Andrew Carnegie for a new library.

In the late nineteenth and early twentieth centuries, Andrew Carnegie became a kind of library messiah. Carnegie was only twelve when his

impoverished family emigrated from Scotland to America in the late 1840s. Driven to succeed, he had made a fortune in the stock market by the time he was in his thirties. He then turned his attention to the steel industry, where he built an empire by keeping manufacturing costs below those of his competitors. By the close of the nineteenth century Carnegie dominated the American steel industry. After making his fortune many times over, Carnegie gave it away. One of his philanthropic endeavors was funding library buildings. Through the Andrew Carnegie Foundation he financed almost 1,700 libraries across the country, many in rural communities like Montevideo where educational and cultural services were limited.

Carnegie's generosity did not impress everyone, especially those who toiled in his steel plants for meager wages. Margaret Byington, author of *Homestead: The Households of a Mill Town,* paraphrased Carnegie steel-workers who believed employees would rather have had more money in their pockets than libraries: "Many a man said to me, 'We'd rather they hadn't cut our wages and let us spend the money for ourselves. What use has a man who works twelve hours a day for a library, anyway?'" But while Carnegie could have done better by those that labored in his factories, there is no question that numerous generations benefited immensely from his libraries, including the people of Montevideo. By 1906, Montevideo was constructing its first library building, thanks to a $10,000 grant secured from the Andrew Carnegie Foundation.

The Montevideo Carnegie Library was designed by Martin Granum, a local architect who was responsible for the plan of several public and private buildings in Montevideo. Local contractor Everett Iverson erected the structure. Situated near the intersection of Third Street and Sherman Avenue near downtown Montevideo, the library was a 30- by 32-foot Neoclassical-style building. The noble architectural style was popular in the early twentieth century for public buildings, reflecting integrity and democratic ideals. Montevideo's library was a frame structure sheathed in pressed brick and trimmed with Bedford Stone. It had a raised base-ment and a low, hip roof. The east facade held a centrally located entrance embraced by paired Ionic (evident by the volute capitals) columns support-ing a pedimented portico with decorated tympanum, the recessed, trian-gular space between the pediment's cornices. The entrance doors were edged by brick quoins and topped with a semicircular arch. Brick quoins also accented each corner of the building.

The library was dedicated in early 1907. Montevideo residents crowded into the local opera house to enjoy the community orchestra and to hear public officials detail the obligations of humanity. The festivities then moved to the library, continuing well into the evening. When the library officially opened for use, it boasted a collection of roughly 4,000 volumes.

The remaining founders of the Montevideo Library Club must have been beaming. The library served the citizens of Montevideo until 1968, when a larger building was constructed to house the expanding collection. A racquetball club occupied the old library for a time, but vacated the building in 1980. Comprehending the historic significance of the library, Montevideo residents refused to allow it to wither away. A citywide initiative to raise money for the restoration of the structure was successful, and in 1984 the building reopened as a reception hall. As an attractive, Andrew Carnegie–endowed venue for knowledge, the petite Montevideo Carnegie Library was placed on the National Register in 1982.

✳ Minnesota State Reformatory for Men

ST. CLOUD | SHERBURNE COUNTY

"It Could Be You" is a poem attributed to James Martin, an inmate at the Minnesota State Reformatory for Men in St. Cloud in the early 1970s.[58] The melancholy lines reveal an intelligent man who seems lost—a troubled soul who has spent years institutionalized. His brooding work concludes:

> Now I recall what I heard people say
> "To keep him alive we must chain him today"
> But I wonder if they will ever understand
> the chains only tell him he's not a full man
> All it does is destroy what little he does possess
> And the time and waiting will do the rest
> What fools we are to say there's nothing we can do
> What would you want done if that someone was you?

In the evening of March 17, 1974, James Martin hanged himself in his cell.

Although Martin had a history of erratic mental behavior, the absence of freedom likely contributed to his end. Providing prison inmates with televisions, ping-pong tables, and basketball courts is no substitute for loss of liberty. Even so, prisons have come some way since the early years of the penal system, when confinement and punishment were their only purpose. In his 1892 book the *History of Prison Architecture*, John R. Thomas espoused the virtue of prison as reformatory:

> A place of mere confinement is one thing, a place of mere punishment is another; a place which—while the prisoner is securely kept in it, and while he undergoes, at the least, the great punishment of privation of liberty—is also a place of education and a place of reform, in which a prime object is that he shall go out a better and more useful man than he came in. . . .

The Perimeter Wall
at the Minnesota State
Reformatory for Men
continues to remind
passersby it is better to
be outside looking in
than inside looking out.

Most probably agree that a rehabilitative prison is better than one designed solely for confinement and punishment. In 1885, that is what the Minnesota State Legislature concluded after authorizing construction of the state's third correctional facility, a reformatory to be built on a granite quarry a few miles south of St. Cloud in central Minnesota.

Founded in 1851, the Territorial Prison in Stillwater, a St. Croix River community roughly twenty miles east of St. Paul, was Minnesota's first penal institution. The House of Refuge was created sixteen years later in St. Paul, about three miles west of the present capitol building. Unlike the Territorial Prison, the House of Refuge adopted reform practices, an idea sweeping the country by the late nineteenth century. Specifically for very young offenders, the House of Refuge had no bars. Inmates worked the institution's farm raising fruits and vegetables and also attended academic and trade classes. The facility was renamed the Minnesota State Reform School in 1879. Eleven years later it relocated to Red Wing, about forty-five miles southwest of St. Paul. In 1895, it was again renamed, this time as the State Training School. The institution was placed on the National Register in 1973. The Territorial Prison in Stillwater was so honored nine years later.

The Minnesota State Reformatory for Men in St. Cloud bridged the gap between the State Training School and the Territorial Prison. Like the Territorial Prison, it had bars, but as with the training school, it was intended as a reformatory, housing relatively young offenders (sixteen to thirty years of age) believed salvageable from a criminal life. Construction of the first cell block began in 1887 and was completed two years later. Designed by J. Walter Stevens, an architect responsible for the appearance of many buildings in St. Paul's Lowertown, the four-story, rectangular, Romanesque Revival–style cell house featured a gable roof marked with pyramidal-roofed dormers. Trimmed in sandstone, the structure's brick-faced walls were decorated with several window openings topped by semicircular arches. Other early buildings like the Laundry, Kitchen, Chapel, Hospital, and classrooms were wood frame. The first inmates to the reformatory were seventy-five young transfers from the prison in Stillwater.

The original cell block reached capacity by the late 1890s and the state legislature approved construction of another housing unit. Again designed by Stevens, the new building resembled the earlier cell block, although it was built by inmates using granite from the on-site quarry, a common construction practice as the reformatory grew. In 1893, only five years after work began on the second cell house, inmates were building a third housing unit. Stevens planned this unit as a mirror image of the second cell block. Soon after it was finished in 1897, work started on the Romanesque Medieval–Style Administration Building. Due to several work stoppages, the structure required about two decades to complete. The building was designed by Clarence H. Johnston, a prominent architect who created the plans for a number of state institutional facilities such as the Minnesota State Sanatorium for Consumptives near Walker in Cass County, a National Register property exhibiting an impressive collection of Colonial, Tudor, and Spanish Colonial–style buildings. Completed in 1920, the reformatory's five-story, granite Administration Building had a flat roof and a projecting bay at the west facade flanked by octagonal corner towers. As with the cell blocks, many of the windows were crowned by semicircular arches.

Inmates working in the quarry in 1914, probably pulling granite for the Administration Building.

Living in a cell block
is more like existing.

Johnston ultimately designed several buildings at the reformatory, including additional cell blocks and the North and South Dining Halls. He also planned the Infirmary, Power Plant Building, Maintenance Shops, Guard Towers, and various school and trade buildings. Maybe the most imposing edifice designed by the architect was the Perimeter Wall, a thick, 22-foot-high granite barrier that enclosed much of the compound and all but shouted to those on the outside to be good citizens or else. Like many of the other structures at the reformatory, the wall was erected by inmates.

While quarrying taught inmates the stone trade, prisoners also worked the reformatory farm. As time passed more vocational trades developed, like sash and door manufacturing. A license plate plant was initiated in the 1940s. The Intermediate Building, which was constructed in 1933, was geared toward academics, housing schoolrooms and a library. But even though the correctional facility was a reformatory, allowing inmates to prepare themselves to be productive members of society, it still occasionally exhibited the nasty side of prison life. There were brawls among inmates and fights with guards. After the death of an inmate in the late 1940s, which apparently involved reformatory personnel, new policies on humane treatment were instituted, which included the elimination of the lead-core canes some guards carried for protection—and possibly other uses.

In 1958, the reformatory constructed a gym, which was the last building erected at the institution employing inmate labor. Because of high costs and an unsettling escape rate, the farm was finally shut down in the 1960s. Inmates could take college-level classes by 1970, and within a few years a drug rehabilitation course and other social programs were in place. These programs indicate that the correctional facility has evolved from a traditional reformatory into a kind of ultrasecure treatment and educational center, although recent state budget cuts have forced reductions in prison curriculums. A peek at the massive granite wall is likely to convince most that education or treatment elsewhere is preferable. Probably the most prominent landmark in the St. Cloud area, and Minnesota's best example of the prison reform movement, the Minnesota State Reformatory for Men was added to the National Register in 1986.

YESTERDAY'S HOUSE

8

MINNESOTA'S OLDEST RESIDENCE is located at Mendota, a small community near the confluence of the Mississippi and Minnesota Rivers, opposite Fort Snelling. Constructed in 1835, the two-story, gable-roofed, stone house belonged to Henry Hastings Sibley, a prominent personality of New England lineage who arrived in Minnesota a year earlier to supervise operations of the American Fur Company. Sibley is lauded by historian Roger Kennedy as "Minnesota's most intriguing character of the frontier period," a man with "a flair for making and reporting expeditions to exotic places, for hair-raising escapes, and for big game hunting quite beyond the call of the [fur] trade." Widely considered a "founding father," Sibley was Minnesota's first territorial representative in Congress and became the state's first governor in 1858. The house he raised at Mendota was a kind of rustic, scaled-down version of the Federal style, an architecture that became popular in the East toward the end of the Revolutionary War. Although the style mostly faded about 1820, examples were still built for another twenty years or so. It is not surprising that some late versions appeared on the frontier, an expanse far removed from the East and new architectural trends. Now a Minnesota Historical Society historic site open to the public, the stout Sibley House regularly hosts tours and family days.[59]

Although Sibley's residence was hardly opulent, it was considerably more impressive than most frontier dwellings, which were often humble shelters of no particular style formed from building resources in the immediate vicinity. Stone and clay were frequently employed in arid regions, while heavy timber dwellings, such as the Guri and Lars Endreson House, appeared in wooded areas. Adoption of specific architectural styles was not very evident in Minnesota until settlement progressed toward community and usually included modest industry, like sawmilling. As sawmills began marking waterways, wood framing became popular and architecture styles were more common. House designs were bolstered with the coming of the railroad, which delivered relatively inexpensive construction materials from other regions. Moreover, the railroad brought knowledge of architectural fashions in the East, oftentimes in the form of young professionals intent on designing and building a new West.

One of the first building styles to reach Minnesota was Greek Revival, an architecture adapted from the classic Greek temple. The Orville and Sarah Chubb House in Fairmont, for instance, is a simplified Greek Revival–style residence, although it was erected at a time when the architecture was losing its luster. A more lively expression of the style was built by Evert Westervelt in Frontenac in southeastern Minnesota. Constructed around 1855, and now part of the Old Frontenac Historic District, Westervelt's two-story house featured a pedimented gable above each wall, heavy pilasters accenting the corners, and a wide frieze edging the cornice.

By the early 1870s, with an expanding railroad system helping refine Minnesota's cultural palate, French Second Empire architecture gained appreciation, evidenced by the Minneapolis residence of Alonzo Rand, a wood-framed structure sheathed in cast stone that was completed in 1874. A better example of the style, however, was finished two years earlier in St. Paul for Alexander Ramsey. Unlike the framed Rand House, the striking residence of Minnesota's first territorial governor was supported by massive walls of limestone. The brawny structure was detailed with arched window openings, large cornice brackets, hood molds, and an ornate porch. Today, the Alexander Ramsey House is managed by the Minnesota Historical Society and is one of the few National Register properties open to the public.

Ramsey referred to his residence as a "Mansion House." While it was certainly larger than most dwellings in Minnesota at the time it was built, it was not a mansion by today's standards. In truth, it was not even a mansion by the standards of the 1890s. In 1884 James J. Hill began erecting his mammoth Richardsonian Romanesque–style residence on Summit Avenue in St. Paul. When the building was completed eight years later, it made the Ramsey House look Lilliputian. Another National Register structure administered by the Minnesota Historical Society, the Hill House was an exception in Minnesota. Certainly other fantastically large residences were constructed in the state, like the National Register property "Glensheen," Chester and Clara Congdon's estate in Duluth, but Minnesota's affluent crowd typically avoided grossly overt displays of prosperity.

Most Minnesotans, of course, did not suffer the burden of hiding wealth behind semimansions. Yet, many had homes with modest flourishes, often classical elements of one kind or another. The Lena O. Smith House, for example, was a rather reserved two-and-a-half-story dwelling erected in Minneapolis in 1912. Still, the National Register structure was accented with gable returns and featured a porch with Ionic columns. The Smith House, though, made it to the historic listing because of its occupant, not its architecture.

A number of architectural styles were prominent in America at the beginning of the twentieth century, including Colonial Revival, Neoclassical, and Tudor. The Gothic Revival and Italianate inclinations had mostly passed by the mid-1880s. Victorian styles like French Second Empire, Stick, and Shingle had generally given way to other designs as well, although Queen Anne architecture remained popular until about 1910. Prairie style, one of the few truly American architectural forms, was fully embraced during the first decade of the 1900s. The foremost authority on the Prairie-style house was Frank Lloyd Wright, a curious, and exceptionally gifted, architect who was described by writer Laurence Schmeckebier in 1944 as "a handsome little man with flowing white hair, who has a genius for insulting people as well as for building beautiful houses to suit himself for other people to live in." Originating in the Midwest, Prairie School architecture, with its horizontal lines and widely overhanging eaves, was welcomed in the central states more than anywhere else.

From the grandiose to the exceptionally plain, Minnesota has many residences exhibiting the diverse architecture of the last century and a half. The notable houses the state has lost, however, is unsettling. The Oscar Schmidt House in Mankato in south-central Minnesota was an impressive Georgian Revival–style building razed in 1988. The unassuming Philander Prescott House in Minneapolis was removed eight years earlier, even though its original occupant was one of Minnesota's earliest settlers. Both of these structures were on the National Register. Fortunately, the historic listing still retains some fine extant examples of Minnesota houses, honored either for their architecture, association with a significant person, or because they recall a substantial event. The Anne Bickle House in Glenwood in west-central Minnesota, for instance, is an unexceptional American Foursquare. Nevertheless, it is tied to a prominent citizen from the city's past. The Martin T. Gunderson House in Kenyon in the southeastern section of the state is also associated with a leading personality, although the house is significant for its architecture as well. The Gunderson House is a superb example of the Queen Anne style. Like the Bickle and Gunderson Houses, the residences on the ensuing pages demonstrate the varied criteria that make a property historic. From the incredible Paul Watkins House in Winona to the unusually meek Hinckley Fire Relief House in Sandstone, the state's history is evident in the structures Minnesotans have called home.

✳ Rensselaer D. Hubbard House

MANKATO | BLUE EARTH COUNTY

It is evident to all that no man is entirely the arbiter of his own destiny, but to a large degree is the creature of heredity, environment, and association, yet some there are with the will power to overcome adverse surroundings and carve out for themselves positions of honor and influence in their community; such men may appropriately be denominated self-made. To this class belonged R. D. Hubbard. . . . He depended upon his unaided exertions for whatever success he achieved. The fact that he became wealthy and eminent proves that he possessed rare qualities of mind and stability of character.

Although hyperbole oozes from parts of this 1909 biography of Rensselaer Dean Hubbard, there is no question he was a go-getter who succeeded. Born in Ostego County, New York, in 1837, Hubbard was making his own way by the time he was fifteen years old. By 1854 he was a farmhand in the Sacramento Valley in California. He soon tried his luck on his own farm, but quickly lost his crops to drought. After spending a brief period on the Fraser River in British Columbia searching for gold, Hubbard returned to Sacramento and worked as a clerk and manager in a grocery store. He moved back to New York in 1863, marrying Mary Cook of Ostego County and settling in Sydney Plains to raise tobacco. Within a few years the couple immigrated to Corey, Pennsylvania, where Hubbard invested $2,000 in a grocery enterprise. By 1870, that investment was worth $30,000. That same year the couple relocated to Mankato, Minnesota, where Hubbard constructed a warehouse and engaged in the wheat trade. In 1872 he and some partners established the Mankato Linseed Oil Company. Seven years later Hubbard created the Mankato Milling Company, predecessor to Hubbard Milling Company, which became one of the largest milling concerns in southern Minnesota.[60]

In 1871, as Hubbard was on his way to becoming a Mankato somebody, he decided to build a house that would turn heads. He purchased property at the corner of Third and Warren Streets for $3,100 from A. T. Lindholm, an employee of the First National Bank. Lindholm had completed a residence on the site only a year earlier, but Hubbard wasted little time removing it. Although the name of the architect is unknown, construction of the Hubbard House began in spring and was completed by fall. The residence was not a mansion, but it was still an impressive example of the French Second Empire style.

The 1860s and 1870s represented the heyday for Second Empire architecture in this country. A Victorian style, it takes its name from France's Second Empire, the reign of Napoleon III, a regime that undertook a major building initiative in Paris in the mid-1800s, creating grand boulevards and buildings. Unlike other building styles from the period, which typically drew inspiration from past architecture, Second Empire was considered modern, even though its most distinctive characteristic, a mansard roof, was a design first developed by seventeenth-century French Renaissance architect François Mansart. The boxlike shape of the mansard roof creates an attic offering a full floor of usable space. Dormers almost always mark the roof, allowing sunlight to penetrate the attic. Columns, balustrades, arched window openings, and decorative cornice brackets are also common characteristics of the style. Towers, or narrow bays extending from the facade, are incorporated into some designs as well.

Second Empire architecture was popular mainly in the Northeast and Midwest. The Pringle House in Fredonia, New York, was an early example of the style, erected around 1857. Alexander Ramsey began building his

The 1871 Rensselaer D. Hubbard House denotes French Second Empire style with its concave mansard roof, polychromatic shingles, dormers, ornate brackets, and projecting pavilion.

Second Empire–style house in 1868. Unlike the heavy, stone construction of the Ramsey House, Rensselaer Hubbard's roughly $10,000 home was composed of brick set upon a foundation of stone. The mansard roof of the two-story house essentially created a three-story dwelling. The roof, sheathed in polychromatic slate and pierced by dormers, was crowned with a balustrade. The base of the roof was accented with a cornice resting upon large, ornate brackets. A balconet with a fanciful balustrade edged the rectangular window openings at the first floor of the east facade. Balustrades also embraced a small, covered porch extending from the main entrance, which was set into the base of a projecting bay that resembled a truncated tower. The porch's entablature was supported upon columns and topped with another balustrade. Like the facade's first-floor window openings, first-floor openings at other sides of the building were also rectangular. Second-floor window openings, however, were arched.

Over time, the decorative building became larger, likely reflecting Hubbard's growing status as a Mankato industrialist. In 1888, Mankato architect F. Thayer designed a sympathetic addition to the building, including a wing at the dwelling's south side, replacing a smaller wing that was part of the original construction. A one-story bay window with balustrade was built at the north side. A full porch was eventually added to the dwelling's facade. The main entrance porch was either removed in favor of a larger section, or it was extended. The balustrade atop the porch's roof was also removed. The balconets that edged the windows to the north and south of the main entrance were replaced with porch sections protruding farther from the building.

Unfortunately, Mary Hubbard was not around to enjoy the larger residence, having died in 1877. The following year, Rensselaer married Miss Frank Griffith of Mankato. The couple spent more than twenty-five years together before Rensselaer died on a business trip to Chicago in 1905. While not a millionaire, he had assets valued at more than $350,000. Frank continued to live in the Hubbard residence until her death in 1934, when the house passed to her daughter, Esther Richter, who was also living in the home with her children. Frank willed the remaining property to her grandchildren upon Esther's death, with the peculiar condition that they be unmarried and non-Catholic. Esther's children soon departed for California, although it is uncertain if any eventually tied the knot or regularly recited the "Salve Regina." In 1938 the Blue Earth County Historical Society acquired the house from Esther, quickly passing ownership of the building to the city, which agreed to maintain the house for use by the historical society. Presently, the picturesque dwelling serves as a county museum. A monument to one of Mankato's major industrialists and an excellent example of French Second Empire architecture, the Rensselaer D. Hubbard House was placed on the National Register in 1976.

Hanna C. & Peter E. Thompson House

BARNESVILLE | CLAY COUNTY

When the Great Northern Railway (GN) established a division point at Barnesville in 1885, it seemed both blessing and curse. Barnesville, located in the Red River Valley in northwestern Minnesota, roughly thirty miles southeast of Fargo-Moorhead, was a tiny agricultural community when the GN increased prosperity in the area by constructing railroad maintenance shops a few blocks east of the town. But for some Barnesville merchants and residents being close to the shops was not close enough, so they uprooted their interests and moved even closer, angering those who stayed behind. Animosities between the two factions never erupted into a Hatfield-McCoy–type feud, but those who abandoned the old for the new punctuated their move by incorporating as a village in 1886. Separated by mere blocks, "New Barnesville" and "Old" Barnesville appeared to have, according to the local newspaper, the *Review,* "a tacit agreement to disagree and live apart forever in single blessedness." It was all rather silly and by 1889 the anger had dissipated. In March of that year the two sides came together and—the *Review* again—"a love feast [was] indulged in by men who had been suspicious and jealous of one another." Since the "ill feeling that had existed for years [had] melted away like snow in April sunshine," the two communities soon merged and incorporated as the city of Barnesville, with Peter E. Thompson as mayor.[61]

Thompson was an obvious choice to lead the city, an exemplary example of the progressive personality common to many infant Minnesota communities in the late 1800s. He and his wife, Hannah, managed a general store in Barnesville for almost two decades. He was the town's first postmaster, as well as the first justice when Barnesville incorporated as a village in 1881. Thompson also served on the village council for several years. Mayor seemed the next step in his progression as a leader, although he would trump that in 1891 when he was elected to the state legislature, serving two terms. A vital cog in the development of Barnesville, he was later praised by a local newspaper: "His advice has been more often sought and his suggestions more fully carried out than any other man who has ever lived in Barnesville." Hannah, too, was no slouch. In an age that limited leadership roles for women, she excelled as a social conscience, frequently ministering to those in need. Even after the family's financial success was secured "she did not interpret that as an opportunity for ease and an idle life, but rather as a call for a greater public service to the community." She was devoted to improving the public cemetery and during the First World War she traveled the county securing aid for the American Red Cross.

During their first few years in Barnesville the Thompsons resided in quarters in the rear of their general store. They then lived in a house on

Front Street for a time. Later, they speculatively built houses, dwelling in each for a brief period before selling. By the early 1900s the family was ready for a statement house, one that would stamp their mark on Barnesville. The Hancock Brothers of Fargo, North Dakota, maybe the most prominent architectural firm in that city in the early twentieth century, was commissioned to design the dwelling.

George Hancock established the architectural enterprise in Fargo in 1882. Walter Hancock, George's younger brother, was initially an apprentice in the business but later became a partner. In the early years of the company George was responsible for designing several Gothic Revival–style churches, including St. Stephen's in Casselton, North Dakota, a structure erected in 1885 and financed by George W. Cass, president of the Northern Pacific Railway. The architectural firm also designed in Stick style, an architecture partly characterized by "stick work," where boards are applied vertically, horizontally, or diagonally over horizontal siding to create a decorative pattern. In time, Richardsonian Romanesque architecture became a favorite of the brothers. The style, which emphasizes massiveness and strength through heavy, rough-faced stone construction, may even have been introduced into North Dakota by the Hancocks. The Hancocks soon discovered a fondness for Classical Revival style, an architectural form that became immensely popular after the 1893 Columbian Exposition in Chicago, an event featuring many buildings exhibiting classical designs. Classical Revival architecture takes inspiration from antiquity, typically Greek or Roman themes, and is partly characterized by generally symmetrical buildings with columned porticoes with pediments, or entries embellished with columns and an entablature. Often used for institutional buildings and sometimes commercial structures, such as banks, the architecture was also applied to dwellings. The Hancock Brothers, for example, planned many wood-framed houses in Fargo using the style, including the Thomas Baker Jr. House (ca. 1897), John C. Hunter House (1898), William Rentschler House (1899), and the Frank F. Grant House (1899). It was not surprising, then, when the brothers opted for a Classical Revival–style residence for Hannah and Peter Thompson in 1902.

The large, two-and-a-half-story, wood-framed Thompson House was completed in 1903 on the northwest side of Second Street Northeast in the eastern part of Barnesville. Resting on a granite foundation, the clapboard-sided building had a boxlike main section with a truncated hip roof crowned with a widow's walk. A hip-roofed rectangular wing projected from the structure's rear. The generally symmetrical southeast facade featured a one-story porch covered by a wide entablature with a smooth frieze and dentils. The entablature shielded a centrally located main entrance and was supported upon Tuscan columns, and an open balustrade with turned balusters edged the porch and linked clapboard-covered column pedestals. Windows

Home to a prominent Barnesville couple, the Classical Revival–style Hannah C. and Peter E. Thompson House was designed by the Hancock Brothers, a well-known turn-of-the-twentieth-century architectural firm in Fargo, North Dakota.

were chiefly rectangular, a feature common to most of the house, although the center wall at the facade's second floor was pierced with an oval window with a keyed surround. A hip-roofed dormer with two small window openings holding multipane windows was situated a few feet above the oval opening, interrupting the slope of the roof. The dwelling's northeast and southwest sides were marked by two-and-a-half-story projecting bays, each capped with a polygonal roof. The small window openings at the top of each bay held windows formed of multiple diamond-shaped panes. Another porch with entablature braced upon Tuscan columns was positioned at the southwest side of the rear wing, where a second entrance was located. The porch was surrounded by an open balustrade, and another balustrade edged the top of the entablature.

The house was a fine example of Classical Revival architecture, but Peter E. Thompson did not take pleasure in his ornate home for long, dying of heart failure less than two years after it was completed. He was only fifty-two years old. Like most, friend Charles S. Marden was stunned: "Peter E. Thompson is dead! It seems almost impossible to believe the evidence of our own senses. . . . Barnesville has lost her foremost citizen and the people their best friend." Hannah continued in the house until she passed away in 1920, but the structure remained within the family at least into the mid-1970s. Carefully restored by the late 1990s, the house fetched a handsome price. The Thompson House is the only remaining property in Barnesville tied to Peter and Hannah Thompson, two of the community's most prominent early citizens. "An intact and locally rare example of the Classical Revival style," it was placed on the National Register in 1996.

✳ Casiville Bullard House

The Casiville Bullard House was erected in the years 1909–10 and is located on Folsom Street in the Como Heights neighborhood in St. Paul, roughly four blocks east of Lake Como. It is a simple American Foursquare–style dwelling that was constructed by its owner, Casiville Bullard. Bullard was an exceptional man, but it is doubtful many history books mention his name. A gifted stonemason and bricklayer, Bullard was one of the few skilled African Americans working in the building trades in St. Paul in the early twentieth century.[62]

Born in 1873 in Memphis, Tennessee, Casiville Bullard was the eldest of seven children. When he was old enough to understand racial prejudice he realized his life would be harder than most. He spent much of his childhood picking cotton with his parents, who were former slaves, and tending his younger siblings; when Casiville finished picking one cotton row, he would carry his baby brother to the end of the next row and again start picking. Not surprisingly, Casiville's formal schooling was brief and he obtained only a third-grade education. Casiville, however, was smart and talented, and even though he matured in an age with few opportunities for African Americans, he succeeded.

Bullard had one advantage: a cultural heritage of excellence in skilled trades. As slaves, blacks were forced to complete traditional agrarian chores, but they were also required to make things for others, from clothing to buildings. Many slaves became proficient in spinning, weaving, shoemaking, carpentry, painting, blacksmithing, and the "trowel trades," like stonemasonry, bricklaying, and plastering. Throughout much of the nineteenth century, including the period immediately following emancipation, blacks in the American South dominated these crafts, passing skills down from one generation to the next. One African American who passed on considerable knowledge to younger generations was former slave Lewis Adams. In the late 1800s, Adams established a modest school in his tinsmith/blacksmith shop in Tuskegee, Alabama, the seed that eventually blossomed into the prestigious Tuskegee Institute, which is now Tuskegee University.

An uncle in Memphis taught Bullard the trowel trades. Bullard was also schooled in carpentry. He became so skilled that he could cut and lay just about any masonry, including brick, marble, and granite. He could also cut and lay pine and oak flooring. But in the South in the late 1800s, carpentry rapidly became a poor endeavor for African Americans. Racism in the Brotherhood of Carpenters and Joiners Union was so strong that locals were segregated and few black carpenters were given jobs outside poor black neighborhoods. In fact, as historian Darryl Paulson explains, "separation between black and white carpenters was so complete that when not enough white workers were available for a job, the white local would call in out-of-town tradesmen rather than turn to local black carpenters." The attitude of the Brotherhood of Carpenters and Joiners reflected the approach of most trade unions at the time, and the dominance black craftsmen once enjoyed in the market rapidly diminished. The trowel trades unions were unique, however, maintaining nondiscrimination policies, influenced in part by the almost total supremacy of black artisans in these fields. Nevertheless, housing discrimination, segregation laws, and the loss of political power and legal rights forced southern black craftsmen of all trades to look north for a better life. Between 1890 and 1910 many skilled black workers were part of a substantial migration of African Americans to northern cities. Although the number of blacks moving into Minnesota was only a small percentage of the nearly 200,000 African Americans traveling north during this period, St. Paul's tiny black population still swelled by almost 500 percent. One of these migrants was Casiville Bullard, who was initially drawn to the area by the opportunity to work on architect Cass Gilbert's fantastic Minnesota State Capitol Building.

Bullard arrived in St. Paul around 1898, when construction began on the capitol building. He maintained his residence in Memphis, however, returning to the South when work on the capitol slowed in winter. He must have found the job climate or social atmosphere in Minnesota appealing, though, for around 1902 he and his wife, Addie, made St. Paul their permanent residence. About this time Bullard began work on the Great Northern Railway's Dale Street Shops in St. Paul. He would remain busy for the greater part of his career and by the time he retired he had completed stone- or brickwork on numerous St. Paul structures, including the St. Paul Public Library and Hill Reference Library, St. Paul Union Depot, Federal Courts Building (Landmark Center), St. Paul Cathedral, and various Como Zoo buildings and structures. His daughter later recalled that when she and her father drove through town he often pointed out various buildings he helped construct. Bullard stayed so active in the building trades because he was one of the few skilled black masons in St. Paul and his exceptional ability working with both stone and brick made him valuable. When former building contractor James Milsap was a young man he watched Bullard work, impressed with the older man's innate ability to lay brick: "Today bricklayers use tools like brick saws to cut and fit the brick. Not Mr. Bullard. He took a brick hammer and knocked the corners off the brick and laid them. . . . When he finished, it was impeccable."

By 1904 the Bullards were living in a wood-framed house Casiville had constructed on Folsom Street in the Como Heights Addition. Much of the addition was undeveloped and the Bullards were the only black family in the area. Acquiring the property had been difficult and Casiville refused to talk about it because it was painful. Once the family was rooted on the

Casiville Bullard, one of St. Paul's pioneer black craftsmen, in his later years.

Most of the residences surrounding the Casiville Bullard House were built in the 1920s, more than a decade after the Bullards constructed their home.

property, however, the neighborhood accepted them. In 1909, Casiville began building a new, larger house on the lot, a necessity since the family was growing. Eventually, the Bullard family would include ten children. Casiville labored on the dwelling in the evenings after work, Addie holding a lantern for him while he laid the brick. Completed in 1910, the house was a 24- by 26-foot, two-and-a-half-story, wood-framed, American Four-square with a brick veneer. Popular between 1900 and 1920, the American Foursquare is a subtype of the Prairie style. Featuring a low-pitched hip roof and a boxlike plan, it is sometimes called the Prairie Box. The Bullard House was a vernacular version of the style, incorporating hip-roofed dormers and a single-story, hip-roofed porch at the west facade.

The Bullards were happy in the Como area and spent much time pic-nicking in Como Park and skating on Lake Como. Casiville often enter-tained the family by playing the harmonica and guitar. Addie died in 1918, a victim of the influenza pandemic that decimated communities through-out the world in the early twentieth century. Two years later the family moved to another home Casiville constructed on Maryland Avenue, a few blocks south of the Folsom Street residence. The new house was on a large parcel, giving the Bullards more space to raise dairy cows, chickens, and a vegetable garden. In 1927, Casiville married Fannie Josephine Russell, an acquaintance from Memphis. In 1937, the year the couple moved to a one-story house on West Central Avenue in St. Paul, Fannie passed away. Casiville and his children operated the Sweet Shop, a restaurant at the cor-ner of Central and Western Avenues, from 1940 to 1943. Casiville began living with one of his daughters in 1948, around the same time he retired from stone- and brickwork. He died in 1959 at age eighty-six. The Casiville Bullard House on Folsom Street remains, however, as does the dwelling on Maryland Avenue. As the earliest extant residence associated with the life and career of one of St. Paul's pioneer black craftsmen, the Casiville Bullard House on Folsom Street was added to the National Register in 1997.

✳ Paul Watkins House

WINONA | WINONA COUNTY

Way back in 1868 when Minnesota was young, when Indians roamed her plains and hills and when great forests covered many parts of this State, a new business was started by a young man. This young man, J. R. Watkins, was a pioneer in this new kind of business and was the originator of a novel and highly effective system of distribution—organized house-to-house selling. . . . The trying reconstruction period had barely started when young Watkins launched his new enterprise, the manufacture and sale of a wonderful Liniment. He had great faith in his Liniment, and with youth's ardent zeal he set about to convert people to its use.

The remainder of this company history written by J. R. Watkins Company (now simply called Watkins) of Winona, Minnesota, is even more romantic, but by the time it was published in 1928 the business deserved to be a little sentimental and self-ingratiating. After all, the tiny one-person operation begun by Joseph Ray Watkins in 1868 had mushroomed into a mammoth commercial enterprise by the late 1920s, with offices, factories, and distribution centers in Winona, New York, Chicago, Newark, Columbus, Kansas City, Memphis, Oakland, Montreal, Hamilton, Winnipeg, and Vancouver. The company would eventually branch into Europe and South America as well. In the first half of the twentieth century, the door-to-door "Watkins Man" became about as common in some communities as the local postal carrier. As the business expanded, so did the product line championed by the Watkins Man, which came to include food products, spices, extracts, toiletries, and more. (Today both men and women make up the company's sales force.) As Joseph Ray Watkins wore out the soles of his shoes peddling his liniment in the early days of his business, it is doubtful he dreamed his company would grow so large.[63]

The J. R. Watkins Company was already a multimillion-dollar machine when Paul Watkins joined his uncle's business as vice president in 1892. In 1911 he succeeded Joseph Ray Watkins as president. Although Paul Watkins inherited a successful enterprise, it was under his guidance that most of the branch offices and distribution centers were established, making the J. R. Watkins Company one of the largest direct-selling companies in the world. But even though the business had offices in major urban centers like New York and Chicago, the headquarters remained about 115 miles southeast of the Twin Cities in the Mississippi River town of Winona. It was here that the incredible Paul Watkins House was built, designed by noted architect Ralph Adams Cram of Cram and Ferguson, Boston.

Ralph Adams Cram is best known for his Gothic forms. Indeed, the *Macmillan Encyclopedia of Architects* boldly states that he was the "foremost Gothic revival architect of the United States." His office designed numerous churches in the style, including All Saints, Ashmont (1892) in Dorchester, a suburb of Boston, as well as St. Thomas Church (1906) on Fifth Avenue in New York City. Still, Cram did not confine himself solely to Gothic architecture. Richmond Court (1898), Cram's own apartment house in Brookline, Massachusetts, was designed in Tudor style, and the Federal Building (1930) in Boston was developed as an Art Deco skyscraper. Cram's penchant for Tudor architecture was further evidenced when he designed the Paul Watkins House as a Jacobethan Revival–style structure, although that architectural designation had yet to be coined when the dwelling was planned in the early 1920s. Architectural historian Marcus Whiffin explains that Jacobethan Revival architecture was "compounded from Jacobean and Elizabethan," English styles from the reign of Elizabeth I (1558–1603) and James I (1603–25).

Constructed between 1924 and 1927, the obscenely gorgeous Paul Watkins House was described by its architect as "a modified English sixteenth-century form, partly Tudor, partly Elizabethan." In other words, Whiffin's Jacobethan. The style frequently employs steeply pitched roofs, with gables rising above the roofline. Bay windows and large rectangular

Now used for elder care, the Paul Watkins House exults in architectural excess, almost wallowing in self-importance, which would seem insulting if the mansion was not so captivating.

"The main stairway
is unusually massive
and very richly carved,"
the mansion's architect,
Ralph Adams Cram,
wrote in 1928.

window openings divided by stone mullions are common as well. Decorative chimneys are often very high, with individual shafts for each flue.
Entrances are regularly embellished with classical detailing, although classical forms are usually absent from other parts of the structure. All of these
elements were found in the mansion Cram designed for Paul Watkins. Facing northeast on East Wabasha Street near the center of Winona, the large,
T-shaped house was formed of Harvard brick with stone trim. The facade
was dominated by two-story window bays surmounted with balustrades
and large, steeply pitched dormers, complementing the house's slate gable
roof, which was steeply pitched and pierced at the ridge by two chimneys.
The facade was further marked by rectangular window openings with multipane windows, a feature common to most of the building. The arched

main entrance was covered by gates of hand-wrought-iron and topped with an ornate entablature resting upon fluted stone pilasters with decorative capitals. A two-story, hip-roofed section with chimney branched from the building's east side and the opposite side featured a two-story, hip-roofed porte cochere with chimney. The building's rear section had very large multi-pane windows and a projecting window bay.

The thirty-nine-room interior was as fantastic as the exterior, featuring carved wood paneling throughout, hand-carved stair railings, parquet floors, marble bathrooms, chandeliers, molded plaster ceilings, and more. Watkins apparently had one of the most experienced master plasterers in the country working on his home, a craftsman who boasted that his family had been molders since the time of Christ. "My father, my father's father, his father's father and down through the centuries we have been plasterers," the man explained. The most extraordinary interior space was the Great Hall or Music Room, which occupied the entire rear section of the house and exhibited an open-timber roof. Cram described it as "suggestive of the hall in an old English manor house." The room had a huge stone fireplace and an Aeolian pipe organ composed of nearly six thousand pipes.

Paul Watkins only enjoyed his grand house for four years, passing away on Christmas Eve 1931. Florence Watkins, Paul's wife, remained in the home until she died in 1956. Their children donated the property to the Central Methodist Church of Winona, which employed the residence for elderly care. An almost glorious architectural piece, and home to one of the most influential citizens in Winona's history, the Paul Watkins House was added to the National Register in 1984. Incidentally, after suffering through bankruptcy in the late 1970s, the business begun by Joseph Ray Watkins in 1868 rebounded and continues to provide spices, extracts, and other home and health products worldwide.

✳ Merton S. Goodnow House

HUTCHINSON | McLEOD COUNTY

Merton S. Goodnow was a native of Hutchinson, a south-central Minnesota community about sixty miles west of Minneapolis in McLeod County. Born in 1870, Goodnow graduated from the local high school and eventually attended the University of Minnesota, graduating with a degree in dentistry in 1897. That same year he returned to Hutchinson and set up a dental practice, which he maintained for many years. A member of the Masons, as well as the Modern Woodmen of America, a fraternal benefit society founded in Omaha, Nebraska, in 1890, Goodnow was a civic-minded citizen who served on the local school board and the public library board. One of Hutchinson's notable residents in the early twentieth century, today he

One of Purcell and Elmslie's earliest creations, the 1913 Merton S. Goodnow House reflects Prairie School style in its horizontal lines, exaggerated eave overhangs, projecting beams, broad chimney, and its mixed brick and stucco exterior.

would likely frown with the knowledge that his name is celebrated more for his house than for his professional and public service.[64]

While the residence Goodnow constructed on South Main Street in 1913 is not breathtaking, it is still a handsome example of the Prairie style. Prairie School architecture was popular mainly between 1900 and 1920, although Frank Lloyd Wright, generally acknowledged as the principal spokesman of the style, employed Prairie characteristics as early as 1893, when he designed Winslow House in River Forest, Illinois. One of the few truly American architectural styles, it was developed by a group of Chicago architects who wanted to express building design as an extension of the midwestern prairies. The style is apparent from its predominantly horizontal character, which is demonstrated by widely overhanging eaves and windows arranged in horizontal rows. The windows sometimes feature leaded glass and geometric patterns. Although some Prairie-style buildings are covered with gable roofs, most feature low-pitched hip roofs. Roofs are often pierced with large, rectangular chimneys. Prairie houses are frequently two-story structures with one-story wings and are usually sheathed with brick, stucco, or wood, but a combination of these materials is also employed at times. One-story porches, porte cocheres, or terraces add to the horizontal appearance of Prairie houses. Often walls extend from the building, seeming almost a part of the landscape, and further stress the structure's horizontal character.

Not surprisingly, Prairie architecture was most common in and around Chicago, especially in the suburbs of River Forest and Oak Park. The style found its way into other communities as well. The Martin House in Buffalo, New York, is a very large Prairie-style home that was constructed in 1904, and the Jeremiah Jones House in Dallas, Texas, which was built circa 1920, features a wide front gable that hides a hip-roofed unit at the rear. Even though many examples of Prairie architecture are located throughout the country, the style remains uniquely midwestern and it is in the heartland where most Prairie-style structures were built, including many that were designed by Purcell and Elmslie, a prominent Minneapolis architectural firm that planned the Merton S. Goodnow House.

Purcell and Elmslie were two of the trendsetting Chicago architects who helped develop the Prairie style. In 1909, William Purcell and George Feick Jr. were operating an architectural firm in Minneapolis when they were joined by George Elmslie. Feick left the partnership in 1913, but Purcell and Elmslie remained together until 1922. During that time the partnership became, in the words of architectural historian Rolf T. Anderson, "one of the leading architectural practices of the early twentieth century and emerged as the most important Minnesota firm within the Prairie School." The duo was responsible for the design of numerous public and private Prairie-style buildings in Minnesota and elsewhere, and counted the Woodbury County Courthouse in Sioux City, Iowa, as one of their major accomplishments. Completed in 1918, the structure was "the only major civic building constructed by any of the architects of the Prairie

The interior of the Goodnow House continues the horizontal theme of Prairie School style.

School." Other Prairie-style buildings developed by the firm were the Jump River Town Hall, completed in Jump River, Wisconsin, in 1915, and the Kasson Municipal Building, constructed in 1917 in Kasson, Minnesota. Residential structures designed by the partners included the J. W. S. Gallagher House, built in Winona in 1913, and Lake Place, Purcell's own home in Minneapolis, which was also erected in 1913. The architectural significance of all of these buildings has been recognized through their listing on the National Register.

The Merton S. Goodnow House was completed the same year as the Gallagher House and Lake Place and typified most of Purcell and Elmslie's early residential designs. These dwellings "were distinguished by simple massing, compact plans and, if possible, the use of inexpensive materials," and were inspired by Frank Lloyd Wright's "Fireproof House for $5,000," a 1907 piece published in the *Ladies' Home Journal*. Purcell and Elmslie's two-story Goodnow House featured a medium-pitched, cross-gabled roof with wide overhanging eaves accented with large beams. A large, rectangular chimney pierced the roof's ridge. Resting on a concrete foundation, first-floor walls consisted of dark brown brick, while second-floor walls were yellow-tinted stucco. Window openings held one-over-one windows, with the windows of the upper walls arranged in horizontal rows. A one-story, gable-roofed sunroom projected from the east facade and a wing extended from the south side. The slope of the roof at the south side was broken by a gable-roofed dormer and a through-cornice dormer. A semicircular-arched main entrance, a nod to Romanesque style, marked the east side of the south projecting wing. The entrance door was embellished with leaded glass panels featuring the initial "G" for "Goodnow."

Purcell and Elmslie's reputation grew in the years following construction of the dwelling on South Main Street in Hutchinson, but later notoriety was rooted in the firm's early work, which makes the Goodnow House more significant than most residences. Today, the house is occupied by its seventh family, a household intent on maintaining and restoring many of the architectural qualities that make the house historically important. A worthy example of the Prairie style attributed to Purcell and Elmslie, as well as a community landmark, the Merton S. Goodnow House was added to the National Register in 1985.

✳ Muret N. Leland House

WELLS | FARIBAULT COUNTY

"If I'd known then what I know now we'd never [have] bought the place." Kenneth Brehm was probably only half serious when he made that comment to the *Wells Mirror* in 1984, five years after he and his wife, Yvonne, purchased the Muret N. Leland House on Second Avenue Southwest in Wells, Minnesota, a Faribault County town roughly twenty-five miles northwest of Albert Lea. By 1979, almost a century after the Leland House was constructed, the residence required major restoration. Nevertheless, Yvonne had fallen in love with the place and welcomed the challenge of bringing it back to life. Kenneth was less enthusiastic. In 1984 the couple was still laboring and Kenneth was likely grumbling about better ways to spend one's retirement. But the duo soldiered on. Unfortunately, Yvonne passed away in 1987, leaving Kenneth to fulfill the potential she had seen in the dwelling many years earlier. Kenneth soon completed Yvonne's dream—the house as elegant as it was that summer day in 1890 when the Leland family began making memories within its walls.[65]

The architect is unknown, but the Leland House was built in 1883 by Frankie Watson, a medical doctor who used the building as both residence and office. Little is available concerning the doctor, except that his home was sold to Muret N. Leland seven years after it was completed. Leland was one of those men about whom early county histories wax poetic, a prominent citizen who helped shape the success of the community. Born in Quincy, Michigan, in 1849, Leland's father was a member of the state senate. In 1870, after gaining experience in various mercantile establishments, Leland moved to Wells and opened his own store. Later that year he married Libbie Townsend from Coldwater, Michigan. Since Wells was platted only a year before Leland arrived, his business was one of the community's first commercial enterprises, prospering as the town grew. He must have been a significant commercial influence in the region by the mid-1890s because a local newspaper tagged him the "merchant prince of southern Minnesota." Leland was also politically active, serving as mayor and school board member for many years. In 1884 he was elected to the Minnesota legislature.

Not as boisterous as the
Queen Anne–style John G.
Lund House in Canby in
Yellow Medicine County,
the late-nineteenth-century
Muret N. Leland House
nevertheless whispers
"look at me."

The attractive two-and-a-half-story Queen Anne–style dwelling Leland
acquired from Watson was one of the larger residences in Wells and
seemed befitting for one of the community's leading citizens. Queen Anne
style, a subtype of Victorian architecture, became popular about 1880.
Even though most Victorian styles passed from favor by the beginning of
the twentieth century, Queen Anne architecture remained somewhat common until about 1910, although the Samuel R. DuBois House in Vassar,
Michigan, was a particularly late example, completed around 1915. A decorative style, even gaudy at times, Queen Anne architecture often features
irregular massing, multiple rooflines, one-story wraparound porches, bay
windows, patterned chimneys, and towers. The fanciful Leland House
exhibited all of these characteristics.

While the Leland House was large, it was not quite large enough, and
even before the family moved into the dwelling a sympathetic addition was
made to its south side, making the irregularly shaped building even more

irregularly shaped. The wood-framed house was covered with clapboard siding and had a multigabled roof and numerous windows set into rectangular openings. Sitting upon a limestone foundation, the main entrance at the dwelling's east facade was shielded by a covered porch supported upon classical columns. A portion of the porch roof was embellished with a pediment. The porch wrapped around the house's northeast corner, merging with a pyramidal-roofed porte cochere with ornate finial, turned posts, and bracketed eaves. The porch columns were linked by balustrades with decorative spindles. A bay window projected from the first floor of the east facade, just south of the porch. The facade was further accented by a partially shingled, second-story corner tower with conical roof and finial. The east facade of the south addition was set back several feet from the facade of the main section. The entrance at the addition's first floor was covered by another attractive porch with balustrades and pedimented roof section. A patterned chimney hugged the addition's south wall.

The Leland House was the venue for many festive occasions, including the weddings of at least two of the Lelands' daughters. The prominent structure was even host to the local high school prom in 1900. The Lelands' resided in the house until about 1902 or 1903, when Muret retired and the family moved to Minneapolis. At least one family member left her mark on the house. When Rosamond Leland graduated from high school her father presented her with a diamond, which she used to carve her name into a section of the large window in the front sitting room. The Brehms left the mark as remembrance of the Lelands. After Libbie Leland died about 1918, Muret began spending much of his time in California, where he passed away in 1921.

The Leland House served a succession of owners and renters after Libbie and Muret departed Wells. Nearing its century mark, it was battered. But then an enthusiastic woman convinced her doubting husband that they could restore the house to its original elegant form. It was difficult—and expensive; so expensive that almost a decade after the Brehms began the restoration project Kenneth refused to total the costs: "I've got the figures but I've never added them up. I'm afraid to!" Even though Kenneth groused a bit about the labor and expense, he said the restoration project was still a "labor of love and a time of learning." Associated with one of the pioneer citizens of Wells and a sterling example of Queen Anne architecture, the Muret N. Leland House was placed on the National Register in 1980.

Often a feature of the Queen Anne style, towers are rarely practical, just delightfully showy.

Rosamond Leland did not want to be forgotten, and all subsequent occupants of the Muret N. Leland House have honored her wish.

✳ Lena O. Smith House

MINNEAPOLIS | HENNEPIN COUNTY

The Lena O. Smith House is a two-and-a-half-story, rectangular, wood-framed and side-gabled structure situated near the intersection of Fifth Avenue South and Thirty-ninth Street East in South Minneapolis, only a few blocks east of Interstate Highway 35W. Constructed in 1912, the comfortable dwelling is dressed in clapboard siding and rests upon a stone foundation coated in cement. Rectangular windows mark the walls and a gable-roofed dormer protrudes from the roof at the west facade. Although not as ornate as the Classical Revival–style Hanna C. and Peter E. Thompson House, the dwelling still exhibits classical detailing, including gable returns and Ionic columns that support the front porch's hip roof. The structure's unpretentiousness belies its importance, since it was once home to one of Minnesota's most prominent African Americans, Lena Olive Smith.[66]

Like Casiville Bullard, Smith bettered the lives of African Americans in Minnesota. But while Bullard's contribution was subtle, demonstrating through his daily labors that blacks were just as talented as whites, Smith's offering was unabashedly vocal. Moving from Kansas to Minnesota with her mother and siblings around 1906, Smith sought her niche in occupations like hairdressing and dermatology. She even learned the art of embalming. Such vocations were unsatisfying for one with a social conscience that compelled action, however. Graduating from Northwestern College of Law (now William Mitchell College of Law) in 1921 at age thirty-five, she became one of only a handful of black attorneys who practiced law in Minneapolis in the late nineteenth and early twentieth centuries. Moreover, she was the first African American woman licensed to practice law in Minnesota. For the next forty-five years she crusaded against racial injustice, battling and educating a social system fraught with bigotry and intolerance.

In 1920 three black circus roustabouts accused of assaulting a white woman were lynched from a telephone pole in Duluth while a mob cheered. The event made a profound impression on the idealistic Smith, strengthening her resolve to seek justice for the underrepresented. Four years after leaving law school she helped found the Minneapolis chapter of the Urban League, an organization established in 1910 to better the social and economic position of African Americans. When the Urban League in Minneapolis came into existence the black population was still small, totaling less than four thousand. Most African Americans were concentrated in two main areas. The near north neighborhood enveloped the business and entertainment areas on Lyndale and Sixth Avenues, and the south side neighborhood spread out around Fourth Avenue South and Thirty-eighth Street. Most of these citizens worked as porters, waiters, and laborers, although the city did have some black professionals and businessmen, including a few restaurant owners and several barbers. A small number of black lawyers, physicians, and dentists also worked in the community. The city employed some blacks in the police and fire departments, and about thirty African Americans worked for the post office.

In 1931 Smith assumed the case of one black postal employee whose prior legal council was anything but stellar. The family of A. A. Lee was suffering the wrath of their new neighbors and others because they had the audacity to move into an all-white section of the city. After dropping their first attorney, a professional offering the remarkably unprofessional advice that the family sell their home on Columbus Avenue South and scat, the Lee family received aid from the National Association for the Advancement of Colored People (NAACP), another national group committed to helping African Americans. Smith would become president of the Minneapolis chapter of the NAACP in the mid-1930s, but in 1931 she was the organization's representative in the Lee case, providing counsel to the family and lending her voice to the media covering a sensational happening that never should have been a sensational happening. In July 1931, standing outside the Lee home, facing the press and a bigoted crowd estimated at around 3,000, Smith was quoted by the *Minneapolis Star:* "[Lee] has no intention of moving now or later, even after we are assured the feeling in the district has subsided. He has nothing to trade, barter or sell. I believe we have made that clear to all parties involved." Although the words were forceful, and Smith and the Lee family were determined, the harassment proved too much and the family eventually moved from the hostile neighborhood.

In July 1937 Smith investigated the case of Curtis Jordan, a waiter who had been beaten by two off-duty police officers. Apparently the officers were

The prominent dormer has gable returns.

intoxicated and had accosted others on Sixth Avenue North before noticing Jordan. The *Minneapolis Spokesman,* a local black newspaper, offered an account of what happened next:

> Both officers, cursing violently, ordered everybody off the street. Most people left the scene of the trouble. [The officers] suddenly espied Curtis Jordan, a waiter at the Hotel Curtis, seated alone at the counter in a cafe. They went into the cafe, dragged him to the door, asked him questions which they didn't give him time to answer, slugging him as they dragged him into a squad car.

The *Spokesman* also noted that Curtis "was injured so badly that the police kept him at Northside Station, to give his face wounds time to heal, for a day and night." Surprisingly . . . or maybe not, a municipal judge eventually dismissed charges against the two police officers.

These were the types of battles Lena Olive Smith spent a lifetime waging, most before the inspiration of Reverend Martin Luther King Jr. and

Modestly embellished with classical detailing (note the porch's Ionic columns), the Lena O. Smith House was home to the first black woman licensed to practice law in Minnesota.

other African American leaders helped unite civil rights groups into a formidable national voice. But although Smith sometimes lost, she also won, as when she filed suit against the Nicollet Hotel for refusing to serve a black man at a mixed-race convention. Smith successfully argued that even though the Nicollet had a nondiscrimination policy it was still responsible for damages to her client. Smith also helped end segregation within the balcony of the Pantages Theatre in Minneapolis, and she brought suit against the hamburger chain White Castle for service discrimination.

When Smith passed away in 1966, she was no longer living at her residence on Fifth Avenue South. She had lived long enough to witness the Civil Rights Act of 1964, legislation signed into law by President Lyndon B. Johnson prohibiting discrimination in employment and education, as well as segregation in public places. In a piece for *Hennepin History* in 1995, architectural historian Jacqueline Sluss aptly expressed Smith's starring role on the local civil rights stage:

> *Smith was an original in the field of law in the Twin Cities and no doubt, within the state. . . . The years between 1920 and 1940 witnessed the maturation of major civil rights organizations including the NAACP, and Lena Smith's proactive posture in the courts contributed to the development of the local chapters of the NAACP. . . . Her work made her a champion of the major historical changes of her time.*

As home to one of Minnesota's principal African American leaders, a lawyer who became an ardent defender of civil rights, the Lena O. Smith House was added to the National Register in 1991.

✳ Hinckley Fire Relief House

SANDSTONE | PINE COUNTY

A simple, one-and-a-half story, rectangular, wood-framed house with a gable roof stands at the corner of Court Avenue and Sixth Street in Sandstone, Minnesota, a Pine County community roughly eighty miles north of St. Paul. Its face hidden behind a broad arborvitae, the residence is the antithesis of the Paul Watkins House. Most probably pass the unassuming dwelling with barely a glance, but the clapboard-covered residence is special, an 1894 reminder of the region's most tragic event, an episode historically recorded as the "Great Hinckley Fire."[67]

Platted adjacent to the Kettle River in 1887, Sandstone was an outgrowth of the Kettle River Sandstone Company Quarry, today a National Register property that was the most extensive sandstone quarrying operation in the state in the late nineteenth and early twentieth centuries. Sandstone was prospering by the early 1890s, a stop along the route of the Eastern Railway of Minnesota, which was essentially an extension of the Great Northern Railway (GN). The Eastern line ran from Hinckley, about ten miles south of Sandstone, north to Duluth and Superior. This road, along with the St. Paul and Duluth Railroad (StP&D), which operated a line only a short distance west of Sandstone, was hailed as a savior when the massive forest fire of 1894 swept through the area.

Much of Pine and Kanabec Counties had been enveloped in smoke several times during the summer of 1894, a consequence of small fires smoldering in the dry, wooded countryside. As a result, few seemed apprehensive when the skies around Hinckley and Sandstone clouded with ash and smoke on September 1 that same year. An Eastern train was making a regular afternoon run north on the GN tracks to Hinckley, where it would pick up its own line to Lake Superior, while a train for the StP&D was headed south from Duluth. Thickening smoke eventually forced the StP&D train to light its cab and coach lamps, but the engineer was not alarmed until within sight of Hinckley, where a number of panicked people rushed his train pleading for transport out of the area. Frank B. Daugherty, one of the train's passengers, explained: "As [Hinckley residents] were assisted into the cars we gathered from them that the whole surrounding country seemed to be on fire and that Hinckley was burning up." With a few hundred people piled into the passenger cars, the engineer reversed direction, but the surroundings erupted in fire, igniting part of the train. Even so, the engineer kept the train moving until he reached a swamp called Skunk Lake, a few miles north of Hinckley. Passengers rushed from the coaches into the swamp, a decision that saved their lives. The train, however, was devoured by the blaze.

The Eastern train had a similar experience. Overloaded with those fleeing the area, it barely escaped disaster, passing over the Kettle River Bridge at Sandstone only minutes before the structure's timber approach spans collapsed in flames. The train and its passengers eventually reached safety. Many in Sandstone, Hinckley, and other nearby towns were less fortunate. Patrick Regan, a citizen of Sandstone, followed his family to the Kettle River as fire engulfed the town, witnessing an awful episode along the way: "As I was running, I saw a woman coming from another direction, evidently making for the river. I thought I would wait for her and try to help her along, but the flames traveled faster than she did; they soon overtook her and she dropped in her tracks, her clothing all on fire." Regan's own clothing was on fire by the time he plunged into the Kettle River.

After the fire passed, relief parties arrived, meeting with a terrible sight. Approximately five hundred square miles of Pine and Kanabec Counties had been obliterated, including the communities of Sandstone, Hinckley,

Mission Creek, Pokegema, Finlayson, Miller (Groningen), and Partridge (Askov). Eighteen bodies were discovered in a well at Sandstone, twelve of them children. At a nearby farm a mother and her five children perished as they tried to escape their blazing cellar. Hundreds of remains were found in Hinckley. Amidst all the carnage, however, emerged an astonishing discovery. Reverend E. Anderson of Sandstone, a member of a party gathering the deceased, recalled the group's surprise at recovering an unexpected survivor: "One of the most remarkable cases was a babe which we found yet clinging with its little arms about its mother's neck, not very much hurt, though its mother, lying face down, was burnt in front to a black fire brand." But such recoveries were rare. While the loss of life around Sandstone and Hinckley was not as great as that experienced from the forest fire near Peshtigo, Wisconsin, in 1871, it was still devastating. For the next several months, citizens in the region continued to stumble upon bodies in remote locations. The death toll eventually reached 418.

On September 3, 1894, Minnesota Governor Knute Nelson appointed a State Fire Relief Commission to administer state aid, as well as the donations that poured in from throughout the country and the world. The sultan of Turkey even contributed, providing three hundred Turkish pounds. One responsibility of the commission was the construction of modest, wood-framed houses for victims who had lost their homes and had little or no insurance for rebuilding—akin to an early version of our modern Habitat for Humanity. The adopted plan was for a house measuring about 16 by 24

Fire relief houses were not beautiful, but they were welcomed by desperate families in late 1894.

feet and costing between $95 and $150, not including labor. Many of the
houses were single-story structures, but one-and-a-half-story buildings were
erected for larger families. Another smaller section was added if the family
was especially large.

The one-and-a-half-story house at the intersection of Court Avenue and
Sixth Street in Sandstone featured a single-story section at the rear. Completed at a cost of $181, the residence was occupied by the six members
of the Edward Halverson family, who escaped the inferno that destroyed
their original home by wading into the Kettle River. Like most victims, the
Halversons received temporary housing and other assistance in Duluth
while carpenters for the State Fire Relief Commission built their new house.
Once finished, the home was supplied with simple furniture, utensils, bed-
ding, and a store of food.

Today, most of the more than two hundred fire relief houses erected in
the months following the 1894 blaze have been razed or drastically altered.
The Halverson House, however, maintains a high degree of historic integrity,
making it a good representative of the humanitarian efforts that marked
the aftermath of one of the worst natural disasters in Minnesota's history.
The humble residence, now more commonly known as the Hinckley Fire
Relief House, was placed on the National Register in 1980.

✳ Lorenz & Lugerde Ginthner House

WABASHA | WABASHA COUNTY

Wabasha has a curious heritage. Situated on the Mississippi River in Wabasha County in southeastern Minnesota, around thirty miles southeast of Red Wing, much of the community's early residential character differed substantially from neighboring towns. Even more, its most prominent early citizens generally came from the merchant-tradesman class. Maybe that does not seem unusual, but in mid- to late-nineteenth-century Minnesota selling clothing or laboring as a tinsmith was not the short path to wealth and veneration. No, most Minnesota towns either flourished or failed under the guidance of grain merchants, land speculators, financiers, and the like—those who often made fortunes quickly.[68]

Wabasha already had about a hundred citizens by the time it was platted in 1854. Benefiting from its river location, amidst a region of prized timber and fertile soil, the community rapidly evolved into a distribution point for lumber and wheat. But unlike pacesetters in Reads Landing, Lake City, and Red Wing to the north, most town leaders in Wabasha remained detached from the land. Moreover, this large collection of merchant-tradesmen erected houses that frequently contrasted with residences of the prominent personalities in those other communities. While elites in Red Wing and Lake City constructed mostly wood-framed Victorian dwellings, their counterparts in Wabasha were chiefly drawn to red brick houses with Romantic flourishes. Initially, this meant somewhat modest homes with Greek Revival or Federal-style influences, but by the 1870s home design was more fanciful and had turned to the Italianate.

Italianate style, as the name implies, was drawn from the architectural fashions of Italy, a country described by the wonderfully witty architectural historian Roger Kennedy as "a popular place for travelers first to wonder at and then to ransack." Kennedy notes that beginning in the late nineteenth century it was not uncommon for the American wealthy to travel to Italy, crate up an entire room, and sometimes a whole house, and ship it to America. Of course, only the richest of the rich could transport all of the constituents of a grand residence across an ocean and piece them back together again. But even though the semi-rich had fewer resources with which to pillage the land of romance, they were still able to construct ornamental Italian-looking houses, thanks in part to the house-style pattern books of Andrew Jackson Downing that were published in the 1840s and 1850s.

Low-pitched roofs and narrow windows often set within arched openings crowned with ornate, U-shaped window hoods are identifying characteristics of Italianate style. Some examples have square towers or cupolas as well. The most common feature is the widely overhanging eaves accented with large, decorative brackets, which explains why Italianate architecture

is occasionally called Bracketed style. Wabasha's most exuberant example of Italianate architecture is located at the corner of West Third Street and Allegheny Avenue, a building commissioned by Lorenz (also spelled Lawrence) and Lugerde Ginthner.

Lorenz Ginthner was one of Wabasha's foremost late-nineteenth-century merchants, a tailor praised by the local newspaper: "By a long course of honest and fair dealing, [Lorenz] Ginthner has established a business which draws custom from all parts of Wabasha and Buffalo counties. As a citizen Mr. Ginthner stands the peer of any man, and is held in universal respect." Unfortunately, almost nothing is known of his wife, Lugerde, which underscores one of history's monumental gaffes—the extraordinary dearth of information on women.

Lorenz was a native of Baden, Germany, the same city that produced fellow Wabasha merchant Lucas Kuehn. Both arrived in America in 1852, each settling in Wabasha three years later, a year after the community was platted. Lorenz soon married Lugerde, while Kuehn married a Ginthner. Both men eventually established mercantile businesses that slowly grew as Wabasha grew. In time, each constructed his own business block.

Like Ginthner, Kuehn also erected an Italianate-style trophy house. The fact that Kuehn built his home in 1878, twenty-three years after he came to Wabasha, while Ginthner's was not completed until 1882, twenty-seven years after he arrived, implies that making wealth as a merchant in nineteenth-century Minnesota often required considerable time.

Fixed atop a limestone foundation and featuring a hip roof embellished

Very large houses were rare in early Minnesota, but prosperous owners often erected dwellings with considerable ornamentation. The Ginthner House still retains decorative elements such as large brackets, limestone hoods, and oculus windows.

with false gables at the southwest facade and northwest side, the Ginthner House is more detailed than the Kuehn House and is a somewhat better example of Italianate architecture. The two-story, L-shaped main section is joined at the northeast rear by a one-and-a-half-story wing, which in turn is contiguous with a smaller wing. A wood veranda with decorative pillars and cornice is located at the facade. The walls of the facade hold rectangular windows that are surmounted by decorative U-shaped limestone hoods, a window design common to much of the building. A bay window projects from the first floor of the northwest side and a limestone oculus is positioned within the wall beneath each false gable, lighting the attic. The widely overhanging eaves of the roof are accented with large, ornamental brackets appended to the dentiled cornice.

The architects for many of Wabasha's impressive nineteenth-century brick residences are unknown, including the designers of the Ginthner House, Kuehn House, and the two Italianate-style residences belonging to Kuehn's daughters. While regrettable, it is not odd, since Wabasha did not attract architects until the twentieth century. It is possible that prominent architects like Charles Maybury of Winona or Ewin Alexander of Lake City designed some of Wabasha's distinguished homes. The contractor for the Ginthner and Kuehn Houses is also uncertain, although James H. Evans was the dominant mason/contractor in Wabasha at the time the homes were built and likely was involved in their construction. In fact, by the mid-1880s, Evans had worked on almost three-quarters of the brick buildings in Wabasha. Furthermore, he constructed a brick Italianate-style residence for himself. Not surprisingly, the contractor who became mayor was also a merchant, a part owner of a local meat market.

In 1987 historian Paul Clifford Larson completed a study of Wabasha's late-nineteenth-century red brick residences associated with merchant-tradesmen, an intriguing examination that eventually led to National Register listing for several Wabasha dwellings. The Kuehn House was one of the honorees, as was the most detailed Italianate-style residence in the community, the Ginthner House. While the Kuehn House was not added to the historic listing until 1994, the Ginthner House gained membership into the exclusive club only a year after Larson finished his study. Today, the Ginthner House looks much as it did when it was constructed 125 years ago, thanks mainly to Jay Anderson, a preservation-minded individual who has owned the structure for more than three decades. Anderson is fortunate, since he owns, in Larson's words, "the single most outstanding nineteenth-century residence in Wabasha."

GATHERING PLACES 9

IN THE 1870S AND 1880S many religiously devout settlers in Scambler, Dunn, and Pelican Townships in Otter Tail County in west-central Minnesota assembled in local residences for church services. Sometimes the Union Church of Christ in Scambler (later First Congregational Church) employed the local school as spiritual center. The church disbanded in 1884, never having constructed a building solely for religious services. Three decades later residents in the region formed the People's Union Church and worshiped in a modest, but nevertheless charming, wood-framed building in Scambler Township. Almost ninety years later the religious gathering place constructed and managed by women remains and likely will soon find a place on the National Register.[69]

As demonstrated by the people in the townships of Scambler, Dunn, and Pelican, a formal gathering place can be located most anywhere, even in an informal setting. This characteristic was most evident in newly settled areas, since the population did not always have the resources to construct a venue simply for congregating. Centers designed primarily for assemblage became more prominent as prosperity increased and a strong sense of community developed. Some of the earliest buildings constructed as meeting locales were government structures like town halls. Oftentimes lonesome buildings with little neighboring improvements except rural roads, town halls are the setting from which township boards govern the township community. Board meetings usually attract a gathering of township citizens exercising their right to participate in the democratic process. Town halls, however, rarely served strictly governmental functions and have often been used to host celebratory get-togethers as well, such as wedding receptions, banquets, and dances. At other times, they are employed for solemn events, like funeral dinners.

Town halls are not the only government buildings to be used as sites for festival or reflection. Remember, the Howard Lake City Hall, while home to vital city functions, also held the community auditorium, which doubled as a basketball court. Commercial buildings, too, have frequently made room for entertainment, socializing, or other community needs. As noted earlier, the basement of the First National Bank in Blooming Prairie was specifically designed as a meeting center, while the basement of the First National Bank in Fulda evolved into one. The Big Store in Minneota was topped with an opera house, an elegant name for a facility that was mostly a place to watch traveling vaudeville acts or listen to guest speakers or bands, or maybe enjoy a banquet.

The importance of social and entertainment sites was more apparent when they were built as stand-alone community features. In the early 1900s, after years of housing cultural activities in commercial buildings, the town of Belview in Redwood County in southeastern Minnesota erected the Odeon Theater independent of other buildings, suggesting its dominance as the town's cultural heart. In 1915, Herman Jochims, a resident of Luverne, the county seat of Rock County, constructed the Palace Theater on the corner of Main Street and Freeman Avenue. An especially large building for the time, the two-story structure featured a Classical Revival–style exterior and an Art Nouveau–style interior. Both the Odeon and Palace Theaters originally hosted live entertainment before adapting to motion pictures. Each has subsequently been added to the National Register.

Gathering sites intended mostly for specific groups have always been common to Minnesota. While the most obvious examples are church buildings, which were constructed for those wishing to celebrate a higher order, fraternal society buildings mark many towns as well. The Grand Army of the Republic (G.A.R.), for instance, erected meeting halls throughout the state. A kind of early version of the American Legion, the G.A.R. was an organization of Union Civil War veterans. Initially a political lobby, the G.A.R. is probably best remembered for its charitable and patriotic efforts. In a country of immigrants, ethnic lodges also found a home. Ethnic lodge buildings dot even the most remote corners of Minnesota, serving to perpetuate the cultural values of the "old country."

Another type of ethnic gathering locale was the settlement house. The moniker is something of a misnomer since settlement houses were frequently quite large and did not always resemble houses. Forerunners to modern social service organizations, settlement houses were places to teach American culture and practices to newly arrived immigrants to this country, although the Phyllis Wheatley House in North Minneapolis was specifically contructed to serve a disenfranchised African American population. At one time, Minneapolis and St. Paul, like many large urban areas, had several settlement houses in neighborhoods most in need of social and economic support.

Through listings on the National Register, Minnesota has recognized the social and architectural contributions of many gathering places to the state's heritage. Winter Saloon, for example, is an austere "watering hole" constructed in Norwood in Carver County around 1890. The building's second floor was used as a fraternal meeting hall for the Modern Woodmen of America and other groups. St. Mary's Church, an elegant Beaux Arts–style building in New Trier in Dakota County, was erected in 1909. St. Mary's became known as the "Mother Church" for other nearby Catholic congregations.

This section tells the stories of other National Register gathering places, including the North East Neighborhood House, the only settlement house in Minnesota honored with a historic designation. Unfortunately, gathering places as a specific property type have received little contextual study from Minnesota scholars, a void that is surprising given the prominent role of meeting sites in communities. Then again, such study would be very broad. Historians mostly judge the historic value of properties by comparison with identical properties—evaluating town halls against other town halls, for instance. Even so, the concept of gathering place seems to warrant in-depth scholarship, especially since we have an almost instinctive desire to gather, regardless of venue.

✳ Church of St. Boniface (Church of St. Mary)

MELROSE | STEARNS COUNTY

In May 1989 Father Ralph G. Zimmerman learned he soon would become the pastor at St. Mary's Catholic Church in Melrose, a small town in Stearns County around thirty miles northwest of St. Cloud. He had passed the church many times, viewing its twin towers from the freeway as he drove by the city. But now it was different. St. Mary's was to be his parish and he felt compelled to call on the striking building and gather a sense of its history before assuming his new role.[70] Five years and many sermons later, he penned his thoughts of that visit:

It was late in the afternoon when I walked up the long steps of the main church entrance. No one was around and I was alone in the building. I walked slowly up and down the long aisles and sat down on one of the sanctuary steps to get the feel of the place I would call my church home. All of a sudden I had the distinct impression that someone was watching me. I looked over my shoulder and stared right into the "Eye of God" stained glass window. The strong spring sun was brilliantly shining though it. God was watching!

Father Zimmerman was taken with the church's splendor, but he was more impressed by the sense of God that it engendered. The pastor understood that it was not the stunning architecture of the place that created, in his words, "magnificence and beauty." Instead, it was the "People of God" that made the church a special place. True—but stunning architecture doesn't hurt.

St. Mary's is gorgeous. Its Romanesque Revival–style design is indicative of the impressive cathedrals and chapels that mark so many of the small agricultural communities of Europe. Specifically, its architecture reflects the ideals of America's German Catholic immigrants in the late nineteenth century, a population generally committed to grand architectural expressions of faith. Formed of red pressed brick and resting upon a foundation of gray St. Cloud granite blocks, the building's dominant features are its two square towers that flank its east facade. Each tower supports an octagonal belfry capped by a metal onion dome. Both domes are crowned with cupolas that are surmounted with Coptic crosses. Three widely spaced entrances set within arched openings punctuate the facade. A steeply pitched pediment of painted pressed metal accents each opening. The central pediment is marked at its base with volutes (scroll-like ornaments) and gargoyle-type faces. A rose window is situated above the central pediment. The facade and towers also hold several arched window openings filled with leaded and stained glass windows, a feature also found at other parts of the building. Each side of the church has a tower-like bay that holds a confessional. A polygonal bay supporting a rounded apse with a conical roof commands the church's west rear.

The building's impressive interior features several decorative clustered columns bracing a vaulted plaster ceiling. The choir loft and Moller pipe organ are located at the east end and the chancel with its high altar and two side altars are stationed at the west end. A polygonal sacristy, a room where sacred vessels and vestments are stored, is positioned behind the chancel. Elaborately carved wood doors cover entrances to the confessionals and oak pews provide seating for a thousand on the main floor.

St. Mary's did not start out beautiful. In fact, St. Mary's did not start out as St. Mary's. It actually began as St. Boniface, named for the English-born missionary who converted many nonbelievers in Germany to Christianity. St. Boniface was a fitting patron for the new congregation since its mem-

The onion domes and Coptic crosses of St. Boniface are visible to travelers on Interstate Highway 94.

A modern-day view of the church's stunning interior, a superb example of the German Catholic affinity for magnificence in spiritual architecture

bers all emigrated from Germany. The church was founded by about a dozen families in 1878 and was guided by Father Paul Rettenmeier. Initially, the families attended St. Patrick's, Melrose's first organized church, which was established by several Irish families in 1872. The German members of the church eventually broke from St. Patrick's because the congregation never allowed a sermon in German. For all the similarities the Irish and Germans shared regarding their religious beliefs, their attitudes varied greatly when it came to cultural identity. The Irish in America had an advantage over the Germans—they spoke English. Additionally, Irish Catholics not only fled their homeland in the last half of the nineteenth century because of poverty and starvation, but also because of religious persecution. As a result, Irish Catholics generally embraced assimilation into American society. The Germans, however, although also seeking a better life, came from a region of Europe with strong religious traditions. The Germans did not long to change; they simply wanted to transplant the old country's traditions to their new home.

The congregation of St. Boniface erected its church in 1879. It was a modest 30- by 90-foot, wood-framed structure costing around $3,000. The church prospered from the beginning, chiefly due to a rising German population in the community. While New Englanders, and then the Irish, initially dominated Melrose, by the 1880s new settlers were overwhelmingly German. Over time, Germans supplanted the Irish in Melrose as the largest ethnic group. St. Patrick's suffered when many Irish left Melrose soon after the turn of the twentieth century. The congregation totaled 250 in 1884, but by 1910 membership was down to 45. Melrose would lose more Irish families when breadwinners lost jobs after the Great Northern Railway moved its division headquarters from Melrose to St. Cloud in 1923.

While the years would be hard on St. Patrick's, they proved rosy for St. Boniface. Within a few years of its founding, the church expanded to include a combination convent and parochial school. The Sisters of St. Benedict in nearby St. Joseph served as instructors at the school. In 1889 the congregation also built a parsonage. About this time the parish consisted of roughly 130 families. In 1895, to accommodate the copious congregation, the church was enlarged. But some in the parish must already have been thinking about an even larger, more elaborate house of worship. Only three years after expanding the original church, the cornerstone for the present building was laid. On May 1, 1898, Bishop James Trobec presided over a grand ceremony and mass to mark the occasion. A procession of five thousand wound through the streets of Melrose from the old church to the new site, even though the new site was just across the street. A band led the way, followed by schoolchildren, nuns, and religious and laypeople from various religious societies. The bishop was granted the honor of placing the cornerstone.

The new church was constructed under the direction of Father Bernard J. Richter. Its designer was German-born George Bergmann of St. Cloud, an architect who specialized in creating building designs for German communities. Carl Kropp of St. Cloud laid the foundation and local contractor Ed Richmond was charged with erecting the superstructure. The building was finished in early June 1899. Another regal gathering celebrated its completion. On June 6, an escort party on horseback met Bishop Trobec just outside Melrose and guided him and his entourage to the new St. Boniface. Again, schoolchildren and members of Catholic societies were part of the parade. Alone, the bishop entered the church and performed the consecration. The following morning the church was officially dedicated with a mass. The largest church in the Diocese of St. Cloud was just not large enough to accommodate everyone, but about fifteen hundred people managed to wedge themselves inside St. Boniface for the service.

The elegant new church was a source of pride in the German community, clearly reflecting the German Catholic penchant for religious architectural grandeur. Even more, it bespoke the success of St. Boniface parish, a success that would continue throughout the 1900s. By the middle of the twentieth century even St. Patrick's was doing well. By then the congregation occupied a good-sized brick building that was constructed in 1916. Services were actually held in the basement because the upper floors were used as a school and auditorium. The pastor at St. Patrick's was mulling over plans for a new church when the bishop nixed the idea. Bishop Peter W. Bartholeme decided it was time for the Catholic community in Melrose

Positioned between St. Patrick and St. Boniface, the Virgin Mary "keeps the peace."

to come together under one roof, which was easier to accomplish by this time since the demographics had changed. St. Boniface was now dominated by an American-born congregation that did not have the same allegiance to German traditions as earlier generations. Actually, as early as the 1920s English had replaced German as the primary language for services in the church. But Bishop Bartholeme also had another reason for merging St. Patrick's congregation into that of St. Boniface. Already the Catholic Church was suffering from a lack of priests and joining the parishes at Melrose was a practical measure. St. Boniface was renamed St. Mary's in 1958, with Father Julig, the former pastor at St. Patrick's, as its guiding hand. Father Julig placed a statue of St. Boniface on one side of the altar and a statue of St. Patrick on the other. Between the two was a statue of the Virgin Mary. As one writer noted, her role was "to keep the peace." The Church of St. Boniface was placed on the National Register in 1993.

✸ Odeon Theater

BELVIEW | REDWOOD COUNTY

On December 19, 1925, the citizens of Belview in western Minnesota were treated to a movie at the Odeon Theater. The motion picture featured one of the hottest film stars of the period, Rin-Tin-Tin, the "wonder dog." The movie *Tracked in the Snow* was a "Red-Blooded Story of a Fighting Dog."[71] Although the story line in the film's promotion was a bit fuzzy, the advertisement in the local newspaper left little doubt the movie would be exhilarating:

> *The wonder dog of the screen today stands alone: the motion picture star who is truly in a class by himself. And never was he more sensationally thrilling than in his latest picture. You'll quiver with excitement and tingle with glee when you see Rin-Tin-Tin on Saturday—He'll Claw His Way Into Your Heart.*

Whether or not Rin-Tin-Tin succeeded with his clawing only those who attended the movie can say. But more substantial than the film was the venue where it was shown. The Odeon Theater was a distinctly small-town gathering place, an event hall that served as all things to all people.

Belview was born when the Minneapolis and St. Louis Railway was constructed across western Minnesota in the mid-1880s. In 1887 a grain company in Minneapolis sent Fred Simpson to Redwood County to establish a grain warehouse near the railroad line in Kintire Township. Only a short time earlier a local farmer named Hibbard Jones had constructed a boxcar depot in the vicinity. Jones soon also erected a general store to serve area farmers. He followed that with another grain warehouse, while Simpson built a lumber and coal yard. A post office was established in the general store by 1888. One year later, Jones platted a four-block townsite. He divided the blocks into lots and advertised the properties for sale. The town was christened "Belview," apparently inspired by the name of Fred Simpson's sister, Lily Belle.

Belview would never evolve into a thriving metropolis, but a few years after its founding it had become a modest agricultural community. Like many towns, Belview judged its success, at least in part, by the amenities it could offer its citizens. In the late nineteenth and early twentieth centuries, a chief amenity was a theater or opera house. Rural theaters and opera houses were synonymous and rarely did they host highbrow productions. Instead, these facilities were meant as social centers, venues where the public could come together to enjoy the arts, celebrate or mourn, or engage in political debate. Frequently, the theater or opera house was part of a larger establishment, like a merchant building—the Big Store, for example. Belview, too, housed its two small theaters, Simpson's Hall and Kolin's Hall, in commercial establishments. Sometimes, however, communities opted to separate the social center from any other building, plainly signifying its importance as the town's cultural core. This was what Belview did in the early 1900s.

By 1901 the Belview Dramatic Club was looking for a new home. It had outgrown the limited space of both Simpson's and Kolin's Halls. In mid-September, the village council called a public meeting in Simpson's Hall "for the purpose of more freely finding out the sentiments and wishes of the people in the matter of building [a new] opera house." The villagers overwhelmingly supported the idea. In fact, citizens were so enthused that officials purchased lots for the new building before voters officially approved the project. The community's eagerness almost proved economically disastrous. The new building was actually completed before financing could be

This 1906 image of the Odeon's interior was taken from the gallery.

obtained, and for a time it appeared that money to pay for the structure was not forthcoming. The dedication of the theater was postponed for many months as officials searched for funding. Financing was finally arranged in late 1902, and the theater was formally opened in October of that year.

The Odeon Theater was unpretentiously elegant, reflecting a simplified Queen Anne style. The rectangular building measured 40 by 90 feet and rested upon a stone foundation. The clipped gable roof was crowned with a truncated tower that sported a balustrade. Several rectangular window openings holding two-over-two windows marked its clapboard-covered walls. The entrance was surmounted by a fanlight. A 12- by 22-foot stage and two dressing rooms occupied the east one-third of the building's interior. The main floor was made of hardwood maple and held movable chairs. More seating was available in the 20- by 36-foot gallery. A checkroom, box office, and smoking room flanked the theater's main entrance. Designed by August F. Pattratz, a local man who arrived in Belview in 1892, the structure cost roughly $3,800. The contractor was Olie Johnson, a resident of the community since 1891. Johnson was a prominent carpenter in Belview and was responsible for building several residences and commercial buildings in the village, although he considered the Odeon his crowning achievement. Soon after its dedication the *Belview Independent* boasted that "the Odeon is one of the best halls along the Minneapolis and St. Louis Railroad between Morton, Minnesota, and Watertown, South Dakota."

The dedication of the Odeon drew the largest crowd ever to Belview, pulling in people from all over Redwood and Renville Counties. Many were unable to enjoy the festivities within the hall because it filled to capacity before they could get in. Officials gave speeches and the Redwood Falls Cornet Band provided music. The revelry also included a rooster chase as well as a football game between Redwood Falls and Vesta. (Vesta was grossly overmatched, losing 33 to 0.) During the evening local actors presented the stage show "Fort Sumter to Appomattox." The event was capped by a dance, with numbers played by Tibbetts Orchestra of Redwood Falls.

Initially, the Odeon hosted plays, vaudeville acts, guest speakers, and bands, including Belview's own Silver Cornet Band. In the 1920s the hall functioned as a sports arena as well, serving as the hometown's basketball facility. Silent movies also became popular at the Odeon in the 1920s, when the theater was wired for electricity and a film projector installed. For a time the Odeon, like many theaters, married live acts with a movie, giving patrons a double feature of entertainment. Eventually, however, interest in traveling shows waned. Radio, movies, and finally television brought an end to most live variety exhibitions. In the 1930s large motion picture houses in nearby towns proved too tempting for moviegoers and the Odeon suffered. In 1940 the projector was removed from the theater. The gallery was taken out a decade later. Even though the theater continued to be used

Thanks to the Belview Preservation Commission and other like-minded individuals, the Odeon Theater remains an integral part of Belview.

for some events, it was no longer the attraction it once had been. By the 1970s the Odeon was in poor physical shape. Fortunately, preservation-minded individuals came together to form the Belview Preservation Commission. One of its first tasks was rehabilitating the Odeon. Still used as a community gathering locale, hosting wedding dances, suppers, and special events like "Old Sod Day," an annual preservation fundraiser, the Odeon now looks as charming as it did a century ago. As an exceptional example of an early-twentieth-century cultural center, the Odeon Theater was placed on the National Register in 1974.

✳ Lodge Boleslav Jablonsky No. 219

POPLAR GROVE TOWNSHIP | ROSEAU COUNTY

When members of Lodge Boleslav Jablonsky No. 219 gathered for meetings in their tiny hall in Poplar Township, about ten miles east of Strathcona, a small Roseau County community in northwestern Minnesota, they conducted business in much the same way as other fraternal organizations, taking roll and listening to the reports of officers.[72] Patriots of Bohemia in central Europe, they sometimes honored the homeland in song:

> *Where is my home?*
> *Waters flow through meadows,*
> *Pines cover cliffs and rocks.*
> *In garden, spring blossoms,*

An earthly paradise in view.
It is a beautiful land, Czech land, home of mine.
Our region blessed by God,
Gentle souls, right and successful,
With strength that defies and can destroy.
Czech fame races on among the Czechs,
Among the Czechs is my home.

Although the lyrics are slightly different than those above, "Where Is My Home?" is now the national anthem of the Czech Republic. The song was a unifying influence, reminding Bohemian immigrants in northwestern Minnesota of their shared Czech heritage. The lodge hall was a venue for reflecting on that heritage, a unique gathering place that was a kind of ethnic preservation center.

Founded in 1914, two years before the meeting hall was constructed, the lodge was named for Boleslav Jablonsky. Born in 1813 in Kardasova Recice, Kingdom of Bohemia, Austrian Empire, Jablonsky was the oldest of six children. Encouraged by his parents to become a priest, he entered a Prague monastery in 1834. One year later he abandoned the monastic life to study law and begin a writing career. Financial difficulties and his parents' disappointment with his vocational direction soon convinced him to return to the monastery. Completing his theological training in 1841, he was overseeing a convent in Zwierzyniec, near Cracow, Poland, by 1847, an institution that remained his home until his death in 1881. Throughout his priesthood he wrote prolifically, his poetry published in contemporary periodicals like *Lumir* and *Kvety ceske*. His book of poetry, *Basne*, was published the same year he finished his formal theological education. Committed to the Czech nationalist movement, which advocated political separation from Austrian-German rule, his writings were often laced with Czech history and patriotism. His words touched many of his native peoples, including those who emigrated from Bohemia to extreme northwestern Minnesota in the late 1800s and early 1900s.

The poet-priest was a somewhat curious lodge patron, since Lodge Boleslav Jablonsky No. 219 was founded chiefly by "freethinkers," Czech-Americans who cut formal ties to organized religion and advocated free thought. But although Jablonsky was a priest, he was also a nationalist, and it was this attribute that likely came to mind when members sought a lodge patron. Interestingly, the freethinking philosophy of the lodge was not a requirement for membership and many Czechs who were aligned with a particular denomination were welcomed. For members of Lodge Boleslav Jablonsky No. 219, religious differences made no difference.

The oldest free-thought fraternal society was the Czechoslovak Benevolent Society (*Cesko-Slovanska Podporujici Spolek*), more commonly known as the C.S.P.S., which was established in St. Louis, Missouri, in 1854. C.S.P.S.

lodges offered an atmosphere where Czechs could socialize, organize, and work to preserve native language and culture. Additionally, the society provided life insurance to male members. In 1897, however, a new freethinking fraternity splintered from the C.S.P.S. Known as the Supreme Lodge of the Western Bohemian Fraternal Association (*Zapadni Cesko-Bratrska Jednota,* or Z.C.B.J.), it differed from the C.S.P.S. over insurance premium standards. The new group also offered insurance to female members. Lodge Boleslav Jablonsky No. 219 was organized as a constituent of the Z.C.B.J.

In 1916, after two years of meeting in the homes of its members, Lodge Boleslav Jablonsky No. 219 erected a formal meeting hall on a one-acre parcel in the southwest corner of Poplar Township, about a mile north of the Roseau-Marshall county line. Erected upon a concrete foundation, it was a one-story, rectangular, wood-framed building covered in lap siding and divided into two sections. Topped with a gable roof, the main section was edged at the north end by a smaller, hip-roofed component. The lodge's walls were marked by several rectangular windows. With its gable-roofed

The unassuming Lodge Boleslav Jablonsky No. 219 was modestly treated with a partial false front when constructed in 1916.

main section and south facade modestly embellished with a partial false front, the building almost duplicated Lodge Jan Hus No. 50 in Lindsey, Nebraska, a lodge named for a Czech Catholic reformer who was branded a heretic and put to death in 1415.

In some ways Lodge Boleslav Jablonsky No. 219 functioned much as an organized church. The lodge was not only a bastion of Czech language and culture, but also a benevolent institution, aiding Czech immigrants transitioning to a new country, as well as helping to fund nursing homes, orphanages, and cemeteries. When Nazi Germany occupied Czechoslovakia in 1938 and 1939, lodge members pleaded with U.S. officials to recognize Czech independence. Members also donated money to both the American and the Czech Red Cross during the World War II. Of course, the lodge was also the conduit for death benefits to local lodge families.

Over the years, the lodge building was frequently employed for weddings, dances, theatrical performances, fundraisers, holiday celebrations, and more. The elders even initiated a Juvenile Department, which was designed to instill a sense of Czech heritage in younger members. But while Czech heritage remained a core commitment of the lodge, the organization eventually became less exclusive, a policy shift initiated when the Supreme Lodge of the Western Bohemian Fraternal Association changed its name to Western Fraternal Life Association and began offering insurance and membership into the society to all ethnicities. The meeting hall erected by Lodge Boleslav Jablonsky No. 219 changed as well when a gable-roofed porch was added to the main entrance and a chimney was installed near the north rear. Interior spaces were made more accommodating.

Today the lodge operates much as it always has, and near the close of the twentieth century its membership was larger than it had ever been, totaling almost 160. In part, membership increased when the Czech lodge in nearby Badger merged with the Poplar Township group. The meeting hall erected by Lodge Boleslav Jablonsky No. 219 continues to house fraternal meetings and other social gatherings. It is in remarkably good shape after so many years and still reflects its period of construction. Moreover, it remains a symbol of the efforts of early Czech residents in Roseau County to maintain their ethnic identity. The building was added to the National Register in 2002.

✳ ## Grand Army of the Republic Hall

LITCHFIELD | MEEKER COUNTY

When "Johnny" victoriously came marching home in 1865 after enduring the Civil War, four years of one of the bloodiest conflicts the world had ever known, he expected to be rewarded. He was—sort of. Communities north of the Mason-Dixon line sponsored grand parades honoring the conquering heroes, while officials waxed poetic about great deeds and selfless courage. Federal soldiers who had stifled secession and freed a race of people from slavery were showered with praise from a grateful, indebted (though still divided) nation. But how much debt did the country owe its Union veterans? In the federal government's view, not much. Individuality was America's defining trait and the government felt no responsibility for discharging hundreds of thousands into civilian status with little more than a handshake. As hordes of soldiers came home they quickly discovered a

Litchfield's tiny castle is a monument, continuing to remind generations of the sacrifices of members of the G.A.R.

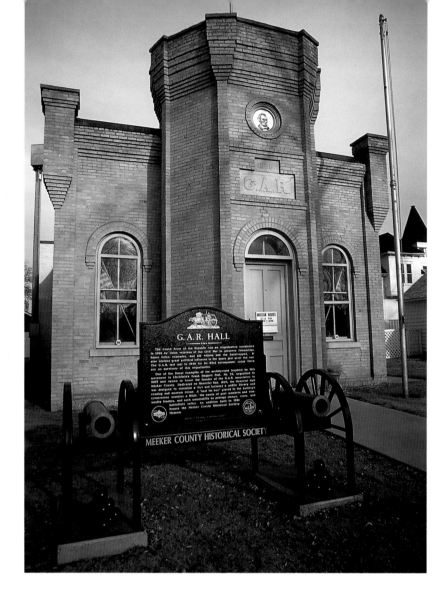

society ill-prepared to take them back. Joblessness among these "heroes" soared. In Wisconsin, the *La Crosse Democrat* noted that unemployed veterans were "sitting on door steps, and in alley ways, eating crackers, cheese, raw pork, and hard bread." Other newspapers like the *New York Tribune* and the *Philadelphia Inquirer* all but begged the federal government and private industry to make room for soldiers. Almost nothing happened. Some veterans responded to their plight by rioting or engaging in other antisocial public acts. Others organized.[73]

By 1866 several veterans' groups had been formed to champion the cause of soldiers, including the Grand Army of the Republic (G.A.R.), which was established in Decatur, Illinois. Benjamin F. Stephenson and William J. Rutledge are often credited with creating the society, but the real power behind its founding was Governor Richard J. Oglesby of Illinois and John Alexander Logan, a politically ambitious former general in the Union

Army. Both understood the power veterans could wield in the political arena if they united, and both wanted the soldiers on their side. As membership in the G.A.R. strengthened, the constituency helped advance the political agendas of Oglesby and Logan. Few of the society's members realized the partisan motives of its organizers, although they all understood the advantage the G.A.R. offered veterans. The pressure the group exerted on Congress forced the government to provide benefits the veterans believed they were owed. But even though the G.A.R. served a political purpose, it also had a less self-seeking mission to "preserve fraternal feelings, aid needy or disabled comrades, and provide for support and education of soldiers' orphans and maintenance of their widows." Furthermore, the G.A.R. was a patriotic voice, encouraging "allegiance to the United States and a respect for its Constitution."

Membership in veterans' groups, including the G.A.R., waned in the 1870s as soldiers began to feel they had accomplished much of what they intended. By the end of the decade, however, Congress was again ignoring them. George Lemon, publisher of a veterans' newspaper called the *National Tribune,* developed an intimate relationship with the G.A.R., convincing the group to seek out former soldiers and persuade them to enlist in the society. Lemon's activism worked. In 1879 enrollment in the G.A.R. was slightly less than 45,000, but one year later it was almost 61,000, and by the mid-1880s it was over 230,000. The G.A.R. had become the dominant veterans' organization in the country. One of the precinct clubs that was established during the early 1880s was Frank Daggett Post No. 35 in Litchfield, a Minnesota community sixty-five miles west of Minneapolis.

The G.A.R. chapter in Litchfield was named for Frank Daggett, a lieutenant in the Sixth Minnesota Volunteer Infantry and a local newspaper publisher. Daggett helped found the veterans' society in Minnesota. He was a disciple of abolitionist John Brown and during the war he commanded two African American artillery regiments. When he returned home he brought a black soldier with him, Albert Van Spence. Spence became a member of Litchfield's G.A.R., making the post unique, since most were segregated.

Although the post was established on July 8, 1883, members did not have a hall to store their records and to serve as a meeting place. The group found a location for a permanent building on Marshall Avenue, just north of Litchfield's business district. G. H. Phelps, one of the society's members, drew the plans for the building. The structure's cornerstone was laid on May 30, 1885. The Henry Ames Brickyard supplied the brick and a local mason named McNeal erected the building, completing it near the end of the year.

The finished G.A.R. Hall, also known as "Memorial Hall," was a singular building in Litchfield. Measuring about 28 by 60 feet, it resembled a petite medieval castle. Formed of cream-colored brick, its main entrance was set within an arched opening at the base of a central tower. An arched glass transom crowned the entrance. Small turrets were situated at the roof at each front corner and two additional turrets marked its north and south side. Arched windows flanked the central tower, a window design also found at the north and south sides. An inscribed stone was set just above the main entrance, about halfway up the tower. It read: "G.A.R. 1885."

The building's interior consisted of a library, anteroom, and dressing room, with a meeting room occupying the structure's rear. An elaborate kerosene-lit chandelier hung from the ceiling of the meeting area. One legend holds that the chandelier was taken from a bordello in New Orleans as a spoil of war, but a more likely story was that the fixture was purchased from a Boston hotel. The new building cost between $4,000 and $5,000, with funds donated by society members and local citizens.

The hall was essentially a monument, reflecting the post's desire to be remembered. The G.A.R., unlike many fraternal organizations, was not self-perpetuating—when its last member died, so would the G.A.R. The Litchfield chapter wanted an ornate building that would cause future generations to pause and consider the sacrifices made by members of the organization. A resolution passed by the fraternity explained: "It is the purpose of the Post to erect a building that shall worthily perpetuate the memory of the soldiers."

The G.A.R. Hall in Litchfield quickly became the center of social activity in the community and nearly every veteran in Meeker County was a member. Obviously, Memorial Day parades began at the building. On Saturday evenings members hosted dances and card games, rising for religious services in the hall the following morning. Issues surrounding the economic

The ornate kerosene chandelier was hung when the G.A.R. Hall was completed in 1885.

and social direction of the town also drew crowds. Litchfield even housed its library within the hall, a community benefit made possible by the far-sightedness of G.A.R. members, who deeded the building to Litchfield. The agreement allowed both the veterans' group and the community to use the facility. In return, Litchfield was responsible for maintaining the structure, even after the G.A.R. faded into history.

By the middle of the twentieth century the G.A.R. in America was all but gone. In 1952 three frail old men were all that remained of the proud fraternity. The men would not see the 1960s. Litchfield's G.A.R. chapter disbanded in 1949. During the latter years of the chapter the hall was venue to many member funerals. By this time it was being managed by the Meeker County Historical Society. The building was in disrepair by then, but with help from volunteers and the city the historical society was able to restore the structure. Today, the historical society operates the hall as a museum. The building is filled with items that belonged to members of Post No. 35, as well as other Civil War artifacts. Items from the Dakota Conflict of 1862 are also housed within the building. The historical society constructed a brick addition at the rear of the hall in the early 1960s to hold its growing collection. Litchfield's Grand Army of the Republic Hall is one of the few such buildings remaining in Minnesota and its stalwart architecture dutifully reflects the greatness of the organization it served. It was added to the National Register in 1975.

✳ North East Neighborhood House

MINNEAPOLIS | HENNEPIN COUNTY

On Labor Day 1914 Robbins Gilman was in Northeast Minneapolis over-seeing the remodeling of Drummond Hall, a building that would soon reopen as the North East Neighborhood House (NENH). Gilman was from the East, a social reformer who a short time earlier was working in New York. He had probably given little thought to moving to the Midwest, happy to be doing what he was doing where he was doing it. Sometimes, though, life throws a curve. So when Gilman lost his job as headworker of the prestigious University Settlement, he took a chance on an opportunity in Minnesota, becoming the first headworker for a new settlement house in the most ethnically diverse section of Minneapolis. He would remain in that position for thirty-four years.[74]

Like so many social work disciples in the early twentieth century, Gilman owed a great deal to Stanton Coit. Coit was a philosopher who initiated the settlement house movement in this country when he established the Neighborhood Guild on New York's Lower East Side in 1886. Coit believed that social betterment of the lower classes, especially the burgeon-

Maybe Robbins Gilman was sharing wisdom with these local boys in 1927, or maybe all were just talking football.

ing immigrant population, could be achieved if selfless individuals established residence within social institutions that were strategically positioned within troubled urban centers; in other words, if they "settled" within the neighborhoods occupied by those most in need of support. Aiding the needy was hardly a new concept. Religious organizations had been providing assistance to the downtrodden for centuries, but such aid often came with a helping of moral instruction. In late-nineteenth-century America, with its ever-growing immigrant population comprised of diverse nationalities and different religions, a faith-based approach to social welfare was less likely to succeed than a secular one. This became one of the driving principles of the settlement house movement—aid without pious obligation. As Coit's idea took off and settlement houses began to dot the urban landscape in many of this country's larger cities, some of the facilities proved more faithful to this principle than others. Some of the institutions, although designed to be free of religious instruction, were sponsored by a particular denomination and the benefactors occasionally nudged aside the secular philosophy. Most settlement houses, however, even those sustained by religious groups, generally abided by the founding ideals of the movement.

The NENH finds its roots in Immanuel Sunday School. Plymouth Church, a Minneapolis congregational church that still exists, established the school in 1881 near the intersection of Second Street Northeast and Broadway Street. The school building was replaced in the late 1890s by a more spacious structure that was christened Drummond Hall. The new structure was erected near Second Street Northeast and Fifteenth Avenue. With a larger facility, the church expanded its curriculum beyond religious education. Clubs for boys and girls were started, as well as classes in gymnastics. Instruction in industrial education also became popular. By the 1910s, however, the demographics of Northeast had changed. Gone were many who had emigrated from France, Germany, and Scandinavia, replaced by newcomers chiefly from Eastern Europe. Although the new population still required social services, their religious doctrine was rooted in Catholicism and few families would accept a helping hand that came with Protestant ministrations. As a result, attendance at Drummond Hall plummeted, forcing the facility to close in 1913.

Plymouth Church refused to surrender, initiating a study to discover what it could do to create a successful social organization in Northeast. The study concluded that Northeast required an institution to acquaint new immigrants with American cultural norms and offer services like education, health care, and recreational activities. The primary point of the study, however, was neighborhood unity. Since Northeast was home to diverse nationalities, antipathies between the various ethnic groups had to be soothed if the community was to develop into a cohesive whole. With a fresh plan, Plymouth Church established a settlement house, tapping Robbins Gilman to lead the charge, a man of conscience who had recently been fired from his position at University Settlement for supporting the grievances of the International Workers of the World.

Gilman enthusiastically embraced this new opportunity. Under his supervision, Drummond Hall reopened in January 1915 as the NENH, an organization providing nonsectarian social services that would strive to unite a community separated by ethnicity and religion. Gilman's wife, Catheryne Cooke Gilman, a distinguished social activist in her own right, wrote: "The situation demanded neutral leadership by a group entirely disassoci-

In the 1920s the children visiting North East Neighborhood House and enjoying its many activities, including story time, were mostly from Eastern European immigrant families.

ated with any nationality dominant in the area. The finger of destiny pointed to the North East Neighborhood House, which functioned on a non-partisan basis, with but one purpose, that of helping all of the people to help themselves to the social, civic, and economic opportunities available to them on an equal basis."

The NENH steadily grew, gaining the confidence of many in Northeast. Services included a dental clinic, job placement department, nursery, and more. Recreational activities and clubs drew many children to the facility. Probably the most important services offered were classes that taught immigrants how to adapt to their new country. Instruction in English, as well as American culture, was vital to creating successful and productive citizens.

Although some in the community remained wary of the NENH, the success of the settlement house was evident in August 1919, when its staff moved into a large, new building recently erected a short distance from Drummond Hall. Kenyon and Maine, a prominent Minneapolis architectural firm, designed the impressive Georgian Revival building. The structure consisted of a main section that fronted Second Street Northeast and a north wing that edged Twentieth Avenue. The $80,000 building was greatly appreciated, especially by Gilman, who had threatened to resign unless a new facility was constructed. While there were some difficulties transitioning from one building to the other, it did not bother Gilman, as he gleefully recorded: "All inconveniences, delays, non-deliveries and mistakes of whatever kind, were joyously, I might say rapturously, overlooked because we were in one of our dreams, the largest one."

Drummond Hall continued as an extension of the NENH for several years, but was finally sold in 1927 when Pike and Cook Company, a Minneapolis contracting concern, completed two additions to the main facility. The additions included a south wing and gymnasium. Costing about $60,000, the new building sections matched the original structure so well that they hardly appeared to be additions at all.

For the next several decades the NENH continued with its mission of helping those most in need. The settlement house became a focal point for aid when the Great Depression hit and management at the institution adopted many of the citywide and nationwide relief programs. Around this time Gilman seemed to become more vocal in his moral judgments. For instance, he was pleased with Prohibition, articulating that saloons had "done more to retard our national progress, debauch our citizenship and piteously outrage the innocent . . . than anything the modern world has known." Even though the headworker's moral righteousness sometimes showed, there was little doubt he and the NENH were providing a valuable service.

After dedicating more than half his life to the NENH, Gilman retired in 1948. Although he and his wife had accomplished much over the years, he still felt that the neighborhood never came together as he had hoped. In the 1950s an anonymous report written by one of the staff members of the NENH validated this belief. The report noted that neighborhood cohesiveness had improved during Gilman's tenure, but the core problem of ethnic differences was never satisfactorily resolved.

After Gilman retired the NENH went through a transformation. When Lyndon Johnson advocated his "New Society" the government began dominating social services. Moreover, the social problems of the fifties, sixties, and seventies were generally more severe than those in the early part of the twentieth century. The NENH, like most settlement houses, had to adapt to

Near the end of the twentieth century the North East Neighborhood House looked much as it did in its early years, although additions at the roof covered a non-original elevator shaft and emergency exit.

this evolving social service landscape. Many did this by merging with other settlement houses. In the early 1960s, the NENH merged with another Minneapolis settlement house, the Margaret Barry House. The combined enterprise was organized as East Side Neighborhood Service, Inc. (ESNS). ESNS offers a wide variety of programs to meet the needs of its diverse clientele, although its geographic influence is much greater than that of the original NENH. In 2001, ESNS moved out of the Georgian Rival building and into a new structure only a couple blocks away. The NENH was listed on the National Register the same year. The old building was refurbished and is now used as apartments. Drummond Hall also is still standing, but it barely resembles its original form. Presently a Buddhist temple, Drummond Hall's most notable feature is its concrete railings that edge either side of the walkway in front of the building. Now each is adorned with the figure of a dragon.

✳ Gran Evangelical Lutheran Church

POPPLE TOWNSHIP | CLEARWATER COUNTY

In 1973 members and guests of the Clearwater County Historical Society assembled near a tiny church and cemetery situated amongst spruce trees near the northern edge of Section 22 of Popple Township, only a short distance northwest of Minnow Lake near Bagley, a small town about twenty-five miles west of Bemidji. The purpose of the gathering was to place a plaque on the log church as a memorial to its founders and first pastor.[75] Valborg Nesseth, the pastor's son, honored the memory of the long-departed souls with a passage from the biblical "Parable of the Talents":

> *Well done, thou good and faithful servant: thou hast been faithful over a few things, I will make thee ruler over many things: enter thou into the joy of thy Lord. (Matt. 25:21)*

The words aptly described the religious commitment of the early Norwegian parishioners of Gran Evangelical Lutheran Church, hardworking people determined to eke out a modest living in the sparsely settled lands of northwestern Minnesota in the late 1800s, and yet so dedicated to their Christian values they refused to believe God came second to their hardships. As demonstration of this devotion, one of their earliest efforts was the construction of a house of worship.

Appearing a little weathered at the beginning of a new century, Gran Evangelical Lutheran Church is a humble acknowledgment of the importance of spirituality to the Norwegian pioneers of Popple Township.

The interior's elevated floor is a simple chancel, a space for altar and clergy.

The first minister of Gran Evangelical was G. P. Nesseth. A man of Norwegian stock, Nesseth was educated at Luther College in Decorah, Iowa. He was a member of the Norwegian Lutheran Evangelical Church of America, more commonly known as the "Norwegian Synod." Upon completing his studies in Decorah, he attended the Synod's seminary in the Twin Cities. Soon after leaving the seminary his ministry led him to the pine country of western Beltrami County. When Nesseth entered the region in the 1890s lumber companies had just arrived, having exhausted the timber in the north-central part of the state. Settlement in the area was light and was dominated by Norwegian immigrants. In 1895 Nesseth and some of the Norwegian settlers banded together to form Gran Evangelical Lutheran Church, the region's first congregation. During its first two years the group held services in homes of various members. In April 1897, the congregation decided to build a church. Members donated about $20 total toward construction. The land, timber, and labor were also freely given by the congregation. Member Ole Eneberg supervised construction. The first church in what would soon become Clearwater County was completed by July.

Whereas the Church of St. Boniface in Melrose was a resplendent architectural offering, Gran Evangelical was a remarkably simple confirmation of faith. In fact, Gran Evangelical is an exemplary model of early church construction in the newly settled regions of Minnesota. Rarely did rudimentary nineteenth-century settlements possess the financial resources to construct elaborate monuments to pious conviction, but often citizens sacrificed whatever money and material they could to bring at least a modest religious gathering place to the community. It is this selflessness that is embodied in Gran Evangelical and it is what makes the humble church so appealing. Measuring only about 25 feet long and 20 feet wide, the church

The walls of the church were erected using dovetail notching.

had no architectural embellishment. It had a gable roof and rested upon a fieldstone foundation. A fieldstone chimney marked its east side. The building's only entrance was at its north facade, and a few window openings marked the other walls.

Although an unadorned structure, the church exhibited design qualities unique to its period and place of construction. Its timber walls were formed from hand-sawed and squared logs linked at each corner in a dovetail notch, like the Lars and Guri Endreson House in Kandiyohi County (see page 23). The small gaps between the squared timbers were chinked, or sealed, with cement. About five years after it was completed, Clearwater County was carved from the southwestern portion of Beltrami County. So, technically, the church was built in Beltrami County but actually stands in Clearwater County.

G. P. Nesseth remained with his congregation in Popple Township until his death in 1937. That same year the church's fieldstone chimney was rebuilt. The original wood entrance door was finally replaced in the 1970s. The congregation eventually expanded its membership to include Lutherans of other ethnic backgrounds. Services continued in the church until 1953, when the congregation merged with another in nearby Ebro to form Our Savior's Lutheran Church. Although vacant for some time, the unassuming church has been maintained as a community historic site. The historical significance of Gran Evangelical Lutheran Church was recognized in 1988 when it was placed on the National Register.

✳ Deerwood Auditorium

DEERWOOD | CROW WING COUNTY

Sometimes communities rely on the generosity of private citizens to bring cultural amenities to the larger population. In Detroit Lakes, Minnesota, for example, early-twentieth-century entrepreneur Elon Galusha Holmes built an opera house. In Deerwood, a central Minnesota town about twenty miles northeast of Brainerd, the community not only relied on the giving spirit of one of its residents for its cultural center but also on the generosity of the federal government. Without Uncle Sam's help, the delightfully rustic Deerwood Auditorium might never have been built.[76]

As early as 1933, officials in tiny Deerwood, a village named for its plentiful white-tailed neighbors, considered erecting a community hall. Like the Odeon Theater in Belview, the hall would be the town's formal gathering place. In July 1934 local resident Beriah Magoffin donated two lots on East Forest Road to the village as a site for the new building. It was possibly the most prominent plot of land in Deerwood. First occupied by a residence, the land was later sold to Charles W. Potts, a local man who intended to construct an office building on the site. Potts died before he could follow through with his plan and the property passed to M. H. Hilyar, a businessman who filled the lots with a gasoline service station. After Hilyar relocated his business, Magoffin purchased the lots and gave them to the village. Magoffin extended his goodwill when he bought the brick boiler building at the Meacham Mine from the Evergreen Mining Company and donated the structure's materials to Deerwood for a new auditorium.

Magoffin's gift was extremely generous, but the village still had little money for a community hall. Cash-strapped Deerwood was not much different than most towns in the mid-1930s. After the stock market crumbled in late 1929, loudly proclaiming the arrival of bad economic times, few communities could afford public improvements. But the country had a president who understood that pouring federal dollars into public works programs provided a modicum of hope to a disenfranchised population who believed the world was coming apart. Franklin Roosevelt's New Deal initiatives were not simply designed to keep people occupied by putting them to work, however. The programs also were intended to create lasting components of society, structures that would serve the public good for

The fieldstone-faced Deerwood Auditorium is a fine example of a Depression-era federal relief project that used native materials to defray costs.

generations. Roads, bridges, public parks, municipal buildings, and more were erected with federal money. As deflating as the Great Depression proved to the American psyche, it was still a time of remarkable infrastructural development. In 1939, the Works Progress Administration (WPA), one of Roosevelt's many relief programs, published *Accomplishments, Minnesota, 1935–1939,* a pictorial record of many of the structures the agency had completed in the state. Not surprisingly, one of the buildings highlighted was the handsome Deerwood Auditorium.

In 1935 Deerwood received early funding for its auditorium through the State Emergency Relief Administration (SERA), the same relief organization that initially supervised the Beltrami Island Project in northern Minnesota. Soon after work began on Deerwood Auditorium, however, the building programs of the SERAs gave way to the WPA. So while the Minnesota SERA began the community building in Deerwood, the WPA finished it.

The auditorium was designed by Carl H. Buetow, a St. Paul architect who was tutored for a time by Clarence H. Johnston, a well-known architect responsible for a number of state institution buildings, including several at the Minnesota State Reformatory for Men in St. Cloud (see page 183). The *Deerwood Enterprise* noted that Buetow "sought the [auditorium's] motif in the work of the master builders of the past and brought forth a design in stone that in dignity, charm and beauty is unsurpassed." The comment was a bit romantic, maybe, but the fieldstone design was certainly pictur-esque and an excellent example of how many communities during the Depression tried to cut costs by using local materials.

Local men began collecting fieldstone for the auditorium in early March 1935. Most of the eight hundred tons of stone required to face the building was pulled from the nearby golf course. Construction continued through-out much of the year, although work was halted for a short time in early August pending additional funding. At least some of the material from the old Meacham Mine building was used in the new structure. The brick, for instance, was employed to form the walls. Work was interrupted a few more times in 1936 as officials waited for more federal money. For a time it appeared that Deerwood would be unable to celebrate an important event in the building as planned. By early October, however, the local newspaper announced that additional funding was secured and a double crew was working on the hall, which "ensure[d] the holding of the eighth annual lute-fisk supper in the new auditorium on Thursday evening, October 29. . . ."

Final touches to the $43,000 auditorium were completed in early 1937. The head-turning building was a two-story, rectangular structure measur-ing 75 by 140 feet. Supported by steel framing, the brick walls were faced with split fieldstone set into concrete. The gable roof rested upon steel trusses and its north end was marked by a louvered belfry, a constituent of the one-story fire station that comprised the rear of the building. While the sides of the auditorium were mostly unadorned, lined with rectangular multipane windows, the south facade was embellished with a projecting one-story main entrance with two sets of doors surmounted by multipane transoms. The projecting bay was accented with cast stone quoining and topped with a cast stone panel displaying "AUDITORIUM." Pilasters with cast stone quoining flanked the entrance, rising to embrace the triangular pediment at the roof. The design of the three windows situated above the projecting entrance at the second floor generally matched those at the sides of the building. Broad pylons delineated the facade's corners.

The auditorium's interior reflected its multipurpose design. The largest space was a basketball court and auditorium with a stage at the north end. A second-floor balcony edged either side of the court and provided spectator seating, and the first-floor area just beneath was occupied by the kitchen, library, locker rooms, and council room. Within its first few years of operation the facility hosted lectures, company meetings, exhibits, fraternal gatherings, graduations, and awards banquets. Of course, it was also home to the annual lutefisk dinner.

The building has undergone a few modifications over the decades. The roof covering the fire station at the rear of the building has been changed and the louvered belfry is gone, replaced by a siren. At some point, framed glass doors replaced the original wood doors of the main entrance. Also, the two vehicle entrances into the fire station were modified into one large entrance, likely necessitated when fire engines became larger. Even with these alterations the building's historic integrity is remarkable. Moreover, the structure still retains its original purpose as the principal gathering place in Deerwood. The most prominent building in the community, and one of the finest examples of federal relief architecture in Minnesota, Deerwood Auditorium was honored with a National Register listing in 1995.

✳ Mahnomen County Fairgrounds

VICINITY OF MAHNOMEN | MAHNOMEN COUNTY

It is probably impossible to determine what gathering was first termed a "fair." The word is drawn from the Latin *feria*, which relates to "holiday," while holiday is derived from "holy day." It seems possible, then, maybe even likely, that the earliest fairs were religious assemblages of some sort. Over time, the term was also applied to commercial gatherings. Commercial fairs of the Middle Ages are well documented. In the last couple centuries, however, fairs have come to represent an educational or exhibitive event as well, like the Chicago Exposition of 1893, a grand affair dressed in a classical theme. The classical building styles exhibited at that fair greatly influenced architecture in this country well into the first part of the twentieth century. Of course, the Chicago Exposition was also commercial, a characteristic that has become common to many fairs.[77]

Maybe the most practical type of fair is the agricultural fair. Primarily a rural institution, these gatherings are marked by displays of agricultural products and livestock, as well as exhibits by government agencies, agricultural schools, and manufacturers. The chief purpose of the agricultural fair is to promote better farming practice and to improve rural life. Still, an agricultural fair is not strictly an educational experience. It is also an occasion for social mingling and recreational activity. In rural areas, where day-

to-day life is centered on agriculture and residents often spend long hours
in the field, leaving little time for socializing, the local fair is possibly the
most significant annual event.

The generally practical nature of agricultural fairs is often expressed
by the utilitarian look of the fairgrounds. In Lincoln County, Minnesota,
for example, the fairgrounds, which were added to the National Register
in 1980, are comprised of many structures that are "starkly simple in
appearance." The Ticket Booth, Horse Barn, Barrow Show Barn, Children's
Barn, American Legion Canteen, 4-H Canteen, Commercial Building,
and Grandstand exhibit little architectural embellishment. There are a few
visually distinctive buildings as well. The Exhibit Building has two one-
and-a-half-story rectangular wings, each resembling a country schoolhouse.
The gable roof of each wing supports a cupola capped by a pyramidal roof.
A one-story concourse links the wings, giving the Exhibit Building a horse-
shoe appearance. Maybe the most impressive facility on the grounds is the
4-H Club Building, a handsome two-story, rectangular structure with a gable
roof and several wall dormers. The first-floor walls are made of random
coursed stone, while board-and-batten siding is utilized for second-floor
walls. The 4-H Club Building was a federal relief undertaking, constructed
by the Works Progress Administration (WPA) in 1937. Only a year earlier
the WPA had been hard at work in northwestern Minnesota near the city
of Mahnomen, constructing several fair buildings for Mahnomen County.

Mahnomen County's fairgrounds were essentially rebuilt during 1936.
A new stone gateway and fence were included in the effort. The Grand-

stand was enlarged as well. Further work included a water system for fire protection. The WPA endeavor was one of many federal relief programs that were initiated in the county during the 1930s. In 1937 the city of Mahnomen received a WPA-constructed city hall, a wonderful example of public architecture utilizing locally quarried stone. Coincidentally, the Mahnomen City Hall was listed on the National Register in 1988. During the economically dismal 1930s, workers in Mahnomen County, like elsewhere, were happy for the labor the WPA provided.

Planning for Mahnomen County's new fairgrounds began in January 1936. The federal government promised the Mahnomen County Fair Board almost $35,000 if the local officials could obtain an additional $2,500. Curiously, county commissioners were unwilling to help raise the funds. The Fair Board managed to come up with $1,000 and the remaining money was raised through private subscription. Work was underway by late February 1936. The project architect was George H. Carter of Moorhead, and Carl Nelson, a local contractor, served as foreman. Initially, the twenty-two-man work crew spent the days clearing the ground of snow so construction on the Livestock Pavilion could begin. Although a considerable amount of work was completed by May, construction was slightly behind schedule due to a lumber shortage. Thankfully, when the county's twentieth annual agricultural fair opened at the beginning of July many of the buildings were finished, including the Livestock Pavilion, the fair's most impressive structure.

The Pavilion was comprised of three sections connected by covered walkways. The framed, hip-roofed building had exposed rafter tips and was sheathed in clapboard siding. The large main building section was T-shaped and was covered by three intersecting roofs that were capped by hip-roofed clerestories punctured with louvered ventilators. A gable projection marked the east wall and held the building's main entrance, which was crowned by a fanlight. The many window openings were shielded from the inside with

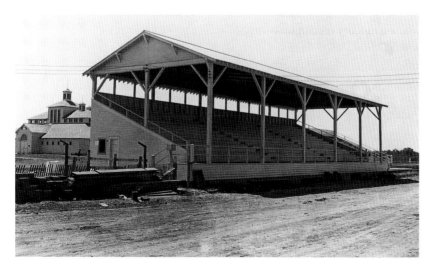

Destroyed by fire in 1987, the enlarged Grandstand as it appeared in 1938.

hinged, wooden covers that could be raised to help ventilate the structure. The other two building components were identical in design and flanked the main section. Each was rectangular and somewhat smaller than the main building section. Boards were hinged near the eaves and opened inward for ventilation. Fairgoers were taken with the attractive and spacious new building, prompting the *Mahnomen Pioneer* to gush: "We daresay that no other fair association in the Northwest has a building that will compare with it."

The other components of the new construction were a bit more modest than the Pavilion. The rectangular 4-H Building had a hip roof and clapboard siding. Gable-roofed wall dormers were located on its north, east, and west elevations, each marking building entrances accented with transoms. Both the north and south walls held eight window openings. The Poultry Judging Building was a tiny rectangular structure with clapboard siding and a gable roof. Small, rectangular openings punctuated the building's sides. Two small, gable-roofed, clapboard-sided bathrooms were also part of the construction effort. Additional work included an oval racetrack for the Grandstand. The dirt racetrack had a grass interior and was edged by a simple wood railing. Besides the Pavilion, the most distinctive new structure was the fair's main entrance, which consisted of two curved walls formed of rough-faced ashlar (finely dressed squared stones) capped with concrete. Stone columns marked either end of each wall. A small, stone Ticket Office with a pyramidal roof was situated near the south wall. The entrance and Ticket Office exhibited superior craftsmanship.

Through the years the Mahnomen County Fairgrounds has hosted various events. Other than the fair, the grounds have been used for softball tournaments and 4-H activities. Stock car racing is popular on the oval racetrack. Today, the site continues to look much as it did when the WPA improved it more than sixty-five years ago. A few additional buildings have been added but the original Grandstand was destroyed by fire in 1987. The entrance to the Livestock Pavilion has changed slightly and ventilators are no longer part of the building's roof. But the alterations to some of the fair buildings are simple and reflect the evolving nature of Mahnomen County's annual agricultural get-together. The Fairgrounds clearly echo the county's agrarian heritage and many of the structures are fine examples of WPA architecture. In fact, the Mahnomen County Fairgrounds may be the most architecturally cohesive example of fair-associated buildings in the region. The Fairgrounds were placed on the National Register in 1989.

TOURISM & ROADSIDE ARCHITECTURE

MINNESOTA ATTRACTED TOURISTS even before it was a state. By the 1850s this tourism mostly consisted of vacationers wishing to view the Mississippi River region. While excursions to St. Anthony Falls and Minnehaha Falls were popular, as were visits to Fort Snelling at the junction of the Mississippi and Minnesota Rivers, St. Paul was the biggest attraction. Awed by its nearly unceasing commercial and construction activity, many tourists were almost convinced that St. Paul was morphing from a settlement into a metropolis before their eyes. The rapid growth of St. Paul and other nearby communities accentuated the vanishing frontier in Minnesota in the mid-nineteenth century and at least some of the holidaymakers wanted to see the boundary's leading edge as it receded toward the Dakotas, halfway between the Atlantic Coast and extinction.[78]

In 1856 the *Congregationalist,* a Boston publication, printed the account of a New Englander who had recently visited the St. Paul area, a tourist enamored with the "tremendous energy with which all the enterprises of life and business [were] conducted" in the Mississippi River town. The vacationer observed that trips to St. Paul had become "fashionable," not only for refined Easterners but also for genteel Southerners "who formerly resorted to Saratoga, or Newport" to wait out the steamy months. The finer hotels in burgeoning St. Paul provided a base for launching outings into the wilds, which were only a carriage ride away but getting farther each day.

Of course most could not afford a fashionable trip to Minnesota in the mid-nineteenth century. Actually, much of the population did not vacation at all, since disposable income was a benefit few enjoyed. No, tourism for the masses chiefly awaited the twentieth century. Before then, however, elites welcomed the guilty pleasures of leisure and recreation in places like Saratoga Springs, New York, where they mingled with their own class in lavish hotels and cottages, or enjoyed boating excursions, games, or therapeutic spas. Minnesota's appealing landscape of rivers, lakes, and woods became an attractive vacation destination primarily after the region was perceived as being stable and unthreatening—that is, after it became more settled. While early tourism in Minnesota was limited, it eventually evolved into one of the state's top income-producing industries.

Although northern Minnesota ultimately became the state's vacation hub, tourism was mostly foreign in the area until the early part of the twentieth century. Besides extravagant hotels in St. Paul, early vacationers to Minnesota stayed in upscale accommodations bordering White Bear Lake, just northeast of the capital city, or at the resorts edging Lake Minnetonka, about ten miles west of Minneapolis. Frontenac, too, became a significant summer holiday destination. Israel Garrard's tiny baronial empire adjacent to Lake Pepin in southeastern Minnesota, about ten miles east of Red Wing, became immensely popular with the affluent crowd after the Civil War.

Modest tourism in northern Minnesota was evidenced at least by the 1880s. In 1884, the Hotel Minnesota, a gorgeous wood-framed building, was erected in Detroit Lakes in Becker County in northwestern Minnesota. Unlike most hotels in the region, which usually catered to traveling salesmen and railroad personnel, the Hotel Minnesota was a true tourist facility, a multistory, balconied statement of luxury in the heart of northwestern Minnesota lake country that was designed to pilfer sophisticated clientele from resorts in the Twin Cities. The task was made easier by the Northern Pacific Railway, which had reached Detroit Lakes several years earlier and made the trip from the Twin Cities a mere jaunt. The Hotel Minnesota, however, remained an exception in northern Minnesota for several years, as many continued to believe tourism was an economic sideshow compared to the iron ore and timber industries. Moreover, many farmers had not yet grasped the fact that much of the soil in upper Minnesota simply could not sustain a decent agricultural existence.

By the early part of the twentieth century, residents in northern Minnesota began accepting that the gift of iron ore and timber Mother Nature bestowed was running out. The poor agricultural conditions were slowly being realized as well. Associations were formed to try to bring industry to northern Minnesota, but tourism seemed to happen almost by chance. Fisherman and hunters arriving in areas with little or no accommodations often sought shelter and food from private residents. Some of these residents did not have to be hit with an anvil to realize there was money in farming out spare bedrooms or allowing vacationers to pitch tents on their property. Moreover, families from warmer parts of the country began looking beyond the Twin Cities to the picturesque settings and relatively cool climes of northern Minnesota for summer refuge. Fishing and hunting lodges, lakeside resorts and cottages, and campgrounds began sprouting up in parts of northern Minnesota as locals realized the scenic landscape provided economic opportunity that was unlikely to disappear as quickly as the white pine forests and timbering. And with natural amenities like Lake Superior and the North Shore, as well as the Arrowhead region, which stretches from the great lake west to Bemidji, northern Minnesota's backdrop was difficult to match in other parts of the country.

With a growing middle class, tourism for the larger population became more popular in the first half of the twentieth century. Tourism received an added boost as automobiles became more affordable. Although the railroad had aided tourism throughout Minnesota, rail lines could not compete with vehicles that could travel in almost any direction, oftentimes on the most minimal of minimum-maintenance roadways. With the founding of the Minnesota Department of Highways in 1917 and the subsequent creation of the state trunk highway system, Minnesotans took to the road in record numbers. The proliferation of automobiles on the roadway had an interesting side effect: roadside architecture. Although the definition is a little hazy, it generally refers to conspicuous roadside structures, some much more conspicuous than others. While fascinating, and sometimes odd, creations are now commonplace, the earliest examples often find their way to the National Register.

Minnesota has many National Register listings tied to tourism and roadside architecture. Larson's Hunters Resort near Wheaton in Traverse County, for example, is a turn-of-the-twentieth-century lodge established by a farming family to accommodate sportsmen hunting game birds. Winibigoshish Resort in Bena, a community on the Leech Lake Indian Reservation in Cass County, is a motor court with a gas station/general store that looks something like a red, white, and blue pagoda. The wood squirrel carvings decorating parts of the structure only enhance its appeal. The Lindholm Oil Company Service Station in Cloquet in Carlton County is a property type most expect to appear utilitarian. This gas station, however, is a graceful Prairie-style structure designed by the Prairie School master, Frank Lloyd Wright. Each of these properties helps tell the story of Minnesota's maturation into a land of leisure, recreation, and curious—often playful—visuals, as do the National Register listings on the succeeding pages.

✳ Frontenac

GOODHUE COUNTY

About three decades before Bernard H. Pietenpol took to the air in his homebuilt airplane, Jeptha Garrard was building flying machines in a barn behind his brother's house in Frontenac, a quaint, quiet, virtually hidden community in Goodhue County snuggling the western shore of Lake Pepin and edged to the north by a rocky bluff known as Point-No-Point. According to local history, Jeptha's most promising creation resembled an inverted umbrella and featured a hanging platform where the pilot stood, navigating the aircraft by "rocking with a bird-like motion." It failed to work, of course, but the designer was smart enough to hire someone else to test it. Piloted by a parachute jumper, the contraption was launched from Point-No-Point over . . . well, into, Lake Pepin. Even though Jeptha never achieved wide recognition for his aeronautic experiments, he was still his brother's brother, and his brother was Israel Garrard, cofounder and developer of Frontenac, Minnesota's earliest resort community.[79]

Nestled against Lake Pepin, Frontenac looks warm and inviting from Point-No-Point.

Israel Garrard was not the first to take residence beneath the shadow of Point-No-Point adjacent to Lake Pepin, a water body between Wisconsin and Minnesota that is actually a swelling of the Mississippi River extending roughly from Red Wing to Wabasha. Native Americans had roamed the land for centuries and in the 1830s and 1840s a fur trader named James "Bully" Wells, who later became a territorial legislator, managed a trading post in the area, which at that time was called Waconia. Wells sold his holdings to Dutch immigrant Evert V. Westervelt in 1852. A decade later, and no longer a legislator, Wells was farming in Rice County when he was killed during the Dakota Conflict.

Two years after purchasing Wells's property, Westervelt was introduced to Israel and Lewis Garrard, when the two refined Southerners arrived at Waconia while on a hunting expedition. The sons of a former Kentucky governor, the Garrard brothers traced their lineage to the prominent Ohio Garrards. Moreover, their maternal grandfather, Israel Ludlow, was one of the founders of Cincinnati. Lewis remained at Waconia for only months, but returned a few years later. Israel made the site his home from the outset, establishing a hunting retreat/house that he shared with his wife Catherine. The lodge was named for St. Hubert, the patron saint of hunting, who, if the story conveyed in the 1909 *History of Goodhue County, Minnesota,* is true, had "dared to desecrate Good Friday by a riotous hunt, was stopped by a spirit stag with a crucifix on his forehead, after which the knight, awe-struck, dropped to his knees in the forest, surrounded by his retainers, and devoted his life to the cause of religion, the wild hunters becoming monks, and Hubert their abbot. . . ."

The French Colonial–style St. Hubert's Lodge was completed in 1855, only a short time after Westervelt built the Greek Revival–style Locust Lodge on a neighboring parcel. In 1857 the two men partnered to purchase an additional 4,000 acres, setting aside 320 for the townsite of Westervelt. The following year Evert Westervelt sold half his land to Lewis, while Israel sold half his holdings to Kenner Garrard, another brother. In 1859 the townsite of Westervelt was renamed Frontenac in honor of a seventeenth-century French count who was governor of New France (Canada).

Israel intended to transform Frontenac into more than a modest hunting getaway, but the Civil War stalled his plans. Before the conflict finished its second year, however, German, Swiss, and Scandinavian craftsmen from Cincinnati completed several structures, including a sawmill, grain warehouse, saloon, general store, and brewery. Two of the more impressive buildings erected at this time were the Greystone and Dakota Cottages. The only

Israel Garrard's St. Hubert's Lodge, where the general strolled the veranda surveying his vacation hideaway, has changed little since his death.

major house in Frontenac not built of wood, Greystone was constructed two blocks south of Locust Lodge and was formed with walls of grout, which gave rise to the moniker "the Grout House." Reflecting Southern Georgian style, Dakota Cottage, four blocks north of St. Hubert's Lodge, was a two-story building with upper and lower verandas—hardly a cottage. It was home to Lewis Garrard and the family matriarch, Sara Ludlow Garrard McLean. After Israel outfitted the Seventh Ohio Volunteer Cavalry and went to war, construction at Frontenac ceased. Jeptha joined his brother, fighting with his own Federal regiment, the Sixth Independent Ohio Calvary. Kenner, a soldier long before the war began, fought for the Union as well.

Israel and Jeptha returned to Frontenac when the conflict ended, both with the rank of general—not bad for a few years of service, but then affluence has certain advantages. Kenner, also a general, but seemingly more deserving of the rank, retired from the army and also retreated to Frontenac. Under Israel's supervision, postwar Frontenac quickly evolved into an exclusive vacation hideaway. In 1867, two years after fighting between the North and South concluded, Israel converted the town's grain warehouse into the three-story Lakeside Hotel, a fitting, if unoriginal, name. Nuzzling the lakeshore, the hotel provided lodgings for the Garrards' wealthy acquaintances and others from cities like St. Louis, New Orleans, and Memphis who arrived by riverboat with horses, carriages, and servants. Frontenac's growing popularity was evidenced a few years later when the hotel was enlarged. A number of cottages from other parts of Frontenac were moved closer to the Lakeside, providing even more accommodations. Unlike Dakota Cottage, or the large Greek Revival–style Winona Cottage, which was built for Israel's son George and his wife Virginia in 1889, the buildings actually resembled reserved dwellings. The Lakeside offered hunting, fishing, and sailing excursions. Horse racing was a popular digression sponsored by the hotel as well, but it is unclear where the track was situated.

Even though Frontenac was a recreational haven, Israel and other prominent residents also accommodated spirituality by erecting a few churches, including Christ Episcopal, a simple, Gothic-style structure constructed near Frontenac's western edge in 1868. Israel's commitment to virtuousness was clearly demonstrated in 1890 when he donated 124 acres near Frontenac for Villa Maria, a Catholic girls' school established by the sisters of the Ursuline Academy in Lake City. Located by Point au Sable, the school was dominated by a high tower capped with a pyramidal roof. Fire destroyed the landmark in 1969, a year before the school closed.

Frontenac remained an exclusive recreational retreat largely because Israel refused to allow the Chicago, Milwaukee, and St. Paul Railway to construct a line through the town in 1871. Instead, he donated land about three miles to the southwest for a railroad right-of-way. The village that soon sprang up near the line was called Frontenac Station, a community that drew mercantile activity away from the old town, which was welcomed by most in Frontenac.

On September 21, 1901, ten days after being burned in a fire, the baron of Frontenac died. Westervelt had passed away thirteen years earlier and Catherine Garrard had been gone for over three decades. Israel was laid next to his wife. In 1933 historian Frances Densmore poetically, although somewhat confusingly, described Israel's gravesite setting:

> *Under the snow of winter and the sweet shadows of summer trees the master of St. Hubert's Lodge lies asleep. There is dignity and seclusion in his resting place. A wooded, winding road separates it from the cemetery, which consists of one avenue. On either side of this avenue, in land given by General Garrard, are many who knew and served him. Today their graves are between him and the world of people.*

No longer a resort community, Frontenac remains secluded, a characteristic treasured by residents as much now as it was when Israel strolled St. Hubert's veranda surveying his picturesque fiefdom. Many of the prominent buildings still stand, including Locust and St. Hubert's Lodges, Dakota and Winona Cottages, Greystone, and Christ Episcopal Church. The Lakeside Hotel is extant as well, although it is suffering neglect and the rear section has been removed. The hotel may be rehabilitated, however, and possibly employed as lodgings for a bed-and-breakfast.

Over forty years ago historian Lucy Cook penned a detailed account of Frontenac, at one point colorfully observing the town's refusal to fall into line: "Nestled like a piece of antique jewelry in a bend of Lake Pepin, Frontenac has quietly withstood the pressures of progress like an old fashioned lady who cherishes her way of life and feels no need to conform to modern design." The metaphor still applies. Predating all other resort communities in Minnesota and retaining the charm of a bygone era, Frontenac was placed on the National Register in 1973.

Today, Christ Episcopal Church at the western edge of Frontenac mirrors its 1868 design.

✳ Lake Bronson State Park

PERCY TOWNSHIP | KITTSON COUNTY

Newspaperman Clifford W. Bouvette was a staunch Democrat. He was so committed to the ideals of his political party that when Democrat Adlai Stevenson was trounced by Republican Dwight Eisenhower in the 1952 presidential election Bouvette ran the front-page story "Best Man Loses" in the *Kittson County Enterprise*. The act offended many, including the Minnesota Editorial Association, which demanded Bouvette apologize to the readership. Bouvette later expressed regret, although it was for misspelling

Eisenhower's name in the article. Even though some in Kittson County were put off by Bouvette's unrelenting liberal philosophy, he was a genuine personality whom almost everyone considered friend. Wanting only the best for his northwesternmost corner of Minnesota, Bouvette was a driving force behind much development in Kittson County. R.C. Nelson, one of Bouvette's many friends, later remarked: "Cliff had lots of guts. He was not afraid to ask anyone in government for something for his community." One thing he asked for was a reservoir dam, which eventually led to the creation of Lake Bronson State Park, a beautiful recreation area just over a mile east of the small town of Lake Bronson and about twenty miles south of the Minnesota-Manitoba border.[80]

Kittson County is naturally lakeless, which seems odd in a state nationally recognized for its abundant water supply. In the early 1930s, as the Great Depression continued to greatly depress everyone, Kittson County was drier than usual, the region suffering through a terrible drought. As wells dried up and crops withered, officials concluded the county needed a safety net, a water storage facility on the South Branch of Two Rivers, near Bronson (later Lake Bronson). For more than a year, supporters of the plan lobbied the federal and state government for funds for the project. One of the leading voices was the mayor of Bronson, O. T. Danielson. Danielson was joined in the effort by county engineer J. E. Dishington and several other prominent Kittson County residents. It was not until Clifford Bouvette became part of the chorus in early 1936, however, that major progress was achieved. The newspaperman was then serving as mayor of Hallock, the county seat of Kittson County, roughly twenty miles northwest of Bronson. The mayor had powerful friends, including Floyd B. Olson, Minnesota's Democratic governor at the time, as well as Adolph Bremer, a St. Paul banker and the president of Schmidt Brewing Company—and a man who had Franklin Roosevelt's ear. While Olson set up state funding for the project, Bremer secured a meeting between Bouvette and the president. The vocal Democrat from Hallock greatly impressed the chief executive, receiving a White House blessing and federal dollars for construction of a reservoir dam. By early April 1936, construction equipment was moving toward the dam site on the South Branch of Two Rivers.

While water relief was the original intention of the endeavor, by the time construction began the plan had evolved into a reservoir/recreation area project. After all, Kittson County was mostly devoid of recreational facilities and officials now had an opportunity to create a scenic attraction for county residents and tourists. By mid-April, Works Progress Administration (WPA) crews were erecting a temporary camp for the workers who would build the dam and other facilities. The camp was completed by the end of the month and serious study of the dam site began in May. The location was occupied by Anderson Bridge, a pinned, Pratt, pony truss that

A gravity dam constructed on the South Branch of Two Rivers in 1937 impounded a large reservoir christened Lake Bronson, now a tourist attraction in northwestern Minnesota.

would likely be eligible for the National Register today. The bridge was removed and workers delved into the river bottom in search of a stable foundation for the dam. Not finding one, officials concluded the dam could still be built at the site, but it had to be modified to squeeze the water from the "quicksand" foundation. The unique structure was designed by the Division of Drainage and Waters, although the agency possibly received help from engineer Clifford Holland, creator of the vehicular tunnel in New York City bearing his name.

After diverting the river around the dam site, pumps pulled water from the quicksand through well points placed into the river bottom, resulting in a dry, hard foundation. At least one pump was kept running at all times during construction to prevent the sand from becoming wet and soft again. The pump was only a temporary measure, for the reinforced concrete dam was designed with ten seepage pipes, which were driven vertically into the foundation and extended upward through the dam into a horizontal drainage tunnel passing through the structure's three spillways. Engineers believed the dam's weight coupled with the hydrostatic load pressing against the upstream side of the structure would squeeze the water in the sand foundation up through the seepage pipes and into the drainage tunnel. From there the water would be diverted into the river at the dam's upstream side. The fact that the dam has not vanished into the river bottom after more than six decades is testament to its design.

Completed in June 1937, the $275,000 dam impounded a roughly 325-acre reservoir. Measuring about 130 feet long and 40 feet high, the base width of the dam was 58 feet, although it tapered near the crest, which held a two-lane roadway. The dedication on June 20 was a huge event, attracting nearly eight thousand visitors from around the region. The crowd enjoyed the music of the Bronson Community Band and participated in water sports, boating, and bicycle races. Dignitaries were introduced by Bouvette and included Minnesota WPA administrator Victor Christgau and regional WPA representative R. C. Jacobson. The *Bronson Budget* bragged that the "completion of the project [gave] the area a lake . . . destined to become an important recreational center, as well as assuring the community a source of pure water."

As exciting as the new dam and lake proved to the people in the region, there was more to come. The reservoir and surrounding acreage was designated a state park soon after dedication and another $40,000 was appropriated for park facilities. Additional funds for park improvements were secured over the next few years, including a $123,000 federal grant in 1939, the same year the community of Bronson renamed itself "Lake Bronson" in honor of its new water playground and reservoir. A roughly 45-foot-high hexagonal water tower with observation deck, the most prominent edifice in the park, was constructed only a short time prior to receiving the grant, its fieldstone decoration indicative of other park structures, like the Latrine and Bath House, both erected in 1938. A fieldstone Office and Garage was built the same year as the water tower, and a fieldstone picnic shelter followed in 1940. The coming years would bring additional improvements.

Today, the once lakeless county has become a prime destination in the northwestern section of the state, as its scenic state park pulls in tourists from Minnesota, North Dakota, and southern Canada. Fishing, swimming, canoeing, and water skiing have become popular pastimes on Lake Bronson. Snowmobiling and cross-country skiing are featured during the winter. With 53 kinds of mammals, 24 species of reptiles and amphibians, and more than 200 species of birds, the park is a cornucopia of wildlife. Of course Lake Bronson continues as Kittson County's security against exceedingly dry weather. A model of WPA relief efforts during the Depression and a superb representation of how a region can transform itself, Lake Bronson State Park was placed on the National Register in 1989.

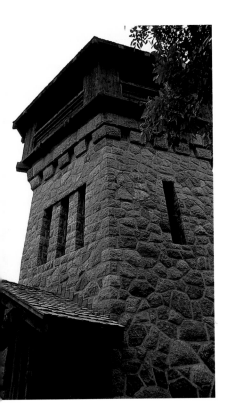

The most dominant feature at Lake Bronson State Park is the fieldstone-faced water tower finished in 1939.

✳ Paul Bunyan & Babe the Blue Ox

BEMIDJI | BELTRAMI COUNTY

During the opening credits of *National Lampoon's Vacation,* a 1983 comedy about a dysfunctional family on holiday, the theater audience is treated to several images depicting American roadside attractions. While Lindsey Buckingham belts out "Holiday Road," an image flashes across the movie screen that is familiar to just about everyone in the theater. The statues of Paul Bunyan and Babe the Blue Ox in Bemidji, Minnesota, are the quintessential example of the roadside colossus in the Upper Midwest, and the producers of the Chevy Chase comedy classic fittingly included the figures at the beginning of the movie. Surprisingly, the first tangible representation of Paul Bunyan was not as a northern Minnesota tourist attraction. Instead, the mighty woodsman was initially employed in an advertising campaign. In other words, Paul Bunyan was an early-twentieth-century Pillsbury Doughboy™.[81]

Bemidji had a modest tourist industry as early as the 1890s. Located in north-central Minnesota, the city was situated within a region graced by vast woodlands and lakes, natural attractions tempting to hunters and anglers from the Twin Cities and other urban areas. After completion of rail lines into the region in 1898, promoters developed lakeshore sites for summer cottages and resorts. Bemidji further benefited from the construction of a

Bemidji's Paul and Babe look reserved compared to some roadside colossi today, but the duo were originals when erected in 1937.

state highway system and the proliferation of the automobile. By the 1920s, tourism in and around Bemidji was booming, although good times waned a bit when depression gripped the country by the end of the decade.

While tourism in Bemidji was generally good during the summer, many were not anxious to visit the city during the frigid months. In 1936, several civic organizations and businesses came together to convince out-of-towners to come to the community during winter and enjoy its many amenities, including its new sports arena for figure skating, hockey, and curling. The group sponsored a four-day winter carnival in mid-January 1937. The carnival's theme was drawn from Bemidji's history as a lumbering center. The symbols chosen to reflect this timber heritage were the mythical figure of Paul Bunyan and his blue ox, Babe.

The legend of Paul Bunyan and his four-legged companion was not born in Minnesota. Stories of the redoubtable strength and skill of the giant lumberjack were often told in the logging camps of New England, where Paul was said to be able to fell stands of timber with a single swing of his ax. The stories migrated with the logging companies as the industry moved west in search of timber in the mid-nineteenth century. Along the way Paul's legend grew. The Great Lakes were supposedly carved from the prancing hoofs of his ox companion, and the Dakotas are shy of timber because Paul cleared much of the land to make room for Babe to lie down. One of the giant's adventures pitted him against a species of mammoth mosquito. Another campaign took him overseas, where he helped preserve democracy in Europe during the First World War—the Kaiser's army was likely stunned at the size of the Yank. The tall tales surrounding Paul were a reflection of the spirit and history of a people, at least according to poet Carl Sandburg. Paraphrasing Sandburg, author Karal Ann Marling noted: "Paul Bunyan got his massive stature from the frontier savvy and the native grit of a nation, from the energy of a whole people endowed with the indomitable legacy of the westering pioneers."

Although Paul Bunyan did not originate in Minnesota, he was embraced as a native son when the Red River Lumber Company in Akeley, Minnesota, immortalized the lumberjack in print in 1914. Copywriter and ex-lumberjack W. B. Laughead created a pamphlet of Paul's gigantic deeds, highlighting his Minnesota exploits. Laughead also sketched the lumberjack. His illustration was of a somewhat portly woodsman with a stiff mustache that extended well beyond either side of his face, like the whiskers of a cat. He clenched a pipe in his teeth, although the mustache hid his mouth. Laughead and the Red River Lumber Company never envisioned the sensation that would follow publication of the pamphlet. It quickly became a hit with the public, making Paul and Babe national celebrities. Over the next three decades Laughead's stories would sell almost 125,000 copies. The Red River Lumber Company created an icon when all it had intended to do was to sell lumber. Laughead later remarked: "It was just another advertising job. It never occurred to me it was 'folklore.' All I wanted to do was to sell lumber."

Capitalizing on the popularity of Paul Bunyan, organizers of the 1937 Winter Carnival in Bemidji employed Cyril M. Dickinson of the Dickinson Lumber Company to create an 18-foot-high statue of Paul. Jim Payton, manager of a local power company, was responsible for making the 10-foot-high, 23-foot-long Babe. The statue constructed by Dickinson was not unlike

The lightweight and maneuverable Babe that toured Minnesota in the late 1930s before being hard-coated and anchored next to Paul.

Laughead's drawing, although Dickinson's wood-framed statue was less rotund and brawnier. Cement stucco gave shape to the figure. Paul was anchored in a municipal park overlooking Lake Bemidji, while Babe was mounted atop a Model A Ford automobile and driven around the carnival.

Bemidji's winter celebration proved a huge success, as many from out of town poured into the community to enjoy horse races, sled-dog races, curling, figure skating, lumberjack competitions, hockey games, dances, and fireworks. About two hundred visitors and a band came by chartered train from Duluth. Both Paul and Babe were a smash with the festival crowd. Paul was even wired for sound so he could greet visitors. After the carnival ended, Babe and the Model A spent a good part of the next year traveling around the state and appearing in parades. Around 1938 or 1939, Babe was also hard-coated and placed on permanent display next to Paul. Eventually, *Life* magazine caught wind of the gigantic pair and presented the figures in a full-page spread, adding to their celebrity.

Today, Paul and Babe are synonymous with Bemidji, although that fact may perturb some in Akeley. In 1949, Akeley built a huge cradle and claimed itself the birthplace of the giant. Brainerd followed in 1950 with an enormous Paul Bunyan figure of its own. Akeley finally constructed a Paul Bunyan statue in 1984. Even though Akeley's Paul is on one knee, it still measures 33 feet high. The theme has continued. Paul's big Black Duck is located, fittingly, in Blackduck. He apparently left his anchor in Ortonville, and his sweetheart, Lucette Diana Kensack, in Hackensack. Those who wish to pay their last respects to the legend can visit his grave in Kelliher. The tombstone simply states: "PAUL BUNYAN, 1794 to 1899, Here Lies Paul, and That's All." This good-natured Paul Bunyan rivalry has helped tourism in northern Minnesota, since it takes a powerful will to pass a roadside colossus without stopping for a photograph and a souvenir or two . . . or three.

Oversized statues have now become rather commonplace. What separates Bemidji's Paul and Babe from all of the others is the knowledge that they were "pioneering efforts in the field . . . The 'prototypical' expressions of the genre," according to architectural historian Jeffrey A. Hess. Paul and Babe continue to draw visitors to Bemidji, and their importance to the history of the community and the folklore of the state was officially recognized in 1988 when the duo was placed on the National Register.

❋ Cascade River Wayside

VICINITY OF GRAND MARAIS | COOK COUNTY

In a 1930s promotional pamphlet, management at Cascade Lodge, a rustic getaway about ten miles southwest of Grand Marais in Cook County, emphasizes the resort's lovely locale, describing it as "a beautiful place of primeval wilderness on the shores of Lake Superior and beside the beautiful Cascade River, which winds its way thunderously through Cascade Park. . . . The rugged beauty of this famous North Country has remained unspoiled. It is an ideal combination of natural beauty and comparative detachment from the outer world." The comments are a little gushy, maybe, but hardly an exaggeration.[82]

Minnesota's North Shore was gorgeous in the 1930s and it is gorgeous today. This land of "rugged beauty" is accessed via State Highway 61, a rather ho-hum-sounding thoroughfare with an agreeable alias, "North Shore Drive." In 1959 the National Association of Travel Organizations named North Shore Drive one of America's most scenic highways. More recently, the Federal Highway Commission designated the route an All-American Road, and the Minnesota Department of Transportation (MnDOT) named it a Minnesota State Scenic Byway. Although four billion years of an undulating earth gave Minnesotans the North Shore, MnDOT's forerunner, the Minnesota Department of Highways (MHD), provided the popula-

Although a state park was not established until the 1950s, it was always part of the original planning, as demonstrated by this circa 1935 sign.

tion with the scenic byway. MHD did not simply grade and pave a route, it thoughtfully coursed its way to the Canadian border, blending the road with the land's picturesque geography. What MHD did is officially called "roadside development," defined by historians at Gemini Research in Morris, Minnesota, as "a field of landscape architecture and highway design that is concerned with improving highway safety and aesthetics." Improving highway safety and aesthetics includes adding wayside rests, which not only give tired eyes respite from the asphalt, but frequently widens them by accenting natural surroundings. Maybe nowhere did MHD do this better then on the North Shore Drive when it created the Cascade River Wayside near the Cascade River, just east of Cascade Lodge.

By the time work began on the Cascade River Wayside in 1934, MHD had already improved much of State Highway 61, a roadway that previously existed as Minnesota Highway 1, which was actually a series of crude, gravel roads stretching to Canada. In the early 1930s, MHD moved large sections of the route nearer Lake Superior, improving efficiency while taking advantage of the scenic landscape. Near the Cascade River, the highway realignment included shifting the river's mouth roughly 325 feet east and erecting a reinforced-concrete, filled-spandrel arch bridge over the waterway. In the years 1933–34, some realigned sections of the roadway, including that passing the Cascade River, were surfaced with asphalt.

Land for the Cascade River Wayside was acquired the same year construction started. The more than 2,000-acre parcel was considerably larger than needed for a wayside, but farsighted government officials intended to eventually transform much of the acreage into a state park. Although work on the facility was overseen chiefly by the Roadside Development Division of the MHD, the state agency was joined in the effort by the National Park Service and the Civilian Conservation Corps (CCC), the same Depression-era relief organization that built Norris Camp on Beltrami Island in 1935 (see page 176). One of the designers of the wayside was Arthur R. Nichols, a consultant to the MHD who is often credited with helping establish the landscape architecture profession in Minnesota. Designer of numerous state parks, campuses, and private estates, Nichols was a strong advocate of the emerging roadside development concept within MHD, as were residents of Cook County. In August 1934, the *Cook County News-Herald* boasted:

> *Here, in a naturally wild and beautiful setting, closely skirting the lake shore, new ideas in highway beautification and safety will be put into practice. . . . The highway, instead of being a raw gash through the woods, will be made to harmonize with the scenery so that the edge of the right of way will blend imperceptibly with the wilderness. . . . At Cascade a roadside parking area large enough to accommodate 40 automobiles will be constructed. A native stone concourse will overlook the lake, while on the other side of the highway foot trails will lead back into the woods along the river banks.*

Operating from a camp called Caribou Lake, about eight miles west of the planned wayside, CCC Company 2702 started work in July 1934, initially concentrating on surveying, as well as roadside cleanup and landscaping of a ten-mile stretch of State Highway 61 from Lutsen, roughly eight miles southwest of the wayside site, to about two miles above the mouth of the Cascade River. Four months later, Company 2702 moved to Spruce Creek Camp, a staging area closer to the wayside site that was completed by the CCC and the U.S. Army and was named for the nearby stream of Spruce Creek. In fall 1934, while roadside landscaping continued, the CCC was constructing foot trails through the woods near the Cascade River. Work on the huge overlook wall above Lake Superior was underway as well. The wall was pieced together using gabbro, a local stone also known as "green granite," "black granite," and "trap rock." During spring and summer 1935, as roadside landscaping, foot trail construction, and overlook work continued, the CCC began building a picnic area, including picnic tables, fireplaces, and latrines. During this period a 25-foot-long, gabbro, arched footbridge over Babineau Creek and another narrower, timber and steel bridge over the Cascade River were completed. The 50-foot-long Cascade River crossing linked the foot trails at either side of the waterway while providing a vantage from which hikers could view the river's impressive falls and rapids.

The gabbro overlook as it appeared soon after its completion

The curved overlook was completed in summer 1935, the eastern end of its parapet merging with the southern headwall of the arched roadway bridge spanning the Cascade River. The first Rustic-style highway overlook constructed by the Roadside Development Division of the MHD, the structure measured 535 feet long and was accented with two lookout bays, which provided spectacular views of Lake Superior and the mouth of the Cascade River. The foot trails across the highway from the overlook were finished

in 1935 as well, quietly blending into their forested surroundings. Trails
near Lake Superior were also completed. The dirt trails included stone and
timber steps at various locations. Timber lookout platforms were incorporated into the trails, as were log guardrails along especially steep sections
of path. Besides the Cascade River Footbridge and the pedestrian crossing
over Babineau Creek, the trails also included more modest wood bridges.

Work on the wayside halted between January and August 1936, but then
resumed for two months as finishing touches were made to the roadway
bridge over Cascade River and picnic tables, picnic fireplaces, and latrines
were completed. The popularity of the wayside, even before it was completed, was documented in the *Minnesota State Park and Recreational Plan*
published in 1939: "This tract is used largely by the pleasure touring public. Some indication of its use may be obtained from the attendance records
taken in 1935, which show that on July 4th, 258 people used the foot trails
up the river gorge; and that 172 cars, 25% of which were from out of state,
used the highway concourse in a period of fourteen hours. The use is
undoubtedly increasing." The report continued: "The exceptionally beautiful natural characteristics and the extent of the area, suggests that it should
be established as a State Park." Although this had always been part of the
original plan, curiously, it was not implemented until the mid-1950s.

While Cascade River Wayside has received a few alterations over the
decades, it still looks much as it did when finished in 1936. A remarkable
piece of planning, the wayside complements its setting, subservient to the
stunning geography of the North Shore near Cascade River. One of the

largest and most attractive waysides built by the Roadside Development Division of the MHD, the Cascade River Wayside is a recent honoree to the National Register. Ironically, its 2003 addition to the historic listing comes at time when the state is suffering a financial shortfall and is considering closing some of its wayside rests. Hopefully, Cascade River Wayside will be spared.

✳ Naniboujou Club

VICINITY OF GRAND MARAIS | COOK COUNTY

In summer 1932 George Cormack, president of the Naniboujou Club, announced that the resort would soon open to the general public. This was good news for many vacationers, perhaps, but it was an ominous sign for the North Shore retreat. Planned as an exclusive hideaway for the affluent, the Naniboujou Club did not achieve the financial success its founders envisioned. Now, three years after it opened, officials of the rustic escape 125 miles northeast of Duluth, where the Brule River empties into Lake Superior, hoped the common folk would keep the lodge from failing.[83]

By 1927 the Naniboujou Holding Company owned over three thousand acres nuzzling the shore of Lake Superior. Formed by Duluth businessmen, the holding company leased the property to the Naniboujou Club, which commissioned a prospectus written by John Stone Pardee to tout the restricted getaway the Zenith City entrepreneurs intended to erect adjacent the Brule River and Lake Superior. The author exuberantly described the setting prospective members of the club would find: "In the valley of the Arrowhead, one hears the rustle of the pines, the brawling and babbling

Although the Lake Superior side of the common area has been altered somewhat from its original design, after almost seventy-five years the Naniboujou Club remains a distinctive architectural and social feature of the North Shore.

of the stream, the muffled murmur of the breakers on the beach. There is the breath of balsam, the scent of the pine, the tang of the cedars. . . ." With lines such as "birches like Greek columns and cedars like Gothic pillars," Pardee's waxing made the florid prose of nearby Cascade Lodge's 1930s promotional literature seem almost unimaginative. The Duluth group named the resort for Naniboujou, a Cree Indian god of the woods who, according to Pardee, was a "genial, friendly spirit" whose favorite haunt was the North Shore.

With a sales pitch thoroughly wrapped in Indian mythology, the enterprise began accepting memberships from the elite, including journalist Ring Lardner, heavyweight boxing champion Jack Dempsey, and the "Sultan of Swat," George Herman "Babe" Ruth. Only 25 percent of the planned one thousand members could come from Minnesota, an effort to ensure space for those from other states. Swayed by the Duluth group's grandiose vision of a complex comprised of a 150-room lodge, cabin sites, bathing houses, several tennis courts, a golf course, swimming pool, and even an electric generating plant on the Brule River, membership reached about six hundred by the time ground was broken for the club house in July 1928. Troubling financial signs were already appearing, however. Initially planned as a $500,000 facility, the complex was now reduced to a $250,000 project. Moreover, memberships to this point seem to have been less than expected. Nevertheless, the local newspaper painted a rosy picture: "The enrollment has been far beyond expectations and, as a result, building operations have been started this summer instead of a year from now as originally planned."

Designed by Duluth architects Holstead and Sullivan, the club house was completed by Duluth contractor Arthur T. Dinsmore in early summer 1929. The large, generally U-shaped, two-story structure was covered in cedar shakes and featured a gambrel roof pierced by dormers. A rectangular sleeping wing extended diagonally from either end of the rectangular common area. The intersecting walls of the sleeping wings and common area were punctuated with two-story, polygonal towers capped with hip roofs. The walls of the common area were accented with French doors surmounted with large, multipane sashes with pointed crowns. The window-door combination offered the impression of a two-story arcade. Although the exterior clearly signaled a substantial building, it was the interior of the common area that grabbed attention. With a ceiling shaped like an inverted canoe, the common area was brilliantly decorated in multicolored Cree Indian motifs by French-Canadian Antoine Gouffee. A 12-foot-high fireplace formed of rounded, water-washed stones dominated the space. The 200-ton hearth was embellished with a stone sunburst, the Cree welcome symbol.

Minnesota Governor Theodore Christianson, a member of the resort, was expected to speak at the club house dedicatory celebration on July 6,

The Cree welcome symbol embedded within the huge fireplace greets visitors to the common area.

With a ceiling shaped like an inverted canoe, and colors and patterns that leap out at guests, Naniboujou's common area is a treat for the eyes.

1929, but fell ill and could not attend the event. More depressing for lodge officials, however, was the stock market crash in October, which brought the "Roaring Twenties" to a whimpering close and ultimately spelled the end for the Naniboujou Club as a province of the well-to-do. Business at the resort was lacking by the following summer and the *Cook County News-Herald* sounded bitterly desperate: "If the wonders of Naniboujou's domain were known in Chicago, St. Louis, Tulsa and other cities of the mid-continent, the Club house would be much too small and every one of the beautiful cottage sites would be snapped off in a months time."

It is uncertain if the newspaper's grousing helped, but the common folk did their part, at least for a time. The lean economics of the 1930s eventually proved too much and vacations became a luxury of the few. The

Naniboujou Club, only a fraction the size its optimistic founders fancied, closed in 1939. But the Great Depression was not so great that it lasted indefinitely, and the Naniboujou Club eventually reopened, passing through a succession of owners. The rustic jewel continues to grace the shores of Lake Superior, amidst the birches like Greek columns and the cedars like Gothic pillars. Now called the Naniboujou Lodge, it looks warm and inviting astride the inland sea. Moreover, its common area, a popular North Shore fine-dining restaurant, still retains the dazzling Cree geometrics and mammoth hearth, compelling visitors to pull out the camera. As a fantastically conceived 1920s northern Minnesota retreat, the Naniboujou Club was added to the National Register in 1982.

✳ Graystone Hotel

DETROIT LAKES | BECKER COUNTY

Elon Galusha Holmes was an entrepreneur. A former Civil War veteran, Holmes was working as a clerk in a mercantile exchange in St. Paul in the early 1870s when he decided to seek his fortune in northwestern Minnesota, a region endowed with inviting woodlands and lakes. At this time the Northern Pacific Railway (NP) was pushing west across the state. Holmes, understanding that financial opportunity flows where the railroad goes, speculated that the line would pass through Ottertail City. With his new bride, Lucy Sherman, he moved to the rural community where he soon established a store and newspaper and awaited the railroad. But the railroad didn't come. Instead, the NP laid its line to the north, through Detroit (renamed Detroit Lakes in 1926) in Becker County. No matter, Holmes simply uprooted his interests and moved to Detroit. By 1872 he had reestablished his store, as well as his newspaper, which he christened the *Detroit Record*.[84]

Holmes quickly made a name in Detroit Lakes. Since owning a store and newspaper hardly satiated his vocational appetite, he also entered into finance, joining the Bank of Detroit as a cashier. He would become president of the institution in 1884. Meanwhile, he continued to expand his endeavors. Between 1876 and 1880, he was clerk of district court. Three years later he was elected to the county board. About this time he contracted with the NP to provide the railroad with lumber and ties, a venture that made him wealthy. He also platted four additions to Detroit Lakes and founded the community's first light company, which he later sold to the city. In addition, he was responsible for developing much of Block 6 of the Original Townsite of Detroit, a parcel that ultimately became one of the city's principal commercial locales. By the close of the 1880s Holmes was one of the most prominent men in northwestern Minnesota. In fact, in

1889 his popularity won him election to the state legislature as Becker County's first senator.

Given Holmes's enterprising nature, it was not surprising when he and a few other forward-thinking individuals formed the Hotel Minnesota Company in the early 1880s. The stock company was born for the sole purpose of bringing a large, elegant hotel to Detroit Lakes, a facility in stark contrast to the area's first hotel. In 1870 Merwin M. Tyler had erected a residence in Detroit Township, a short distance east of present-day Detroit Lakes. The 12- by 14-foot log cabin was meant only as his home, but when the NP showed up the following year, home life for Tyler changed. Settlers soon began arriving in the area by rail and they needed a place to stay, as did personnel of the NP, so Tyler's tiny cabin became a common lodge. Realizing that his sparse quarters would not do, Tyler built an addition to his cabin and Tyler's Hotel was born. The community that rose up around the hotel was called Tylertown.

Not long after Tyler erected his building, another hotel was constructed to the west in the new town of Detroit Lakes. The Commercial Hotel wasn't swank, but it was nicer than Tyler's. More importantly, it was located in a town that new settlers to the region found more appealing than Tylertown. Eventually, those in Tylertown also concluded that Detroit Lakes was the place to be. As Tylertown slowly emptied, so did Tyler's Hotel. Tyler finally gave up the unprofitable enterprise and by the early 1890s the building was in disrepair.

While Tyler's Hotel struggled in faltering Tylertown, the Commercial Hotel prospered in booming Detroit Lakes. The hotel catered to newly arriving settlers, traveling merchants, and railroad employees. In the late 1800s, it was the classic small-town hotel. But when E. G. Holmes and his partners built the Hotel Minnesota in 1884 they were thinking on an altogether different plane. Their mission was to draw tourists to Detroit Lakes and they wanted a hotel as fine as the getaways on Lake Minnetonka and White Bear Lake near the Twin Cities. The wooden, multistory Hotel Minnesota was ornamented with verandas and balconies and an observatory tower that afforded a spectacular view of the community and nearby lakes. Since Detroit Lakes was only a train ride away from Minneapolis and St. Paul, the hotel quickly became a popular destination for well-heeled residents of the Twin Cities. The upscale hotel also triggered a trend in the community. Others around the city began building choice hotels and cottages and by the early twentieth century Detroit Lakes boasted about a dozen lodging facilities geared toward those searching for relaxation and recreation. None, however, was as grand as the Hotel Minnesota.

The Hotel Minnesota was a landmark in Detroit Lakes until 1915, when the ornate building was consumed by fire after employees accidentally ignited clothing on an oil stove. Holmes had sold his interests in the business six years earlier and moved to California. Now, community leaders prodded him to return and build again. Holmes obliged, moving back to Detroit Lakes and constructing a fabulous hotel on Block 6 of the Original Townsite of Detroit, a parcel he had already personalized with the Holmes Block, a building that housed Blanding's, a mercantile business that ultimately became a major commercial enterprise in the town. Coincidentally, the Holmes Block was placed on the National Register in 2001.

The Graystone Hotel was completed only a year after the Hotel Minnesota was lost. Unlike its predecessor, however, it was a fireproof building. The concrete-framed building was designed by Duluth architect Edward F. Broomhall and constructed by Detroit Lakes contractor August S. Randolph. The first-floor exterior was faced with off-white ashlar, while the upper floors featured beige brick with gray pebble aggregate. The main entrance was situated within one of two bays that slightly projected from the north facade. A shouldered gablet crowned the bays, rising above a parapet wall with a stone coping that encircled the building. The hotel's lobby featured a tile floor, walls of marble wainscoting, and a large brick fireplace trimmed with oak. The first floor held a barbershop, writing room, dining room, cafe, and more. Sample rooms, a nod to traveling merchants, and a ballroom occupied much of the basement. A terrazzo stairway led to the hotel rooms on the second and third floors.

The concrete-framed, ashlar- and brick-faced Graystone Hotel circa 1920—the elegant outcome of a painful loss

GRAYSTONE HOTEL, DETROIT, MINN. 169.

The Graystone had no equal in Detroit Lakes and may have been unequaled anywhere in northwestern Minnesota. Situated within the downtown, it was less a hotel than an urban resort. It offered guests the experience of a relaxed, small-town atmosphere in elegant surroundings while also providing its clientele with excursions to nearby woods and lakes. It became quite popular with hunters, anglers, sunbathers, and others who wanted to spend their days enjoying the natural environment outside the city and then retreat to the posh comforts of the hotel in the evenings. The Graystone became so popular that it was often featured in regional and state tourism literature like *Recreation Days*. Capitalizing on this success, management expanded the hotel by acquiring an adjoining building. Dubbed the Graystone Annex, this two-story structure was modified to resemble the Graystone Hotel. Between 1926 and 1927, the building was given a third floor, and its new facade duplicated the original hotel. The annex was employed for guests who wished to stay at the Graystone for extended periods.

When Holmes died in 1931, ownership of the hotel passed to his niece, Grace Wright. Grace soon transferred the business to her son, Frederick H. Wright. Not long after Frederick assumed control he purchased the Edgewater Beach Hotel located on Detroit Lake. He managed both hotels with help from his wife, Marie. The duo operated a shuttle between the facilities, an effort that allowed their guests to experience the perks of each hotel. The future looked bright for the Graystone in the early 1940s, but dimmed considerably by the 1950s. With the development of the interstate highway system in the years following the Second World War, Americans took to the road in staggering numbers, a phenomenon giving rise to the motor court. The appealing rates and convenient locations of motor courts doomed many urban hotels, including the Graystone. The Wrights eventually sold the hotel and in the 1970s it was converted into apartments. Two decades later its physical integrity was suffering. In 1998, Midwest Minnesota Community Development Corporation of Detroit Lakes purchased and rehabilitated the building. Today, it serves as affordable rental housing, with much of the look of its glory days restored. As one of the historic gems in Detroit Lakes, the Graystone Hotel was listed on the National Register in 1999.

✳ Jun Fujita Cabin

WENDT ISLAND, VOYAGEURS NATIONAL PARK |
ST. LOUIS COUNTY

Jun Fujita was something of a mystery, a talented photographer and poet with whom many were acquainted, but few seemed to know. Fortunately, Fujita left behind a small body of work that provides some insight into this man of alien culture who existed within the sometimes chaotic confines of early-twentieth-century Chicago while periodically escaping to the tranquility of northern Minnesota's border country for inspiration and reflection.[85]

In 1996 *Chicago History* celebrated Fujita in picture and verse. Images from "Jun Fujita's Chicago" capture the brazen gang violence of the Windy City in the early 1900s, as well as the sometimes shocking consequences of racial intolerance. The photographer's pictures of the grim aftermath of the

Fujita separated himself from a harsh world when he visited his cabin on Wendt Island on Rainy Lake during the 1920s, '30s, and '40s.

Eastland tragedy, the worst maritime accident in Chicago's history, stab at the heart. Yet Fujita also welcomed inspiration from the seemingly unexceptional, simple patterns found in a midwestern farm field sprinkled with haystacks, or the repetition of a rigidly straight rail line vanishing into a flat rural landscape. Expressing feeling in words, Fujita embraced *tanka,* a minimalistic Japanese poetry consisting of five lines and thirty-one syllables:

> *Into the evening haze,*
> *Out of the giant stacks, the smoke*
> *Winds and fades.*
> *Din and whistles have dwindled away*
> *And stillness chants an empty echo.*

Fujita's small book of poetry, *Tanka: Poems in Exile,* was published by prominent Chicago printer Will Ransom in 1923.

Even with the works Fujita left for us, we know surprisingly little about him. Born in Hiroshima, Japan, in 1888, he immigrated to Canada as a teen, working as a photographer for a Japanese publication. By 1915 he was employed as a photographer for the *Evening Post* in Chicago, where he composed some of his most captivating images, including his 1915 photographs related to the capsizing of the U.S.S. *Eastland* and his 1929 pictures of the St. Valentine's Day Massacre, when several gangsters were lined against a wall and machine-gunned. His 1919 images of the race riots on Chicago's South Side are brutal, some depicting a black man being stoned to death by a mob of angry white men. It required uncommon courage for a man of Japanese ancestry to record the atrocious events of the riots. Fujita left news photography in the 1930s, opening a commercial studio in one of the Columbian Exhibition buildings on Harper Street. His client list included Stark Nurseries, Johnson Motors, and Sears, Roebuck and Co. Fujita completed photography for Johnson Motors on Rainy Lake in northeastern Minnesota, a remote location near the Canadian border where the photographer had a vacation cabin on the eastern tip of a small island.

Eventually called Wendt Island, for a time the four-acre land mass roughly thirty miles east of Ranier, was popularly known as "Jap Island," an overtly racist slur likely tied to Fujita's time there. Fujita first came to the island in 1928, when his longtime companion, Florence Carr, purchased the property. A Euro-American woman, Carr studied at the University of Chicago and became a social worker. She and Fujita began living together in the early or mid-1920s, eventually marrying in 1940. The island was placed in Carr's name for fear that it could be confiscated under state laws restricting alien land ownership. Curiously, neighbors at Rainy Lake never recalled meeting Carr, implying that Fujita was the sole occupant of the island.

Fujita constructed a 13- by 16-foot, one-story cabin on the island soon after Carr acquired the property. Framed with cedar poles and covered in drop siding, the gable-roofed structure blended subtly into its surroundings of large rocks, pine trees, and wildflowers. Several multipane windows marked the cabin's walls and a chimney comprised of native rubble was centered on the building's west side. Two log additions were made to the building over the next several years. A screened porch with shed roof spanned the north facade and a 7- by 8-foot addition with a hip roof projected from the structure's east side. The floor in the small addition was slightly higher than in the rest of the cabin and it is possible Fujita used the space as a shrine. The alcove had three large windows, which allowed an excellent view of the island's landscape, as well as the long view of Rainy Lake. Although Fujita's cabin was similar to other area cabins, it also exhibited architectural elements typical of Japanese construction, including modest decoration and a simple foundation of dry-laid stones. The moderately pitched roofs of various designs and the veranda along the facade were also indicative of Japanese building methods.

Fujita erected his cabin when the Rainy Lake region was still evolving into a vacation spot. Regular travel into the area became possible in 1907, when the railroad reached International Falls, about five miles southwest of Ranier. By the early 1920s passable roads had been constructed into the region from the Minnesota towns of Duluth, Baudette, and Bemidji. Several tour operations sprang into being and the area soon became a popular hunting and fishing retreat. The location also attracted those interested in vice, like gambling, drinking, and prostitution. Indeed, International Falls and Ranier became well known for tolerating vice.

Fujita may have used the log addition as a shrine.

The photographer and poet found peace in the cabin's simplicity, an aesthetic still evident today.

As the Rainy Lake region grew in popularity, Fujita was still afforded considerable privacy on the island. He enjoyed the silence and beauty of his surroundings and spent much of his time reading and meditating. Although he received visitors, most remained for brief periods, respecting his desire for solitude. While it is uncertain if Fujita used his island as subject for any of his artistic work, it seems likely the picturesque setting influenced his creative sensibility. Fujita abandoned the island to friends shortly before the Second World War, possibly because of its great distance from his Chicago home and the prevalent anti-Japanese sentiment of the period. In fact, it was rumored that a Rainy Lake local threatened him. Fujita died in 1963, dividing his remaining years between his studio in Chicago and a vacation cabin in the Indiana Dunes in northwestern Indiana, only about an hour drive from his home. Associated with one of the first prominent Japanese-Americans in the Midwest and also tied to the early development of recreation in the Rainy Lake region, the Jun Fujita Cabin was added to the National Register in 1996.

✳ White Castle Building No. 8

MINNEAPOLIS | HENNEPIN COUNTY

"Progress chips away little pieces of our lives. The tangible things that unite today with yesterday become dust, and in the end our past is just a scrapbook." Minneapolis resident M. Howard Gelfand's 1984 statement is largely correct, although a program like the National Register of Historic Places is designed to save at least a modicum of our nation's heritage. Gelfand was mourning the loss of a wonderfully garish building marking the intersection of Central Avenue and Fourth Street Southeast in Northeast Minneapolis. After more than three decades on the site, the petite White Castle building formed of steel and porcelain was being removed in favor of a new, larger restaurant a few blocks away. But even though the old building was lost to Northeast, it would not vanish altogether, for a local remodeling company rescued it from demolition when it transported the entire structure to South Minneapolis. One of only a handful of early White Castles that remain in the country, the novel building is now a jeweler's office on Lyndale Avenue South.[86]

In 1930, Edgar Waldo "Billy" Ingram commissioned a study at the University of Minnesota to determine the nutritional value of cooked ground beef. For eight weeks a university student survived only on water and hamburgers. When the experiment was over the student was found to be healthy. Ingram was thrilled, promoting the study as scientific proof that hamburgers are nutritious. Few today would go so far, but Ingram was obsessed with convincing Americans to eat more burgers. He was, after

all, one of the founders of White Castle, the first fast-food restaurant chain in America.

Ingram and his partner, Walter Anderson, began altering the nation's eating habits in 1921, when the duo established White Castle in Wichita, Kansas. The partners faced a daunting challenge. Americans were still queasy after reading *The Jungle,* Upton Sinclair's 1906 novel publicizing the polluted conditions of the meat processing industry. Moreover, since ground beef was often spoiling cuts of meat ground together with preservatives, few were anxious to take a bite. But Ingram and Anderson wanted to make ground beef a staple of the American diet and they began by constructing tiny, hygienically white, brick buildings with stainless steel interiors. The castle-like appearance of the hamburger restaurants was drawn from the castle-like Chicago Water Tower, an architectural design that implied permanence. The buildings were immaculate and employees were adorned in spotless uniforms. For a time, staff even ground high-quality cuts of meat in view of customers, ensuring diners they were getting only the best.

While cleanliness and first-rate ground beef helped pull Wichita residents into the restaurants, a tasty burger kept them coming back. The enterprise was a sensation and by 1923 the company had branched into Omaha, Nebraska, meeting with the same success it had in Wichita. Other midwestern cities were soon conquered as well, including Minneapolis, which welcomed its first White Castle in 1926. Only one year later, the city received its eighth White Castle, which was constructed at 616 Washington Avenue Southeast, near the University of Minnesota's Memorial Stadium. The glazed brick building remained until 1936, when it was replaced by an innovative White Castle design that became a company signature.

Since White Castle pioneered the fast-food industry, there was no existing infrastructure to aid the proliferation of the business. The company established centralized bakeries and warehouses and materials were purchased in large quantities at reduced rates and stored until needed. Paperlynen, a concern that made all the paper products required for the operation of the restaurants, was formed as a White Castle subsidiary. White Castle even created a company to manufacture its buildings. Porcelain Steel Buildings built movable, prefabricated structures framed with rolled steel channels covered by metal panels sheathed with porcelain. Billy Ingram later remarked: "As far as we have been able to learn, this building [design] represented the first successful use of porcelain as an architectural material." The unique and durable buildings could be quickly assembled at any White Castle site, and the design was employed at 616 Washington Avenue Southeast in Minneapolis. Measuring only 28 by 28 feet, the new White Castle Building No. 8 featured octagonal buttresses, crenellated towers, and a parapet wall. "White Castle Hamburgers" signs in black Gothic lettering marked all four sides of the building, some even reminding patrons to "Buy 'em by the sack."

Now a jeweler's office, the petite porcelain fortress punctuates a small lot adjacent to Lyndale Avenue in South Minneapolis.

The steel and porcelain building occupied the Washington Avenue location until 1950, when the landowner refused to renew the lease. The reluctance of metropolitan landowners to extend leases on small parcels was precisely the reason White Castle manufactured movable buildings. Another site for White Castle Building No. 8 was found in Northeast Minneapolis, near the intersection of Central Avenue and Fourth Street Southeast. The building was disassembled and transported to the new site, where it was re-erected. It was also renamed White Castle Building No. 16. By this time the hamburger chain's fortunes had turned. Labor and food shortages during World War II triggered a substantial decrease in patronage, and the number of White Castles plummeted from 130 before the conflict to 87 immediately after. With rising costs and fears of another food shortage during the Korean War, the company conserved by punching five small holes into its hamburger patty and reducing its overall size. Surprisingly, the measure proved popular with the public, but the novel hamburger patty was only a small success in an otherwise dismal period.

White Castle blundered when it failed to capitalize on the considerable population shift from metropolitan centers to suburbs in the 1950s. While upstart quick-service restaurants realized stunning financial successes in burgeoning new communities, White Castle was trying to survive in declining urban neighborhoods. Aggressive marketing eventually helped pull White Castle out of its financial rut. Finally pushing into suburbs brought new life as well. The company also began constructing larger restaurants with less ornamentation but more customer seating. Many of the newer buildings were formed of materials other than steel and porcelain. The White Castle in Brooklyn Park, a suburb of Minneapolis, was comprised of rusticated concrete block. The larger restaurants spelled the end for many of the more fanciful and intimate older castles.

In 1983 company officials erected a new, large building only a few blocks from Northeast's cozy White Castle. Since the city would lose a significant piece of its social and architectural history with the demolition of White Castle Building No. 8, the Minneapolis Heritage Preservation Commission found an organization willing to purchase and move the building to a new site adjacent to Lyndale Avenue in South Minneapolis. In 1986 the blatantly conspicuous structure was added to the National Register as one of the few remaining examples of the building type in America. And even though removing a building from its traditional site is often a National Register no-no, the federal program recognizes that White Castle specifically constructed its early restaurants to be movable.

NOTES

1. Ian Johnson, "In China, 350 Years Isn't Old Enough When You're a House," *Wall Street Journal*, October 27, 2000; U.S. Department of the Interior, *National Register Bulletin No. 15: How to Apply the National Register Criteria for Evaluation*, rev. ed. (Washington, D.C.: Government Printing Office, 1997), 1; Laura Weber, "Wins and Losses: The National Register of Historic Places in Minnesota," *Minnesota History* 55 (Fall 1997): 305–6; Norman Tyler, *Historic Preservation: An Introduction to its History, Principles, and Practice* (New York: W. W. Norton and Company, 2000), 33–36, 42, 44–45; Robert E. Stipe, "Historic Preservation: The Process and the Actors," in *The American Mosaic: Preserving a Nation's Heritage,* ed. Robert E. Stipe and Antoinette Lee (Washington, D.C.: U.S. Committee, International Council on Monuments and Sites, 1987), 3; Larry Millett, *Lost Twin Cities* (St. Paul: Minnesota Historical Society Press, 1992), 1–2, 160–63; State Historic Preservation Office (hereafter SHPO), *The National Register of Historic Places: Minnesota Checklist* (St. Paul: Minnesota Historical Society, 1997), ii–iii; Clark A. Dobbs, "Precontact American Indian Earthworks, 500 BC–AD 1650," ca. 1996, and Mark J. Dudzik, "American Indian Rock Art," March 1995, National Register of Historic Places (hereafter NRHP) Multiple Property Documentation Forms, both available at SHPO, Minnesota Historical Society (hereafter MHS), St. Paul.

NATIVE AMERICANS

2. MHS, *Minnesota Statewide Archaeological Survey, Summary: 1977–1980* (St. Paul: Minnesota Historical Society, 1981), ix; Lloyd A. Wilford, "The Prehistoric Indians of Minnesota," *Minnesota History* 25 (June 1944): 153; Scott Anfinson, "Indian Communities and Reservations" (draft), May 1994, historic context available at SHPO, MHS, St. Paul, 1–4, 8–9; J. V. Brower, "Prehistoric Man at the Headwaters of the Mississippi River," *Collections of the Minnesota Historical Society*, vol. 8 (St. Paul: Minnesota Historical Society, 1898), 234; Theodore C. Blegen, *Minnesota: A History of the State* (Minneapolis: University of Minnesota Press, 1963), 96.

3. JEFFERS PETROGLYPHS SITE Elden Johnson, "Jeffers Petroglyph Site," April 1970, NRHP Registration Form, available at SHPO, MHS, St. Paul; Dean R. Snow, "Petroglyphs of Southern Minnesota," *Minnesota Archaeologist* 24 (1962): 103, 119; Gordon A. Lothson, *The Jeffers Petroglyphs Site: A Survey and Analysis of the Carvings* (St. Paul: Minnesota Historical Society, 1976), 3–4, 6–7, 29–33, 40; Newton H. Winchell and Warren Upham, *The Geology of Minnesota, Volume 1 of the Final Report* (Minneapolis: Johnson, Smith and Harrison, State Printers, 1884), 501; Kevin L. Callahan, *The Jeffers Petroglyphs: Native American Rock Art on the Midwestern Plains* (St. Paul: Prairie Smoke Press, 2001), 26, 30, 35, 45, 61; "Report on the Sojourn of the 'Mound Creek Exploring Party,'" *New Ulm Review*, August 12, 1885; Nick Coleman, "Petroglyphs Preserve Stories in Stone," *St. Paul Pioneer Press*, May 7, 1999.

4. LITTLE RAPIDS (INYAN CEYAKA OTONWE) Amy L. Ollendorf, "Inyan Ceyaka Otonwe," April 1997, NRHP Registration Form, available at SHPO, MHS, St. Paul; Paul Klammer, "What a Find," *Minnesota Archaeologist* 1 (July 1, 1935): 3–4; Janet D. Spector,

What This Awl Means: Feminist Archaeology at a Wahpeton Dakota Village (St. Paul: Minnesota Historical Society Press, 1993), 11, 36–38, 46; Theodore C. Blegen, *Minnesota: A History of the State* (Minneapolis: University of Minnesota Press, 1963), 133.

5. BIRCH COULEE SCHOOL Michael Koop, "Birch Coulee School," February 1989, NRHP Registration Form, available at SHPO, MHS, St. Paul; Samuel D. Hinman letter to Bishop Henry Benjamin Whipple, December 1, 1887, available in Box 20, "Henry B. Whipple Papers, 1833–1934," MHS, St. Paul; Samuel D. Hinman letter to Bishop Henry Benjamin Whipple, October 31, 1861, available in Box 2, "Henry B. Whipple Papers, 1833–1934," MHS, St. Paul; Betty Paukert Sheppard and Edward L. Sheppard, *The Mission at the Lower Sioux: 1860–1980* ([Minnesota]: Episcopal Diocese of Minnesota, Bishop Whipple Mission, 1981), 3–7, 10–11, 15–16, 21, 24; Wallace F. Simpson, "Redwood County, Now and Then," 1968, booklet produced by County Superintendent of Schools Office, Redwood Falls, Minnesota, 9.

6. SUGAR POINT (BATTLE POINT) Christy A. Hohman-Caine, "Battle Point," March 1990, NRHP Registration Form, available at SHPO, MHS, St. Paul; William E. Matsen, "The Battle of Sugar Point: A Re-Examination," *Minnesota History* 50 (Fall 1987): 269–75; Louis H. Roddis, "The Last Indian Uprising in the United States," *Minnesota History Bulletin* 3 (February 1920): 276–87, 289–90; William Watts Folwell, *A History of Minnesota*, vol. 4 (St. Paul: Minnesota Historical Society, 1930), 314–17, 321–22; Diane Mundt, "Historic Site Status Sought for Last Indian Battle Locale," *Minneapolis Star Tribune*, September 2, 1985.

BEFORE THE RAILROAD

7. John H. Randall, "The Beginning of Railroad Building in Minnesota," in *Collections of the Minnesota Historical Society*, vol. 15 (St. Paul: Minnesota Historical Society, 1915), 215, 220; Timothy Rowley, "The Ordeal of Pioneering," *Minnesota History* 10 (December 1929): 403; Harold A. Meeks, "Railroad Expansion and Agricultural Settlement in Minnesota, 1860–1910," *Proceedings of the Minnesota Academy of Science* 27 (1959): 26, 28; Demian Hess, "Minnesota Red River Trails," July 1989, NRHP Multiple Property Documentation Form, available at SHPO, MHS, St. Paul; Robert Hybben and Jeffrey A. Hess, "Overland Staging Industry in Minnesota, 1849–1880," July 1990, NRHP Multiple Property Documentation Form, available at SHPO, MHS, St. Paul; John Grossman, "Pickwick Mill," May 1970, NRHP Registration Form, available at SHPO, MHS, St. Paul; Ted Lofstrom, "Zoar Moravian Church," January 1978, NRHP Registration Form, available at SHPO, MHS, St. Paul.

8. GURI & LARS ENDRESON HOUSE Susan Granger, "Lars and Guri Endreson House," July 1985, NRHP Registration Form, available at SHPO, MHS, St. Paul; Guri Endreson, letter to daughter in Norway, December 2, 1866, in "Notes and Documents," *Minnesota History* 10 (December 1929): 427–28; *Anniversary Album, 1859–1944, Lebanon Lutheran Church, New London, Minnesota* (New London, Minn.: [Lebanon Lutheran Church?], 1944), 52, 58–60; *Centennial History of Kandiyohi County, 1870–1970* (Willmar, Minn.: Centennial Committee,

1970), H; Virginia McAlester and Lee McAlester, *A Field Guide to American Houses* (New York: Alfred A. Knopf, Inc., 1984), 63; Roger Kennedy, *Minnesota Houses: An Architectural and Historical View* (Minneapolis: Dillon Press, 1967), 20–21.

9. ST. CLOUD & RED RIVER VALLEY STAGE ROAD: KANDOTA SECTION Robert Hybben and Jeffrey A. Hess, "St. Cloud and Red River Valley Stage Road: Kandota Section," July 1990, NRHP Registration Form, available at SHPO, MHS, St. Paul; Robert Hybben and Jeffrey A. Hess, "Overland Staging Industry in Minnesota, 1849–1880," July 1990, NRHP Multiple Property Documentation Form, available at SHPO, MHS, St. Paul; Dickens's description of stagecoach travel is found in Kenneth E. Colton's "Stagecoach Travel in Iowa," *Annals of Iowa* 22 (January 1940): 187; "The Frazer River Trail," *Weekly Pioneer and Democrat,* July 7, 1859; Richard S. Prosser, *Rails to the North Star* (Minneapolis: Dillon Press, 1966), 17.

10. JEFFERSON GRAIN WAREHOUSE David C. Anderson, "Jefferson Grain Warehouse," April 1994, NRHP Registration Form, available at SHPO, MHS, St. Paul; Kevin Schultz, "Grain Warehouse Outlives Town, Steamboat Travel," *The Land,* March 3, 1995.

11. GOOD TEMPLARS HALL Susan Pommering Reynolds, "Good Templars Hall–School District 24," June 1979, NRHP Registration Form, available at SHPO, MHS, St. Paul; a copy of the circa 1857 poster promoting Nininger is in *Honoring the Late Ignatius Donnelly: Poet, Author, Statesman, Philosopher,* circa 1938 pamphlet published by the *Hastings Gazette,* available at MHS, St. Paul, n.p.; Mike Barrett, "Nininger Township Hall is a Place of History," *St. Paul Dispatch,* October 3, 1978; Milly Smith and Gary Phelps, "National Register Sites in Dakota County (Part 1)," *Over the Years* 27 (June 1987): 15; Dudley S. Brainard, "Nininger, a Boom Town of the Fifties," *Minnesota History* 13 (June 1932): 127–151; W. H. Mitchell, *Geographical and Statistical Sketch of the Past and Present: Dakota County* (Minneapolis: Tribune Printing Company, 1869), 82; Thomas Prinz, "Ignatius Donnelly," February 1967, typescript history available in "Good Templars Hall" file at SHPO, MHS, St. Paul, 1–6; Miriam Allen DeFord, "The Amazing Ignatius Donnelly," January 1929, published history in Minnesota Historical Society Pamphlet Collection, copy available in "Good Templars Hall" file at SHPO, MHS, St. Paul, 44; J. Fletcher Williams, *History of Dakota County and the City of Hastings,* (Minneapolis: North Star Publishing Company, 1881), 439; "A Commission from the Independent Order of Good Templars," n.d., web page available at http://users.1st.net/dhancock/templar.html; "Origin of the Independent Order of Good Templars," in "Weekly Recorder," March 28, 1889, web page available at http://www.rootsweb. com/~nyononda/MANLIUS/ goodtemplars.html; "The Panic of 1857," in "Today in History," n.d., at the American Memory Library of Congress website, web page available at http:// memory.loc.gov/ ammem/today/aug24.html.

12. LANESBORO STONE DAM Robert M. Frame III, "Lanesboro Historic District," February 1981, NRHP Registration Form, available at SHPO, MHS, St. Paul; Donald C. Jackson, *Building the Ultimate Dam* (Lawrence, Kans.: University Press of Kansas, 1995), 13–20; *History of Fillmore County* (Minneapolis: Minnesota Historical Company, 1882), 464; Charles R. Drake and Vienna L. Drake, *River Valley Echoes* (Rochester, Minn.: Whiting Printers and Stationers, 1969), 8–9; Lanesboro Historical Preservation Association, "A Guide to Lanesboro's Historic Structures and Locations, Past and Present," 1992, typescript history available

at MHS, St. Paul, II-28; "Historic Lanesboro from its Beginning Until 1902," early 1900s Lanesboro history reprinted by Lanesboro Historical Preservation Association in 1992, available at MHS, St. Paul, 1.17; Jeffrey A. Hess, "Minnesota Hydroelectric Generating Facilities, 1881–1928," October 1989, NRHP Multiple Property Documentation Form, available at SHPO, MHS, St. Paul; Richard S. Prosser, *Rails to the North Star* (Minneapolis: Dillon Press, 1966), 14, 21.

13. ORVILLE P. & SARAH CHUBB HOUSE Susan Granger and Kay Grossman, "Chubb, Orville P. and Sarah, House," August 1994, NRHP Registration Form, available at SHPO, MHS, St. Paul; Ruth Hein, "Fairmont Group Works to Qualify Home for Register," *Worthington Daily Globe,* September 14, 1995; Jim Samuelson, "Chubb Home Slated for Demolition," *Sentinel,* ca. 1990, newspaper clipping available at Martin County Historical Society, Fairmont, Minnesota; "Death Claims John Dalton, 100 Years Old," *Fairmont Daily Sentinel,* February 23, 1931; Virginia McAlester and Lee McAlester, *A Field Guide to American Houses* (New York: Alfred A. Knopf, Inc., 1984), 177–81.

14. HASTINGS FOUNDRY Susan Pommering Reynolds, "Hastings Foundry–Star Iron Works," June 1979, NRHP Registration Form, available at SHPO, MHS, St. Paul; Edward D. Neill and J. Fletcher Williams, *History of Dakota County and the City of Hastings, Including Explorers and Pioneers of Minnesota, and Outlines of the History of Minnesota* (Minneapolis: North Star Publishing Company, 1881), 270; Milly Smith and Gary Phelps, "National Register Sites in Dakota County (Part 2)," *Over the Years* 27 (June 1987): 4–5; Richard S. Prosser, *Rails to the North Star* (Minneapolis: Dillon Press, 1966), 12; Jack El-Hai, *Lost Minnesota: Stories of Vanished Places* (Minneapolis: University of Minnesota Press, 2000), 164–65; "Foundry and Machine Works," *Hastings Independent,* September 29, 1859; "The Stella Whipple," *Hastings Independent,* August 29, 1861; "Great Loss by Fire," *Hastings Independent,* May 29, 1862; "Editorial Correspondence," *Farmer and Gardener* 1 (May 1861): 142; Hazel Jacobsen, comp., "Star Iron Works," n.d., compilation of historical records available at SHPO, MHS, St. Paul.

RAILROADS & AGRICULTURE

15. James J. Hill, "History of Agriculture in Minnesota," in *Collections of the Minnesota Historical Society,* vol. 8 (St. Paul: Minnesota Historical Society, 1898), 279–80; Richard S. Prosser, *Rails to the North Star* (Minneapolis: Dillon Press, 1966), 3–4, 7–9, 12, 17, 35, 135–36, 161–62, [187-91]; *The Hill Roads* (New York: Harris, Forbes and Company), 3-15; Joseph W. Zalusky, "The Railroads West of the Mississippi—Part I," *Hennepin County History* 25 (Summer 1965): 5–7; Harold A. Meeks, "Railroad Expansion and Agricultural Settlement in Minnesota, 1860–1910," *Proceedings of the Minnesota Academy of Science* 27 (1959): 26–37; "Railroads in Minnesota," *Roots* 4 (Winter 1975–76): 2, 4, 10–11; Harold F. Peterson, "Early Minnesota Railroads and the Quest for Settlers," *Minnesota History* 13 (March 1932): 41; Denis P. Gardner and Charlene K. Roise, "Northern Pacific Bridge No. 95," July 2000, Historic American Engineering Record (hereafter HAER) documentation completed for United States Army Corps of Engineers (hereafter USACOE), available at USACOE, St. Paul, 6–7; Edward Van Dyke Robinson, *Early Economic Conditions and the Development of Agriculture in Minnesota* (Minneapolis: University of Minnesota Press, 1915), 137; Thomas Harvey, "Sioux City and St. Paul Railroad Section House," March 1979,

NRHP Registration Form, available at SHPO, MHS, St. Paul; Thomas Harvey, "Wulf C. Krabbenhoft Farmstead," October 1979, NRHP Registration Form, available at SHPO, MHS, St. Paul; Michael Zuckerman, "Henry Damon Round Barn," June 1978, NRHP Registration Form, SHPO, MHS, St. Paul; Lamont Buchanan, *Steel Trails and Iron Horses: A Pageant of American Railroading* (New York: G. P. Putnam's Sons, 1955), 43.

16. NORTHERN PACIFIC RAILWAY SHOPS Norene A. Roberts, "Northern Pacific Railroad Shops Historic District," June 1988, NRHP Registration Form, available at SHPO, MHS, St. Paul; Denis P. Gardner and Charlene K. Roise, "Northern Pacific Bridge No. 95," July 2000, HAER documentation completed for USACOE, available at USACOE, St. Paul, 6, 25; Warren Upham, *Minnesota Place Names: A Geographical Encyclopedia* (St. Paul: Minnesota Historical Society Press, 2001), 157; Denis P. Gardner, "Duluth and Iron Range Rail Road Company Shops, Roundhouse" in "Duluth and Iron Range Rail Road Company Shops," September 2001, HAER documentation completed for USACOE, available at USACOE, Detroit, 13; "Gone Up in Flames," *Brainerd Dispatch,* April 2, 1886; American Association for State and Local History, technical leaflet 95, "Bridge Truss Types: A Guide to Dating and Identifying," *History News* 32 (May 1977): n.p.

17. VIOLA COOPERATIVE CREAMERY Garneth O. Peterson, "Viola Cooperative Creamery," June 1999, NRHP Registration Form, available at SHPO, MHS, St. Paul; *Godahl Community and Nelson and Albin Mercantile Association: Fourscore Years Since 1894* (n.p., 1974), 13, 23; "Viola Creamery Burns Early Saturday Morning," *Elgin Monitor,* February 29, 1924; "Open New Creamery at Viola Monday," *Elgin Monitor,* August 8, 1924.

18. MINNEAPOLIS, ST. PAUL & SAULT ST. MARIE DEPOT (SOO LINE DEPOT) Heather Esser, Elizabeth A. Butterfield, and Barbara M. Kooiman, "Minneapolis, St. Paul and Sault Ste. Marie Depot," 1995, NRHP Registration Form, available at SHPO, MHS, St. Paul; "Arrested at Depot," *Thief River Falls News-Press,* March 6, 1913; "Material for New Depot Arrives," *Thief River Falls News-Press,* July 24, 1913; "Soo Depot Completed," *Thief River Falls News-Press,* April 30, 1914; "Soo Line Depot," *Minnesota Monthly,* March 1997, 16; "Much Railroad Talk Here in April 1903," *Thief River Falls Times,* March 10, 1953; Richard S. Prosser, *Rails to the North Star* (Minneapolis: Dillon Press, 1966), 43, 162.

19. JOHN BOSCH FARMSTEAD Susan Granger, "John Bosch Farmstead," July 1985, NRHP Registration Form, available at SHPO, MHS, St. Paul; David L. Nass, ed., "Recollections of Rural Revolt," *Minnesota History* 45 (Winter 1975): 304–8; John Bosch, "The National Farm Holiday Association," July 1970, typescript history of the Farm Holiday Association, available in "John Bosch Farmstead" file at SHPO, MHS, St. Paul; Harvey Wasserman, *Harvey Wasserman's History of the United States* (New York: Four Walls Eight Windows, 1988), 61–110.

20. STEAMBOAT BRIDGE Robert M. Frame III, "Great Northern Railway Company Bridge," April 1980, NRHP Registration Form, available at SHPO, MHS, St. Paul; David Plowden, *Bridges: The Spans of North America* (New York: Viking Press, 1974), 31; "Park Rapids and Leech Lake Railway Company," in "Minnesota Railroad Companies," n.d., notebook of synopsis railroad histories, available at MHS, St. Paul; "Great Northern Railway Company: Bridge List, Lake District, Mesabi Division," available in Folder 1, Box 133.F.19.14F, Great Northern Railway

Company Collection, MHS, St. Paul; J. A. L. Waddell, *Bridge Engineering,* vol. 1 (New York: John Wiley and Sons, Inc., 1916), 408, 411; *A Walk Through Time: Walker Centennial, 1896–1996* (Walker, Minn.: Walker Centennial Book Committee, 1995), 21; Jeffrey A. Hess, "Stillwater Bridge," NRHP Registration Form, available at SHPO, MHS, St. Paul; "Minnesota's Cass County," 1980, unpublished history available at MHS, St. Paul, 9.

21. NANSEN AGRICULTURAL DISTRICT Christina Slattery, Kathryn Franks, and Amy Squitieri, "Nansen Agricultural Historic District," January 1999, NRHP Registration Form, available at SHPO, MHS, St. Paul; Harold Severson, *We Give You Kenyon: A Bicentennial History of a Minnesota Community* (Kenyon, Minn.: Security State Bank of Kenyon, 1976), 13, 92; Richard S. Prosser, *Rails to the North Star* (Minneapolis: Dillon Press, 1966), 12, 18.

22. SOO LINE HIGH BRIDGE Herschel L. D. Parnes, "Soo Line High Bridge," April 1976, NRHP Registration Form, available at SHPO, MHS, St. Paul; "Laborer Killed," *Stillwater Gazette,* November 9, 1910; "Did Bridge Nearly Fall?" *Stillwater Gazette,* March 8, 1911; "New Bridge Now in Service," *Stillwater Gazette,* June 14, 1911; Patrick Dorin, *The Soo Line* (Seattle: Superior Publishing Company, 1979), 20; David Plowden, *Bridges: The Spans of North America* (New York: Viking Press, 1974), 67, 177–78; Denis P. Gardner, "Duluth and Iron Range Rail Road Company Shops, Oil House" in "Duluth and Iron Range Rail Road Company Shops," September 2001, HAER documentation completed for USACOE, available at USACOE, Detroit, 8; Denis P. Gardner and Charlene K. Roise, "Portage Lake Bridge," April 1999, HAER documentation, completed for the Michigan Department of Transportation (hereafter MDOT), available at MDOT, Lansing; J. A. L. Waddell, *Bridge Engineering,* vol. 1 (New York: John Wiley and Sons, Inc., 1916), 619; photographs Runk 1212 and Runk 1225, John Runk Collection, available at MHS, St. Paul.

INDUSTRY & TECHNOLOGY

23. James J. Hill, "History of Agriculture in Minnesota," in *Collections of the Minnesota Historical Society,* vol. 8 (St. Paul: Minnesota Historical Society, 1898), 275–77; "Becoming an Industrial State," *Roots* 7 (Fall 1978): 3; Theodore C. Blegen, *Minnesota: A History of the State* (Minneapolis: University of Minnesota Press, 1963), 31, 74–75; Federal Writers Project, *Minnesota: A State Guide* (New York: Hastings House, 1938), 92–93, 95, 98, 100–102; SHPO, "Historic Context: Northern Minnesota Lumbering, 1870–1930s," ca. 1990, context available at SHPO, MHS, St. Paul, n.p; Michael Koop, "Kettle River Sandstone Company Quarry," August 1990, NRHP Registration Form, available at SHPO, MHS, St. Paul; John J. Hackett, "Phelps Mill," November 1974, NRHP Registration Form, available at SHPO, MHS, St. Paul; Dennis Gimmestad, "Kern Bridge," January 1980, NRHP Registration Form, available at SHPO, MHS, St. Paul; Jeffrey A. Hess, "Lake Zumbro Hydroelectric Generating Plant," October 1989, NRHP Registration Form, available at SHPO, MHS, St. Paul.

24. PINE TREE LUMBER COMPANY OFFICE BUILDING Thomas L. Jenkinson and Norene Roberts, "Pine Tree Lumber Company Office Building," March 1985, NRHP Registration Form, available at SHPO, MHS, St. Paul; Thomas L. Jenkinson and Norene Roberts, "Charles A. Weyerhaeuser and Richard Drew Musser Houses," March 1985, NRHP Registration Form, available at SHPO, MHS, St. Paul; Mary Swanholm, *Lumbering in the Last of the White-Pine States* (St. Paul: Minnesota Historical Society,

1978), 7–10, 13, 21, 32; Charles Vandersluis, comp., *Mainly Logging* (Minneota, Minn.: Minneota Clinic, 1974), 177; "Peter Musser, Prominent Pioneer Lumberman, Passes to Rest," *Muscatine News-Tribune*, September 29, 1910; "Welcome to 'Linden Hill,'" n.d., promotional pamphlet for Linden Hill Conference and Retreat Center in Little Falls, Minnesota, available at SHPO, MHS, St. Paul, n.p.

25. PEAVEY-HAGLIN EXPERIMENTAL CONCRETE GRAIN ELEVATOR Robert M. Frame III, "Peavey-Haglin Experimental Concrete Grain Elevator," May 1978, NRHP Registration Form, available at SHPO, MHS, St. Paul; Robert M. Frame III, "Grain Elevators in Minnesota," September 1989, NRHP Multiple Property Documentation Form, available at SHPO, MHS, St. Paul, E.1–E.7, E.45; Ruth J. Heffelfinger, "Experiment in Concrete: A Pioneer Venture in Grain Storage," *Minnesota History* 37 (March 1960): 14–18; Kenneth D. Ruble, *The Peavey Story: A History of Pioneering Achievements in the Grain Industry Since 1874* (Minneapolis: Peavey Company, 1963), 5–15, 33–39, 42; Robert Riley, "Grain Elevators: Symbols of Time, Place and Honest Building," *AIA Journal* 66 (November 1977): 50–52.

26. SEVENTH STREET IMPROVEMENT ARCHES Jeffrey A. Hess, "Seventh Street Improvement Arches," August 1988, NRHP Registration Form, available at SHPO, MHS, St. Paul; W. A. Truesdell, "The Seventh Street Improvement Arches," *Association of Engineering Societies* 5 (July 1886): 317–24; "William Albert Truesdell," *Association of Engineering Societies* 28 (January 1909): 369–72; several 1916 articles in untitled newspapers, as well as various correspondences on the history of the NP bridge component of the East Seventh Street Bridge also proved useful. The articles and correspondence can be found in the "Seventh Street Improvement Arches" file at SHPO, MHS, St. Paul.

27. HILL ANNEX MINE SHPO and Rolf Anderson, "Hill Annex Mine," May 1985, NRHP Registration Form, available at SHPO, MHS, St. Paul; David A. Walker, *Iron Frontier: The Discovery and Early Development of Minnesota's Three Ranges* (St. Paul: Minnesota Historical Society Press, 1979), 1, 8, 13–14, 16–17, 23–38, 51, 76–86, 252; Hill Annex Mine Staff, "A Teachers' Guide to the Hill Annex Mine," 1986, typescript history in "Hill Annex Mine" file at SHPO, MHS, St. Paul, 6–7, 9, 17; Fremont P. Wirth, *The Discovery and Exploitation of the Minnesota Iron Lands* (Cedar Rapids, Iowa: The Torch Press, 1937), 173–74.

28. SCHECH'S MILL Robert M. Frame III, "Schech's Mill," June 1977, NRHP Registration Form, available at SHPO, MHS, St. Paul; Warren Upham, *Minnesota Place Names: A Geographical Encyclopedia*, 3rd ed. (St. Paul: Minnesota Historical Society Press, 2001), 242, 246; Mason A. Witt, ed., *Historical Notes of Interest: Houston and Area* (n.p., 1974?), 4–5; *The Advantages and Resources of Houston County, Minnesota* (Hokah, Minn.: Reynolds and Wertz, 1858), 3–4, 22; Edward D. Neill, *History of Houston County, Including Explorers and Pioneers of Minnesota, and Outline History of the State of Minnesota* (Minneapolis: Minnesota Historical Society, 1882), 455; Robert M. Frame III, "Millers to the World: Minnesota's Nineteenth Century Water Power Flour Mills," 1977, study completed for the MHS, St. Paul, 28–35, 49–51, 58, 75–79, 133.

29. GOODSELL OBSERVATORY Thomas Lutz and Ruthmary Penick, "Goodsell Observatory," March 1975, NRHP Registration Form, available at SHPO, MHS, St. Paul; Ian R. Bartky, "The Invention of Railroad Time," *Railroad History* 148 (Spring 1983): 13–15; Mark Greene, *A Science Not Earthbound* (Northfield, Minn.:

Carleton College Office of Publications, 1988), 4–7, 10–12, 14–15, 18–19, 23–24; "The Northfield Observatory," ca. 1878, *Minneapolis Tribune* editorial available in "Goodsell Observatory" file at SHPO, MHS, St. Paul; Richard P. Brennan, *Dictionary of Scientific Literacy* (New York: John Wiley and Sons, Inc., 1992), 270, 300.

30. UNIVERSAL LABORATORIES BUILDING Cynthia de Miranda and Jeffrey A. Hess, "Universal Laboratories Building," August 1995, NRHP Registration Form, available at SHPO, MHS, St. Paul; "Funeral Today for L. R. (Les) Peel, Dassel Business-man," *Dassel Dispatch*, December 3, 1959; "Major Industries in Dassel," *Dassel Dispatch*, September 18, 1941.

31. BERNARD H. PIETENPOL WORKSHOP & GARAGE Robert M. Frame III, "Pietenpol, Bernard H., Workshop and Garage," February 1981, NRHP Registration Form, available at SHPO, MHS, St. Paul; telephone interview with Bernis Hoopman Finke, daughter of Orrin Hoopman, friend to B. H. Pietenpol and fellow flyer, by the author, December 31, 2001; Noel E. Allard and Gerald N. Sandvick, *Minnesota Aviation History, 1857–1945* (Chaska, Minn.: MAHB Publishing, 1993), 11, 115–16; Bernard H. Pietenpol, "Plans for the Pietenpol Sky Scout," *Modern Mechanics and Inventions* (April 1931): 124; Mike Williams, "Airplane Garage is Considered National Historic Candidate," *Agri-News*, November 13, 1980.

32. HIBBING DISPOSAL PLANT Rolf T. Anderson, "Hibbing Disposal Plant," 1990, NRHP Registration Form, available at SHPO, MHS, St. Paul; Denis P. Gardner and Charlene K. Roise, "The Hershey Sports Arena, Hershey Park, Pennsylvania," December 1999, history available at Hess, Roise and Company, Minneapolis, Minnesota, n.p.; Charles Foster, "The Hibbing Sewage Treatment Plant," *Improvement Bulletin* (February 1940): 31–32; David P. Billington, *The Tower and the Bridge: The New Art of Structural Engineering* (Princeton: Princeton University Press, 1983), 173–93.

MARITIME MINNESOTA

33. Norman Beasley, *Freighters of Fortune* (New York: Harper and Brothers Publishers, 1930), 1; James Cooke Mills, *Our Inland Seas: Their Shipping and Commerce for Three Centuries* (Chicago: A. C. McClurg and Company, 1910), 53–60, 63; Dana Thomas Bowen, "Great Lakes Ships and Shipping," *Minnesota History* 34 (Spring 1954): 9–10; Matti Kaups, "North Shore Commercial Fishing, 1849–1870," *Minnesota History* 46 (Spring 1978): 46–48; Jeffrey A. Hess, "Scott, Jim, Fishhouse," July 1985, NRHP Registration Form, available at SHPO, MHS, St. Paul, n.p; Charlene K. Roise, Denis P. Gardner, and Abigail Christman, "National Register Eligibility Assessments of Seven Wisconsin Lighthouses," December 1999, National Register eligibility study prepared for General Services Administration (hereafter GSA), Property Disposal Division (1PRM-5), available at GSA, Property Disposal Division (1PRM-5) offices, Chicago, Illinois, n.p; John J. Hackett, "Minnesota Point Lighthouse," November 1974, NRHP Registration Form, available at SHPO, MHS, St. Paul, n.p.; Stephen R. James Jr., "U.S.S. Essex," September 1992, NRHP Registration Form, available at SHPO, MHS, St. Paul, 7.1; Scott F. Anfinson, "The Wreck of the *USS Essex*," *Minnesota History* 55 (Fall 1996): 95–103; Alan R. Woolworth and Nancy L. Woolworth, "Grand Portage National Monument: An Historical Overview and an Inventory of Its Cultural Resources, Volume I," August 1982, report prepared for the National Park Service, U.S. Department of the Interior, 89–91.

34. AERIAL LIFT BRIDGE Tom Lutz, "Aerial Lift Bridge," March 1973, NRHP Registration Form, available at SHPO, MHS, St. Paul; Frank A. Young, "The Duluth Ship Canal: One Hundred Years of History," *Duluthian* 7 (August-September 1971): 6–9, and "Duluth's Most Famous Landmark," *Duluthian* 9 (July 1973), 10–13; Dwight E. Woodbridge and John S. Pardee, eds., *History of Duluth and St. Louis County: Past and Present*, vol. 2 (Chicago: C. F. Cooper and Company, 1910), 509; Noam Levey, "Duluth Lift Bridge Faces Costly Repairs," *St. Paul Pioneer Press*, December 28, 1995; Jeffrey A. Hess, "Stillwater Bridge," August 1988, NRHP Registration Form, available at SHPO, MHS, St. Paul, 8.3–8.4; Charlene K. Roise, Denis P. Gardner, and Abigail Christman, "National Register Eligibility Assessments of Seven Wisconsin Lighthouses," December 1999, National Register eligibility study prepared for GSA, Property Disposal Division (1PRM-5), available at GSA, Property Disposal Division (1PRM-5) offices, Chicago, Illinois, n.p.; "A Brief History of Duluth From the 1500s to 1870," in "History of the Duluth Police Department," n.d., website, located at http://www.ci.duluth.mn.us/city/police/website/history/duluth.htm.

35. MADEIRA SHIPWRECK Brina J. Agranat and Kevin J. Foster, "*Madeira*," May 1991, NRHP Registration Form, available at SHPO, MHS, St. Paul; "Minnesota Maritime Historic Resources," *Preservation Matters* 2 (August 1986): 1.

36. TWO HARBORS LIGHT STATION Charles K. Hyde, "United States Coast Guard Lighthouses and Light Stations on the Great Lakes," October 1979, NRHP Registration Form, available at SHPO, MHS, St. Paul; Hugh E. Bishop, *By Water and Rail: A History of Lake County, Minnesota* (Duluth: Lake Superior Port Cities, Inc.), 6, 20–32, 48; Frank A. King, *The Missabe Road: The Duluth, Missabe and Iron Range Railway* (San Marino, Calif.: Golden West Books, 1972), 15–31, 198; Two Harbors Light Station file, available at Lake County Historical Society, Two Harbors; "Local Dashes," *(Two Harbors) Iron Port*, May 30, 1891; "Local News," *(Two Harbors) Iron Port*, June 11, 1891; "Local Dashes," and "The Light House," *(Two Harbors) Iron Port*, July 16, 1891; "Local News," *(Two Harbors) Iron Port*, October 31, 1891; Charlene K. Roise, Denis P. Gardner, and Abigail Christman, "National Register Eligibility Assessments of Seven Wisconsin Lighthouses," December 1999, National Register eligibility study prepared for GSA, Property Disposal Division (1PRM-5), available at GSA, Property Disposal Division (1PRM-5) offices, Chicago, Illinois, n.p; *Two Harbors in 1910* (St. Paul: Minnesota Historical Society, 1910), 16–17.

37. U.S. ARMY CORPS OF ENGINEERS DULUTH VESSEL YARD Christopher Marzonie, C. Stephan Detmer, and Gary G. Robinson, "U.S. Army Corps of Engineers Duluth Vessel Yard," April 1993, NRHP Registration Form, available at SHPO, MHS, St. Paul; Charlene K. Roise, Denis P. Gardner, and Abigail Christman, "National Register Eligibility Assessments of Seven Wisconsin Lighthouses," December 1999, National Register eligibility study prepared for GSA, Property Disposal Division (1PRM-5), available at GSA, Property Disposal Division (1PRM-5) offices, Chicago, Illinois, n.p; Frank A. King, *The Missabe Road: The Duluth, Missabe and Iron Range Railway* (San Marino, Calif.: Golden West Books, 1972), 52, 198.

38. TUGBOAT EDNA G. John J. Hackett, "Tugboat '*Edna G.*,'" March 1975, NRHP Registration Form, available at SHPO, MHS, St. Paul; "Tug Sails to Glory After Sinking: *Edna G.* Still Going Strong after Mishap 56 Years Ago," *Duluth News Tribune*, December 7, 1952; "Tour Narrative," undated history of the Tugboat *Edna G.* used by historical interpreters when providing tours of the *Edna G.*, available in the "Tugboat '*Edna G.*'" file at SHPO, MHS, St. Paul; C. Patrick Labadie, "History of Tugs and Shipping on the Great Lakes," undated history located in "Tugboat '*Edna G.*'" file at SHPO, MHS, St. Paul; "The Tugboat *Edna G.*: A Look at a Minnesota Landmark," *Minnesota Monthly* (July 1995): 20; "Duluth and Iron Range Rail Road Company: Appropriations," ca. 1919, in "Duluth and Iron Range Rail Road Company Records," collection available at MHS, St. Paul; Frank A. King, *The Missabe Road: The Duluth, Missabe and Iron Range Railway* (San Marino, Calif.: Golden West Books, 1972), 7.

39. JIM SCOTT FISH HOUSE Jeffrey A. Hess, "Scott, Jim, Fish House," July 1985, NRHP Registration Form, available at SHPO, MHS, St. Paul; Alexander Ramsey's words concerning the potential of North Shore commercial fishing, as well as other detailed information about the Lake Superior fishing industry, is found in Matti Kaups's "North Shore Commercial Fishing, 1849–1870," *Minnesota History* 46 (Spring 1978): 43, 45, 57–58; June Drenning Holmquist, "Commercial Fishing on Lake Superior in the 1890s," *Minnesota History* 34 (Summer 1955): 246; "Scott Fish House Under Consideration for N. Registry," *Cook County News-Herald*, August 21, 1986; "James G. Scott Dies at 66," *Cook County News-Herald*, January 16, 1947; interview with Ernie Olson, grandson of Andrew Jackson Scott, by Pat Zankman, Cook County Historical Society curator, spring 1999; Willis H. Raff, "Jim Scott's Fish House," 1984, unpublished research report available at SHPO, MHS, St. Paul; e-mail letter to Denis P. Gardner from Pat Zankman, August 15, 2001.

40. ONOKO SHIPWRECK Gordon P. Watts et al., "*Onoko*," June 1991, NRHP Registration Form, available at SHPO, MHS, St. Paul; Julius F. Wolff Jr., *Julius F. Wolff Jr.'s Lake Superior Shipwrecks*, ed. Thomas R. Holden (Duluth: Lake Superior Port Cities, Inc., 1990), 154–55; Lake Carriers' Association, "*Onoko* Mystery," *Bulletin*, November 1958, 5–8; "Steamer *Onoko* Sinks in Mid-lake; Cause Unknown," *Duluth Herald*, September 15, 1915; "Blaming Germany for Loss of *Onoko* Looked on as Preposterous," *Duluth Herald*, September 16, 1915.

COMMERCIAL HISTORY

41. Richard Longstreth, *The Buildings of Main Street: A Guide to American Commercial Architecture* (Washington, D.C.: Preservation Press, 1987), 12–13; Carole Rifkind, *Main Street: The Face of Urban America* (New York: Harper and Row, Publishers, 1977), 63; MHS, SHPO, and Minnesota State Planning Agency, *Historic Preservation for Minnesota Communities* (St. Paul: Minnesota State Planning Agency, 1980), 24; Susan Roth, "Lake City City Hall," January 1981, NRHP Registration Form, available at SHPO, MHS, St. Paul; Susan Granger and Patricia Murphy, "Blooming Prairie Commercial Historic District," September 1993, NRHP Registration Form, available at SHPO, MHS, St. Paul; Susan Granger, "Hotel Atwater," May 1985, NRHP Registration Form, available at SHPO, MHS, St. Paul.

42. THE BIG STORE (O. G. ANDERSON & COMPANY STORE) Susan Roth, "O. G. Anderson and Company Store," December 1980, NRHP Registration Form, available at SHPO, MHS, St. Paul; Nick Coleman, "The Big Store: Retirement Looms Before a Southwest Minnesota Landmark," *Minneapolis Tribune*, July 23, 1972; Margaret Pennings, "The Big Store: A Story of Icelandic Immigration in America," (senior thesis, University of

Minnesota, 1985), 4, 6–7, 13–16, 18–19, 21, 34–36, 38; Gunnar Bjornson, "O. G. Anderson, Minneota's Foremost Citizen Responds to Final Summons," *Minneota Mascot*, September 11, 1903; telephone interview with Daren Giflason, member of the Society for the Preservation of Minneota's Heritage, by the author, May 28, 2002.

43. J. A. JOHNSON BLACKSMITH SHOP Susan Granger and Kay Grossman, "J. A. Johnson Blacksmith Shop," September 1995, NRHP Registration Form, available at SHPO, MHS, St. Paul; Jean Lemmon, "Blacksmith Shop Donated to Wilkin Historical Society," *Wahpeton-Breckenridge Daily News*, July 17, 1992; Cale Dickey, "The Smithy's Forge Still Glows," *Fergus Falls Daily Journal*, April 15, 1971; John C. Hudson, *Plains Country Towns* (Minneapolis: University of Minnesota Press, 1985), 34; telephone interview with Gordon Martinson, president of the Wilkin County Historical Society, by the author, August 1, 2002.

44. FIRST NATIONAL BANK Susan Roth, "First National Bank," December 1980, NRHP Registration Form, available at SHPO, MHS, St. Paul; "First National Bank Opens in New Location," *Fulda Free Press*, May 2, 1919; Fulda Centennial Book Committee, *Fulda Centennial History, 1881–1981*, ed. Gary Richter (n.p., 1981), 61–63; Denis P. Gardner and Charlene K. Roise, "State Bank of Edinburg," January 2001, NRHP Registration Form, available at Historic Preservation Division, North Dakota Heritage Center, Bismarck; telephone interview with Margaret Popp, officer at First National Bank, by the author, July 27, 2002.

45. BARNARD MORTUARY Camille Kudzia, "Barnard Mortuary," August 1984, NRHP Registration Form, available at SHPO, MHS, St. Paul; "Ed T. Barnard, Early Pioneer Citizen Dies," *Fergus Falls Daily Journal*, May 9, 1953; "Historical Museum Is His Monument," untitled newspaper, May 12, 1953, available at SHPO, MHS, St. Paul; "Death Claims One of City's Early Pioneers," *Fergus Falls Daily Journal*, September 25, 1959; "E. T. Barnard Recalls First Journal Press," undated feature in *Fergus Falls Journal*, available at SHPO, MHS, St. Paul; "The Barnard Mortuary," *Fergus Falls Daily Journal*, November 25, 1930; "E. T. Barnard to Erect Modern Mortuary Here," *Fergus Falls Daily Journal*, August 16, 1930; Virginia McAlester and Lee McAlester, *A Field Guide to American Houses* (New York: Alfred A. Knopf, Inc., 1984), 409–10.

46. NELSON & ALBIN COOPERATIVE MERCANTILE ASSOCIATION STORE Susan Granger, "Nelson and Albin Cooperative Mercantile Association Store," February 1986, NRHP Registration Form, available at SHPO, MHS, St. Paul; *Godahl Community and Nelson and Albin Mercantile Association: Fourscore Years Since 1894* (n.p., 1974), 12–18, 20–23; telephone interview with Ruth Anderson, director of the Watonwan County Historical Society, by the author, June 29, 2002.

47. ORIGINAL MAIN STREET Jeffrey A. Hess and Heather E. Maginniss, "Original Main Street Historic District," September 1993, NRHP Registration Form, available at SHPO, Minnesota Historical Society, St. Paul; Sinclair Lewis, *Main Street* (San Diego: Harcourt Brace Jovanovich, Publishers, [1989]), v, 285; Henry Anatole Grunwald, "Main Street, 1947," *Life* 22 (June 23, 1947): 101–2, 108, 110, 113.

48. Beverly Vavoulis and Cece Krettek, *The First 100 Years . . .* (Minneapolis: Minnesota State Bar Association, 1983), 57, 132; R. W. Sexton, ed., *American Public Buildings of Today* (New York: Architectural Book Publishing Company, Inc., 1931), 1–5; Theodore C. Blegen, *Minnesota: A History of the State* (Minneapolis: University of Minnesota Press, 1963), 219.

49. HOWARD LAKE CITY HALL John J. Hackett, "Howard Lake City Hall," January 1978, NRHP Registration Form, available at SHPO, MHS, St. Paul; Franklyn Curtiss-Wedge, *History of Wright County, Minnesota* (Chicago: H. C. Cooper, Jr. and Company, 1915), 811–15; *100 Years of the Good Life, 1878–1978* (n.p., ca. 1978), 3–4, 27; Robert Roscoe, "Howard Lake Begins Campaign for City Hall Re-use Study," *Preservation Matters* 14 (January/February 1998): 1, 18; Hay-Dobbs, "Howard Lake City Hall Historic Structures Report," April 2001, historical and technical report prepared for the city of Howard Lake, copy available in "Howard Lake City Hall" file at SHPO, MHS, St. Paul, 9–14; "A Destructive Fire," *Howard Lake Herald*, January 21, 1904; "Fire Demon at Work," *Howard Lake Herald*, February 18, 1904; "Facts and Figures," *Howard Lake Herald*, February 25, 1904; "Council Meetings," *Howard Lake Herald*, July 28, 1904; "Howard Lake's New City Hall" *Howard Lake Herald*, September 15, 1904; "Howard Lake Roller Mills Reduced to Ashes," *Howard Lake Herald*, September 29, 1904; "Dedication of Hall," *Howard Lake Herald*, December 22, 1904; "Dedication of the City Hall" and "Grand Opening Ball," *Howard Lake Herald*, December 29, 1904; "The New City Hall Formally Opened," *Howard Lake Herald*, January 6, 1905.

50. LOUISBURG SCHOOL Susan Granger, "Louisburg School," January 1985, NRHP Registration Form, available at SHPO, MHS, St. Paul; Jon Willand, *Louisburg, Minnesota: An Illustrated History* (Louisburg, Minn.: Louisburg Centennial Committee, {(Washington, D.C.: Preservation Press, 1984), 36; "Louisburg Locals," *Bellingham (Minnesota) Times*, July 13, 1911; "Louisburg," *Bellingham (Minnesota) Times*, July 27, 1911; "Louisburg," *Bellingham (Minnesota) Times*, September 7, 1911; "Louisburg," *Bellingham (Minnesota) Times*, September 14, 1911.

51. FERGUS FALLS STATE HOSPITAL COMPLEX Stuart MacDonald, "Fergus Falls State Hospital Complex," September 1985, NRHP Registration Form, available at SHPO, MHS, St. Paul; Robert Roscoe, "State Hospital, Fergus Falls, Minnesota," *Architecture Minnesota* 27 (November–December 2001): 21, 58, 60; Emery Johnson, Jr., comp., *A Short History of the Fergus Falls State Hospital, Fergus Falls, Minnesota* (Fergus Falls, Minn.: n.p., 1972), n.p.; Kathy Zachmeier, "Historic Register Nomination Advances," *Fergus Falls Daily Journal*, February 21, 1986; Robert Franklin, "What to do with a City of Ghosts?" *Minneapolis Star Tribune*, February 16, 2003.

52. PIPESTONE WATER TOWER Thomas Harvey, "Pipestone Water Tower," March 1979, NRHP Registration Form, available at SHPO, MHS, St. Paul; The Engineering Record, *Water Tower Pumping and Power Station Designs: The Engineering Record's Prize Designs, Suggestive for Water Towers, Pumping and Power Stations* (New York: The Engineering Record, 1893), [1–2]; The Centennial Committee, *Pipestone: Minnesota Centennial, 1858–1958* (Pipestone, Minn.: The Committee, 1958), 6, 9, 32; MHS, "Minnesota's National Register Properties," 2001, website available at http://nrhp.mnhs.org; letter to Charles W. Nelson, Minnesota Architectural Historian, from Harold E. Lee, Pipe-

stone City Clerk, February 27, 1973, available at SHPO, MHS, St. Paul; "New Buildings and other Improvements in Pipestone Last Year Cost More than $1,000,000," *Pipestone County Star*, January 13, 1920; "Council to Push New Water Plant," *Pipestone County Star*, June 8, 1920; "Law Held Invalid: City Work Stops," *Pipestone County Star*, May 7, 1920; "Contract for New Reservoir Awarded," *Pipestone County Star*, August 17, 1920; "Hunt and Sons to Erect Water Works Building," *Pipestone County Star*, September 14, 1920; "Campbells to Build Tower and Tank," *Pipestone County Star*, April 1, 1921; "Council Sells $54,000 Worth of City Bonds," *Pipestone County Star*, March 4, 1921; J. N. Hazelhurst, *Towers and Tanks for Water-Works: The Theory and Practice of Their Design and Construction* (New York: John Wiley and Sons, 1901), 119–21; Edmund C. Percey, "The Emancipated Water Tower," *Concrete* 9 (September 1975): 22.

53. NEW ULM POST OFFICE Brooks Cavin, "Federal Post Office Building," March 1970, NRHP Registration Form, available at SHPO, MHS, St. Paul; J. H. Strasser, *New Ulm in Word and Picture: J. H. Strasser's History of a German-American Settlement* (1892), eds. Don Hienrich Tolzmann and Fredric R. Steinhauser (Indianapolis: Max Kade German-American Center, Indiana University-Purdue University at Indianapolis, and Indiana German Heritage Society, 1997), v; Elroy E. Ubl, ed., *Historical Notes: A Glimpse at New Ulm's Past*, vol. 1 (New Ulm, Minn.: self published, 1982), 31–32, 105–10; "New Ulm Must Wait," *Brown County Journal*, April 18, 1908; "Start P. O. Building," *Brown County Journal*, April 25, 1908; "Foundation This Fall," *Brown County Journal*, July 25, 1908; "New Federal Post Office Building at New Ulm," *Brown County Journal*, May 21, 1910.

54. FIREMEN'S HALL B. Michael Zuckerman, "Firemen's Hall," July 1978, NRHP Registration Form, available at SHPO, MHS, St. Paul; Gerry Souter and Janet Souter, *The American Fire Station* (Osceola, Wisc.: MBI Publishing, 1998), 16–20; W. Fred Conway, *Firefighting Lore* (New Albany, Ind.: Fire Buff House Publishers, 1993), 19–21; Bicentennial Heritage Committee, *Chronicles of Cannon Falls, 1976* (Cannon Falls, Minn.: *Cannon Falls Beacon*, 1976), 91–93. A reprint of the *Cannon Falls Beacon's* newspaper stories describing the fires of 1884 and 1887 can be found in Connie Bickman's *Roots and Wings* (Cannon Falls, Minn.: Yatra Publications, 1996), 61, 70–72.

55. ROCK COUNTY COURTHOUSE & JAIL Charles W. Nelson and Susan Roth, "Rock County Courthouse and Jail," November 1976, NRHP Registration Form, available at SHPO, MHS, St. Paul; Arthur P. Rose, *An Illustrated History of the Counties of Rock and Pipestone, Minnesota* (Luverne, Minn.: Northern History Publishing Company, 1911), 85–86, 105–6, 111–12; Rock County Historical Society, *A History of Rock County* (Luverne, Minn.: Rock County Historical Society, 1977), 14, 38, 59; [Local News], *Rock County Herald*, February 24, 1887; [Local News], *Rock County Herald*, March 4, 1887; Irid Bjerk, *Luverne: A Look at our Historical Past* (Luverne, Minn.: Luverne Chamber of Commerce, ca. 1993), [8–10]; "Courthouse Remodeling Could Cost $1 Million," *Star-Herald*, July 2, 1984.

56. NORRIS CAMP Rolf T. Anderson, "Norris Camp," April 1993, NRHP Registration Form, available at SHPO, MHS, St. Paul; R. W. Murchie and C. R. Wasson, "Beltrami Island, Minnesota, Resettlement Project," *Minnesota Bulletin* 334 (December 1937): 7, 12, 15; "Federal Resettlement Project in Minnesota Approved," *Improvement Bulletin* 80 (November 8, 1935): 9; "Beavers Aid in Building Dams," *Baudette Region*, August 6, 1937.

57. MONTEVIDEO CARNEGIE LIBRARY Charles W. Nelson and Susan Roth, "Montevideo Carnegie Library," May 1982, and Susan Granger, "Madison Carnegie Library," September 1984, NRHP Registration Forms, available at SHPO, MHS, St. Paul; "Our New Library Building," *The Commercial*, April 12, 1907; "Our New Library Opened," *Montevideo Leader*, April 12, 1907; L. R. Moyer and O. G. Dale, eds., *History of Chippewa and Lac qui Parle Counties*, vol. 1 (Indianapolis: B. F. Bowen and Company, Inc., 1916), 344–46; Chris Potter, "You Had to Ask," 1999, website, located at http://andrewcarnegie.tripod.com/hadtoask292000.html; Robert V. Bruce, "Carnegie, Andrew," 2000, website, located at http://historychannel.com/perl/print_book.pl?ID=34873; telephone interview with June Lynne, executive director of the Chippewa County Historical Society, by the author, July 10, 2002.

58. MINNESOTA STATE REFORMATORY FOR MEN Robert C. Mack and Barbara E. Hightower, "Minnesota State Reformatory for Men Historic District," September 1985, NRHP Registration Form, available at SHPO, MHS, St. Paul; Theartrice Williams, "Investigation Report of the Deaths of Rick Fultz and James Martin," May 1974, study completed for Minnesota Department of Corrections, copy available at MHS, St. Paul, 1, 11, 17, 20–21; John R. Thomas, *The History of Prison Architecture* (New York: Press of J. J. Little and Company, 1892), 4; Nathan G. Mandel, "A Historical Chronology of Corrections," in "Corrections and Behavior: A Historical Perspective," May 1966, study completed for Minnesota Department of Corrections, copy available at MHS, St. Paul, 4–6, 8; John J. Dominik Jr., *Three Towns into One City*, ed. Ed L. Stockinger (St. Cloud, Minn.: The St. Cloud Area Bicentennial Commission, 1976), 113–17.

YESTERDAY'S HOUSE

59. Virginia McAlester and Lee McAlester, *A Field Guide to American Houses* (New York: Alfred A. Knopf, Inc., 1984), 63, 153, 179, 197, 211, 241, 255, 263, 289, 321, 343, 355, 439–40; Roger Kennedy, *Minnesota Houses: An Architectural and Historical View* (Minneapolis: Dillon Press, 1967), 36, 38, 40, 49, 97, 109; Theodore C. Blegen, *Minnesota: A History of the State* (Minneapolis: University of Minnesota Press, 1963), 134–35; Donald R. Torbert, *A Century of Minnesota Architecture* (Minneapolis: Minneapolis Society of Fine Arts, 1958), n.p.; Laurence Schmeckebier, "Art on Main Street," *Minnesota History* 25 (March 1944): 7; SHPO, MHS, "Lost National Register Properties in Minnesota," March 1989, report highlighting historic properties lost to development and neglect during the 1980s, available at SHPO, MHS, St. Paul, n.p.

60. RENSSELAER D. HUBBARD HOUSE Marcia T. Schuster and Charles W. Nelson, "R. D. Hubbard House," February 1976, NRHP Registration Form, available at SHPO, MHS, St. Paul; Thomas Hughes, *History of Blue Earth County* (Chicago: Middle West Publishing Company, 1909), 441–42; Dennis J. Hagen, "The Hubbard House," n.d., unpublished history available at Blue Earth County Historical Society, copy at SHPO, MHS, St. Paul, 3, 6, 11–14; Miller-Dunwiddie Architects, Inc., "Historic Preservation Feasibility Study of the Rensselaer D. Hubbard House," April 1977, technical report prepared for the city of Mankato, copy available at SHPO, MHS, St. Paul, 6–7, 9–12; Virginia McAlester and Lee McAlester, *A Field Guide to American Houses* (New York: Alfred A. Knopf, Inc., 1984), 241–42, 246; John C. Poppeliers, S. Allen Chambers Jr., and Nancy B. Schwartz, *What Style Is It?* (New York: John Wiley and Sons, Inc., 1983), 52.

61. HANNAH C. & PETER E. THOMPSON HOUSE Barbara Kooiman, Elizabeth Butterfield, Susan Granger, and Kay Grossman, "Hannah C. and Peter E. Thompson House," June 1993 and July 1995, NRHP Registration Form, available at SHPO, MHS, St. Paul; *Pictorial Barnesville* (Barnesville, Minn.: H. H. Snell, 1898), [8–10]; "Our Counselor is Gone," *Barnesville Record-Review*, January 26, 1905; "Hannah C. Thompson," *Barnesville Record-Review*, June 24, 1920; Denis P. Gardner, "Franklin School," March 2002, NRHP Registration Form, available at Historic Preservation Division, North Dakota Heritage Center, Bismarck; John J.-G. Blumenson, *Identifying American Architecture: A Pictorial Guide to Styles and Terms, 1600–1945* (New York: W. W. Norton and Company, 1977), 47, 55.

62. CASIVILLE BULLARD HOUSE Susan Granger and Kay Grossman, "Bullard, Casiville, House," February 1996, NRHP Registration Form, available at SHPO, MHS, St. Paul; Darryl Paulson, "Masters of It All: Black Builders in This Century," *Southern Exposure* 8 (1980): 9–10; Virginia McAlester and Lee McAlester, *A Field Guide to American Houses* (New York: Alfred A. Knopf, Inc., 1984), 439.

63. PAUL WATKINS HOUSE Robert M. Frame III, "Watkins, Paul, House," August 1984, NRHP Registration Form, available at SHPO, MHS, St. Paul; J. R. Watkins Company, *The Open Door to Success* (Winona, Minn.: J. R. Watkins Company, 1928), 2, 13, 23, 26, 28; Ralph Adams Cram, "House of Paul Watkins, Winona, Minn.," *American Architect* 134 (August 20, 1928): 223–24, 227; Douglas Shand Tucci, "Cram, Ralph Adams," in *Macmillan Encyclopedia of Architects*, vol. 1, (New York: Free Press, 1982), 471–72; Marcus Whiffen, *American Architecture Since 1780: A Guide to the Styles* (Cambridge: Massachusetts Institute of Technology, 1969), 178–79; Beulah Buswell, "United Methodist Home, Winona, Minnesota," n.d., historical and descriptive pamphlet of the Paul Watkins House, available at SHPO, MHS, St. Paul, 5, 15; "Celebrating 25 Years of Concerned Care," *News and Views*, May 1983; "Watkins Returns to its Wellness Roots," *Minneapolis Star Tribune*, July 7, 1997.

64. MERTON S. GOODNOW HOUSE James A. Sazevich, "Merton S. Goodnow House," November 1983, NRHP Registration Form, available at SHPO, MHS, St. Paul; Franklyn Curtiss-Wedge, ed., *History of McLeod County* (Chicago: H. C. Cooper Jr. and Company, 1917), 581–82; Rolf T. Anderson, "Purcell and Elmslie," in "Historic Profiles through the Decades," *Architecture Minnesota* 18 (November–December 1992): 44–45; Kay Johnson, "Preserving our Past," *Hutchinson Leader*, January 18, 2000; "Merton S. Goodnow House," March 2001, unpublished history available at McLeod County Historical Society, copy at SHPO, MHS, St. Paul; Virginia McAlester and Lee McAlester, *A Field Guide to American Houses* (New York: Alfred A. Knopf, Inc., 1984), 439–40, 444–45; John C. Poppeliers, S. Allen Chambers Jr. and Nancy B. Schwartz, *What Style Is It?* (New York: John Wiley and Sons, Inc., 1983), 80–83.

65. MURET N. LELAND HOUSE Susan Roth, "Leland, Muret N., House," November 1979, NRHP Registration Form, SHPO, MHS, St. Paul; Gay Steckelberg, "Stately Home: Couple Busy Renewing Historic Wells House," *Wells Mirror*, May 31, 1984; Marlene Behle, "TLC Restores Wells House to Former Beauty," *Albert Lea Tribune*, June 12, 1988; "A Handsome Home," *Wells Advocate*, July 24, 1890; "[Local News?]," *Wells Forum*, December 26, 1895; "The Pearl of Joyous Wedding Bells," *Wells Advocate*, June 21, 1900; "M. N. Leland Pioneer Resident of Wells Died Suddenly in California," *Wells Forum Advocate*, October 6, 1921; *A Souvenir—Wells, Minnesota* (Minneapolis: Wall and Haines, 1901), n.p.; Virginia McAlester and Lee McAlester, *A Field Guide to American Houses* (New York: Alfred A. Knopf, Inc., 1984), 238–39, 263; Christine Curran, Denis P. Gardner, and Charlene K. Roise, "Intensive-Level Survey Report: M-15 Corridor, City of Vassar, Michigan," November 1998, study completed for the MDOT and Michigan Bureau of History, copy available at MDOT, Lansing, 5.

66. LENA O. SMITH HOUSE Jacqueline Sluss, "Smith, Lena O., House," July 1990, NRHP Registration Form, available at SHPO, MHS, St. Paul; Jacqueline Sluss, "Lena Olive Smith: Civil Rights in the 1930s," *Hennepin History* (Winter 1995): 30–33; Ann Juergens, "Lena Olive Smith: A Minnesota Civil Rights Pioneer," *William Mitchell Law Review* 28 (2001): 398, 401–2, 413; Rosalind Bentley, "Lena O. Smith," in "Do Remember Me," *Minneapolis Star Tribune*, February 15, 1997; "Lee to Keep Home, Attorney Vows," *Minneapolis Journal*, July 20, 1931; "Brutal Attack by Mill City Police Stirs Entire City," *Minneapolis Spokesman*, July 23, 1937; "Lena O. Smith, Attorney Here 45 Years, Dies," *Minneapolis Spokesman*, November 10, 1966.

67. HINCKLEY FIRE RELIEF HOUSE Mark E. Haidet, "Hinckley Fire Relief House," March 1980, NRHP Registration Form, available at SHPO, MHS, St. Paul; Michael Koop, "Kettle River Sandstone Company Quarry," August 1990, NRHP Registration Form, available at SHPO, MHS, St. Paul; Richard S. Prosser, *Rails to the North Star* (Minneapolis: Dillon Press, 1966), 28; William Wilkinson, *Memorials of the Minnesota Forest Fires in the Year 1894, With a Chapter on the Forest Fires in Wisconsin* (Minneapolis: Norman E. Wilkinson, 1895, 81, 95–96, 129–31, 137, 240–43; Grace Stageberg Swenson, *From the Ashes: The Story of the Hinckley Fire of 1894* (Stillwater, Minn.: Croixside Press, 1979), 97, 109–10, 127, 132, 137; Muriel Langseth, ed., *Sandstone, the Quarry City* (Sandstone: Sandstone History Club, 1989), 68.

68. LORENZ & LUGERDE GINTHNER HOUSE Paul C. Larson, "Ginthner, Lorenz and Lugerde, House," July 1987, NRHP Registration Form, available at SHPO, MHS, St. Paul; Paul C. Larson, "Red Brick Houses in Wabasha, Minnesota Associated with Merchant-Tradesmen," July 1987, NRHP Multiple Property Documentation Form, available at SHPO, MHS, St. Paul; *Wabasha Herald Annual*, 1889 (Wabasha: O. F. Collier and Company, 1889), n.p.; Roger Kennedy, *Minnesota Houses: An Architectural and Historical View* (Minneapolis: Dillon Press, 1967), 139–40; Virginia McAlester and Lee McAlester, *A Field Guide to American Houses* (New York: Alfred A. Knopf, Inc., 1984), 177, 211.

GATHERING PLACES

69. Charles Martin, et al., comps., "Scambler Church," 2002, collection of sources on the history of the People's Union Church, copy available at SHPO, MHS, St. Paul, 6, 100, 102; Henry M. Harren, "Odeon Theater," February 1974, NRHP Registration Form, available at SHPO, MHS, St. Paul; Thomas Harvey, "Palace Theater," November 1978, NRHP Registration Form, available at SHPO, MHS, St. Paul; Lynne VanBrocklin Spaeth, "Winter Saloon," February 1978, NRHP Registration Form, available at SHPO, MHS, St. Paul; Milly Smith and Gary Phelps, "National Register Sites in Dakota County (Part 1)," *Over the Years* 27 (June 1987): 14.

70. CHURCH OF ST. BONIFACE (CHURCH OF ST. MARY) Susan Granger and Patricia Murphy, "Church of St. Boniface," June 1993, NRHP Registration Form, available at SHPO, MHS, St. Paul; Jean Paschke, *Magnificent and Beautiful Structures: St. Mary's Church and Rectory, Melrose, Minnesota* (Melrose, Minn.: Melrose Area Historical Society, 1994), c, 1–2, 4–5, 7–9, 23–24, 27; "St. Boniface Church, Melrose," n.d., typescript history in "Church of St. Boniface," file, available at SHPO, MHS, St. Paul, n.p.

71. ODEON THEATER Henry M. Harren, "Odeon Theater," February 1974, NRHP Registration Form, available at SHPO, MHS, St. Paul; Belview Civic Club, *The History of the Belview Community, Swedes Forest Township and Kintire Township* (n.p., ca. 1984), 1–2, 157; "Big Holiday Attractions Presented by the Odeon Theatre, Belview, Minn.," *Belview Independent,* December 18, 1925; Aiken and Schmahl, "Odeon Dedicated," *Redwood Gazette,* November 5, 1902; "Odeon, Finest Hall West of Cities, Opened," *Redwood Gazette,* November 12, 1902; "Odeon, 1902–1977: Rededication October 22, 1977, Belview, Minnesota," 1977, promotional pamphlet in "Odeon Theater" file at SHPO, MHS, St. Paul; telephone interview with Lori Ryer, Belview City Clerk's Office, by the author, August 21, 2003.

72. LODGE BOLESLAV JABLONSKY NO. 219 David C. Anderson, "Lodge Boleslav Jablonsky No. 219," March 2002, NRHP Registration Form, available at SHPO, MHS, St. Paul; "The Early Years and the Emergence of the Sales Force," *Fraternal Herald,* February 1997; letter to Susan Roth, Minnesota National Register Historian, from Daniel Necas, Assistant Curator, Immigration History Research Center, University of Minnesota, May 16, 2002, available at SHPO, MHS, St. Paul; letter to David C. Anderson, Architectural Historian, from Frances Forst, Secretary, Lodge Boleslav Jablonsky No. 219, February 21, 2002, available at SHPO, MHS, St. Paul; letter to David C. Anderson, from Linda Grove, Fraternal Manager, Western Fraternal Life Association, January 3, 2002, available at SHPO, MHS, St. Paul.

73. GRAND ARMY OF THE REPUBLIC HALL Mary R. Dearing, *Veterans in Politics: The Story of the G.A.R.* (Baton Rouge: Louisiana State University, 1952), 50–51, 53, 56–57, 81–88, 185, 268–73, 498; John J. Hackett, "G.A.R. Hall," November 1974, NRHP Registration Form, available at SHPO, MHS, St. Paul; "Grand Army of the Republic Hall and Meeker County Historical Society Museum," n.d., promotional pamphlet available in "G.A.R. Hall" file at SHPO, MHS, St. Paul, n.p.; telephone interview with Cheryl Almgren, curator at the Meeker County Historical Society, by the author, February 23, 2002; "Grand Army Museum in Litchfield Displays a Proud Past," *Minneapolis Star Tribune,* January 9, 1995; "The G.A.R. Hall at Litchfield, Minnesota," n.d., typescript history available in "G.A.R. Hall" file at SHPO, MHS, St. Paul, 1–4; "Litchfield's Memorial Hall," *National Arsenal* 1 (March 5, 1887): n.p.

74. NORTH EAST NEIGHBORHOOD HOUSE Denis P. Gardner, "North East Neighborhood House," March 2001, NRHP Registration Form, available at SHPO, MHS, St. Paul. Catheryne Cooke Gilman's words noting the importance of the North East Neighborhood House were recorded in Winifred Wandersee Bolin's "Heating Up the Melting Pot," *Minnesota History* 45 (Summer 1976): 60; biographical information on Robbins and Catheryne Cooke Gilman is located in "Who's Who in East Minneapolis," *North East Argus,* June 17, 1927, as well as Elizabeth

Gilman's "Catheryne Cooke Gilman: Social Worker," in *Women of Minnesota: Selected Biographical Essays,* eds. Barbara Stuhler and Gretchen Kreuter (St. Paul: Minnesota Historical Society Press, 1971), 190–207.

75. GRAN EVANGELICAL LUTHERAN CHURCH Jeffrey A. Hess, "Gran Evangelical Lutheran Church," January 1987, NRHP Registration Form, available at SHPO, MHS, St. Paul; Ralph A. Larson, *The Story of Clearwater County, 1902–1952* (Bagley, Minn.: Farmers Publishing Company, n.d.), 3; Valborg Nesseth, untitled typescript of oration given at 1973 ceremony honoring the founders of Gran Evangelical Lutheran Church, available in "Gran Evangelical Lutheran Church" file at SHPO, MHS, St. Paul.

76. DEERWOOD AUDITORIUM Rolf T. Anderson, "Deerwood Auditorium," April 1995, NRHP Registration Form, available at SHPO, MHS, St. Paul; Warren Upham, *Minnesota Place Names: A Geographical Encyclopedia,* 3rd ed. (St. Paul: Minnesota Historical Society Press, 2001), 158; "$43,000 Community Hall Project Now Underway," *Deerwood Enterprise,* March 1, 1935; "Work on Hall Resumed with Full Crew," *Deerwood Enterprise,* October 9, 1936; "Community Hall Assured," *Deerwood Enterprise,* August 17, 1934.

77. MAHNOMEN COUNTY FAIRGROUNDS Michael Koop, "Mahnomen County Fairgrounds Historic District," July 1987, and Susan Roth, "Lincoln County Fairgrounds," May 1980, NRHP Registration Forms, both available at the SHPO, MHS, St. Paul; Wayne Caldwell Neely, *The Agricultural Fair* (New York: Columbia University Press, 1935), 3–4, 19, 21; "$34,500 Project at Fair Grounds Will Start this Month," *Mahnomen Pioneer,* January 3, 1936; "Work Advancing Rapidly at Fair Grounds," *Mahnomen Pioneer,* May 22, 1936; "County Fair Gets Underway with Many Exhibits," *Mahnomen Pioneer,* July 3, 1936.

TOURISM & ROADSIDE ARCHITECTURE

78. Charles M. Gates, comp., "The Tourist Traffic of Pioneer Minnesota," *Minnesota History* 16 (September 1935): 272–73, 278–80; Eileen Patricia Walsh, "The Last Resort: Northern Minnesota Tourism and the Integration of Rural and Urban Worlds, 1900–1950" (Ph.D. diss., University of Minnesota, 1994), 1, 7, 10–11, 16–17, 28, 30–31, 36–37, 41, 50, 61–64, 69–71; Thomas Lutz, "Old Frontenac Historic District," March 1973, NRHP Registration Form, available at SHPO, MHS, St. Paul; Denis P. Gardner and Charlene K. Roise, "Graystone Hotel," January 1999, NRHP Registration Form, available at SHPO, MHS, St. Paul; Susan Granger, "Larson's Hunters Resort," November 1984, NRHP Registration Form, available at SHPO, MHS, St. Paul; Eric Dregni, *Minnesota Marvels: Roadside Attractions in the Land of Lakes* (Minneapolis: University of Minnesota Press, 2001), 27, 51; Department of Administration, *Minnesota Guidebook to State Agency Services, 1992–1995,* ed. Robin Panlener (St. Paul: State of Minnesota, 1992), 441.

79. FRONTENAC Thomas Lutz, "Frontenac," March 1973, NRHP Registration Form, available at SHPO, MHS, St. Paul; Beth Gauper, "Tranquil Frontenac," *St. Paul Pioneer Press,* May 10, 1998; "Historic Frontenac," unpublished and undated history prepared by the Goodhue County Historical Society, available at SHPO, MHS, St. Paul, 3; Robert Roscoe, "The Saga of the Lakeside Inn: An Imperilled Lake Pepin Landmark," *Preservation Matters* 9 (December 1993): 9, 11; Frances Densmore,

"The Garrard Family in Frontenac," *Minnesota History* 14 (March 1933): 34–35, 37, 40, 43; Sister M. Catherine McCarrick, "The Villa Maria," *Goodhue County Historical News* 3 (June 1969): n.p.; Franklyn Curtiss-Wedge, ed., *History of Goodhue County* (Chicago: H. C. Cooper, Jr., and Co., 1909), 177–78; Lucy Cook, "The Town That Time Forgot," *Twin Citian*, July 1961.

80.   LAKE BRONSON STATE PARK   Rolf T. Anderson, "Lake Bronson State Park WPA/Rustic Style Historic Resources," September 1988, NRHP Registration Form, available at SHPO, MHS, St. Paul; Nelson's comment about Bouvette, as well as detailed information on Lake Bronson State Park, is found in Kittson County Historical Society, *Our Northwest Corner: Histories of Kittson County, Minnesota* (Topeka, Kans.: Josten's/American Yearbook Company, 1979), 409–15; Robert D. Florance, "Building the Bronson Dam," in *Kittson County WPA Commemorative Celebration, 1937–1987* (Lake Bronson, Minn.: Kittson County Historical Society, 1987), n.p.; "Work Goes Forward on Bronson Lake," *Bronson Budget*, April 16, 1936; "Bronson Lake Camp Site now Complete," *Bronson Budget*, April 30, 1936; "$250,000 dam nearing completion," *Bronson Budget*, April 1, 1937; "Plans Complete for Bronson Dam Dedication," *Bronson Budget*, June 17, 1937; "8,000 Attend Bronson Dam Dedication," *Bronson Budget*, June 24, 1937; "Two Rivers State Park Receives $40,000," *Bronson Budget*, July 1, 1937; "New Tower Being Built at Two Rivers State Park Here," *Bronson Budget*, February 9, 1939; "Two Rivers Park Receives $122,852 Federal Grant," *Bronson Budget*, August 31, 1939; "Lake Bronson Name is now Official," *Bronson Budget*, January 5, 1939; Minnesota Office of Tourism, *Kittson County: Where Minnesota Begins!* (St. Paul: Minnesota Office of Tourism, n.d.), n.p.

81.   PAUL BUNYAN & BABE THE BLUE OX   Jeffrey A. Hess, "Paul Bunyan and Babe the Blue Ox," January 1987, NRHP Registration Form, available in SHPO, MHS, St. Paul; Karal Ann Marling, *The Colossus of Roads—Myth and Symbol Along the American Highway* (Minneapolis: University of Minnesota Press, 1984), 1–3, 9, 12–15; Bob von Sternberg, "Tall Tale: Paul's Legend Flows from an Adman's Prose," *Minneapolis Star Tribune*, May 24, 1987; Marty Kohlmeyer, "Paul and Babe on the National Register," *Bemidji Pioneer*, May 10, 1988; Susan Hauser, "Paul Bunyan: Just the Facts," *Minnesota Monthly*, August 1987, 35.

82.   CASCADE RIVER WAYSIDE   Susan Granger, Scott Kelly, and Kay Grossman, "Cascade River Wayside," January 2003, NRHP Registration Form (draft), available at SHPO, MHS, St. Paul; Susan Granger, Scott Kelly, and Kay Grossman, "Historic Roadside Development Structures on Minnesota Trunk Highways," December 1998, report completed for the Minnesota Department of Transportation, copy available at SHPO, MHS, St. Paul, 2.2; "New Ideas in Road Beautifying," *Cook County News-Herald*, August 23, 1934; Minnesota Department of Conservation, Division of State Parks, *The Minnesota State Park and Recreational Area Plan* (n.p., 1939), 97.

83.   NANIBOUJOU CLUB   Charles W. Nelson and Mark E. Haidet, "Naniboujou Club Lodge," May 1982, NRHP Registration Form, available at SHPO, MHS, St. Paul; John Stone Pardee, "In the Tip of the Famous Arrowhead Country: The Naniboujou Club," ca. 1927, prospectus published by the Naniboujou Club, copy available at SHPO, MHS, St. Paul, [5–6], [11]; "Naniboujou Adopts 'Open House' Policy," *Cook County News-Herald*, June 30, 1932; "Duluth Group Announces Big Development," *Cook County News-Herald*, November 24, 1927; "Ground to be Broken Sunday for Naniboujou," *Cook County News-Herald*, July 12, 1928; "Naniboujou Club Opened Sunday," *Cook County News-Herald*, July 11, 1929; "Naniboujou Club Opens for Summer," *Cook County News-Herald*, June 26, 1930; Adelheid Fischer, "Indian Lore: The Naniboujou Resort Conjures North Shore Fantasy in Mythological Trappings," *Architecture Minnesota* 18 (March/April 1992): 45.

84.   GRAYSTONE HOTEL   Denis P. Gardner and Charlene K. Roise, "Graystone Hotel," January 1999, NRHP Registration Form, available at SHPO, MHS, St. Paul; "Elon G. Holmes Passes Away Early Today at His Summer Residence," *Detroit Lakes Tribune*, September 24, 1931; Richard Carlson, "The Graystone Hotel," unpublished history available at Becker County Historical Society, Detroit Lakes, n.p.; Ken Prentice, *Horse and Buggy Days at Detroit Lakes* (Detroit Lakes: Lakes Publishing Company, 1971), 9.

85.   JUN FUJITA CABIN   John Hurley, "Fujita, Jun, Cabin," July 1994, NRHP Registration Form, available at SHPO, MHS, St. Paul; Eileen Flanagan, "Jun Fujita's Chicago," *Chicago History* 25 (Summer 1996): 34–35, 38, 42–43, 46–49, 52, 54–55.

86.   WHITE CASTLE BUILDING NO. 8   Kristin L. Wilson and Nella L. Bean, "White Castle Building No. 8," June 1986, NRHP Registration Form, available at SHPO, MHS, St. Paul; Tom Balcom, "A Castle Preserved," *Southside Journal*, April 1984; David G. Hogan, "White Castle: Billy Ingram's Burger," *Timeline* 16 (March-April 1999): 4–5, 7, 12, 14–16, 18–19.

INDEX

Advisory Council on Historic Preservation, xxii

Aerial Lift Bridge, Duluth, description, 109–10; added to National Register, 110

African Americans, in skill trades, 196; and NAACP, 210, 212; and union segregation, 196–97; and Urban League, 210; discrimination against, 197; northern migration of, 197; settlement in Minneapolis, 210

Agate Bay, 113–15, 121

A. Guthrie and Company, see Hill Annex Mine

Allard, Noel, and Gerald Sandvick, historians, 100. See also Pietenpol, Bernard H.

Allen, T. D., architect, 175

American Bridge Company, 70

Anderson, Olafur Gudjon, merchant, 131–32, 134–35

Anderson, Sigurdur Arne, merchant, 131–32, 135

Anderson, Theodore William, merchant, 134–35

Anderson, Walter, businessman, 277

Andrew Carnegie Foundation, 182

Antiquities Act, xxi

Architectural styles, evolution of, 130–31, 188–89. See also specific architectural styles

Arndt, Armin, preservationist, 7

Arthur Mining Company, see Hill Annex Mine

Askin, John, commercial shipper, 106

Bacon, Gen. John M., 18–19

Bancorporation, see First National Bank, Fulda

Bank architecture, 139–40

Barnard, Edward T., 141, eulogized, 141; early career, 142–43; dies, 144

Barnard Mortuary, Fergus Falls, 143; description, 143–44; added to National Register, 144

Barnesville, 193; and Great Northern Railway, 193

Battle Point (Sugar Point), 16, 19; artifacts found at 20; added to National Register, 20

Beaux Arts Classicism, architectural style, 140

Belview, 225–26

Belview Dramatic Club, 226

Beltrami Island, Lake of the Woods Co., description, 176; and logging, 176

Beltrami Island Project, 176; relocation effort, 178; success of, 179

Beltrami Island State Forest, 177

Bemidji, tourism in, 259–60

Bennett, A. C., and Ralph Wilcox, 98

Bergmann, George, architect, 224

Bernard H. Pietenpol Workshop and Garage, description, 99; added to National Register, 101. See also Pietenpol, Bernard H.

Bickle, Anne, house, 189

The Big Store, Minneota, 131; closes, 131; and O. G. Anderson Company, 132–34; description, 133–34; and opera house, 134; Margaret Pennings comments on, 134–35; declines, 135; added to National Register, 135

Birch Coulee School, Lower Sioux Community, 15; description, 15; added to National Register, 16

Blakely, Russell, businessman, 27

Blinn, John, miller, see Schech's Mill

Bosch, John, farmer advocate, 57, 59–60; dies, 61

Bosch, John, farmstead, described, 59; added to National Register, 61

Bouvette, Clifford W., newspaper publisher, 255–56

Brainerd, 47–48, 50

Brainerd Water Tower, Brainerd, 168

Brehm, Kenneth, retiree, 206, 208

Brehm, Yvonne, retiree, 206

Bremer, Adolph, banker, 256

Bridges, plate girder, 62–63; movable, 63–64; arched, types, 69, 82. See also various bridges

Broomhall, Edward F., architect, 271

Brower, J. V., archaeologist, 4

Buetow, Carl H., architect, 244

Bug-O-Nay-Ge-Shig (Hole-in-the-Day), 16–20

Bullard, Casiville, 196–97; house, 196, 198; house added to National Register, 199; dies, 199

Bulk freighter, first of type, 126; description and evolution, 126–27

Burlington Northern Railroad, 49, 64

Byington, Margaret, historian, 182

Callahan, Kevin L., archaeologist, 9

Calumet Hotel, Pipestone, 166

Cannon Falls, 52; and fire, 172; community admonished, 172. See also Firemen's Hall

Carleton College, Northfield, 92–94

Carnegie, Andrew, industrialist, 181–82

Carr, Florence, see Fujita, Jun

Carter, George H., architect, 247

Casa Grande Ruin, xxi

Cascade Lodge, Cook County, 262

Cascade River Wayside, Cook County, 263; construction and description, 264–65; added to National Register, 266

Center Building, St. Peter, 161

Central Pacific Railway, 45

Central Park Methodist Episcopal Church, St. Paul, xxii

Cesko-Slovanska Podporujici Spolek (C.S.P.S.), 229–30

Cherry Grove, 98

Chicago and Northwestern Railway, 45, 51

Chicago, Dubuque and Minnesota Railroad, 30

Chicago Exposition of 1893, 245

Chicago, Milwaukee and St. Paul Railway, 254

Chief of Duluth, 19

Christ Episcopal Church, Frontenac, 254

Chubb, Lottie, 39

Chubb, Orville P., 37–39; dies, 39

Chubb, Orville P. and Sarah, house, 37, 188; description, 38–39, 40; added to National Register, 40

Chubb, Sarah, 37; dies, 39

Church of St. Boniface, Melrose, evolution of 221–25; description, 222; added to National Register, 225

Civilian Conservation Corps (CCC), 178

Classical orders, 59

Classical Revival, architectural style, 194

Cleveland Shipbuilding Company, Cleveland, Ohio, 120

Coit, Stanton, social advocate, 235–36

Commercial districts, 129–31; Carol Rifkind comments on, 130

Commercial Hotel, Detroit Lakes, 270

Congdon, Chester and Clara, estate, 189

Cook, Lucy, historian, 255

Cooperative (co-op), defined, 50

Concrete thin shells, defined, 101; and Italians and Spanish, 101–2; and Germans, 101–3

Cram, Ralph Adams, architect, 200

Crawford, Harold, architect, 52

Creamery, defined, 50

Crow Creek Reservation, South Dakota, 15

Culver, J. B., politician, 108

Cunningham, Ann Pamela, xviii

Cuyuna Iron Range, 73, 84, 86

Dakota Conflict of 1862, 14, 24
Dakota Cottage, Frontenac, 253–54
Damon, Henry, round barn, 47
Dams, arch and gravity, 35
Dassel, 95
Dawson, 151
Deerwood, 242
Deerwood Auditorium, 242–43; and Beriah
    Magoffin, 242–43; description, 244–45;
    added to National Register, 245
Dennis, Walter R., architect, 143
Densmore, Frances, historian, 255
Detroit Lakes, 250, 269–70
Dickens, Charles, author, 26
Dickinson, Cyril M., lumberman, 261
Dome roofs, evolution of, 101
Donnelly, Ignatius, politician, 31–33;
    house, 34
Dovetail notching, 24
Drummond Hall, Minneapolis, *see* North
    East Neighborhood House
DuBois, Samuel R., house, 207
Duluth, 106, 108, 110, 116; harbor channel,
    108; harbor, 116–18; first ore dock, 117
Duluth Aerial Ferry Bridge, Duluth, 70, 109
Duluth and Iron Range Rail Road, 106,
    113–14, 120–21
Duluth Central High School, Duluth, 160
Duluth, Missabe and Iron Range Railway,
    123
Duluth, Missabe and Northern Railway, 117
Duluth-Superior Harbor Authority, 117
Duluth Union Depot, Duluth, 47
Dunnel, Warren B., architect, 161
Dyckerhoff-Widmann (Dywidag), 103;
    and Zeiss-Dywidag System, 103

East Side Neighborhood Services,
    Minneapolis, *see* North East
    Neighborhood House
Eastern Railway of Minnesota, 213
Endreson, Guri, 24–25; dies, 25
Endreson, Guri and Lars, house, description,
    23–24; altered, 25; added to National
    Register, 26
Ergot, defined, 95; medicinal value, 96;
    exporters of, 96; production in U.S., 97
Erie Canal, *see* Great Lakes
Ethnic lodges, 220. *See also* Lodge Boleslav
    Jablonsky No. 219

Fair, defined, 245; types, 245
Fairmont, 37–38
Faribault, Jean Baptiste, 11
Farmer, E. L. Weston, editor, *see* Pietenpol,
    Bernard H.
Farmers Holiday Association, 60–61
Farmers Union, 58
Federal, architectural style, popularity, 187
Federal Emergency Relief Administration
    (FERA), 177

Fergus Falls State Hospital Complex, Fergus
    Falls, 160–61; description, 161–63;
    receives first patients, 163–64;
    women admitted, 164; and declining
    admissions, 164–65; added to National
    Register, 165
Finke, Donald, aviator, *see* Pietenpol,
    Bernard H.
Firemen's Hall, Cannon Falls, 172;
    description, 173; closes, 173; added to
    National Register, 173
First National Bank, Blooming Prairie,
    130, 220
First National Bank, Fulda, 139, 141, 220;
    description, 140; and Bancorporation,
    141; added to National Register, 141
Flathouses, 78
Flora, 18
Flute, Jerry, Dakota elder, 9
Fort Abercrombie, 27
Fort Snelling, 4
Foster, Charles, engineer, 103
Frame, Robert M., III, architectural histo-
    rian, 73
French Second Empire, architectural style,
    188, 191
Fresnel, Augustin, physicist, 115
Frontenac, 252, 255; developed, 253–54;
    added to National Register, 255
Frontenac Station, 255
Fujita, Jun, photographer, 273–74; and
    poetry, 274; and Florence Carr, 274;
    dies, 276. *See also* Jun Fujita Cabin
Fulda, 139; early banking in, 139
Fur trade, 23, 72

Garrard, Israel, 252–54; dies, 255
Garrard, Jeptha, 252, 254
Garrard, Kenner, 253–54
Garrard, Lewis, 253–54
Gateway District, Minneapolis, xxii
Gelfand, M. Howard, 276
Gerlach, H. G., architect, 133
Gilbert, Cass, architect, 152
Gilman, Catheryne Cooke, social advocate,
    237–38
Gilman, Robbins, social advocate, 235, 237;
    prohibitionist, 238
Ginthner, Lorenz, merchant, 217
Ginthner, Lorenz and Lugerde, house,
    217–18
Glensheen, *see* Congdon, Chester and Clara,
    estate
Globe Shipbuilding Company, Cleveland,
    Ohio, 126–27
Goodnow, Merton S., 202; house, 203–6;
    added to National Register, 206
Goodsell Observatory, description and
    moniker, 93; donation from James J.
    Hill, 93; added to National Register, 95
Good Templars Hall, Nininger, description,
    32–33; added to National Register, 34

Gouffee, Antoine, artist, 267
Grain elevators, 78
Gran Evangelical Lutheran Church, Clear-
    water Co., 240–41; description, 241–42;
    added to National Register, 242
Grand Army of the Republic (G.A.R.), 220,
    231–33; founders, 232–33; ceases, 235
Grand Army of the Republic Hall, Litchfield,
    founded and named, 233; description,
    233–34; operation, 234–35; added to
    National Register, 235
Grand Marais, 106
Granger, Susan, architectural historian,
    130, 138
Granum, Martin, architect, 182
Graystone Hotel, Detroit Lakes, 271;
    description, 271, decline, 272–73; added
    to National Register, 273
Great Chicago Fire, 171
Great Hinckley Fire, 212–14; and State Fire
    Relief Commission, 214; and fire relief
    houses, 215
Great Lakes, shipping, 105–6; fishing, 106;
    and Erie Canal, 106; and St. Mary's Falls
    Ship Canal, 106, 116
Great Northern Iron Ore Properties,
    see Hill Annex Mine
Great Northern Railway, 21, 46, 54–56,
    61–62, 81, 193, 224
Greek Revival, architectural style, 32–33,
    38, 188
Greysolon, Daniel, Sieur du Lhut, 107
Greystone Cottage, Frontenac, 253–54
Griffin, 105
Grossman, Kay, architectural historian, 138
Grunwald, Henry Anatole, writer, 149–50
Gull Lake Mounds Site, Cass Co., 5
Gunderson, Martin T., house, 189–90

Haglin, Charles F., engineer, *see* Peavey,
    Frank Hutchinson
Hancock Brothers, architectural firm, 194
Hastings, 22, 40, 66
Hastings Foundry, 40–42; and A. R. Morrell,
    40–42; description, 41–42; and *Stella
    Whipple*, 42; and later owners, 42; added
    to National Register 42
Hastings Spiral Bridge, Hastings, 41
Hess, Jeffrey A., architectural historian,
    150, 262
Hibbing, 103
Hibbing Disposal Plant, and PWA, 103;
    description, 103–4; added to National
    Register, 104
Highland Park Water Tower, St. Paul, 165
Hill Annex Mine, Itasca Co., 86; and Arthur
    Mining Company; and Great Northern
    Iron Ore Properties, 86; and Inter State
    Iron Company, 87; and A. Guthrie and
    Company, 87; closes, 87; as state park,
    87; added to National Register, 87

Hill, James J., 46, 55, 61, 71, 86; house, 188
Hinckley Fire Relief House, 212, 215;
    added to National Register, 215
Hinman, Rev. Samuel Dutton, 13–15
Holland, Clifford, engineer, 257
Holmes, Elon Galusha, entrepreneur,
    269–70, dies, 272
Holmes Block, Detroit Lakes, 271
Holmquist, June, historian, 124
Holstead and Sullivan, architectural firm,
    267
Hoopman, Orrin, aviator, see Pietenpol,
    Bernard H.
Hotel Atwater, Atwater, 131
Hotel Minnesota, Detroit Lakes, 250, 270
House of Refuge, St. Paul, 184
Houston County, Minn., description and
    industry, 87–88
Houston, Minn., 22, 87
Howard Lake, 154; village hall, 154–55;
    fire in, 154–55
Howard Lake City Hall, 155, 220; descrip-
    tion, 156; added to National Register, 157
Hubbard, Rensselaer D., 190, house,
    190–91; house description, 192;
    dies, 192; house added to National
    Register, 192
Hubbard Milling Company, 190
Hudson, John, historian, 136
Humphreys, Lt. Chauncey B., 18
Hutchinson, 202
Huxley, Thomas Henry, 180

Immanuel Sunday School, Minneapolis,
    see North East Neighborhood House
Independent Fire Company of Baltimore,
    Maryland, 173
Independent Order of the Good Templars,
    32–33
Indian Knoll, Kentucky, 7
Ingram, Edgar Waldo, businessman, 276–77
Interior Elevator, Minneapolis, see Peavey,
    Frank Hutchinson
Inter State Iron Company, see Hill Annex
    Mine
Iron ranges, 84–85. See also various ranges
Ishpeming, 108
Italianate, architectural style, 216–17

Jacobethan Revival, architectural style, 200
J. A. Johnson Blacksmith Shop, Rothsay,
    136–37, description, 137; added to
    National Register, 138
Jay Cooke and Company, 47
Jeffers Petroglyphs Site, Cottonwood Co.,
    5–9; added to National Register, 9
Jefferson, 29–30
Jefferson Grain Warehouse, Houston Co.,
    28–30; description, 29; and William
    Robinson, 29–30; and R. P. Spencer,
    29–30; added to National Register, 30

Johnston, Clarence H., architect, 76, 185–86,
    244
Johnson, Johannes Arndt, 136–37; and
    W. A. Redmann, 138; dies, 138
J. R. Watkins Company, Winona, 199
Jun Fujita Cabin, Rainy Lake, description,
    274–75; added to National Register, 276.
    See also Fujita, Jun

Kennedy, Roger, architectural historian, 216
Kenyon and Maine, architectural firm,
    56, 238
Kern Bridge, Mankato, 73–74
Kettle River Sandstone Company Quarry,
    Sandstone, 73, 212
Kirkbride, Thomas S., mental-health
    practitioner, 161
Klammer, Paul, archaeologist, 9–10
Kolin's Hall, Belview, 226
Krabbenhoft, Wulf C., farmstead, 47
Krugmire, Ivan, see Schech's Mill

Lac qui Parle, courthouse, 151–52
Lake Bronson, 256
Lake Bronson Dam, Kittson Co., 256;
    designer of, 257; description, 257–58
Lake Bronson State Park, Kittson Co., 256,
    258; added to National Register, 258
Lake City, city hall, 129
Lake Pepin, 252
Lakeside Hotel, Frontenac, 254
Lake Superior, 106, 108, 116; and commer-
    cial fishing, 123–24; fishing declines, 125
Lake Superior and Mississippi River
    Railroad, 108
Lake Zumbro Hydroelectric Generating
    Plant, Mazeppa, 74
Land O'Lakes Creameries, Inc., see
    Minnesota Cooperative Creameries
    Association
Lanesboro, 34; and Lanesboro Townsite
    Company, 34
Lanesboro Stone Dam, 34–36; added to
    National Register, 37
Larson, Paul Clifford, architectural historian,
    217
Larson's Hunters Resort, Wheaton, 251
La Salle, Robert Cavalier de, 105
Laughead, W. B., copywriter, 260
Leech Lake, 16, 19, 62
Leland, Muret N., 206; house, 207–8;
    house added to National Register, 208;
    dies, 208
Leland, Rosamond, 208
Lewis, Sinclair, author, 148
Lewis, Theodore, surveyor, 7, 10
Lighthouse Service, 115
Lincoln, Abraham, politician, 14

Lincoln County Fairgrounds, 246
Lindholm Oil Company Service Station,
    Cloquet, 251
Litchfield, 45
Little Portage, 107–8
Little Rapids (Inyan Ceyaka Otonwe), 9–12;
    trading post at, 11; and Mazomani, 11;
    and Dakota women, 12; added to
    National Register, 12
Locust Lodge, Frontenac, 253
Lodge Boleslav Jablonsky No. 219, Roseau
    Co, 228, 230; fraternal song, 228–29;
    namesake, 229; and "freethinkers," 229;
    added to National Register, 231
Logging, and Pillager band of Ojibwe, 16–17;
    in Cass Co., 63–64; in Minnesota, 72;
    early development in America, 74;
    Mary Swanholm comments on, 74; and
    Mississippi and St. Croix Rivers, 74; and
    St. Anthony Falls, 74; and Minneapolis,
    75; environmental impact in Minnesota,
    77; in Houston County, 88; near Beltrami
    Island, 176. See also Pine Tree Lumber
    Company
Longfellow, Henry Wadsworth,
    "Evangeline," 136
Lothson, Gordon A., archaeologist, 7
Louisburg, 157; prohibition fight in, 157, 159;
    founders and evolution of, 158
Louisburg School, Louisburg, 158; closes
    160; added to National Register, 160
Lower Sioux Agency, 14–15, 24
Lower Sioux Community, 16
Lower Sioux Reservation, 4
Luverne, 220

Maatafa, 112
Maatafa Storm, 111–12
Madeira, 111; description, 111; and
    International Bridge, 111; and William
    Edenborn, 111–12; sinks, 112; added to
    National Register, 112
Madison, 151; and county courthouse, 151–52
Madison Carnegie Library, Madison, 153
Maginniss, Heather E., architectural
    historian, 150
Magoffin, Beriah, 242–43
Mahnomen City Hall, Mahnomen, 153, 247
Mahnomen County Fairgrounds, 246–47;
    and WPA, 246–47; description, 247–48;
    added to National Register, 248
Mankato, 22
Mansart, François, 191
Marine Lumber Company, St. Croix River,
    74
Marling, Karal Ann, historian, 260
Martin, James, "It Could Be You," 183
Mazomani, see Little Rapids
McCleary, James T., federal official,
    see New Ulm Post Office
McGilvray, Thomas F., engineer, 109

McGregor Western Railway, 45

McLean, Sara Ludlow Garrard, 254

McSpadden, William George, settler, 87–88

Melrose, and Great Northern Railway, 224

Mendota, 187

Merritt, Leonidas, 86

Merritt family, 86

Mesabi Iron Range, 73, 84–86, 106, 116–17

Milling, 71–72, 88; major mills, 90

Milwaukee and Prairie du Chien Railway, 45

Minneapolis and Cedar Valley Railroad, 44

Minneapolis and St. Louis Railway, 151, 225

Minneapolis, St. Paul and Sault Ste. Marie Depot, Thief River Falls, description, 56; reuse, 57; added to National Register, 56

Minneapolis, St. Paul and Sault Ste. Marie Railway 54, 69; and agriculture, 54–56; incorporated, 55; and Great Northern Railway, 55–56; decline, 56–57

Minneapolis Union Railway, 61

Minneota, 132

Minnesota and Pacific Railroad, 21, 44

Minnesota Central Railway, 45

Minnesota Cooperative Creameries Association, and Land O'Lakes Creameries, Inc., 50

Minnesota Department of Highways (MHD), 251, 262–63

Minnesota Iron Company, 73, 86, 106, 113–14

Minnesota Point, 107–8, 116

Minnesota Point Lighthouse, 107

Minnesota School Trust Fund, 86–87

Minnesota Stage Company, 27–28

Minnesota State Reformatory for Men, 183–85; construction and operation, 186; added to National Register, 186

Minnesota State Sanatorium for Consumptives, Walker, 185

Minnesota Steamship Company, Cleveland, Ohio, 111

Mission, architectural style, 143

Mission of St. John the Evangelist, Lower Sioux Agency, 14

Mississippi River, as transportation corridor, 22, 28, 40, 74

Modern Woodmen of America, 202

Moe, Richard, President, National Trust, on places, xv, xvii–xviii; and architecture, xvi

Montevideo Carnegie Library, 180; and Montevideo Library Club, 180; and Montevideo Library Association, 180; and Andrew Carnegie, 180, 182; description 182; added to National Register, 183

Morrell, A. R., ironsmith, see Hastings Foundry

Mount Vernon Ladies' Association of the Union, xxviii, xxi

Musser, Peter, industrialist, 75

Musser, Richard, see Pine Tree Lumber Company

Naniboujou Club, Cook Co., 266; and Naniboujou Holding Company, 266; prospectus for, 266–67; description, 267; newspaper comments on, 268; decline of 268–69; added to National Register, 269

Nansen Agricultural District, 64; types of farmsteads in, 66–67; added to National Register, 67. See also Sogn Valley

National Association for the Advancement of Colored People (NAACP), 210, 212

National Farmers' Bank, Owatonna, 160

National Historic Landmarks, xxiii

National Historic Preservation Act, xxii

National Park Service, xxi

National Prohibition Act, 64

National Register of Historic Places, xxiii

National Trust for Historic Preservation, xxii

National Trust for Historic Places, xv, xxi

Native Americans, 3–16, 22; and education, 13–16; and Wanikan culture, 20. See also Ojibwe, Pillager band, and various treaties

Nee Gee, see Scott, James Garfield

Neill, Edward D., historian, 40

Nelson and Albin Cooperative Mercantile Association Store, Godahl, 131, 145–47; description, 146; added to National Register, 147

Nesseth, G. P., minister, 241–42

New Albin, Iowa, 30

New Ulm, 168–69

New Ulm Post Office, 160, 168–69; and James T. McCleary, 168, 170; added to National Register, 170

Nicholson, Peter, architect, 82

Nininger, 31–34

Nininger, John, speculator, 31–33

Nordic Ware Company, Minneapolis, 81

Norris Camp, Lake of the Woods Co., 153, 178; description, 179; added to National Register, 179. See also Beltrami Island Project

North East Neighborhood House, 221, 235; and Drummond Hall, 235, 237–39; and Plymouth Church and Immanuel Sunday School, 236–37; description 238; and East Side Neighborhood Services, 239; added to the National Register, 239

Northern Pacific Railway, 28, 45, 47, 75, 81, 250, 269

Northern Pacific Railway Shops, Brainerd, 47–48, 50; fire at 48; rebuilding, 49; and Burlington Northern Railroad, 49; shops close, 49; added to National Register, 50

Northern Pacific Survey, 44

Northwestern Express and Transportation Company, 27

North Shore Drive, 262–63

Odeon Theater, Belview, 220, 225–28; added to National Register, 228

Ojibwe, Pillager band, 16–17, 19–20

Olson, Floyd B., politician, 256

Onoko, 126; description, 127; sinks, 128; conspiracy, 128; added to National Register, 128

Opera house, defined, 226

Oregon Railway and Navigation Company, 45–46

Original Main Street, Sauk Centre, 147–50; added to National Register, 150

Palace Theater, Luverne, 220

Panic of 1857, and Ohio Life Insurance and Trust Company, 33, 45

Pardee, John Stone, writer, 266–67

Park Rapids and Leech Lake Railway, 62

Paul Bunyan and Babe the Blue Ox, Bemidji, 259–62; added to National Register, 262

Paulson, Darryl, historian, 196–97

Payne, William Wallace, professor, 92; and Popular Astronomy, 94

Payton, Jim, power company manager, 261

Peavey, Frank Hutchinson, 73, 77–81; comments on, 78; and St. Anthony Elevator, 79; and Interior Elevator, 79–80; and Charles H. Haglin, 80–81

Peavey, James Fulton, 78

Peavey-Haglin Experimental Concrete Grain Elevator, description, 80; added to National Register, 81; and National Historic Landmark, 81

Peel, Lester R., 95–96; dies, 97

Pennings, Margaret, historian, see the Big Store

Penstock, defined, 89

People's Union Church, Otter Tail Co., 219

Percey, Edmund C., engineer, 168

Peshtigo, Wisc., fire, 171–72

Phelps, G. H., architect, 223

Phelps Mill, Otter Tail Co., 73

Phyllis Wheatley House, Minneapolis, 221

Pickwick Mill, Pickwick, 23

Pierce, Franklin, politician, 44

Pietenpol, Bernard H., 73, 98; first airplane, 99; and "Air Camper," 99; and E. L. Weston Farmer, 99; and Donald Finke, 99; and Orrin Hoopman, 100; and "Sky Scout," 100; plans published, 100; comments on, 100; dies 101

Pine Tree Lumber Company, Little Falls, 75; and Richard Musser, 75; and Charles A. Weyerhaeuser, 75; operation 76; closes 77

Pine Tree Lumber Company Office Building, Little Falls, description, 76; added to National Register, 77

Pipestone, 166; improvements in, 167; and city hall and county courthouse, 167

Pipestone Indian School Superintendent's Residence, Pipestone, 5
Pipestone Water Tower, Pipestone, 165, 167–68; added to National Register, 168
Plowden, David, historian, 61–62, 69–70
Plymouth Church, Minneapolis, see North East Neighborhood House
Point-No-Point, Goodhue Co., 252
Populist Party, 57–58
Portage Lake Bridge, Houghton, Mich., 70
Porter, Henry H., industrialist, 114
Prairie School, architectural style, 189, 203; examples of, 204–5
Prescott, Philander, house, 189
Prohibition, and Louisburg, 157-59; and National Prohibition Act, 64; Robbins Gilman comments on, 238
Public construction, 152–53
Public Works Administration (PWA), 101
Purcell and Elmslie, architectural firm, 204–6

Queen Anne, architectural style, 207

Railroads, 21–23, 28, 43–46. See also various lines
Rainy Lake, 274–76; and Wendt Island, 274
Ramsey, Alexander, 31–32, 123; house, 188, 191–92
Rand, Alonzo, house, 188
Randall, John, railroad historian, 21–23
Red Lake Game Refuge, 177. See also Beltrami Island Project
Redmann, W. A., see Johnson, Johannes Arndt
Red River Lumber Company, Akeley, 260
Red River of the North, 23
Red River Trail, 23
Red River Valley, 46
Red Rock Ridge, 6–7, 9
Red Wing, 66
Reinforced concrete, defined, 101
Resettlement Administration (RA), 178
Richardsonian Romanesque, architectural style, 194
Rifkind, Carol, historian, see Commercial districts
Roadside architecture, 251
Roberts and Schaefer Company, Chicago, Ill., 103
Robinson, William, see Jefferson Grain Warehouse
Rock art, 5
Rock County, 174; and Blue Mounds, 174
Rock County Courthouse and Jail, Luverne, 174; description, 175; jail constructed, 175; threat of demolition, 176; added to National Register, 176
Roefer, Florence, site interpreter, 7

Roosevelt, Franklin, politician, 61, 101, 177, 243
Root River Valley and Southern Minnesota Railroad, 44
Roth, Susan, Minnesota National Register Historian, 141
Rothsay, 136
Rowley, Timothy, historian, 21–22
Ruskin, John, author, xvi–xvii

St. Anthony Elevator, Minneapolis, see Peavey, Frank Hutchinson
St. Anthony Falls, Minneapolis, 71, 74
St. Cloud and Red River Valley Stage Road: Kandota Section, description, 27; added to National Register, 28
St. Cornelia's Church, Lower Sioux Indian Community, 5, 15
St. Croix River, 74
St. Hubert, legend of, 253
St. Hubert's Lodge, Frontenac, 253
St. Louis River, 108
St. Mary's Church, New Trier, 221
St. Mary's Falls Ship Canal, see Great Lakes
St. Patrick's Catholic Church, Melrose, 223–24
St. Paul, and state capital, 152; as tourist attraction, 249
St. Paul and Chicago Railroad, 40
St. Paul and Duluth Railroad, 81, 213
St. Paul and Pacific Railroad, 21, 28, 45
St. Paul, Minneapolis and Manitoba Railway, 46, 54, 82, 136, 158
St. Peter, and state capital, 152
Sandstone, 212
Santee Reservation, Nebraska, 15
Schech, Michael, miller, 90
Schech's Mill, Houston Co., and John Blinn, 88–89; description 89; and Caledonia Grist Mill, 90; upgraded, 91; and Ivan Krugmire, 91; added to National Register, 91
Schmidt, Oscar, house, 189
Schooner barges, evolution of, 111
Scott, Andrew Jackson, 124
Scott, James Garfield, 124–25; and Nee Gee, 124; fish house, 124–25; dies, 125; fish house added to National Register, 126
Scott, Roger, 124
Settlement house, 221. See also North East Neighborhood House
Seventh Street Improvement Arches, 73, 81; description, 82–83; moniker, 84; added to National Register, 84
Sexton, R. W., architectural critic, 152–53
Sexton, Thomas, 113
Sheldon, 87–88
Sibley, Henry Hastings, politician, 187; and fur trade, 187; house, 187
Sidereal time, 93
Simpson's Hall, Belview, 226

Sinclair, Upton, author, 277
Sioux City and St. Paul Railroad Section House, Dundee, 47
Sluss, Jacqueline, architectural historian, see Smith, Lena O.
Smith, Ann Eliza, 48
Smith, John Gregory, railroad president, 48
Smith, Lena O., 209; legal cases, 210–12; Jacqueline Sluss comments on, 212
Smith, Lena O., house, 189, 209; added to National Register, 212
Smith, William Robertson, biblical historian, 180
Snow, Dean R., archaeologist, 5, 7
Sogn Valley, 65–67
Solar time, 93
Soo Line High Bridge, 67–68; and Wisconsin Central Railway, 68–69; description, 69–70; added to National Register, 70
Southern Minnesota Railroad, 34, 39, 88
Spector, Janet D., archaeologist, 10; awl handle discovered, 12
Spencer, R. P., see Jefferson Grain Warehouse
Staging industry, 23, 26–28; road description, 26; remaining, 28
Standard Railway Time, 91–93
State Capitol Building, St. Paul, 152
State Emergency Relief Administration (SERA), 177, 243–44
State Fire Relief Commission, see Great Hinckley Fire
State Historic Preservation Offices, xxii–xxiii
State Training School, Red Wing, 184
Steamboat Bay, Leech Lake, 62
Steamboat Bridge, and logging, 63; description 63–64; added to National Register, 64
Steamboat Lake, 62
Steamboat River, 62
Stella Whipple, see Hastings Foundry
Stevens, Issac, politician, 44
Stevens, John, house, xxiii
Stevens, J. Walter, architect, 93, 185
Stick, architectural style, 194
Stone Arch Bridge, 61–62
Sugar Point, see Battle Point
Swanholm, Mary, historian, see Logging

Taylor, J. C., architect, 103
Taylor, James Knox, architect, 170
Tedesko, Anton, engineer, 103
Territorial Act of 1848, 86
Territorial Prison, Stillwater, 184
Thayer, F., architect, 192
Thief River Falls, 54, 56
Third Regiment U.S. Infantry, 18–19
Thomas, John R., reformatory advocate, 183
Thompson, Hannah C., 193–94; dies, 195
Thompson, Peter E., 193–94; dies, 195

Thompson, Peter E. and Hannah C., house, 194–95; house added to National Register, 195

Tourism, in Minnesota, 249–51; for upper classes, 250; for middle classes, 251

Tower, Charlemagne, industrialist, 86, 113–14

Town hall, defined, 220

Transit circle, purpose, 93

Transit Railroad, 44

Treaty of La Pointe, 106–7, 113

Treaty of Mendota, 14

Treaty of Traverse des Sioux, 11–12, 14

Truesdell, William Albert, engineer, 81–82; comment on skewed, arch bridges, 82

Tugboat *Edna G.*, 112; sinks, 120; namesake, 121; description and operation, 121–22; retired, 122; added to National Register, 123

Tugboats, 120

Turbines, and waterwheels, 89

Turner, Claude A. P., engineer, 69–70, 109

Two Harbors, 106, 113–15, 121

Two Harbors Light Station, xxiii, description 115; automated, 115; added to National Register, 116

Tyler, Merwin M., and Tyler's Hotel, 270

Union Pacific Railway, 45

Urban League, Minneapolis, 210

U.S. Army Corps of Engineers, 16, 114–17, 118–19

U.S. Army Corps of Engineers Duluth Vessel Yard, Duluth, 118–19; description, 119; added to National Register, 120

U.S. Naval Observatory, as time station, 93–94

U.S.S. *Essex*, 107

Universal Laboratories, and Rice Laboratories, 95; and Eli Lilly Company, 97; and Burroughs Wellcome Company, 97

Universal Laboratories Building, description, 95; added to National Register, 97

Upper Sioux Agency, 11, 14–15, 24

Upper Sioux Reservation, 4

Veblen, Thorstein, economist, 64

Vermilion Iron Range, 73, 84, 86, 106, 113, 116–17, 121

Verzlunarfelag Islendinga (V.I.), 132

Villa Maria, Frontenac vicinity, 254

Viola, 45, 51–52

Viola Cooperative Creamery, Viola, description, 52; production of, 53; declines and closes, 53; added to National Register, 54

Volstead, Andrew, politician, 64

Wabasha, 216; architectural preferences in, 216

Waddell, J. A. L., engineer, 62–63, 69

Walker, David A., historian, 86

Walker, Martin O., businessman, 27

Washburn Park Water Tower, Minneapolis, 167

Water towers, *Engineering Record* comments on, 165; types, 167

Watkins, Joseph Ray, 199

Watkins, Paul, 199; house, 200–2; house donated, 202; house added to National Register, 202; dies, 202

Well, James, fur trader, 252

Wendt Island, Rainy Lake, 274

Westervelt, Evert, house, 188; as settler, 252–53

Weyerhaeuser, Charles A., *see* Pine Tree Lumber Company

Weyerhaeuser, Frederick, industrialist, 75

Whiffin, Marcus, architectural historian, 200

Whipple, Bishop Henry Benjamin, 13–15

White Castle, restaurant chain, 277–79

White Castle Building No. 8, 276; first, 277; description, 278; relocated, 279; added to National Register, 279

White Oak Point Site, Itasca Co., 5

Wigington, Clarence W., architect, 165

Wilcox Motor Company, Minneapolis, 98

Wilkinson, Brvt. Maj. Major Melville C., 16, 18–19

William Edenborn, see *Madeira*

Williamson, Alonzo P., hospital superintendent, 164

Willmar, 45

Willoughby, Amherst, and Simon Powers, 27

Winchell, Newton H., archaeologist, 7

Winnibigoshish Resort, Bena, 251

Winona Cottage, Frontenac, 254

Winter Saloon, Norwood, 221

Wisconsin Central Railway, 68; and bridge over St. Croix River, 68

Wolff, L. P., engineer, 168

Works Progress Administration (WPA), 243–44

Wright Brothers, 98

Wright, Frank Lloyd, architect, 189, 203

Yellowstone National Park, xxi

Zapadni Cesko-Bratrska Jednota (Z.C.B.J.), 230

Zimmerman, Father Ralph G., 221–22

Zoar Moravian Church, Carver Co., 23

PHOTO CREDITS

For institutional listings, the name of the photographer, when known, is given in parentheses, as is additional information about the source of the item.

DENIS P. GARDNER
Pages 32, 33, 49, 90, 96, 97, 98, 99, 100, 114, 115, 143, 154, 169, 171, 215, 217, 243, 252, 253, 254

DAVID LILL, FERGUS FALLS, MINNESOTA
Page 161

JET LOWE
Pages 89, 109, 122 (both), 247

MINNESOTA HISTORICAL SOCIETY COLLECTIONS, ST. PAUL
Pages x, 3, 6, 8 (Gordon Allan Lothson); 10, 12 (Diane M. Stolen); 11 (Klammer and Klammer); 13; 17; 18; 69 (Chester S. Wilson); 70 (Collected by John Runk, photo by Harry Jackson); 75; 84; 87; 134; 142 *(Minneapolis Tribune);* 149 *(St. Paul Dispatch);* 150; 157; 163; 164; 185; 214; 226; 234 *(St. Paul Dispatch-Pioneer Press);* 236; 237; 261 (Niels Larson Hakkerup); 271; 277 *(Minneapolis Star and Tribune)*

DOUG OHMAN
Pages ii–iii, x (right), xi–xiii (all), 15, 21, 35, 36, 37, 38, 39, 40, 41, 43, 51, 52, 53, 55, 56, 57, 58, 59, 61, 65, 66, 71, 76, 83, 92, 93, 94, 105, 110, 116, 117, 118, 119, 123, 124 (both), 125, 129, 132, 133 (both), 135, 145, 146, 151, 159, 162, 166, 167, 177, 179 (both), 180, 181, 182, 183, 184, 186, 187, 191, 198, 200, 201, 202, 203, 204, 205, 207, 208, 209, 210, 211, 219, 222, 223, 224, 225, 228, 232, 235, 240, 241, 242, 249, 257, 258, 266, 267, 268, 272, 273, 274, 275 (both), 278

STATE HISTORIC PRESERVATION OFFICE (SHPO)
Pages 20 (Aaron Fairbanks); 25 (Susan Granger); 27 (Hess, Roise and Company); 29, 230 (David C. Anderson); 34; 62 (Robert M. Frame III); 68 (Liza Nagle and John Hackett); 79, 138, 140, 175, 259 (Michael Koop); 85, 102 (Rolf T. Anderson); 112 (C. Patrick Lavadie, Duluth, Minn.); 121; 127 (E. J. Dowling Collection, University of Detroit); 128 (Institute for Great Lakes Research, Bowling Green State University); 137 (Wilkin County Historical Society); 148, 246 (Joe Van Ryn); 195 (Gemini Research); 197 [family photo provided by Arlee Blakey (née Bullard)]; 239 (Denis P. Gardner); 262, 264 (State Archive Collection, Conservation Dept.); 265 (Gemini Research © 2001)